Psychology of Women

Behavior in a biosocial context

Juanita H. Williams is also the editor of
Psychology of Women: Selected Readings

Psychology of Women

Behavior in a biosocial context

Juanita H. Williams

Director of Women's Studies Program
University of South Florida

W · W · NORTON & COMPANY

New York · London

Library of Congress Cataloging in Publication Data
Williams, Juanita H
    Psychology of women.
    Bibliography: p.   ⟍
    Includes index.
    1. Women—Psychology.   2. Women—Physiology.
3. Women—Sexual behavior   I. Title. [DNLM:
1. Psychology.   2. Women.   3. Sex behavior.
4. Identification, Psychology. HQ1206 W724p]
HQ1206.W72 1977   155.6'33   76-56740
ISBN 0-393-01134-8
ISBN 0-393-09142-2 pbk.

This book was designed by Andrea C. Goodman
The type is Baskerville and Friz Quadrata

567890

To my mother,
Anna Bryant Hingst,
with love
and appreciation

Contents

Preface

During the past decade courses on women have appeared on campuses all over the country. Nurtured by the new feminism and its scholarship, they are bringing the experience of women out of the oblivion of neglect into the various disciplines. They are changing old biases and informing students with new insights and perspectives, as well as generating further research. While much material is now available in the form of journal articles, readers, and collections around special themes, the field of psychology of women is still almost devoid of basic texts. With the publication of this book, the need for an introductory text which analyzes the entire life cycle of women has been fulfilled. Based on recent empirical research, this comprehensive text surveys and integrates the emerging knowledge about women and their behavior, and it examines the influences which affect them in contemporary society.

The first three chapters describe the myths and stereotypes about women in a historical context and present the early psychoanalytic view of women and its critics. From the thesis of biological determinism to the antithesis of sociocultural shaping of woman's behavior, they represent a continuum of ideas which science has only recently begun to test. Beginning with the fourth chapter, the book is organized around research on critical issues and events of the female experience from the prenatal period through adulthood. The determinants of sexual differentiation, early sex differences, and the experience of growing up female are followed by chapters on sexuality and on the psychobiology of birth control and reproduction. The later chapters of the book are concerned with contemporary life styles and their effects on women, delinquency, and mental disorders, and the experience for women of growing older in this society. The last chapter sets out the major variables which determine the psychology of women—and of any particular woman.

The underlying perspective by which the data are integrated is that the behavior of women occurs in a biosocial context and can only be understood within that context. While women have in common certain biological experiences, they live in drastically different social settings under varying moral codes and conditions of life. No understanding of the psychology of women, or of a particular woman, is possible without taking into account this social context with its permissions and prohibitions. Further, the psychology of women cuts across all the subdisciplines in psychology; it looks at the whole spectrum of behavior as it is shaped from all its sources: the personal, the social, and the biological.

Most of the recent research on the psychology of women has been done by women, an observation reminiscent of John Stuart Mill's prophetic comment in The Subjection of Women over a hundred years ago that no understanding of women would ever be possible until women themselves began to tell what they know. Why did women wait so long? One reason, of course, was the dearth of women doing any kind of research. Another was that the definitions of what was important to study were made by men, and historically they did not include the psychology of women. The authenticity of women's knowledge about themselves and of the kinds of questions that science can ask about them is now beginning to be recognized. Women are assuming more instrumental and authoritative roles in seeking out the answers.

The times, indeed, are changing. Deference and passivity as qualities of femininity are no longer fashionable. Women are gaining control of their lives and taking responsibility for their futures. In 1902, the German poet Rainer Maria Rilke wrote that someday the humanity of girls and women would no longer signify only an opposite of the masculine limited to a complementary role, but would unfold to a free-standing identity: the female human being. The realization of that vision is now possible.

For the past five years I have been teaching the course on the psychology of women at the University of South Florida. This book is a result of these years of trial and error. For their interest and their help in the development of ideas, I want to thank my students in that course and in the other women's studies courses which I have taught. In a real sense, this book is for them. Georgia Babladelis of California State University, Martha Mednick of the University of Connecticut, and Mary Brown Parlee of Barnard College read all or part of the manuscript and made many helpful comments. I greatly appreciate their thoughtful attention. My editor at Norton, Don

Fusting, offered invaluable suggestions tempered with patience and good humor throughout the development of the book. Helen Bazin typed all the drafts of the manuscript with equal enthusiasm, and her positive comments always lifted my spirits.

My daughters, Karen, Anita, Gretchen, and Laura were my first inspiration for thinking about the psychology of women and the female condition. Their presence reinforces my conviction of the importance of the subject. Finally, I appreciate the contributions of my husband, Jim, who was unfailingly supportive and helpful in many ways.

J. H. W.

Tampa, 1976

Psychology
of Women

Behavior
in a biosocial
context

Myths, stereotypes, and the psychology of women

1

It is always difficult to describe a myth; it cannot be grasped or encompassed; it haunts the human consciousness without ever appearing before it in fixed form. The myth is so various, so contradictory, that at first its unity is not discerned. . . . [W]oman is at once Eve and the Virgin Mary. She is an idol, a servant, the source of life, a power of darkness; she is the elemental silence of truth, she is artifice, gossip, and falsehood; she is healing presence and sorceress; she is man's prey, his downfall, she is everything that he is not and that he longs for, his negation and his raison d'être.

—————Simone de Beauvoir, *The Second Sex,* 1953

Mythic Woman

Over the millennia women have been variously observed and understood, and the derived wisdom recorded in literature, art, and religion for the enlightenment of all. Mostly, understandings of women have taken the form of strongly held beliefs which served to validate and to order experience, or have emanated from such authoritative sources that few would question them. Thus women have been seen as incarnations of both the highest good and the basest evil, of chastity and of lust, of virtue and deceit, and of the sacred and the profane. Men, and women who are co-opted by the prevalent male view, have rarely been able to perceive women simply as human beings with the same range of idiosyncracies as themselves. Rather, they have had to make myths to explain their awesome differences and their strange powers. Occasionally, in time of great stress, when women's brains, hands, and backs are needed to win a war or tame a frontier, they are seen for a while as simply human— though with certain disabilities, to be sure. But myths do not swirl about the form of the grandmother who matter-of-factly digs a trench for the children to sleep in, nor does a mystique lie about the woman who guides a plow and mule down the rows of some remote farm newly developed from the wilderness.

Aside from such unusual exigencies, however, man has always felt the need to explain and to codify woman, to come to terms with her presence on earth and to accommodate her within his rational system. As he made myths to explain other phenomena of the universe, so he devised explanations of the phenomenon *woman* which expressed significant truths about her, and images such as old maid or virgin that bring to mind the essential features thought to characterize all persons so called. Such beliefs are ways of knowing; they predate but continue to exist alongside the attempts of science to explain human behavior. The tenacity and continuity of these beliefs in different eras and cultures must mean that they serve potent needs in the human experience.

In addition to their explanatory power, myths also provide man with the hope that he can control the frightening and inexplicable phenomena with which they deal. For example, he sees that a natural event like a prolonged drought threatens his existence. If his mythology includes a responsible god who expresses his displeasure by visiting him with droughts, and who can be placated with gifts, then he can end the drought by making sacrifices to that god. Thus he perceives that he has a measure of control over his own destiny. If the procreative and sexual powers of women awe and frighten him, he can hedge them about with taboos, confine them to special places, or devise elaborate rituals whereby he can deal with the mythic female power. Myths thus introduce a semblance of understanding and order into the apparent chaos of the universe.

Myths about the powers, motives, and special qualities of women have been reflected in the literature and religion of most cultures from earliest times. Although they occur in myriad forms, certain themes have been observed to be universal, and to have continuity with the present. They have been analyzed in detail elsewhere (e.g., Campbell, 1959; de Beauvoir, 1953; Diner, 1973; Figes, 1970; Janeway, 1971). After briefly describing a few of these myths, we shall look at one of them more closely because of its relevance to contemporary ideas about women.

Woman as mother nature

The analogy between woman and the earth as sources of life has always inspired the myths and poems of men and caused them to create their earliest religions and figures of worship. Myths of the

Great Mother were part of all the cultures that contributed to the stream of Western civilization. Whether she was called Demeter, Isis, Ishtar, or golden Aphrodite—the goddess of a hundred names—she was the mother and nurturer of both gods and men (Diner, 1973).

A curious reciprocity pervades the mythic concepts of woman and nature. The fecundity of nature, earth bringing forth fruit and grain, sea and river yielding their fishes, all are symbolized by woman. The French author Simone de Beauvoir, tells how an Indian prophet warned his disciples against spading the earth, because it is a sin "to tear the mother of us all in the labors of cultivation" (1953, p. 145). The reciprocity lies in the reversal of these images in the assimilation of nature's forms to woman. One could find hundreds of examples of comparisons of woman and her various parts to the flora and fauna of nature. Surely one of the most beautiful of these is in the Old Testament Song of Solomon:

> Thy belly is like an heap of wheat, set about with lilies . . .
> This thy stature is like to a palm tree, and thy breasts
>   to clusters of grapes (Solomon 7: 2,7).

The identification of nature with woman and the description of woman in terms of nature suggests an affinity between the two. Man could reside and make his mark, could observe and comment, but it was woman who linked him to earth. "Literally woman is Isis, fecund nature. She is the river and the riverbed, the root and the rose, the earth and the cherry tree, the vine-stock and the grape" (de Beauvoir, 1953, p. 145). She was closer to the mysterious scheme of things, to the heart of the matter, than he was. Did not her very body share with the moon its periodicity, and with the earth its power of generation? Thus she was part of that nature which he could not control, which could destroy him with her capricious whims. To effect a separation of the mortal woman from the identity he feared she had with that power, he had to neutralize her magic by setting up systems which would protect him and would give him some control over the unspeakable contingencies emanating from that identity: "That is why she is never left to Nature, but is surrounded by taboos, purified by rites, placed in charge of priests; man is adjured never to approach her in her primitive nakedness, but through ceremonials and sacraments, which draw her away from the earth" (de Beauvoir, 1953, p. 169).

Woman as enchantress-seductress

Myths of the woman who enchants man with her magic charms and seduces him away from the high paths of his holy mission are as old as communication and as persistent as the sex drive itself. On one level, they are stories, simple or epic, about man rendered powerless, having no choice but to surrender to her who has only the frail weapons of her body and her eyes, and, of course, her special connections with potent forces in those occult dimensions which defy the rational mind. On another level, they represent his projections upon her of his own worst fears about himself, of that dark part of his nature with which he constantly struggles, that part most resistant to being tamed into the service of his higher being. Thus for the statement "Against my better judgment I did something that was very bad," he substitutes, "She bewitched me, and caused me to do something which I would otherwise never have done."

Mythic enchantresses, bent upon diverting man from his noble tasks, causing him to abandon reason, and eliciting his essential wickedness, which he had repressed with such pain, are part of our earliest chronicles. The common motif in such accounts is that woman, otherwise powerless, gets what she wants by using devious, cunning means in which her sexual attraction is a strong element to effect the downfall of her prey, man (Figes, 1970). Odysseus, for example, was delayed in his attempt to return home from the Trojan War by the goddess Circe, who, having turned his men into swine, seduced him and kept him on her island for a full year.

Sometimes the fear of being emasculated is brought out in masked form in stories where women cause men to lose their strength, to become like women. Such a woman was Iole who feminized the mighty Hercules in an account by Boccaccio. To get even with him for killing her father and carrying her off, she pretended to love him. "With caresses and a certain artful wantonness," she made him desire her so much that he could deny her nothing. Once he was in this state, she had him take off his lion skin and lay aside his club and quiver of arrows. Defenseless, he submitted to having his beard combed and his body anointed with oils. Adorned with garlands and clad in a purple robe, he came finally to such a pass that he would sit among the women and spin wool. The deceitful Iole had more surely destroyed him than if she had used a knife or poison (Figes, 1970).

Other members of the sisterhood who were invested with the myth were the witch and the prostitute. That vision of women which caused millions of them to be tortured and put to death between the fifteenth and eighteenth centuries was presented most vividly by Jacob Sprenger, a fifteenth-century Dominican and a witchcraft inquisitor. In the *Malleus Maleficarum*—"hammer of witches"—he set forth the doctrine that large numbers of women were in unholy alliance with Satan, and were a horrible threat to man, particularly to his genitals. The worst vice of these women was their insatiable lust, which led them to copulate with the Devil and become his intermediary, working his mischief on the body of man. This idea persisted in less virulent form in later ministerial invocations against the prostitute. She aroused men like Henry Ward Beecher, the famed nineteenth-century American preacher, to passionate rhetoric: "What horrid wizard hath put the world under a spell and charm, that words from the lips of a STRANGE WOMAN shall ring upon the ears like tones of music. . . . [F]rom the lips of the harlot words drop as honey and flow smoother than oil; her speech is fair, her laugh is merry as music. . . . [T]rust not thyself near the *artful woman*, armed in her beauty, her cunning raiment, her dimpled smiles, her sighs of sorrow, her look of love" (Walters, 1974, p. 70).

Woman as necessary evil

The perception of woman as necessary evil, as inferior, insignificant nonperson who is barely tolerated for the services she performs, is true misogyny. Necessary to perform the functions of sex object and child bearer, she is otherwise unimportant, rightfully excluded from the company and affairs of men. While the fortunes of women have varied in different societies at different times, it is a universal observation that men have held women to be lesser persons than themselves and have ascribed to them an inferior status (Bullough, 1973). A very early example is Hesiod's eighth century B.C. account of Pandora, the Greeks' version of the first woman. Pandora came to the first man as a gift from the gods, who had given her a box never to be opened. All too mortal, she could not contain her curiosity and loosed all the evils and diseases which have plagued humans ever since. Hesiod pointed out that it was from her that all women descended, that troublesome tribe who brought man nothing but misery whether he married them or not. A wife was a constant financial drain who could not be trusted in any case. Without her, however, he would have no heirs and no one to nurse him in his old age.

During most of the history of Western civilization, women have been regarded basically as property, with no rights of their own. A strong tenet of Puritan belief, for example, was the requirement that women be kept in a subordinate position. The Puritan poet John Milton insisted on the inferiority of women and the need for men to guard their authority over them to keep them from foolish action. He expressed the not uncommon theme of woman as a kind of intrusive nuisance in man's world in *Paradise Lost,* when he has Adam plaintively ask, after the Transgression, why God created "this novel-tie on earth, this fair defect," instead of filling the world with men, or finding some other way to generate mankind (Rogers, 1966). This mythic perception of woman as necessary evil has persisted through the ages, and has survived the evolution of ideas and intellectual changes. As one of the earliest and most influential views of women, it has dominated not only religious teaching but philosophical thought as well. Schopenhauer, the nineteenth-century German philosopher, is only one example of a cohort of the period whose ideas about women ranged from patronizing to loathing. His essay *On Women* starts out with an innocuous tribute to woman's contribution to man's infancy, maturity, and old age, then gets on with his theme. Women are fitted to nurse and teach children because they are themselves childish and frivolous—an intermediate stage between the child and the full-grown man. Nature lavishes beauty on the young female so that she can capture a man, who, bereft of reason, takes on the burden of her care forever. The fundamental fault of the female character is that she has no sense of justice, being defective in the powers of reasoning and deliberation. In compensation, Nature has caused her to excel in dissimulation, faithlessness, treachery, lying, ingratitude, and so on. Only the man whose sexual impulse has beclouded his reason would call her the fair sex, for she is in fact undersized, narrow-shouldered, broad-hipped, and short-legged. She looks upon everything as a means for conquering man. Thus, she has no genuine interest in any art, and no genius whatsoever.

We shall see later how such vindictiveness encountered a stifling effect with the ascendancy of another myth about women. Even so, the underlying hostility could continue to be vented toward such deviants as old maids—women whom no man had found desirable enough to marry—and feminists, who insisted upon violating the boundaries of woman's place by demanding a role in the institutions which man had created. The basic ideas of woman's inferiority and unfitness to be man's equal continue to be thematically important as determinants of attitudes toward her.

Woman as mystery

The seeming perversity of woman's behavior, the wonderment she excited with her strange powers, the ways she was different from man gave rise to another myth, which was that her mental processes, her behavior, and the whole of what she was, made up a feminine essence which was beyond the power of philosopher, scientist, or any ordinary baffled male to understand. Just as there were other natural phenomena which did not yield to reason or empirical science, so there was woman, with her unpredictable ways and her enigmatic face. This myth, in a way, is a supplement to all the others. Failing any other explanation, she can be viewed as a different order of being, to whom the laws and rules by which behavior and thought are normally understood do not apply.

Simone de Beauvoir in an analysis of the myth of feminine "mystery" pointed out its advantages. First, it permits an explanation which will fit all manner of events. Caprices, moodiness, strange excursions—whatever about her man does not understand, he can attribute to that quality of hers he is sure of, her essential mysteriousness. Instead of admitting ignorance, he can relegate her to that category of events which are simply inexplicable. Second, he can protect himself from disturbing insights. If she changes in her affections, if she talks in riddles, the mystery explains it all. Last, and perhaps most important, it permits man to remain alone as the One who works, judges, and defines reality. She is the Other, and since he cannot understand her, he is exempt from the effort of building an authentic relationship with her. If he cannot understand her, she cannot *be* understood, and authenticity cannot occur in the absence of understanding. Thus even when he is with her he stands alone, in charge, an alternative to the admission and sharing of their common humanity (de Beauvoir, 1953).

Upon what basis could such a myth be founded and perpetuated? The mystery is in the inability of man and woman to communicate across the distance that separates her world from his. As de Beauvoir observed, humans are defined by their acts. When a woman is kept by a man, she is a passive recipient of the advantages he bestows upon her as long as he cares about her. But this role is not a vocation and does not bestow identity upon the woman. Her dependency causes her to dissemble, as all subordinates learn to dissemble with their masters, concealing their real thoughts and feelings under an enigmatic exterior. "And moreover, woman is taught from adolescence to lie to men, to scheme, to be wily. In speaking to them she wears an artificial expression on her face; she is cautious, hypocritical, play-acting" (de Beauvoir, 1953, p. 259).

By defining her as mysterious Other, man spares himself the necessity of analyzing her behavior and understanding it as a consequence of her position vis-à-vis him. To do that would require acknowledgement of her oppression, and a possible shift in their power relationship. The price would be very high.

Behavior theorists of modern times have had much to say about women, some of it helpful, some of it not, in furthering understanding. Freud was less sure than some of his followers that either he or the theories he developed had revealed the mystery. His biographer, Ernest Jones (1955), said that Freud found the psychology of women "more enigmatic" than that of men, and reported him as having asked a female colleague, "The great question that has never been answered and which I have not yet been able to answer, despite my thirty years of research into the feminine soul, is 'What does a woman want?' " (p. 421). And in 1933, in his last paper on female psychology, he spoke of femininity as a riddle—to men but not to women, since they were considered the problem. If one wanted to know more about women, he said, one could ask of one's own experiences, or turn to the poets, or wait for science to give the answers (Freud, 1974).

The influences and remnants of these mythic explanations for woman, as Mother Nature, as spellbinder, as necessary evil, and as mystery, are not difficult to find in the popular culture of today. There is another, however, which has probably had more influence on the lives of women in our society because it is perfectly in keeping with the ideal model for womanhood which has persisted until recent times. It is the myth of female goodness, of woman as the embodiment of virtue. This myth told women how they ought to be and described the rewards. From its beginning with the virtuous wife to today's stereotypes of the feminine woman, this myth more than any of the others has defined woman's place and her behavior in it.

From Myth to Stereotype: The Virtuous Woman

The model of the virtuous woman has occupied writers, priests, and moralists since earliest times. Throughout history there has been remarkable agreement on her characteristics. She is a faithful, loyal, and submissive wife; a dedicated, loving mother; a competent, diligent housewife; and an unquestioning supporter of the moral and religious values of her society. Although emphasis on the importance of each of these qualities has varied in different periods, the basic elements are nearly always discernible. Together they have defined her place. More than the definition of her physical setting, it has included the constellation of personal characteristics and permissible behaviors which distinguish her from the male and describe her status relative to his. As long as she observed her place and behaved in accordance with its prescriptions, no fault was found in her. In fact, during some periods she was so elevated that men were figuratively if not literally on their knees before her, overcome by the moral qualities of her being, so different from their own.

The Book of Proverbs contains an Old Testament description of what constituted goodness in women:

> She riseth also while it is yet night, and giveth meat to her household, and a portion to her maidens.
>
> She considereth a field, and buyeth it; with the fruit of her hands she planteth a vineyard . . .
>
> She layeth her hands to the spindle, and her hands hold the distaff . . .
>
> She stretcheth out her hand to the poor; yea, she reacheth forth her hands to the needy . . .
>
> She looketh well to the ways of her household, and eateth not the bread of idleness.
>
> Her children rise up, and call her blessed; her husband also, and he praiseth her . . .   (*Proverbs 31: 15–28*).

This description of industry and household productivity was supplemented by the statements of early Christian writers on the proper role of women. Women were constantly admonished to obey their husbands. "Wives, submit yourselves unto your own husbands, as it is fit in the Lord" (Colossians 3: 18). St. Augustine, the fourth-century Christian scholar, presented a model of motherhood in a reverential description of his mother, Monica. He praised her for putting up with his father, an unbeliever and adulterer, for praying for him, and above all for never chastising him or showing any temper. Monica had even instructed other women who complained about their husbands that they were bound by the marriage contract to serve, to remember their condition, and not to defy their masters (Figes, 1970).

The ultimate prototype of the model wife, however, was the patient Griselda, whose story was told by the celibate clerk in Chaucer's *Canterbury Tales* of the fourteenth century. Griselda was a serf, whose noble husband had married her on the condition that she would be completely obedient to his every wish. To test her he had her two children taken away, saying that they must be put to death. She acquiesced graciously. He later told her that she must return to her father's hovel, as he had decided to take a younger wife. She agreed to her unworthiness and cheerfully left, thus finally convincing him that she was indeed a good wife. Thereupon he returned her children and brought her back to be his wife. Griselda thanked him copiously, and said that she would die happy knowing that she had found favor in his sight.

During the Middle Ages, there arose the convention of romantic love, a passionate, despairing devotion directed toward an impeccable and unattainable (in theory) lady. Chivalry, the code prescribing that women should be given precedence by a gentle, courteous male, arose from this convention (Bullough, 1973). The man in love, usually a knight, minstrel, or noble, was in a state of total adoration, "in thrall," indeed. Whether he was rewarded or not, the fact that he was in love had great positive value for him, making him more skillful and valiant at his pursuits, usually war or practice for it. The woman, though she herself was a passive recipient of his ardor, had ennobling qualities: she inspired in him courage, skill, and honor. While very few women benefited from this novel adulation, it marked the beginning of the tradition of courtly love, of the feminine mystique, and of the vision of woman on a pedestal which has been one line of approved wisdom ever since.

Rarely have women been idealized and worshiped with such unrelenting fervor as in the American South during the nineteenth century. This attitude spread to other parts of the country as well and was responsible with some modification for the prevalent view of woman during the nineteenth and the first half of the twentieth century.[1] Southern womanhood became a symbol for the Southern male, who imbued her with qualities of purity and goodness which had to be protected and defended against any hint of defilement or threat to her honor. The ideal woman was described in *The Mind of the South* as a combination of "lily-pure maid" and "hunting goddess": "And she was the pitiful Mother of God. Merely to mention her was to send strong men into tears—or shouts. There was hardly a sermon that did not begin or end with tributes in her honor, hardly a brave speech that did not open and close with the clashing of shields and the flourishing of swords for her glory" (Cash, 1960, p. 89).

This romanticization of women was an important social motif in mid-nineteenth-century America, epitomized by the "cult of true womanhood" (Welter, 1973). The true woman, a Victorian adaptation of earlier models of the virtuous woman with strong Puritan and moralistic overtones, had four virtues: piety, purity, submissiveness, and domesticity. So identified, she was secure on her pedestal, and reverential paeans were sung in her honor. Her religious piety made her the moral arbiter of the home and the society; by her doing, souls would be saved; erring men, always more subject to temptation than she, would repent; and fallen women be brought to salvation. Purity meant chastity until the wedding night, an event to

---

[1] The only women who actually had anything to gain from this perception were the affluent classes who could indulge in it. Obviously it did not apply to black women, immigrant women, women working in factories. The flights of rhetoric which made woman an exalted being were meant to pay tribute to white Anglo-Saxon wives of prosperous planters and business and professional men.

which she brought her greatest gift, her virginity. Girls were warned over and over again about the perils of sitting too close to males, of dancing, of inflaming the senses with novels, of listening to "the siren voices of vicious pleasure." For "the sin against chastity was a graver, deeper sin, than any other; . . . the white robe of innocence once soiled, could never again be restored to its former purity" (Brockett, 1869, pp. 213–17). In the sexual relationship, it was woman's responsibility to set the pace and to keep a healthful balance. Physicians taught that women had little or no sex drive and responded to their husbands only to keep them from going to prostitutes. Woman's lack of desire was nature's way of taming man's animal lusts, thus avoiding the drain on his vitality that too frequent or prolonged intercourse would have (Haller, 1974). This view of female sexuality contrasts remarkably with that of its counterpart, the seductress, who was invested with such insatiable appetite that man must be ever on his guard against her.

The third virtue, submissiveness, was the God-imposed role of good women, who deferred to their husbands in all things. The woman who questioned this, or took independent action, was a threat to the sacred order of the universe. It was mostly on this point that the antifeminist argument rested. The suffrage movement, for example, was seen as an assault against Christianity, the home, and the institutions of marriage and the family. The physician James Weir, Jr., in 1895, "proved" that the woman who advocated equality of the sexes had "either given evidence of masculo-feminity (viraginity), or had shown conclusively that she was a victim of psychosexual aberrancy" (Haller, 1974, p. 77). The view that submissiveness was natural and therefore good for women was supported in countless books and treatises which documented sex differences in brain and physique to support the point that woman was delicate, frail, and weak, and that too much intellectual or otherwise assertive activity would damage her health irreversibly (Bullough, 1973). It was common for the medical men of the time to assert that overexercise of the female brain in study would cause mania, sterility, and deterioration of health.

Finally, the true woman was revered for her domesticity. The care of the home and its occupants was her highest calling. To her family she was a comforter and a ministering angel. Gentle, patient, and merciful, she was a perfect nurse, teacher, and inculcator of values. She formed the mind of the infant, the holiest of tasks, and made it possible for the successful man to give her the ultimate accolade, "All that I am I owe to my sainted mother."

The myth of female goodness, building as it did upon the belief in woman's special nature and her moral character, was in fact for women a two-edged sword. On the one hand, it set her apart from the world in a small sphere of her own defined by rigid conventions and artificial pretensions. As long as she observed her place and her duties, she was the object of esteem and adoration, was "better," in fact, than the male whose life was too rough and competitive to permit such refinement of taste and decorum. But this elevated status had very little material reward or prestige, other than that ascribed to her by her husband's position. She had no legal or political power, very little personal freedom, and no way to achieve economic independence. But secure in her place, and venerated as she was, what need had she of these? Thus was she rewarded for her meekness and compliance, and told that she was too good and too delicate to participate in the affairs of men.[2] Women who refused to conform to this model, such as the feminists and other radicals, were castigated in pulpit and press as anarchists and perverts, as unnatural and morally defective.

Another major problem with the myth was that it conflicted with reality. Most Americans of the time still lived on farms, and women did not have the leisure or the means to cultivate the manners and life style of the proper female, as prescribed by the cult of true womanhood (Bullough, 1973). But while probably only a small minority of American women ever lived the myth in all its connotations, it was still the official style of being female and was promoted in the printed media and from the pulpit until recent times. In fact, the same rhetoric has recently reverberated through the land, in support of the arguments of those opposed to the Equal Rights Amendment. Opponents contend that women are a special class of being, and need special protection; not man's equal, they are his superior. Those who demanded equality and liberation from the old shackles of role and place were rejecting their femininity. They were frustrated harridans or lesbians or both. The more things changed, it seemed, the more they remained the same.

From Stereotype to the Psychology of Women

The definition of woman's place and the romanticization of both her and her role in it were descriptive of the favored model of female behavior during the late nineteenth century in both Europe and the

---

[2] The twentieth-century Irish dramatist George Bernard Shaw pointed out the darker consequences for women of being perceived as angels: "It is all very well to be regarded as an angel up to a certain point; but there come moments at which you are seriously inconvenienced by the fact that you are not an angel; that you very seriously require certain accommodations and conveniences which angels can do without; and that when these are denied to you on the ground that you are an angel, you suffer for it (Adams and Briscoe, 1971, p. 197).

United States. At the same time there coexisted the notion of woman as a different order of being. A major feature of her difference was her relative lack of characteristics valued in males, such as originality, creativity, emotional control, and educability—in short, a generalized notion of her inferiority. These two ideas were perfectly compatible with each other, the latter being a rationalization for excluding women from public life and confining them to that sphere in which they could exercise their special qualities of tenderness, nurturance, and devotion to the well-being of others. By virtue of her exercise of these qualities, woman and her place were imbued with a romantic aura which was held to be ample compensation for her inability to do the kinds of things that men did, such as acquiring an education and becoming economically productive. This view of how woman was and how she ought to be was the mode when the young science of psychology began to examine her around the turn of the century.

Psychology is the field of study whose goal is to describe, understand, predict, and control the behavior of humans and other animals. During its early development, in the latter years of the nineteenth-century, little attention appears to have been given to the study of women separate from the study of the adult human. Around 1900, however, there developed in the United States a school of psychology known as functionalism, whose defining feature was its incorporation of evolutionary theory into the subject matter of psychology, emphasizing the concept of adaptation and adjustment to a particular environment. The idea that humans had evolved from lower animals and thus were biologically related to the rest of the animal kingdom influenced the functionalists to apply the concept to behavior as well. Human behavior was seen as the end result of a long process of adaptation and adjustment to the environment, and most important for our subject, it included certain innate components which were biologically based and which humans shared with other animals—such as the maternal instinct. The effect of this trend of thinking gave rise to studies of the biological bases of human behavior, and to studies of individual differences, including the study of sex differences. The significance of the marriage of evolutionary theory and psychology for the beginning of the scientific study of female behavior was demonstrated in a paper which describes the bridge between myth and science, and shows how, in this case, they served each other (Shields, 1975).

The observable sex differences in brain size, in intellectual and cultural achievement, and in nurturing behavior had long been ascribed to the fact, put forth and advocated by the great authorities of religion and philosophy alike, of the inferiority of the female. For the religious authorities she was a lesser being because of her derivative creation and her fateful behavior in the Garden. The European philosophers of the eighteenth and nineteenth centuries, however, attributed her inadequacies to her lack of male virtues, to the fact, ultimately, that she was not male. In either case her inferiority necessitated her subordination to the male and her relegation to the only role that was natural and suitable for her, owing to her biological endowment.

For scientists, such explanations would not suffice, and thus began the search for more sophisticated ways for understanding what was patently observable: the behavioral differences between males and females. The search began, however, with the same old assumptions that woman's lesser cultural contributions to the society and her behavior in the/domestic role were part of the natural order of things. The problem was to find the underlying mechanism to account for these at a level that would satisfy the scientific intellect. To this end did attention turn to topics which had an early relevance to the psychology of women. Three of these were differences in male and female brains, the variability hypothesis, and the maternal instinct. The history of scientific attention to each of these topics shows how their importance as issues lay in the extent to which they explained contemporary beliefs about women and about sex differences (Shields, 1975).

The notion that sex differences in brain size and in development of different areas of the brain explained sex differences in achievement and personality traits was held by neurologists as well as nonscientists until well into the twentieth century. The investigation of its validity became irresistible once tests for measuring intelligence and other abilities became available. Although interest in the issue diminished rather early owing to lack of corroboration within the testing movement, it reappeared, in a paper associating brain size with the maturing of "other powers" (Porteus & Babcock, 1926). Males, because of their larger brains, would have more of these powers and would thus be more competent and achieving. Such proposals, coming from psychologists, fit readily into the social value system and so could be assimilated under the aegis of science.

The variability hypothesis proposed that males vary more from the norm than females do on certain characteristics, including intelligence. This means that a greater percentage of males compared to females would be found at the upper and lower extremes on measures of those characteristics. Thus, for intelligence, the hypothesis is that males would be more likely to manifest both genius and mental deficiency. This explanation would account for the greater achievement and productivity of men, as well as for the observed greater number of men in institutions for the mentally deficient.

The popularity of this hypothesis "did not stem from intellectual commitment to the scientific validity of the proposal as much as it did from personal commitment to the social desirability of its acceptance" (Shields, 1975, p. 744). The corollaries of the hypothesis obviously had strong social implications for women. If genius was a peculiarly male trait, then one would not expect so much from women; therefore, their education should fit them not for the wider world, but for their place in it, and their roles as wives and mothers. The variability hypothesis as one explanation for psychological sex differences has continued to be a topic of interest for psychology. Recent evaluations of the relevant research conclude that the available data are contradictory, and are not in general supportive of the hypothesis (Maccoby and Jacklin, 1974; Shields, 1974).

The concept of maternal instinct, which maintains that women's nurturing behavior is an innate, biological determinant shared with other female animals, was readily incorporated into the early doctrines of psychology. The idea of maternal instinct in human females was quite compatible with evolutionary theory. Along with it went the broader concept that woman's reproductive physiology was intimately and causally related to her behavior in general. That most of her energy, both mental and physical, was consumed by the functions of reproduction accounted for the lack of development of other qualities. The parental instinct of the male was seen as a more abstract, protective attitude toward weak and dependent ones, such as wives and children, whereas it was the nature of the female to respond with specific nurturant behavior to the helpless infant.

The notion of the innateness of maternal behavior was not disputed until the advent of the behaviorist school of psychology in the mid-1920s. The behaviorists successfully challenged the entire concept of instinct in humans, holding that most human behavior was learned. Consequently, interest in the maternal instinct appears now in experimental studies of nurturant behavior in other species. Even so, the idea that women's greatest fulfillment is motherhood has been remarkably persistent: "as much as women want to be good scientists or engineers, they want first and foremost to be womanly companions of men and to be mothers" (Bettelheim, 1965, p. 15).

Explanations of social and behavioral sex differences which rely on differences in brain size, variability, and the maternal instinct seem quaintly archaic to us now, but it is very easy to see how neatly these concepts met the need of behavioral scientists of a few decades ago to understand the social phenomena of their world. In attempting to move from myth to science, they created new myths which would both explain and justify the social order. "That science played handmaiden to social values cannot be denied" (Shields, 1975,

p. 753). Though these issues are now of historical interest only, the search for biological bases of behavior and sex differences continues.

Explanations for the phenomena of female behavior have moved from their mythic beginnings to persistent stereotypes whose acceptance by scientists and lay persons alike impeded deeper understanding, probably being sufficiently satisfying at the time to make further inquiry seem unnecessary. As the influence of functionalism declined from the thirties onward, so too did interest in research on female behavior. Except for continued interest in the topic of psychological sex differences, there was little attention to the scientific study of women by psychologists until the late sixties. Since then research has begun to move beyond the mythic and stereotypic ways of viewing woman toward a sounder understanding of the real determinants of her behavior. In the meantime, however, the next major statement on the psychology of women was made not by psychology but by psychoanalysis, a theory of human behavior whose explanations of female personality are the subject of the next chapter.

Psychoanalysis and the woman question

2

And now you are already prepared to hear that psychology too is unable to solve the riddle of femininity. . . . In conformity with its peculiar nature, psycho-analysis does not try to describe what a woman is—that would be a task it could scarcely perform— but sets about inquiring how she came into being, how a woman develops out of a child with a bisexual disposition.

—Sigmund Freud, "Femininity," 1933

Psychoanalysis has become modern society's most influential theory of human behavior. Developed by Sigmund Freud and his colleagues, it profoundly altered Western ideas about human nature and changed the ways we view ourselves and our experiences. It undermined the treasured belief in the primacy of human reason and in the responsible control of human behavior by free will, the concept that humans freely choose to do good or evil, that their lives are in accordance with a plan of their own devising. Instead, said Freud, we are motivated by strange forces, buried deep in our minds, which are part of the human condition. These shape our behavior and our concepts of ourselves and permeate all our cultural productions and enterprises. Freud's theories opened a new door to the study of human behavior, revealing sources never before explored by science. They have had a far-reaching effect on psychological theory, research, and practice, as well as on many other expressions of contemporary culture.

But ideas which affect the course of human life do not magically spring Athena-like fully mature from the head of their creator. They are the result of a particular combination of a person and a time and place. In this chapter we shall consider the personal and cultural background of Freud's thought, and the development and extension of psychoanalytic theory, particularly as it purported to explain how "a woman develops out of a child."

Sigmund Freud

Freud was born in 1856, the first child of a young mother who gave birth to six other children in the next nine years. His father was a Jewish wool merchant, and the family was solidly middle class. Freud received his medical degree from the University of Vienna, where he had been especially interested in the physiology of the nervous system. In 1886, he opened in Vienna a practice in neuropathology, diseases of the nervous system. In that same year he married Martha Bernays, who became the mother of their six children.

Freud's personal life was conventional and conservative. Martha was a proper Victorian *hausfrau,* loving and subservient to Freud, who was a faithful husband and fond father. His attitudes toward women and his beliefs about the appropriate relationship between the sexes were conditioned by his own personal experiences within the cultural milieu of the time in which he lived. Central European society was strongly patriarchal, distinguishing clearly between the roles of men and women, relegating to men all the duties and privileges of their assignments in the outside world and to women the responsibilities of home and children. Along with this went the assumption that male dominance and superiority were the natural order of things, and that the female, who provided the serene comforts of domesticity, was entitled to the love and protection of the man who married her.

During the early years, Freud was very critical of the feminist argument for equality between the sexes. He reacted strongly to John Stuart Mill's *On The Subjection of Women,* a treatise arguing for the emancipation of women from economic bondage and for their full participation in life outside the home. Freud thought that it was "absurd" to suggest that a married woman could earn as much as her husband, in that her domestic responsibilities demanded the whole of a human being. Further, the earning of a livelihood would require the suppression of her tender attributes, the ideal of womanhood, determined by nature through her beauty, charm, and sweetness. " 'Law and custom have much to give women that has been withheld from them, but the position of women will surely be what it is: in youth an adored darling and in mature years a loved wife' " (quoted in Jones, 1953, p. 176–77). These sentiments and the ideology underlying them were not directly related to the later developed content of psychoanalytic theory, but they help to account for the assumptions inherent in Freud's later formulations of female personality development and female sexuality.

The early development of psychoanalysis

In 1885, Freud went to Paris to study with the famous neurologist Jean Charcot, who was interested in the relationship between hysteria and hypnosis. Hysteria, a commonly observed condition at the time, was thought to afflict mostly women. In fact, the word *hysteria* was derived from the Greek *hystera,* meaning uterus, since early Greek physicians had believed that its symptoms were caused by the wanderings of the uterus through the body and its eventual settling in some part. Hysterical symptoms included a variety of afflictions of the muscles and senses which had no apparent organic or physical cause. They included paralysis, loss of speech or hearing, blindness, loss of sensation, trancelike states, and shaking spells, as well as inexplicable aches and pains and conditions in which the body "mimicked" such normal processes as pregnancy. Although Charcot believed that hysteria was a "real" disease, caused by degeneration of the nervous system, he had observed that the symptoms could be relieved by hypnotic suggestion, an instruction to the hypnotized patient that her symptom would be gone upon emerging from the hypnotic state. Freud was impressed with Charcot's demonstrations, but he found that hypnotic suggestion was ineffectual with many patients. Back in Vienna, he began experiments with a modification of the technique, which involved asking the hypnotized patient to recall the earliest events related to the development of the symptom. He found that if the patient recalled the events, and also felt the emotion appropriate to the original situation, the symptoms would be relieved.

The idea of having the patient, under hypnosis, try to recall the circumstances of the beginning of her illness came to Freud from Josef Breuer, an older physician, who had told him some time before about the case of "Anna O." This young woman, while nursing her ill father, had developed symptoms, including a cough, a squint that interfered with her vision, headaches, and various paralyses and areas of numbness, which Breuer recognized as hysterical. After the father's death, Anna's illness became worse. She began having agitated episodes of hallucination during the day, followed by dreamy, trancelike states in the evening. She and Breuer discovered that if she related to him the details of her hallucinations while she was in the evening trance, she would be relieved and tranquil during the rest of the evening. Later, they found that her troublesome physical symptoms could be removed if she recalled unpleasant events associated with them and talked about them under hypnosis, expressing also the feelings aroused by the memory. Anna called this process the "talking cure," or "chimney sweeping." Breuer named it the *cathartic method*. After a year and a half of treatment, Anna was relieved of her symptoms.[1]

Freud's knowledge of Anna's case and his experience with his own patients led him to the belief that the cathartic method was more effective than hypnosis, and he eventually developed a technique called *free association* in which the patient was instructed to talk about everything that came into her mind, no matter how ridiculous or improper it seemed. Such a train of associations, Freud believed, would lead back to the buried memory that was responsible for the patient's symptom.

Having become quite successful in treating hysterics with this method, Freud persuaded Breuer to work with him on a book which appeared in 1895 as *Studies in Hysteria*. The core of their theory was that hysterics suffered from buried memories of a painful or traumatic nature, and that all such memories with their repressed emotions had sexual features. Freud's association of hysteria with repressed sexual experiences led him to two important discoveries: the effect of unconscious motivation on behavior, and the role of sexuality, particularly in childhood, in human development.

The *unconscious*, Freud proposed, was a repository of memories which were not available to the individual—they could not be recalled at will. Because they represented events that had caused mental pain or shock, they had to be repressed, relegated to the realm of the unconscious. They continued to have effects, however, and were manifested in dreams and in such everyday experiences as forgetting, slips of the tongue, and other "mistakes," which, if analyzed by free association, could reveal their source in the unconscious. If the memories had sexual content, they could produce hysterical symptoms. An understanding of puzzling behavior, and the relief of symptoms with no apparent physical cause, could be effected only by bringing to light their unconscious motivating causes, and by releasing the pent-up emotion with which they were originally invested.

The psychosexual stages

In 1905 Freud presented his general theory of sexual development in *Three Essays on the Theory of Sexuality*. This work, with its later

---

[1] In the meantime, Anna had fallen in love with Breuer, a turn of events which upset the proper physician greatly. When he attempted to terminate treatment she immediately relapsed and presented him with her most dramatic symptom, a hallucination that she was in labor with his child. Breuer hastily left with his wife on a vacation, and never again could he bring himself to use the "talking cure" on a patient. Anna eventually regained her health and became prominent as the first social worker in Germany. A major part of her life's work was spent on women's causes

revisions, and his final book, *An Outline of Psychoanalysis* (1939), deal with infantile sexuality, sexual aberrations, and the stages of sexual development which Freud thought were a universal pattern for all males and females. His later work on the psychology of women grew directly out of this early theoretical unfolding of the development of sexuality through what came to be called the *psychosexual stages.*

Freud postulated the presence at birth of an undifferentiated sexual energy which he called *libido.* Early in life the libido was not directed toward or focused on any particular object, nor was it localized in any part of the body. The selection of sexual aims and objects came later as a result of experience. This generalized sexual potential of the infant, which he called *polymorphous perversity,* made possible the later channeling of sexuality into a variety of expressions, from "normal" heterosexuality to more unusual behaviors such as homosexuality, fetishes, and so on. Freud's theory of psychosexual stages shows how the individual moves from the undifferentiated stage of polymorphous perversity through successive stages in which the libido is organized around certain areas of the body to the final stage, mature genital heterosexuality. This sequence of events, he said, had crucial implications for personality development, and for the later observable psychological differences between the sexes.

The infant's earliest source of gratification and pleasure is in activities associated with feeding. Hunger is an uncomfortable sensation. Relief comes in the form of the mother's breast, rhythmic sucking, and warm milk, all inducing peaceful relaxation. Later, sucking by itself becomes a pleasurable activity, leading Freud to believe that such oral behavior that was not nutritional in its results was sexual in nature. Thus, the mouth and lips are the first area of the body to be associated with sexual pleasure. Freud called areas sensitive to pleasurable stimulation *erotogenic zones.* During the first year of life, the mouth is the primary erotogenic zone, and that period came to be designated the *oral stage* of psychosexual development.

During the second and third years of life the child develops control over certain body functions, notably the retention and expulsion of feces. Successful mastery of bowel activity is greatly valued by the parents, who bestow warm praise for productive and proper performance. Also, the child's self-stimulation by retention and expelling feces, and the rhythmic quality of the action, are themselves pleasurable and gratifying. Thus the anal region becomes an erotogenic zone, and the *anal stage* succeeds the oral stage of psychosexual development.

and emancipation. In 1922, she wrote, "If there is any justice in the next life women will make the laws there and men will bear the children" (Jones, 1953, p. 224).

The three- or four-year-old child has attained mastery over anal functions, and is also physically well coordinated. Now able to manipulate almost any part of the body at will, the child discovers the pleasure potential of the genitals and of infantile masturbation. The locus of sexual pleasure shifts to the genitals, and the child moves into the *phallic stage,* the last sexual stage of infancy, the most likely to be fraught with problems, and the most important for personality development. Although the word "phallic" comes from the Greek word *phallus,* meaning the male genital organ, the phallic stage characterizes the development of both sexes, whose libidinal aim now is the stimulation of the genital regions: for the male, the penis; for the female, the clitoris.

Around age six, the child ceases to display overt sexuality and enters a period which Freud called the *latency stage.* Sexual impulses are not extinct, but essentially lie dormant until their re-emergence at puberty. Infantile sexuality associated with the oral, anal, and phallic stages becomes repressed as a part of the contents of the unconscious, where it may later exercise effects on the individual's behavior, dreams, and personality.

Puberty terminates the latency stage, and the young person enters the *genital stage,* characterized by a resurgence of the sexual impulses. The libido, whose aim has been the self-induction of pleasure through the stimulation of parts of the body, may now be directed toward a member of the other sex. In the normal course of events, the individual has reached psychosexual maturity.

Freud thought that the psychosexual development of boys and girls is the same until they reach the phallic stage, whose events were fatefully linked to the attainment of normal personality and sexuality, and to those behavior patterns called masculinity and femininity. Both have the mother as their first love-object, and both have their earliest identification with her. During the phallic stage, however, the boy develops sexual wishes for the mother, and begins to see his father as a hated and powerful rival. Freud saw in this development a resemblance to the theme of *Oedipus Rex,* a fifth-century B.C. Greek drama by Sophocles. Before Oedipus is born, the Delphian oracle tells his father, Laius, that the expected child will grow up to kill his father and marry his mother. In order to prevent such a horror, Laius tries to get rid of the baby at birth by having him abandoned on a mountain. The child is rescued, however, and as an adult he unwittingly fulfills the prophecy by slaying Laius and marrying his mother, Jocasta, the Queen of Thebes. After fathering four children by her, he learns the truth of what he has done and in his horror he puts out his eyes. Freud saw in this story a universal theme that must be in the experience of every small boy. He named it the *Oedipus complex.*

During this same period that the boy is having unacceptable and anxiety-provoking feelings toward his mother and father, he discovers that girls and women do not have a penis, that organ from which he derives such pleasure. He comes to the conclusion that it has been cut off, probably as a punishment for some misdeed. Such a fate could also happen to him, especially because of his secret desires for his mother and his death wishes toward his father. Thus *castration anxiety* becomes an important feature of this stage, causing unbearable conflict and psychic distress. The resolution of this greatest of childhood's problems, Freud thought, came about through the mechanism of repression, the relegation to the unconscious of the Oedipal wishes and all other sexuality as well, thus ushering in the latency stage. The boy then moved, at an unconscious level, into an identification with the father and his masculinity, and finally into psychosexual maturity.

Freud's theory of female development

And what about the little girl? How did she resolve her phallic stage, move into latency, and develop a feminine identification? Freud first presented a theory of female psychosexual development in *Three Essays.* Much later he wrote three papers in which he integrated these ideas into a theory of female personality. These are "Some Psychical Consequences of the Anatomical Distinction between the Sexes" (1925), "Female Sexuality" (1931), and "Femininity" (1933). During his earlier writings, Freud held to a vague notion of a parallel development of girls and boys, based on the model of the boy and his resolution of the Oedipal conflict. But all along, he spoke from time to time about the puzzle of female psychosexual development. In *Three Essays* he wrote: "The significance of the factor of sexual overvaluation can best be studied in men, for their erotic life alone has become accessible to research. That of women . . . is still veiled in impenetrable obscurity."[2] Almost twenty years later, in a paper on the phallic stage, he confined his descriptions to the male child, because "the corresponding processes in the little girl are not known to us."[3] As late as 1926 we find him saying that this ignorance was no cause for shame: "after all, the sexual life of adult women is a 'dark continent' for psychology."[4]

[2] See Stafford-Clark (1966), p. 195.
[3] *Ibid.*
[4] *Ibid.*

The little girl enters the phallic stage, as does the boy, with the discovery of the genital zone and the pleasures of masturbation. Freud saw no particular psychological significance to this early masturbatory activity in either sex. It began as an inevitable discovery as the child explored its body, and was maintained because it was pleasurable. The psychological consequences came later. Early in this stage, Freud declared, the little girl was destined to make a "momentous discovery." She would notice the penis of a brother or playmate, visible and large, see that it was superior to her own small organ, "and from that time forward fall a victim to envy for the penis" (1974, p. 20).

The psychological consequences of her envy for the penis are of critical importance in her subsequent personality development. She perceives that she has been castrated, a personal wound to her self-esteem, and she develops a permanent sense of inferiority. When she learns that her lack of a penis is shared by all females, she develops a feeling of contempt for her sex. Even later, when she no longer consciously envies the male his penis, she is left with a residual of this envy in the form of jealousy, a character trait that Freud thought was much more important in the mental life of women than of men because of its early reinforcement by penis envy.

Another consequence of the girl's discovery of her genital inferiority is the abandonment of her mother as a love-object. The mother, herself sharing the daughter's inadequacy, is blamed for the lack of a penis. At this time, the girl's libido shifts from her mother to her father. Father is taken as the love-object, and mother is seen as her rival. She will now substitute for her unrealizable wish for a penis the wish for a child. In this transfer of the object of her libido to the male, and in the equating of penis with child, she thus resolves her penis envy and prepares to move along the course of normal femininity.

However, two other lines of development may diverge, which preclude the normal outcome. In the first, the girl finds that the pleasure she took in clitoral masturbation is now spoiled by her envy of the penis. She expresses dissatisfaction with her inferior clitoris by striving against any gratification from it, repressing her sexual impulses, and thereby laying the basis for neurotic problems later in life. In the second, she refuses to accept the fact of her castration, defiantly clings to phallic masturbation, and develops along a principle of activity which Freud called a masculinity complex. By this he meant that she would cling to her threatened masculinity, and to her hope for a penis. The fantasy of being a man in spite of everything would pervade her life, so that she might become homosexual, and be compelled to behave as though she were a man.

Freud thought that the girl had a more difficult transition than a boy to effect in her development toward adult sexuality, for two reasons. First, she had to make the transfer from her original love-object, her mother, to her father; and second, she must change her erotogenic zone from the "phallic" clitoris to the vagina. Thus her libidinal mode of satisfaction had to move from an active to a passive one. Freud's explanation for the necessity of this, and its effects on female sexuality, is rather complicated, but an understanding of it is important for a balanced evaluation of his theory.

Freud began the last of his three papers on women with a discussion of anatomical bisexuality. He noted that male and female genitalia differentiate out of the same embryonic structures, and that vestiges of the male internal reproductive structures are found in the female and vice versa. Anatomically, he said, the human is bisexual, but more one than the other. Likewise, it is common to speak of certain behaviors as masculine or feminine, regardless of who is displaying them. But this distinction is not truly a relevant sexual one, in that what is usually meant by "masculine" is "active" and by feminine, "passive" and, Freud stressed, it is plain that both sexes can display both activity and passivity. Women can be active in many directions, and men must develop considerable passivity if they are to live in community with others. Therefore, Freud concluded, it is incorrect to equate masculinity with activity and femininity with passivity. One can characterize femininity as giving preference to passive aims, but this is not the same as passivity, since considerable activity may be required in the achievement of a passive aim. How is this related to the transfer of eroticism from the clitoris to the vagina? The libido, Freud said, is neither masculine nor feminine. There is only one kind of libido, present in both sexes. The libido by definition is instinctive, and all instincts are active. Thus, following the convention that equates "active" with "masculine," the libido is often thought of as masculine. But Freud cautioned that in this usage it must not be forgotten that it also includes passive aims, which occur in the female when the sexual energy is transferred from the clitoris to the vagina.

During the pre-Oedipal period, the little girl's sexuality is of the same active thrusting kind as the boy's. Upon learning of her "castration" and abandoning her mother as love-object, she also gives up her clitoral sexuality as she moves into the latency period. Freud thought that the vagina was relatively insensitive prior to puberty, deriving what sensitivity it had from the clitoris and the anus. The vagina, in fact, was for most children undiscovered in childhood owing to the primacy of the phallic clitoris. When clitoral sensitivity reappears at puberty, it no longer has the active aim of the earlier period, but now is likely to be used autoerotically in masturbation, or, in heterosexual activities, as part of foreplay preparatory to sexual intercourse. Freud did not believe that the clitoris *lost* its sensitivity, or became anesthetic, but rather that clitoral sexuality was converted into a passive aim as sensitivity was transferred to the receptive vagina (Mitchell, 1974a). A woman might remain "clitoridal" all her life, with no wish for penile penetration, exemplifying arrested development of her femininity. The normal adult woman would be able to have orgasm by vaginal stimulation; to be able to have orgasm only by clitoral stimulation was psychosexually immature.

Freud thought that sexual development of the girl from the active aims of her pre-Oedipal clitoral sexuality to the passive aims of her adult vaginal receptivity was more difficult than that of the boy, and that she was more susceptible to psychological disturbances on account of this. Residuals of the early "masculine" period were common, and some women experienced frequent alternations between the masculine and feminine phases, an expression and a reminder of the bisexuality inherent in the female condition. The psychic energy required to bring about normal femininity had a draining effect on the female, and could account for her lower sex drive and for the frequency of frigidity in women. In some women, a lack of interest in sex or the vaginal anesthesia that characterized true frigidity might be psychogenic, but other cases suggested that such problems might be caused by constitutional or even anatomical factors. In any case, he believed, the accomplishment of the biological aim is effected by the aggressiveness of the male, and is independent to an extent of the cooperation of the female.

Certain features of normal mature femininity, Freud proposed, flow from the girl's pre-Oedipal identification with her mother, her discovery of their common genital inferiority, and the shift of her libidinal aim to her father. The girl's early doll play, for example, is an expression of identification with her mother; she is her mother, and the doll is herself. Later, when penis-envy is established, the doll-baby becomes a baby from the father, the aim of her strongest wish. Because of her identification of penis with baby, motherhood is a special joy, especially if the baby is a boy, bringing with him the longed-for penis. Freud believed that the mother-son relationship is the most perfect and most free of ambivalence of all human relationships. She can realize through her son all the ambition she had had to suppress in herself, and through him she can satisfy all that was left of her old masculine strivings.

But penis envy had long-term consequences, expressed in traits which Freud thought characterized adult women. One of these was narcissism,[5] a preoccupation with the self which was reflected in a strong need to be loved. Another was vanity, seen in the value which women placed on their physical charms, the more important to them as a compensation for their original sexual inferiority. A third was shame, whose original purpose was the concealment of genital deficiency.

Because the girl was spared the boy's traumatic resolution of his Oedipal complex under threat of castration, she never totally had to abandon her libidinal interest in her father. Because she was under less duress, her personality would fail to develop the rigorous components of what Freud called *superego*, which gives rise to conscience, morality, and other traits that mark civilized man. This is why, he proposed, women have little sense of justice and a weak social interest. Finally, Freud offered a comparison of the typical female patient of thirty with her male counterpart. He is still youthful, able to make good use of the possibilities that analysis would open up for him. She, on the other hand, seems rigid and less open to change. No paths are open to further development; the whole process has run its course, as if, Freud said, the development to femininity had exhausted the possibilities of the person.

Freud's theories of female sexuality and personality have drawn heavy fire from feminist critics during the past few years. Because of the key role of penis envy, which is based on the anatomical distinction between the sexes, the events which proceed from it—the suppression of the clitoris, the dependence of further sexual satisfaction on penile penetration, the need for a male child as penis substitute, the derived model of feminine personality with its less than flattering traits—all seem to rest on a biological base which not only limits the range of possibilities but gives scant recognition to the role of social factors as shaping influences of women's behavior. Furthermore, at face value the theories clearly depreciate female sexuality and female genitalia. It is the male who aggressively consummates the biological *raison d'être* of the species. The whole notion of envy of the male organ, and the girl's perception of herself and all those like her as inferior castrates, clearly issues from assumptions of male superiority within the context of patriarchal society. Even Freud's great friend and biographer, Ernest Jones, observed the "phallic" bias of Freud's position.

On the other hand, both the followers and the critics of Freud have generally ignored his cautions of the tentative nature of his exploration of femininity, his call for further validation, and his dis-

---

[5] Narcissism derives its name from the name of the mythological Greek youth Narcissus who fell in love with his own image reflected in a pool of water.

claimers of final answers. He began his 1925 paper by saying that its findings would be of importance "if they could be proved to apply universally," and described them as "in urgent need of confirmation before (their) value or lack of value can be established" (1974, p. 17–18). In conclusion, he said that though he was inclined to "set some value" on these ideas, "this opinion can only be maintained if my findings, which are based on a handful of cases, turn out to have general validity and to be typical" (1974, p. 25).

Although Freud certainly did not stress the effects of society as determinants of personality and behavior, he was not altogether un- aware of such influence. In his later work, as he spoke of those per- sonality traits that seemed to be more characteristic of women, he denied claiming more than an "average validity" for his assertions, and went on to state that "it is not always easy to distinguish what should be ascribed to the influence of the sexual function and what to social breeding" (1974, p. 90).

In another, earlier paper, " 'Civilized' Sexual Morality and Mod- ern Nervousness," Freud showed how the double standard of moral- ity, the Victorian ideal of abstinence, and woman's sexual frustra- tions in marriage brought about neurosis:

> Marriage under the present cultural standard has long since ceased to be a panacea for the nervous sufferings of women; even if we physi- cians in such cases still advise matrimony, we are nevertheless aware that a girl must be very healthy to "stand" marriage. . . . Marital un- faithfulness would . . . be a much more probable cure for the neurosis resulting from marriage; the more strictly a wife has been brought up, the more earnestly she has submitted to the demands of civilization, the more does she fear this way of escape, and in conflict between her desires and her sense of duty she again will seek refuge in a neurosis.[6]

The young girl was educated to be chaste and was not told what her sexual role in marriage would be. Under such circumstances, she could not suddenly become sexually responsive in marriage: ". . . the training that precedes marriage directly frustrates the very aim of marriage."[7] And then, laying frigidity at the very door of civiliza- tion, he wrote, "I do not know whether the anaesthetic type of woman is also found outside the range of civilized education, but I consider it improbable."[8]

A recent analysis of Freud and of several of his important re- cent critics presents a strong argument that orthodox feminist attack on Freud is a serious error (Mitchell, 1974b). Psychoanalytic theory

[6] Quoted in Janeway (1974), p. 66.
[7] *Ibid.*, p. 67.
[8] *Ibid.*

offers an explanation for the oppression of women which explanations relying on biological and cultural roles cannot do. The notion that biology is an innate determinant of personality is not inherent in Freud's feminine psychology (nor in the whole of psychoanalytic theory), because psychoanalysis does not deal with biology but rather with the transformation of biological facts into mental representations. The forms of these mental representations are a function of the social reality of patriarchy, which is synonymous with culture. In other words, psychoanalysis deals with the inheritance of a social order, and with its acquisition by each succeeding generation of males and females. That social order is patriarchy, the law of the father, and psychoanalytic theory is concerned with showing how the boy learns his place as heir to the law of the father, and the girl learns her place within it. Thus their concern is with "how the human animal becomes the sexed social creature—the man or the woman" (Mitchell, 1974b, p. 402). The ways in which this happens are not parallel for the two, in that the resolution of the pre-Oedipal active sexuality and desire for the mother, shared by both, must be asymmetrical, consistent with the asymmetry of their places in the patriarchal society. Thus the boy must give up his desire for the mother knowing that he is heir to the father's place and will some day have a woman of his own. The girl also must renounce her unrealistic love for her mother, not because it is dangerous, but because she has nothing with which to implement it. She learns to identify with her because of their similarities and to expect to take her place. Thus the girl's Oedipus complex occurs almost by default. It is not as strong as the boy's, and there is no reason that she must fully give it up. Its acquisition, in fact, sets her on the path to her feminine destiny under patriarchy. Her subjugation to the law of the father means that she becomes the representative of nature and sexuality. In submitting to the law, she becomes its opposite, loving and irrational. Her task is to provide for the reproduction of mankind within the family, where sex is contained and organized. According to Mitchell's observation, this is the place of all women in patriarchal culture. Differences of class, historical period, or specific social situation may affect the expressions of femininity, but in relation to patriarchy, the law of the father, women's position everywhere is comparable.

Feminist criticism of Freud, that he overvalued the male in taking for granted that the penis is a superior organ and that anyone who did not have one would feel deprived and be envious, and that he was not sensitive to woman's powerlessness and lesser status in society, is ill-conceived, argues Mitchell, for several reasons. Such criticism tries to deal with Freud's statements on feminine psychology

outside the contextual framework of psychoanalysis, thus misin-
terpreting it and distorting its meaning, which can be understood
only as an explanation of the psychology of women in patriarchal society. Far from ignoring social realities, the concern of psychoanalysis is with the mental representations of those very realities. The
little girl's renunciation of her pre-Oedipal sexuality and desire for
the mother are a prerequisite to her assumption of her place in the
real society of ubiquitous patriarchy, just as the destruction of the
boy's Oedipal attachment and identification with the father prepare
him to assume his role.

Furthermore, in arguing that cultural conditioning is solely responsible for woman's inferior role and for the "feminine personality," Freud's critics ignore or by implication deny the unconscious
and infantile sexuality. The struggle between nature and culture
which is the essence of the Oedipal conflict is not conscious or overt,
nor is it dealt with overtly. Its repression and inaccessibility to consciousness give it a power which cannot be matched by superficial
social reforms or by other changes based on understandings which
invoke either biology or conditioning as causes for women's oppression.

Mitchell says that patriarchal ideology, the law of the father,
with its prescriptions for women, is "in the slow death throes of its
own irrationality" (1974b, p. 143). But its final demise will require a
political struggle—a cultural revolution—which may be spearheaded
by revolutionary feminism. When this happens, then it will be possible for those mental representations, reflecting the social realities
which psychoanalysis is all about, to change in fundamental ways.
But for the present and the past, psychoanalysis is an analysis of the
human condition in patriarchal society.

Psychoanalytic research and psychotherapy

Psychoanalytic theory, as developed by Freud and his colleagues, was generated and tested by clinical analyses and investigations of patients. The theories of the unconscious and of infantile
sexuality, for example, grew out of Freud's early experiences in the
treatment of hysterics. The term *psychoanalysis* was applied both to
theory and to a particular kind of therapy, and the two were closely
interrelated. The insights gained in the therapy itself provided data
for the development and modification of theory, and the theory in
turn guided the process of therapy. Unlike the research methods of
modern psychology, which are modeled after those of the physical
sciences with their reliance on controlled observation and quantita-

tive measurement, psychoanalytic research was based on case studies of individuals. Elaborate studies of the single case were presented to "prove" or to elucidate a point. Sometimes, a theoretical innovation would be introduced, based on a small number of cases. For example, Jeanne Lampl-De Groot, a Dutch psychoanalyst, supported a thesis on the Oedipal complex in girls with data derived from the analysis of two female patients, and Helene Deutsch attributed female homosexuality to regression to the "masculine" clitoral stage, based on her study of eleven women.

Another characteristic of psychoanalysis is its use of explanatory concepts which are difficult if not impossible to verify. Penis envy, for example, "explains" certain aspects of female personality, but its actual existence and nature have defied illumination, as witness the fifty-year controversy it has generated.

Related to this is a feature of psychoanalytic psychotherapy, which relies upon overcoming the patient's *resistance* in order to reveal unconscious material, which is then made meaningful by *interpretations* which relate it to the patient's problem feelings and behavior. The free-association process and the analytic skill of the therapist combine to remove resistance to remembering long-buried events, to understand their significance, and to show how their motivating properties have contributed to the presenting symptoms of the patient. But whether or not the interpretation is correct depends on the subjective opinion of the analyst, whose assertion that it is may be impossible to verify. For example, one case described a patient who remembered how as a child he had fainted in the school playground. "This first attack was the unconscious symbolic equivalent of an amorous swoon" (David, 1970, p. 60), which meant his desire for his mother. Obviously such an interpretation taking place many years after the event cannot be checked for accuracy. Freud was aware of such criticisms and offered as a defense his finding that childhood memories persisting into adulthood were screens for important events, usually sexual in nature, and that a correct interpretation of the memory, when recognized by the patient, was often followed by a recession of symptoms. In any case, these characteristics of psychoanalytic theory and therapy have presented obstacles to its acceptance by contemporary psychology just as its male bias, as viewed by feminists, has caused its statements on women to attract withering criticism.

Against all these criticisms however, stands the unassailable fact of the enormous influence that psychoanalysis has had upon Western culture and its interpretations of the human condition. Of women, if it originally did not prescribe how they ought to be but rather analyzed them as they came into being in a patriarchal society, its appraisal continues.[9] Attention is directed not only to Freud's papers on female sexuality and personality but to his own accounts of the cases of the women who were his patients. One in particular exemplifies the development of theory, the process of therapy, and unwittingly, the dynamics of patriarchy as they affect both. In 1905, Freud published "Fragment of an Analysis of a Case of Hysteria," better known as the case of Dora.

Dora was eighteen when she was brought to Freud by her father, whom Freud had treated several years earlier for syphilis. The precipitating reason for the consultation was a letter written by her, and found by her parents, in which she said goodbye to them with the implied intention of taking her life. Although her father doubted that she was serious, he was disturbed enough to insist that she see a doctor. She also had a "nervous" cough, with a history of fainting spells, loss of voice, headaches and depression going back to childhood. Freud diagnosed her collection of symptoms as a typical case of hysteria, and set about an analysis to uncover the cause, which by that time he was already convinced lay in the repressed content of early sexuality. His treatment of Dora lasted for three months, until she abruptly terminated it, much to Freud's disappointment.

Dora's family included her parents and a brother who was one and a half years older. Dora was "tenderly attached" to her father. Her mother, whom Freud never met, was a pallid creature who spent her time obsessively cleaning the house. She and Dora did not get along. Dora was very critical of her, and refused to be influenced by her, at least consciously. The brother took the mother's side in family arguments, and Dora and he had grown apart. Thus were father and daughter aligned against mother and son, a drama with which Freud by now was very familiar. Earlier, a governess had been part of the household. She and Dora had been close until Dora began to believe that the older woman's kindness to her was a strategy to attract her father, with whom the governess had fallen in love.

Dora was precocious as a child, and Freud described her at eighteen as lively and intelligent. She attended lectures and was interested in her studies. Having experienced a variety of medical treatment since childhood for her various symptoms, she now laughed at the efforts of doctors and refused to see them. Her father induced her to see Freud against her will, she told him, and she had decided to "put up with it" until the New Year. Her last session was on December 31, 1899.

---

[9] For example, see Strouse (1974) and Miller (1973).

Dora's father revealed to Freud what he thought had precipitated Dora's most recent illness and the suicide note. Her parents had some time ago formed a close friendship with a married couple, Herr and Frau K. Frau K., an energetic and attractive woman, had nursed Dora's father through a long illness, and Herr K. was especially fond of Dora, going on walks with her and bringing her presents. Dora and Frau K. had spent much time together, and had been confidantes, a type of relationship that Dora had not had with her mother.

Two years before, said the father, Dora had reported that Herr K. had made an indecent proposal to her while they were walking by a lake. She had slapped him in the face and had gone home alone. Confronted by her father, Herr K. denied that any such episode had occurred, suggesting that Dora's imagination had been inflamed by reading books with sexual content, and that she had fantasied the whole thing. Dora's father believed him. But Dora insisted that he break off relations with the K.'s, especially with Frau K. This her father refused to do on the grounds that Herr K. was innocent, and that his own relationship with Frau K. was platonic.

After Dora started in treatment with Freud, she told him of still another episode with Herr K. when she was fourteen. She had gone to his office to watch a street festival, and he had embraced and kissed her. She reacted with disgust and ran home. For some time, she avoided being alone with him.

Freud found Dora well informed about sexual matters, and apparently she was able to talk freely to him. She was insistent on two things: her father and Frau K. had been having an affair for years, and Herr K. had tried to seduce her. To Freud's credit, he believed her: ". . . I came to the conclusion that Dora's story must correspond to the facts in every respect" (p. 57). He thought that the sexual trauma of Herr K.'s initial advance, when she was fourteen, provided an explanation for Dora's symptoms, in accordance with the theory which he and Breuer had derived for the etiology of hysteria. But there was much, much more. Analysis of her dreams was consistent with Freud's theory of the girl's Oedipal love for her father. Dora was reacting to her father's affair with Frau K. as if she were a wronged wife or a betrayed lover—as if she were the woman her father once loved, her mother, or the woman he now loved, Frau K. Since she was neither of these, her reaction, which Freud interpreted as jealousy, was inappropriate. Furthermore, he thought that her reaction to Herr K.'s advances, even when she was fourteen, was "entirely and completely hysterical" (p. 37). Without question this was true of any person in whom an occasion for sexual excitement elicited exclusively negative feelings. Instead of the genital sensation which would have been felt by a healthy girl in such a situation, Dora had felt disgust. Disgust is an oral phenomenon, and this, along with her throat symptoms of coughing and loss of voice, Freud related to her fantasies of her father and Frau K. having oral intercourse.

Although she denied it, Freud insisted that Dora was sexually attracted to Herr K. Her feeling for him reflected both her feeling for her father and her feeling for Frau K. That is, she identified Herr K. with her father, and herself with Frau K. Thus her attraction to Herr K. was a recapitulation of her father's love affair with Frau K.

Freud interpreted Dora's unexpected termination of her therapy as evidence of his newly developing theory of *transference,* the psychic mechanism by which a patient transfers to the therapist old feelings and conflicts which she once felt for significant persons, such as her mother and father. Just as she had transferred her love for her father to Herr K., so she now transferred in the therapeutic situation some of the same feelings to Freud. But these feelings were negative as well as positive, and for her treatment at the hands of the other two she would take her revenge on Freud, by deserting him. She was saying, Freud thought, "Men are all so detestable that I would rather not marry. This is my revenge" (p. 143). Dora's termination caught Freud by surprise. Fifteen months later, she visited him one more time for treatment of a facial neuralgia which had started two weeks earlier. He showed her that exactly two weeks before she had read an article about him in the newspaper. Thus her pain was a self-punishment for the double crime: the long-ago slap at Herr K. when he had compromised her virtue, and her peremptory treatment of Freud in her abrupt termination of their relationship.

Freud never saw her again. But a half century later, Dora reappeared in the psychoanalytic literature. Felix Deutsch (1957) revealed that in 1922 he had been asked to do a "psychiatric study" of a middle-aged woman who turned out to be the Dora whom Freud had made famous. Deutsch found her still complaining of symptoms which he thought were hysterical: dizziness, ear noises, and migraine headaches. She complained that her husband was unfaithful, and denounced all men as selfish, demanding, and ungiving. Many years later, Deutsch, having learned of her death made inquiries about the course of her life during the intervening years, and was told that her symptoms had continued throughout her life. In fact, said Deutsch's informant, she had been "one of the most repulsive hysterics" he had ever met.

Freud published this case, incomplete as it was, because he

thought it was an important demonstration of the sexual origin of hysteria. Dora's Oedipal love for her father, her transfer of this feeling to Herr K. (even though she persistently denied any sexual arousal in her encounters with him), her conscious jealousy of Frau K. and her unconscious identification with her—all these features of the case made it important to Freud. But suppose we examine it from Dora's perspective. How did it feel to be Dora, a teenage girl in turn-of-the-century Vienna? What was the state of her relationships with the significant people in her life?

She and her mother had never been close. Her mother seems to have been unable to help her daughter, and presented such an unattractive model in her role of obsessional housewife that Dora looked elsewhere for a woman she could love and admire. The kindness of her governess was not genuine, but was an exploitative means of winning Dora's adored father. She became very attached to Frau K., who appeared fond of the girl only to betray her in the same way. The once-loved brother abandoned her, joining with the mother in an attitude of rejection. Herr K., family friend and admired adult, made indecent proposals to her, then lied about it. And her father chose to believe *him*, at the same time denying what was obvious to everyone (including Freud), that he was having an affair with a woman who Dora had once thought was her friend. "None of her father's actions," Freud wrote, "seemed to have embittered her so much as his readiness to consider the scene by the lake as a product of her imagination" (p. 57). Freud thought she was over-reacting, but saw that in another respect her reproaches about her father were justified: "When she was feeling embittered she used to be overcome by the idea that she had been handed over to Herr K. as the price of his tolerating the relationship between her father and his wife" (p. 44). Freud himself believed that the two men were engaged in an unspoken conspiracy in which Dora was the pawn: her father would ignore Herr K.'s attempted seductions of his daughter in exchange for Herr K.'s pretended ignorance of his wife's affair with Dora's father. "[E]ach of the two men avoided drawing any conclusions from the other's behavior which would have been awkward for his own plans" (p. 44). Incredibly, Freud also knew the father's motive for bringing Dora to see him. He wanted Freud to talk her out of her notion that there was anything more than friendship between him and Frau K.

Caught in this web of lies, deceit, and betrayal, where could she turn? Her situation as it must have seemed to her was cause enough for depression and suicidal ideas. Freud might have said to her, "You are right, and they are wrong." But Dora had left therapy prematurely, thus it was her fault that she was never cured, that finally, the intelligent, lively girl had earned the epitaph which Deutsch bestowed upon her.

Helene Deutsch

Helene Deutsch was born in 1884, in Poland. Like Freud, she received her medical training at the University of Vienna, and in 1918, she spent a year in analysis with him in Vienna. From that time until he left Vienna in 1933, she worked closely with him, and there is no doubt that this association was the single most important influence on her own work. She was married to Felix Deutsch, Freud's friend and one-time physician (and consultant to Dora). She presented the culmination of her ideas about women in her two-volume *Psychology of Women*, published in 1944 and 1945.

Deutsch was truly a Freudian, one of those women analysts who have been called the "dutiful daughters" (Chesler, 1972). Her early papers were concerned with applying his concepts of the libido, the unconscious, and infantile sexuality to female functions such as pregnancy and childbirth. Though her work is within a Freudian theoretical framework, she greatly expanded the classical concepts as they applied to women. Her data were her clinical experiences with women in her analytic practice, case studies, and analyses of works of literature.

In certain important ways, however, Deutsch revised two key Freudian concepts of female personality development: penis envy and the resolution of the Oedipal conflict. Penis envy, while real, is not the basis of the girl's most essential conflicts, nor does it have a fundamental role in the development of her personality. It is, in fact, a secondary development, growing out of a general tendency to envy, experienced by all children when they observe another child, perhaps a new baby, receiving a great deal of love and attention; or when they see that another child has something of value, and they desire to have it for themselves. Boys experience this more fundamental envy as readily as girls do. When girls express penis envy it is a derivative of the general envy of another who has something one does not have. Some girls, Deutsch observed, even imagine that they have a penis when they are small, but do not need it any more when they are older. The personality trait of envy, described by Freud as a residual of penis envy, is not peculiar to women, said Deutsch.

Freud had assumed that the girl's abandonment of the mother as love-object in favor of her father was accomplished in early childhood. Deutsch believed, to the contrary, that this detachment is never fully achieved. The role of the girl's bond with her mother, and its characteristics, are of crucial importance to her personality development. She tests herself in struggles against it, and it forms a base for her own feminine identification. She must eventually free herself; too persistent a tie is restrictive of healthy emotional development. But the shadowy mother in Freud's system, early rejected by the girl in favor of her robust father, is restored to full and powerful form by Deutsch.

Deutsch's major work on the psychology of women was written when the Western world was in the throes of the Second World War, and women in large numbers were entering the armed services and working in industry. She considered the effects of this and other social changes on female personality, but she remained unimpressed with the importance of cultural factors as sources of change in the feminine psyche. During the war, women had entered the masculine world out of bitter necessity. Competitiveness, that curse of man, had not really got hold of women, who were dominated by tender and erotic motives rather than by aggressive ones. Certain prototypes of women would always recur, as they always had, perhaps showing different aspects in different cultures; the facade might change, but the feminine core would remain.

Psychosexual development

Deutsch accepted Freud's conceptual framework of the psychosexual stages, but it is not central to her own theories of the psychology of women. The interest of psychoanalysis in infantile sexuality was giving way to attention to the development of the child's ego, the growth of self, which mediated adjustment to reality and guided the emotional and intellectual aspects of personality. The infantile period, far from being dominated by sexual development, was also taken up with active attempts to conquer the environment, to adjust to it, and to resolve the inevitable conflicts between the drive for mastery and the necessity of taming the instinctual urges. With the growth of the ego, the child's relationship to the environment gradually became independent of the sexual instincts.

Not convinced that Freud was right about the bisexual nature of the oral and anal periods, Deutsch thought that sex differences were present from birth, becoming psychologically significant in the phallic phase. For the boy, this phase is concentrated around his prominent organ, which is the source of the active, aggressive urges of early childhood. Later, as he learns to adjust to reality through the growth of the ego, these urges are transferred to other needs, opening new possibilities of gratification for him.

Similarly, the girl in this phase has genital urges which are focused on the clitoris, whose structure, tumescent character, and erectibility make it comparable to the penis. It lacks, however, the forward thrusting, penetrating qualities of the penis, and while in some cases it may be touched and seen, it is often so rudimentary that the girl is effectively "organless," with no adequate outlet for her genital urges. Her sexual instincts, while constitutionally less active and aggressive than the boy's are, consist also of active-aggressive components which the clitoris cannot adequately discharge. Thus the impulses that need an active organ are attenuated. The inhibited sexual activity undergoes a transformation into passivity, which is the normal path to femininity. It is important to note, however, that Deutsch explicitly stated that passivity as a psychosexual development did not mean apathy or lack of sexual energy. The latter might be very great, but it would be manifested in the receptive readiness for sexual activity, rather than in the active aggressiveness seen in the male.

Thus the clitoris is deposed in importance by the passive-receptive vagina. In childhood, however, the vagina has no independent function; it is essentially nonexistent, being so far undiscovered. The "awakening" of the vagina to sexual functioning, Deutsch thought, is entirely dependent upon the man's activity; the absence of spontaneous vaginal activity is the physiological basis for feminine passivity. During this period, then, the girl is organless on two counts: first, she lacks an adequate active organ; second, she lacks a passive one. Deutsch thought that masturbation was relatively uncommon in girls, owing to their early renunciation of active clitoral sexuality. Since masturbation involved the clitoral area and hardly ever the vagina, its infrequency was adaptive, since clitoral stimulation would only interfere with the eventual development of vaginal sexuality.

Frigidity (in this case, failure to reach orgasm by vaginal stimulation), which in Deutsch's observation was very common among women, had several possible sources. If gratification by clitoral stimulation persisted, the transfer of sexual sensation to the vagina would be blocked. Or, sexuality may undergo a neurotic repression owing to an early sexual trauma. Many neurotic women were not frigid, however, while many psychiatrically normal women had little or no interest in sex. In some women, the sexual energy might be diverted to reproductive functions and to mothering. In any case, social restrictions on feminine sexuality could intensify a disposition to frigidity.

This review of Deutsch's analysis of the psychosexual development of women reveals the basic premises which her thinking shared with Freud's, and which caused her to share in the criticism directed toward him in later years. The girl's lower sex drive and the inadequacy of her clitoris to handle even her lesser urges were inherent in her femaleness, causing her sexuality to undergo a wave of repression. Its re-emergence later was a transformation, both as to location and to character, from clitoral aggressive activity to vaginal receptive passivity. This is by no means a prescription for frigidity, but it is plain that, for Deutsch, the sexuality of women was not only different from that of men, but also was less important within the overall context of their lives.

Narcissism, passivity, and masochism

Central to Deutsch's theory of femininity is a triad of personality characteristics: narcissism, passivity, and masochism.

Narcissism for Deutsch means taking oneself as the libidinal object, a loving and valuing of the self. Obviously, this can have both positive and negative, healthy and unhealthy aspects. Healthy narcissism is inherent in self-esteem, self-respect, in caring for the self, independently of others' opinions. Unhealthy narcissism is an immature concern for the self that requires constant affirmation from others. It is a manifestation of insecurity and inferiority feelings. Both sexes, of course, can exhibit degrees of each kind of narcissism. In women, narcissism may enrich or impoverish emotional life, but in its most helpful form it serves the woman as a protective function, as that mechanism which supports the instinct for self-preservation.

Adolescence brings a resurgence of sexual urges accompanied by anxiety over unfamiliar feelings and body changes. The ego marshals its defenses against such threats, and an important one of these is narcissism. The girl develops a great preoccupation with herself, with her body, her fantasies, her identity. Even her intense relationships with other girls are narcissistic, the ego drawing advantages for itself from its love for the other. By identifying with another, the girl's ego extends and acquires confidence from the sharing of strength. Healthy narcissism at this age prevents the girl from developing too many identifications, which would interfere with the growth of her own personality. By increasing self-confidence it promotes a strengthening of the ego and a gradual integration of the personal self. Her identity, the "I am I," emerges.

For Deutsch, passivity is the central attribute of femininity, an attitude of receptive waiting and expectancy. The passive person is one who does not act but is acted upon. She did not heed Freud's caution that it was improper to equate femininity with passivity and masculinity with activity. That very equation is at the heart of her psychology of women, a general principle that she said would always assert itself because of its constitutional origins in the body's hormones, anatomy, and reproductive functions. The model had its counterparts in conception and in intercourse, when the aggressive male penetrates the passive female. Woman's greater tendency to identification, her propensity for fantasy, her subjectivity, her inner perception, and her intuition all originate in her passivity. She will abandon her own opinions and tastes, for example, and adopt those of the man she marries. While both sexes fantasize, the male's fantasies are turned more to reality, to dreams of power and conquering the outside world, while hers are preoccupied with her narcissistic needs and with her relations with others. Such preoccupations determine her other characteristics, her subjectivity and perception which come from her feelings rather than from the objective reality of events, and her intuition, a way of "knowing" in the absence of facts. These tendencies are all passive, compared to their male counterparts of independent identity, fewer, more purposeful fantasies, objectivity, perception based on observable events, and rationality.

This is not to say that women do not behave actively. Indeed, the active mother, engaged in all the tasks of motherhood, is a model for her daughter. Woman's activity is harmful, Deutsch thought, only if it comes into conflict with the feminine core, in the form of the "masculinity complex," a protest against acceptance of her feminine self. But her urge toward activity is weaker, and the external inhibitions stronger, than the male's. Above all, the aggressive components are inhibited. The social environment rejects them, and in compensation offers a woman's ego a prize, which is love and tenderness. So the girl gives up her aggressions, partly because of her own weakness, partly because of the taboos of the environment, and mostly because of the love prize she receives in return.

Feminine masochism in Deutsch's thinking must be distinguished from the more familiar model of perversion and neurosis, in that it lacks the components of cruelty, of a seeking out of suffering and pain. In psychoanalysis, masochism means the derivation of pleasure from punishments inflicted by oneself or others. But Deutsch's usage of the term lacks the pejorative connotations. Masochism as she sees it is a normal condition for women, and normal women show no tendency to inflict pain or suffering upon themselves in the pursuit of pleasure. However, women are more attracted to suffering than men are, and are more likely, in the normal course of their lives, to experience it paired with pleasure. The woman's willingness to do this is what Deutsch means by masochism. Thus it is adaptive, an adjustment to the realities of her life, in which many of her normal female biological functions involve a combination of pain and pleasure, even joy, such as childbirth. Defloration, the destruction of the hymen in the first intercourse, can be painful, and pain experienced in the sexual act can lead to a connection with submission and gratification. It is to guard against "surplus" masochism, pain as a condition of pleasure, that narcissism is invoked as a defense. Thus viewed, normal femininity involves a balance between narcissism and masochism, the one in the service of the ego, the other, of reality. The healthy woman, then, will accept the discomfort, even pain, associated with her normal functions, because of the pleasure which accompanies them. And always guarding the gates of the ego is her healthy narcissism, her self-love, which will allow her to accept some suffering, but not too much.

Deutsch's type theory

The personality components of narcissism, passivity, and masochism produce, in delicate balance, the nomal feminine woman; and variations among these account for individual differences. Further, inadequate or incomplete repression of the active-aggressive component of the clitoral phallic stage results in other behavioral manifestations. Thus, various types of women can be described, variously adapted to their constitutional destinies, in harmony or disharmony with their social milieu.

Deutsch grouped her types of women into two basic categories: feminine and masculine. In the first, the types are determined by the relative importance in the personality of the components of narcissism, passivity, and masochism. In the second, the unrepressed active and aggressive tendencies lead to conflicts with the feminine core as well as with the environment, and the forms of these conflicts determine the types. She emphasized that these classifications are only for descriptive purposes. Pure types are not often seen; in each type one can find traces of another. For example, a feminine type may display masculine activity in a need to impose religious and moral values on others.

Feminine types: the erotic woman. The normal feminine woman, as described by Deutsch, is characterized by the predominant trait of eroticism, which means that her chief motive is to love and to be loved. A woman's eroticism may be sexual, but is not necessarily so; sexuality is only one part of her erotic nature. The fundamental elements contributing to the psychological makeup of the feminine-erotic types are the passive-masochistic character of their instinctual life, their narcissism, and the emotional representations of their reproductive functions. The relative weight of each is influenced by childhood history; their interplay directs the ways and means by which the eroticism achieves its aims, and gives each of the types its special qualities.

These types of women have in common a readiness for identification with men and a willingness to experience their own selves through such identification. When the two personalities are harmonious with each other, the woman adapts readily to the man, even if this means renunciation of some of her own needs. If talented, such women may preserve the capacity for being original and productive, but they avoid competitive struggles. The risk, of course, in this kind of adjustment is the effacing of one's own personality. But the healthy feminine woman offsets her tendencies to identification and renunciation, which derive from the passive and masochistic elements of her personality, through the counterplay of her narcissism, which protects her against excessive sacrifice of self. It is the role of narcissism which determines the difference between the first and second of Deutsch's three feminine-erotic types.

The first is easily influenced and won over, ready to give of herself physically and psychologically. But the grateful recipient then finds that those feelings that are most important to her are behind the protective wall of her narcissism. It is the security of this defense which permits her to give of herself initially, in ways that tap only the superficial aspects of her being. The danger for her lies, to use Deutsch's colorful term, in the bribing of her narcissistic guardian, the breaking down of her self-love so that she becomes the victim of her own masochism. Unless she can reinstate her narcissism, she may continue to re-experience such a masochistic fate. Thus is her harmony destroyed and she becomes neurotic, unable to refrain from excessive expenditure of self.

The second type of feminine woman is more cautious at the outset of a relationship, her narcissism immediately protective of her erotic and emotional life. She wants to be sure of the tie between herself and the other before she yields any part of herself. When the bond is secure she can abandon her reserve, knowing that her own personality will remain intact.

The difference between these two types is in where their narcissism makes its stand. Each, when the personality elements are in harmonious balance, is free from envy, competitive feelings, and other aggressive displays. Tolerant of others, they are also self-protective, and will not stay in a relationship which increases their masochistic burden.

The third type differs from the other two in that its masochism tends to be moralistic. That is, instead of aligning itself with passivity in the service of pleasure, it exercises itself against the woman's ego, producing a strong ethical orientation and a readiness to have guilt feelings. This moral masochism takes over some of the work of the narcissistic guardian, being more active in limiting it to self-respect and self-exactions, and in minimizing erotic needs. This woman is less tolerant of both others and herself, and is more likely to feel guilty when she allows herself erotic freedom. Her strong sense of duty requires that she put herself at the service of social values and ethical commitments rather than of eroticism. An important difference between this type and the first two is in the latter's greater openness to erotic experience. The third type is more ascetic and inhibited, and is also more concerned about these qualities in her children.

In delineating these three types, Deutsch took into account both the social milieu and constitutional factors. She thought, for example, that the more moralistic type of feminine woman appeared more frequently in Calvinistic countries, with a tradition of severity of upbringing and strict control of erotic behavior. The other two, in whom eroticism prevailed over moralism, were more likely to be found in Latin and Slavic countries where fewer sanctions were placed on the experiencing of pleasure, and where the attitudes toward sexuality were more relaxed. In the normal course, all have the capacity for warm unambivalent relations with others, both male and female.

Deutsch remarked that all these feminine types had close relationships with their mothers, although the character of the relationship differed between the first two types and the third. The first two tended to have had a smoother time of it, with fewer and briefer periods of conflict. A danger for these women was the possible prolongation of childish dependency, interfering with maturation. For the more moral type, the relationship with the mother, also close, was reactive, following upon stormy periods of conflict. Here it was the active, domineering mother who provoked hatred in her daughter, followed by a guilt reaction and subsequent identification with her.

If the risks in the courses of such relationships could be avoided or resolved, Deutsch thought, then the resulting positive mother-daughter relationship might be ideal; in fact, such a relationship is perhaps basic to the development of the feminine woman.

Active types: the masculinity complex. When the little girl differentiates into a feminine self, Deutsch thought, not all her active-aggressive forces are subject to inhibition. In part, they are preserved and are integrated into a harmonious whole, in no way discordant with her essential femininity. Such uninhibited activities in a nonpathological form may characterize the adjustment of the girl, and later the woman, who identifies with an active mother, and when this adaptation becomes central to the personality, a type emerges who within her family is dominant and managing, not unlike a mythological matriarch. Because her activity is maternal, directed toward nurturing, she may be motivated to have many children, or to care for children on an institutional basis. For Deutsch, this woman is in the line of the earthy mother principle described in the last chapter. Though she may be both feminine and erotic, she is active rather than passive, and her identity is independent of man. Husbands of such women may be pushed out of the role of forceful father, and sons may be passive, and dependent upon her. Especially does her strength attenuate the activity of the men in her family.

Deutsch suggested that there were limits to the activity inherent in such a role, beyond which the woman would sacrifice her feminine erotic qualities. These limits were subject to cultural definitions, however, and only when they pressed too close would the underlying aggression become manifest.

Identification with the father may give rise to active-aggressive drives which manifest themselves in active eroticism, in contrast to the more passive seductiveness of the feminine erotic types. Thus appears the sexually aggressive woman, the coquette, whose seizing of the initiative in encounters with the male is seen as aggressive. Despite the trend in contemporary mores which encouraged less inhibited sexual behavior for women, such aggressiveness, Deutsch believed, was against biological as well as psychological laws. Such a woman was reacting against fear of her own passivity, and would find her neurotic match in the male who wished to escape the responsibility of active courtship, a prerogative of the male role.

While both the matriarch and the coquette have turned their active strivings to the service of the ancient female accomplishments of mothering and seduction, a third type clearly displays what was for Deutsch evidence of the masculinity complex, the predominance in her personality of active and aggressive tendencies which lead to conflict with her environment and with the aims of her feminine self. This woman has goals whose accomplishment is hindered by her femininity, and since she is a woman, she feels inferior because inevitably she will be ineffective in the pursuit of those goals. The classic example of such a woman is the intellectual, who sacrifices her feminine affectivity for the arid pursuit of goals which are defined as masculine: achievement in the arts, business, or the professions. The compulsive character of her activity distinguishes her from women who accomplish a great deal because of their high level of energy and will power, but without sacrifice of their essential femininity.

Psychologically, women who have turned away from femininity, whose active-aggressive drives dominate their behavior and obscure the feminine core, are the result of a fundamental disturbance in their relationship with the mother. Normally, the girl's hatred of the mother because of her preferred position in the family circle gives way to identification with her, smoothing the path to the girl's access to such a position later in her life. But in some cases the girl was blocked from developing an unambiguous feminine identity for lack of an appropriate model. Perhaps her mother was neurotic or hysterical, presenting such an unpleasant model of woman that the girl had to turn from her, and in so doing turned from all aspects of the bogus "femininity" which she represented.

Deutsch illustrated the conflict between masculinity and femininity with an analysis of the life of George Sand, the French novelist whose brilliant work and unconventional life have fascinated many biographers.

Born Aurore Dupin, George Sand was the daughter of an aristocratic intellectual father and a wanton mother of lowly origin. Her paternal grandmother and her mother waged an incessant and deadly war for her father's exclusive love and loyalty, which culminated in the mother's leaving when Aurore was twelve years old to resume her earlier life as a prostitute. Though George Sand was later to defend her mother's behavior and to speak out for the rights of all women, the young Aurore was irreversibly injured by her mother's desertion of her at a critical age. Her unconscious hatred of her mother for this betrayal and her conscious hatred of her grandmother for driving her mother away caused her to identify with the memory of her father (who had died when she was four), whose intellectual interests were certainly closer to her own. Thus she turned from all that was feminine, and adopted masculine dress and habits, alternating at times with the adoption of a maternal role when she was in love.

She sought out feminine men, such as the composer Chopin, for her lovers, and dominated them and mothered them as her grandmother had done to her father. When such men finally left or betrayed her, she was crushed. No such relationship could be successful, because what she really wanted, Deutsch thought, was a strong, powerful, godlike father who could restore her femininity. Her split psyche was a perfect example of the masculinity complex in a woman whose femininity had been compromised by her disastrous relations with her "two mothers." Her intellect was masculine, but the creative intuitiveness she displayed in her novels was feminine. Masculine aggressiveness and feminine maternal needs motivated her search for love and her choice of lovers. Incapable of being a truly feminine woman, she escaped into masculinity, which brought her only grief.

Deutsch interpreted George Sand's tragic life as a psychic failure to integrate the masculine and feminine parts of her personality:

> If we assume that . . . woman and man originate in a common primeval source, we are compelled to conclude that in the psychic economy of the individual, the two components, masculine and feminine, must be united to form a harmonious whole. The feminine component should predominate in women and the masculine in men. When the harmony of the masculine and feminine tendencies is disturbed in an individual, an inner conflict arises (1944, pp. 322–23).

Sexuality and the feminine role

Deutsch's conception of the unfolding of the feminine role is displayed in the subtitles of her two volumes on the psychology of women: *Girlhood* and *Motherhood.* The sexuality of the normal woman was in the service of reproduction, and coitus was the beginning of a process leading to parturition. The central problem of the feminine woman was motherhood, a goal and a condition which eventually would absorb all the active forces of her personality.

Human culture had so modified the natural processes of sex and reproduction, separating them from each other, that their psychophysical unity had been obscured. But this unity was preserved in woman's unconscious, where coitus and childbirth were identified with each other. This relationship was usually imperceptible in normal, feminine women, but sometimes appeared in pathologically distorted forms in disturbed women. The case of Mrs. Andrews was related by Deutsch as an example.

Mrs. Andrews was twenty-nine years old and the mother of six children when she was admitted to the hospital with a number of neurotic symptoms, including fits of anger toward her husband and children. Her greatest expressed concern was an obsessional fear of pregnancy, which had tormented her since puberty. With each pregnancy, she had fought without success for an abortion, had aborted herself a few times, and had even poisoned herself with ergot to bring on her menses. She worked outside the home, forcing her husband to do much of the housework and child care. She associated childbirth with humiliation, saying, "Woman's most degrading position is on the delivery table, with her feet in the stirrups and men taking charge of her" (1945, p. 100).

The oldest of five children, Mrs. Andrews had been victimized and physically abused by her mother and her mother's lovers. She had reacted strongly to her mother's two illegitimate pregnancies, and had early decided that she would never have children. On the one hand, Mrs. Andrews felt an aggressive hatred toward her mother; but on the other, she identified with her, recognizing in herself her mother's temper tantrums and scornful treatment of her husband. It was this identification, Deutsch thought, that caused her pregnancy obsession. Consciously she rejected pregnancy with an overreactive aversive fear; unconsciously, she desired it.

The unconscious wish to be pregnant, Deutsch believed, appeared in the patient's requirements for satisfaction in coitus. She compulsively sought intercourse with her husband, even though she did not love him. But she could attain orgasm only at the moment of his ejaculation, when the semen flowed into her body. Orgasm then, was contingent upon the condition of possible impregnation. Thus was the conscious "No" to pregnancy countermanded by the unconscious "Yes," and in this neurotic woman Deutsch saw revealed what she believed was in the universal female unconscious—the identity of coitus, impregnation, and childbirth.

The case of Mrs. Andrews is presented here because it gives the flavor of Deutsch's interpretations of female behavior. These, of course, attract the same kinds of criticisms as Freud's did of Dora. Was this tormented woman unconsciously desiring and arranging her own pregnancies, while consciously repudiating them, pleading for abortions, and expressing her conflict through her numerous symptoms? Or was her fear a realistic sequel to her wretched childhood, leading to an inability to tolerate the female role prescription of the time, further forced upon her by a string of unwanted pregnancies? There is no way to know how much of her psychiatric illness was caused by the intrapsychic conflict described by Deutsch, and how much was caused by her inability, at that time, to control the events of her body. In any case, no epitaph exists to confirm or to invalidate any of the possible explanations, or to tell of her eventual fate.

For Deutsch, the sexuality of women, culminating in the climax of orgasm, was continuous with its natural consequences, pregnancy and childbirth. Unlike the male, for whom the sexual act was discrete, an end in itself, the female experienced orgasm almost incidentally, as a pleasurable sensation which could be described as a vicarious reflection of her mate's orgasm. Implicit was the notion of adjustment of her sexual activity to his. The expectation of multiple orgasm or of any obligation of the male to bring about sexual satisfaction for the female is absent from her work. Indeed, she termed ridiculous the instruction of "sexologists" that men should heighten their mates' erotic pleasure by their manipulative dexterity (1944, p. 222).

Years later, Deutsch commented on the high incidence of frigidity in women, and the poor results of psychoanalytic treatment for the condition (Chasseguet-Smirgel, 1970). A severe neurosis could be helped without affecting the problem of the patient's frigidity. Some psychotic or very aggressive masculine women had intense vaginal orgasms, while feminine, giving, maternal women did not, even though they expressed sexual gratification through intercourse. Also, analysis often revealed anxiety and depression after vaginal orgasms. By contrast, if the vagina remained passive-receptive, the sex act culminating for the woman in mild, slow relaxation, peaceful sleep usually ensued. Since orgasm, then, seemed to be related to pathological conditions, Deutsch was led to suggest that the passive-receptive kind of gratification for women be accepted as normal. If the intense, vaginal orgasm was not experienced by normal feminine women, then it was incorrect to conclude that frigidity was on the increase; rather, the increase was in the demands for a kind of sexual gratification which was not in harmony with the constitutional purpose of the vagina, an organ of reproduction.

Deutsch shared with Freud certain basic assumptions about women, which were based on the facts of women's anatomy and physiology, and their observable role and function in the society. Since women were biologically equipped to become mothers, and since most did in fact become mothers, such an outcome was the normative base upon which Deutsch built her psychology of women. The active-aggressive components of girlhood were converted to the service of femininity. Some women, such as the matriarch and coquette, channeled their "masculine" aggressiveness into powerful mother or seductress roles, involving activity which was still within the feminine tradition, nurturant and sexual. Others did not successfully integrate the masculine component into the service of femininity. Driven to achievement goals in intellectual or competitive pursuits, their personalities were in constant conflict. Their masculine component, unassimilated and alien, prevented them from accepting the full flavor of their destiny as women. Thus the masculinity complex was clearly a pejorative label, compared to the ideal, an integration of feminine personality and mother role into a harmonious model for womanhood. Inherent in this view is a duality of sex roles, with all the intellectual and other non-domestic activity allocated to the male. Such a designation also leads to the inference that women who thus depart from tradition are not only unfeminine but are not normal as well.

Divested of their value connotations, however, Deutsch's descriptions of types of women and their behavior patterns are unmatched in the psychological literature. Recognizable to clinicians and lay persons alike, these types and patterns do exist, their variety reflecting the interaction of the female condition with particular histories, influenced by the values of their time. Although personality theorists today may regard such a typology as simplistic, the idea persists in the common understanding. Questions such as, "What type of person is she?" and "Is she my type?" attest to to the popularity of the concept.

Erik Erikson

Erik Erikson is a contemporary psychoanalyst who was born in Germany of Danish parents in 1902. In 1927, he went to Vienna and with friends started a progressive school for visiting English and American children, some of whose parents were in analysis or were training to be analysts. He became acquainted with Freud and his family, and underwent a training analysis with Anna, Freud's daughter. He studied clinical psychoanalysis with Helene Deutsch and others who had gathered about Freud in Vienna. He has written extensively about problems of youth and identity, and he has published cross-cultural studies of childhood in American Indian tribes.

In the total context of Erikson's work, his statements about the psychology of women are not extensive. In fact, like Freud, he was in the seventh decade of his life when he published the paper which represented his analysis of female personality development, "The Inner and the Outer Space: Reflections on Womanhood," in 1964. Later, in 1975, he returned to the subject, responding to feminist criticism of his views in "Once More the Inner Space." Though our interest in Erikson concerns mostly these two papers, they should be viewed in the context of his larger contributions.

Erikson's most widely-known book is *Childhood and Society* (1963). In this work he presented his concept of the "eight ages of man," the psychological stages of identity development beginning in infancy and culminating in old age, and analyzed some examples of identity development in America, Germany, and Russia. He brought psychoanalytic insight to bear on child-rearing practices of two American Indian tribes and on the sex differences in play constructions of white American children. These were to provide data for his theoretical formulations about women in the 1964 paper. Our major interest in Erikson's work on identity formation and on childhood lies in those aspects of it that deal with girls and women, and that presumably influenced his later thinking about them.

Psychosocial development: the "eight ages of man"

According to Erikson's conception of the development of the person through the life cycle, the child passes through a series of phases, each with its own conflict, or crisis, to be resolved. Personality, he thought, develops in accordance with the person's readiness for successively increasing interactions with society, which in turn invites these interactions, encourages the rate at which they occur and their unfolding in the proper sequence. These stages,[10] and the period in the life cycle when they appear are shown in Table 2.1. The individual progresses, with variations in tempo and intensity, from one stage to the next, meeting and resolving the conflicts associated with each. The quality of the resolutions depends on what is given or permitted by the caretakers, whose offering in turn is affected by social customs and beliefs. Throughout, Erikson is concerned with the effect of society on the developing person, and thus with commonalities of personality which reflect commonalities of experience, as in child-rearing practices, for example.

The study of identity, Erikson said, is as strategic for our time as the study of sexuality was for Freud's time. Neither, however, precludes the other, as he showed by correlating the psychosocial stages of identity development with their counterpart periods of psychosexual development. While the various components of personality are inseparable, different historical periods evoke attention to different aspects of the whole.

Youth and identity

From this theoretical base, Erikson then proceeded to explore problems of identity by analyzing experiences of youth in three countries, America, Germany, and Russia. Although the "eight ages of man" are also the eight ages of woman, Erikson's examples are all male: in America a certain adolescent "type," a normal middle-class WASP with a mother, a father, and an older sister; in Germany, the young Hitler, who would become the demonic leader of a nation whose collective identity was ready for him; in Russia, the child Maxim Gorky, who grew up to be a famous writer and idol of the

---

[10] Definitions are for the positive aspect of these polarities and are the author's distillation of Erikson's descriptions. For full discussion of the meaning of both poles, see Erikson (1963), pp. 247–74.

Table 2.1 Erik Erikson's life stages

Psychosocial stage	Period
Basic trust vs. mistrust: learning that the provider of comfort is reliable, consistent, and predictable.	Oral sensory
Autonomy vs. shame and doubt: learning to exercise independence and freedom of choice, along with self-control.	Muscular-anal
Initiative vs. guilt: undertaking, planning and attacking a task, for the sake of actively doing it.	Locomotor-genital
Industry vs. inferiority: developing as a worker and producer.	Latency
Identity vs. role confusion: evolving a sense of self that is reliable and consistent, both for oneself and for others.	Puberty
Intimacy vs. isolation: readying oneself for a commitment to affiliation with others, and developing the ethical strength to abide by such commitments.	Young adulthood
Generativity vs. stagnation: using oneself in the establishment and guidance of the next generation.	Adulthood
Ego integrity vs. despair: integrating the earlier stages into an acceptance of one's own life cycle and an assured confidence in one's own life style.	Maturity

Russian people. Each of these boys had mothers, and Erikson's descriptions of the boys' perceptions of them, and how they were affected by them, reveal some of the characteristics of Erikson's psychoanalytic approach to social phenomena.

The mother of the American adolescent boy is somewhat of a "Mom." She has an ideal male image which she believes her son can live up to, but she is not overly dominating or protective, unlike a more virulent strain (Philip Wylie, 1942). She is more willing to extend freedom to the boy than the father is, since she is more sure of the kinds of control she has built into him. The authentic "Mom," however, is also very much on the American scene. She is the one better known to clinicians, who, having been labeled cold, rejecting, or overpossessive, has been identified as the major cause of pathology in the young. Erikson's discussion of the American "Mom" includes both a description of her personality, which Wylie had earlier provided, and, uniquely, a sympathetic explanation of how she came to be that way:

> "Mom," of course, is only a stereotyped caricature of existing contradictions which have emerged from intense, rapid, and as yet unintegrated changes in American history. To find its beginning, one would have to retrace this history back to the time when it was up to the American woman to evolve one common tradition, on the basis of many imported traditions, and to base on it the education of her children and the style of her home life; when it was up to her to establish new habits of sedentary life on a continent originally populated by men who in their countries of origin, for one reason or another, had not wanted to be "fenced in." Now, in fear of ever again acquiescing to an outer or inner autocracy, these men insisted on keeping their new cultural identity tentative to a point where women had to become autocratic in their demands for some order (1963, p. 291).

In frontier communities, desperate men fought over her. At the same time she was responsible for culture, religion, and the education of the young. In a time when life style might be either sedentary or migratory, she had to prepare her children for extremes of milieu, for readiness to seek new goals and to compete mercilessly for them. Thus she was in part a product of a historical situation.

In addition to the requirements of a frontier culture, another force in the making of "Mom," Erikson proposed, was Puritanism, which at first was a system of values "designed to check men and women of eruptive vitality, of strong appetites, as well as of strong individuality" (1963, p. 292). As the country grew older, Puritanism became rigid and defensive, a frigid influence on woman's tasks of pregnancy, childbirth, nursing, and child training. As fathers abdicated their familial and cultural roles for others in business, technology, and the professions, mothers had to assume the paternal role as well. Thus did "Mom" appear on the American scene, to provide a scapegoat for generations of clinicians seeking to explain the peculiar malaise of the American boy.

The older sister hardly figures in Erikson's account of the American adolescent. Her burden is to become a woman and mother without becoming a "Mom." Her success depends on region, class, and the kind of man she marries.

Erikson did not offer an analysis of Hitler's real mother, who hardly figures in his autobiographical *Mein Kampf*. The prototype German mother, he notes, important as she may be to the children, is obsequious and subservient to the father. The child observes her deviousness, as when she selects certain of his misdeeds to report to the father, depending on her whims. For Hitler, there evolved a two-faced mother image: the loving, childlike martyr of the home, and the superhuman goddess whose hands controlled man's destiny. She might dispense good or evil, might be generous or treacherous. "This, I believe, is a common set of images in patriarchal societies where woman, in many ways kept irresponsible and childlike, becomes a go-between and an in-between. It thus happens that the father hates in her the elusive children, and the children hate in her the aloof father" (1963, p. 339).

In Erikson's analysis of the boyhood of young Gorky, it is the grandmother who emerges as the strong, calm, and generous one, who, when she prays, approaches God as an equal, as if He Himself were one of her children who happened to become God. When the boy's mother left him to marry, the *babushka* became mother too, a symbol of survival and persistent endurance. "It is as if she had lived long before passions had made men ambitious, greedy, and in turn, childishly repentent; and as if she expected to outlast it all" (1963, p. 367).

Erikson comments on the "diffusion" of the mother role in peasant Russia, whereby the child is mothered by more than one, "women who are at home in this world because . . . they make it a home for others. Like the big stove in the center of the house, they can be relied upon eternally" (pp. 367–68). He speculates that such an experience of childhood might make the world more reliable, since the child's security was not dependent upon one relationship only. At the same time, the utter reliability of the *babushka* could condition a people who would endure and wait—"so long that reliance becomes apathy and stamina becomes serfdom" (p. 368).

This kind of analysis reveals an essential difference between Erikson and Freud. While both believe in the critical importance of early childhood, Erikson is less concerned with the intrapsychic events described by Freud. Instead, he wants to show how the customs of a society, as they affect what happens to children, result in a kind of shared way of seeing the world, so that, for example, a Hitler can emerge and be accepted by a particular people at a particular time. The "Mom" he describes is not the result of frustrated penis envy, eternally bent upon castrating her sons. She herself is the victim of a confluence of historical trends and events.

Included in *Childhood and Society* are Erikson's studies of childhood among the Sioux and the Yurok, two American Indian tribes. Both are male-dominated societies with sharply differentiated sex roles. The boys are trained to be hunters (Sioux) and salmon fishermen (Yurok), and the girls in both cases are trained to be mothers who will bring up hunters and fishermen. As a child analyst Erikson was drawn to study differences in the ways that different societies handled such universal events of childhood as weaning and bowel training, and the effects of these on adult personalities and values. He observed that even trained anthropologists had until recently failed to see that even primitive tribes *trained* their children in some systematic way—that they did not just grow up like little animals, but were prepared, almost from birth, to assume the role ordained for them in society.

Among the Sioux, for example, the first taboo the child encountered concerned social intimacy between brother and sister. Beginning around age five, the girl was confined to female play, and kept close to the mother and the teepee, while the boy was encouraged to go with the older boys, first for games and later for hunting. Every educational device, Erikson tells us, was used to inculcate self-confidence in the boy. Trust, autonomy, and initiative, the positive poles of the first three psychosocial stages, were assured him first by maternal generosity and later by the older brothers of the tribe. "He was to become a hunter after game, woman, and spirit" (p. 143). The girl, on the other hand, was trained to be a future helper and mother of hunters. She learned to sew, cook, and put up tents. Along with such practical education, she also learned to be shy, reticent, and fearful of men. She must observe certain boundaries in the camp, and as she matured, she had to sleep with her thighs tied together to prevent rape. Not only was virginity highly prized, but the genitalia must not even be touched by a male if the girl were to retain status as a desirable mate. As a mother, she would teach her children the taboos and responsibilities in the relationships between the sexes.

Cultures, then, "elaborate upon the biologically given, and strive for a division of function between the sexes, which is simultaneously . . . meaningful to the particular society, and manageable for the individual ego" (p. 108).

Sex differences and the use of space

At Berkeley, Erikson began to study the play construction of ten-, eleven-, and twelve-year-old boys and girls who were subjects in an ongoing longitudinal study of child development. His method was to invite the children, one at a time, to construct on a table an exciting scene from an imaginary motion picture, using a random selection of small toys and doll figures. He found that the girls tended to build interior scenes, serene and peaceful, of furniture groupings and people and animals in static positions, or doing sedentary things, such as playing the piano. Enclosures consisted of low walls, with gates or vestibules. In some cases, an intruder would cause an uproar, forcing the women in the scene to hide or to become fearful. This intruder was always a man, boy, or animal. Boys, by contrast, erected buildings and towers, and introduced the exciting element of downfall, either causing it to occur or making plain that catastrophe was imminent. Elaborate walls and facades were ornamented with protrusions, such as cones and cylinders. Automobiles and animals moved along the streets.

The spatial tendencies determining these two kinds of productions, Erikson thought, were analogous to sexual anatomy; the males emphasizing erectile, projectile, and active motifs; the females, enclosure, protection, and receptivity (albeit with the ever-present threat of forceful intrusion). He came to believe that this reflection of genital modes on spatial organization was analogous to the sexually different ground plans of the human body, which determined both biological experience and social roles. Later, these data would form the observational basis for his statement on the psychology of women.

Erikson's paper on the dynamics of womanhood and female identity came when America was well into the space age, and it was an observable fact that the exploration of outer space and all its supporting technology belonged to men. In this paper, Erikson proposes that it is the somatic design of the female body, the inner space of its womb and vagina, that determines the identity formation of women and makes it different from that of men. The anatomical plan of her body signifies a biological, psychological, and ethical commitment to take care of human infancy. The core problem of female fidelity is her disposition of this commitment (1964).

The concept of penis envy, Erikson thought, came about when the first clinicians had to understand their female patients with male empathy, leading them to encourage acceptance of reality, of what is not there. But almost all girls and women know of the existence of their productive inner space, set in the center of the female form. This, he said, is more important than the missing external organ. When the clinician finds his female patient beset with feelings of deprivation, he should not interpret them as evidence of her resentment at not being a boy. Rather, such feelings may emanate from the specific loneliness that women may experience if they fear being left empty and unfulfilled.

Thus the inner space, the locus for her potential for fulfillment, may also be the center of despair:

> To be left, for her, means to be empty, to be drained of the blood of the body, the warmth of the heart, the sap of life. How a woman thus

can be hurt in depth is a wonder to many a man, and it can arouse both his empathic horror and his refusal to understand. Such hurt can be re-experienced in each menstruation; it is crying to heaven in the mourning over a child; and it becomes a permanent scar in the menopause   (1968, p. 278).

Thus is anatomy destiny, as it determines the potentials and limitations of physiological functioning, and, to an extent, personality. Further, it is because of her biological function that the female differs from the male in many empirically validated ways. She is healthier and lives longer because she *is* the womb of the species and the nurturer of its helpless infancy. Her psychological superiority, compared to males, in tasks involving concentration on details, sensory discrimination, reactivity, docility, and a tolerance for limitations on her activities equips her especially to respond to the needs of others and is a perfect adaptation to her symbiosis with the infant human.

Her unique attractiveness and the kind of man she seeks affect the progress of her identity formation; but the final closure occurs when she selects what will be admitted to the inner space. In the meantime, such resolution may be postponed while she develops as a person, including participation in the world of men. Since she is never not a woman, her special vision may lead to new areas of inquiry and application of knowledge. Her unique contributions might bring about an evolution of society which would include more human adjustments of work to people, and new kinds of social institutions which would use and cultivate the behavioral referents of woman's inner space: caring, compassion, nurturing, and acceptance.

Who would argue with the merits of such a vision? Surely, the incorporation into the fabric of society's institutions of such feminine values as these would effect a more benign and less brutal environment for the world's children. At the same time, it would profoundly change the ground plan of Western technological society. In analogy to Erikson's own observations on the play construction of girls and boys, a feminine ground plan for society would include the lowering of barriers among people and groups, making peace instead of war, valuing cooperation instead of competition, and attending more to the inner life and less to the outer arena. Though some marginal groups have attempted just such a life style, with greater or less success, it is as difficult to imagine the adaptations of the major institutions of our society to such styles as it is to visualize the forms life might take on another planet.

In recent years Erikson, along with Freud and Deutsch, has attracted considerable negative criticism from feminist writers[11] be-

[11] For example, see Janeway (1971), Chesler (1972), and Doherty (1973).

cause of his views on identity development in women. The concept of inner space, while it refers to what woman is rather than to what she is not, still has in common with the concept of penis envy and the feminine core a view of woman which assumes that her unique biology, with all its prerequisites for biological motherhood, uniquely determines, through the indirect mechanisms of identity formation and commitment, her adaptation to life. Thus it shares with the other two theories the flavor of biological determinism which conflicts with feminist ideology.

On other grounds, the relationship between Erikson's theory and the psychology of women has three major problems. First, his model for psychosocial development and the substance of his work from which it was derived both assume the male as the prototype of humanity. This is not to quarrel with the psychosocial stages themselves, which can theoretically be invoked to explain females as well as males. Rather, the problem is that the model was clearly formulated in terms of a male experiential process which then was adjusted to accommodate women as well. For example, the stage of identity precedes the stage of intimacy. But for women, "the stage of life crucial for the emergence of an integrated female identity is the step from youth to maturity, the state when the young woman, whatever her work career, relinquishes the care received from the paternal family in order to commit herself to the love of a stranger and to the care to be given to his and her offspring" (1968, p. 265). Thus her identity is contingent upon the achievement of intimacy with another, while the male presumably evolves an identity which is independent of that necessity.

In describing the "young adult" of the sixth stage, intimacy versus isolation, he writes: "Body and ego must now be masters of the organ modes and of the nuclear conflicts, in order to be able to face the fear of ego loss in situations which call for self-abandon: in the solidarity of close affiliations, in orgasms and sexual unions, in close friendships and in physical combat" (1963, pp. 263–64). The language of this passage makes it plain that the "young adult" is male.

Further evidence that Erikson's prototype is implicitly male is the pervasive use of male examples. For instance, as noted earlier in the discussion of youth and identity in *Childhood and Society,* all the youths are male; women are discussed as mothers, in terms of the ways they influenced the boys' development. In describing child-training practices among the Sioux and the Yurok, his major interest is in showing how the Sioux boys grow up to become hunters and the Yurok fishermen. Thus he tells how the cultural system of the Sioux limits itself in "specializing the individual child for one main career, here the buffalo hunter" (p. 156), and how "the Yurok child

. . . is to be trained to be a fisherman" (p. 176). In both these examples, *child* means *boy*. Sioux girlhood is dealt with briefly, as preparation for the future roles of wife and mother; Yurok girlhood is not described.

The objectionable part of all this has nothing to do with Erikson's observations of male and female identity development or with his portrayals of the impact of society on the quality of childhood; the value and accuracy of these observations are empirical matters which can be validated by research yet to be done. Rather, it is the identification of a theory of human development with a theory of male development, to which female development is then compared. If women are an exception to the theory, then it is not a theory of *human* development. What the theory does is to provide a background against which women appear as an anomaly.[12] Either separate explanations must be made for her, or she is a silent presence who is lost somewhere among the assumptions underlying the theory.

The second problem is Erikson's persistent identification of woman with mother. Just as Deutsch's conception of woman progressed from girlhood to motherhood, so does Erikson see her identity as achieving its closure within the context of marriage and motherhood, with the disposition of the commitment to care for human infancy. This identification is revealed in a discussion of how men and women can transcend their roles, and each partake of the concerns of the other: "For even as real women harbor a legitimate as well as a compensatory masculinity, so real men can partake of motherliness—if permitted to do so by powerful mores" (1968, p. 286). In man, the female principle, if acknowledged, is mother.

Again, the issue is not whether women do or do not achieve identity through motherhood. No doubt a great many women do so, although almost one in five American women never have children (Lopata, 1971). The problem is the emphasis in the theory on women's reproductive role (which is what the inner space is all about) as *the* main determinant of identity, thus projecting a bias which cannot possibly account for observable exceptions. If one wishes to maintain that the dynamics of inner space are important even for the exceptions, then one must support the assertion with credible evidence. So far, this has not been done. The matter of evidence leads us to the third problem with Erikson's theory.

The concept of the inner space developed, as described earlier, from Erikson's observations of the way prepubescent children make play configurations. Their spatial organization, different for boys

---

[12] For the relationship between theory and anomaly, see Kuhn (1970).

and girls, reflected, it seemed, their different genital modes; the one active, erectile, and thrusting; the other quiet, receptive, and protective. Thus the boys were showing a concern for outer, and the girls with inner, space. But while the modes expressed in play were observably different for girls and boys (although one-third of each sex did not conform to the majority), there is no justification for concluding that these differences are determined by, or even related to, sexual or reproductive morphology. A simpler and less far-fetched explanation would rely on what the children had already learned about toys and play, in a society which gives boys trucks, guns, and telescopes, and girls doll houses, dolls, and everything else they need to rehearse them for motherhood. This explanation would also account for the exceptions, since the experiences that children have are more variable than are their anatomical sex differences. Nowhere in Erikson's description of these experiments does he speak of cultural conditioning as a factor in the play constructions, although he emphasized it elsewhere, as when he told how the Sioux girls were given toys "clearly intended to lead little girls along the path to Indian motherhood" (1963, p. 142), and how they were trained to stay close to home, never to cross certain boundaries, and to maintain a reserved and bashful demeanor. Given such sex-linked differences in socialization it is not possible to know the extent to which innate factors contribute to sex differences in behavior in later childhood.

In response to his critics, Erikson (1975) returned to the subject of inner space, in a paper which is less a defense than an affirmation of the earlier one. He stated, however, that he should not have written about American identity formation without including its meaning for women. Such oversight, he said, should be corrected by looking at the correspondences between female and male experiences in different periods. Thus the statement that woman is never not a woman corresponds to the statement that man is never not a man; and as women have been limited and unfree in making choices, so have men.

To this unarguable point, though, we should observe that the kinds of "unfreedom," or bonds which constrain the two sexes are different. Women have been more confined by definitions of what they can do; men, by definitions of how they can be. Specifically, women have been relegated to the social and work roles of wife and mother, with historically relatively recent permissible incursions into occupational roles consistent with the feminine image, such as teaching and nursing. Men, on the other hand, have had much more freedom of choice among occupational roles, and these contribute heavily to their identification and to the kinds of discriminations that are made among them. But ways of being, at least in American society, are more rigidly prescribed for men than for women. The model of masculinity precludes any behavior which is labeled feminine. All traces of the old mother identification must be expunged. Women, however, have more leeway; a girl may revel in her tomboy years, and the active, competent woman is certainly more favored than is the passive, helpless man.

Corresponding to penis envy (which Erikson did not defend in the earlier paper) is man's anxiety about the worthiness of his organ compared to the competition. And says Erikson, as if this were not enough, he also envies the maternal capacity of the woman. Thus his highest acclaim goes to her for what she can do but he cannot; and his lowest appraisal to any traits of hers which may lurk in his own identity.

As woman has historically assented to an exploitation of the masochistic potential of her roles, to the suffering inherent in them, so has man inflicted on others hardships whose masochistic and sadistic potentials have been disguised as heroism and duty. Thus there are negative and positive elements in the identity development of both sexes, reinforced by the collusion of both, "in both flattering and enslaving each other and themselves" (p. 242).

As a final correspondence, Erikson considers the meaning of two contemporary developments: birth control and arms control, the one going to the core of womanhood, the other to the core of the male identity. As birth control gives women greater role choice, so does arms control imply a liberation of men for roles that are free from the imagery of hunting and conquering. The vision of the future must guide mankind to an order in which chosen children learn to humanize adult inventions. This can come about only "through an equal involvement of women and of their special modes of experience in the over-all planning and governing so far monopolized by men" (p. 247).

From Erikson's re-examination of his own earlier statement on the development of womanhood, we can come to three conclusions. One, the original statement that the ground plan of the body mediates between instinctual genital and reproductive modes and their manifestation in sex-linked behavior continues to represent his position; two, this is not, however, supportive of any argument that women (or men) should be constrained toward certain roles and not others, or confined to roles on the basis of sex; three, the new society will depend not only upon the willingness of men to lay down their arms, but also upon the involvement of women, with their *special* modes of experience, in institutions formerly dominated by men.

"Special" means: "1. Having some peculiar or distinguishing characteristic; out of the ordinary, uncommon; particular. 2. Designed for or assigned to a specific purpose; limited or specific in range, aim, or purpose."[13] Erikson's designation of women's modes as special is not pejorative; it simply means that she is still the Other. In her specialness, she will infuse man's old institutions with her humane values and virtues and presumably guide them toward better solutions for human problems. But the movement that Erikson sees is not unilateral. What about man's mode of experience, even if it is not special? What does it bode for a peaceful society and its microcosm, the family, the single institution in which women ever prevailed, if only in the overseeing of its domestic arrangement, the care of its children, and the maintenance of its harmony and interpersonal relations? Pursuing Erikson's notion of correspondence, as women take up roles in the public world, men must take up roles in the private world of home and family.

One is special only within a context, compared to its norms. Women, to be effective in the public world, will need to incorporate some of the more adaptive features of "masculine" behavior into their previously limited range. Men, if they would participate in that world hitherto designated as female, will need to recognize that *their* mode of experience is special and limited in that context, and that, if they would do at least as well as women have done, they must bring forth and cultivate the residuals of those personality traits usually labeled feminine. The emergence of women and the influence of their special experiential modes now seems, in today's value system, to meet theoretical approval. The corresponding shift for men, and the influence and desirability of their experiential modes, as they adopt role prescriptions previously assigned to women exclusively, has not been explicitly dealt with in the literature. Perhaps the shift for them will be the greater revolution.

These three views of the psychology of women are representative of the traditional psychoanalytic approach to the question. Although they differ somewhat in the concepts they employ, and in the focus of their emphases and the importance they attach to the matter, they have certain characteristics in common.

The first of these is the importance they give to woman's body as a determinant of her personality and behavior. For Freud and Erikson, the relationship is direct, described in the concepts of penis envy and the inner space. For Deutsch, it is mediated by her mother

---

[13] *Funk & Wagnalls Standard College Dictionary* (New York: Funk & Wagnalls, 1968.)

role, real or potential, which is of course made possible by her unique biology. For all of them, woman is very closely identified with her body and its functions.

The second shared quality of these theories is their invocation of a double standard to explain behavior. The male is seen as the norm, as the prototype human being. His sexual anatomy serves sociosexual behavior with greater dedication than it serves reproductive behavior; in fact, he does not necessarily even recognize the relationship between the two. While his sexuality and its many sublimations may affect behavior, no one advances a theory of male personality which rests on his biosocial role as father, because his role in reproduction is only momentarily important, and he does not typically nurture offspring. The norm is the exemption of the male from these functions, whose relative unimportance in his psychic economy means they cannot have determining effects on his personality. On the other hand, woman, in no way exempt, is in a different class. Since her biology allows her to bring forth young and usually causes her to be assigned the social role of mother, she shares with all women a function and role different from the norm, and this difference is seen as having a profoundly shaping effect on her behavior. Thus the female personality is a deviation from the norm, which is the male, and the deviation is explained on the basis of her biological functions.

In psychoanalytic theories of personality, it is implicit that the model is male. Considerations of the female within such a framework have given rise to conceptual spin-offs which sought to bring her under the theoretical umbrella. But such belated attempts at accommodation prove awkward, both for the general theory and for their specific purpose as explanatory concepts meant to deal with the special case of woman. Furthermore, they highlight the embarrassing lack in psychology of serious and systematic attention to the parameters of "female" behavior, as it appears in the great arc of human behavior.

Woman and milieu: innovative views

3

Now, if we try to free our minds from this masculine mode of thought, nearly all the problems of feminine psychology take on a different appearance.
—Karen Horney, "The Flight from Womanhood," 1926

Psychoanalytic theory and its derived views of female personality and sexuality attracted considerable scholarly evaluation and criticism, and several of Freud's colleagues and intellectual heirs abandoned the orthodox position he represented and set forth theories of their own. Of particular interest to us are those whose innovative approach included new interpretations of woman's behavior, her feminine personality, and her experiential history.

Although there was no dearth of criticism of psychoanalysis among the ranks of its early practitioners, almost none of them made the problem of female personality and sexuality, or even of male-female differences, central to their thinking. Few viewed it as a fundamental question of the human experience. However, a few theorists did provide a new direction for thinking about women. Among them were Karen Horney, Clara Thompson, and Alfred Adler, psychoanalysts who took particular exception to Freud, reinterpreting his observations from different perspectives.

Researchers in other social science disciplines as well provided data which led to changes in understanding of human experience, and of concepts of femininity and masculinity. One of the most prolific of these is Margaret Mead, a cultural anthropologist whose observations of non-Western cultures demonstrated decisively the malleability of human behavior.

Although they differ in their theoretical positions—and Mead in her methodology and the nature of her data—they share an appreciation of experiential and cultural influences in the shaping of personality and behavior. The three psychoanalysts set up systems of thinking about human behavior which departed radically from classical Freudian views and Mead showed to students of the individual the importance of the commonalities that one shares with all others within a culture. Among them, they made possible a more balanced approach to the scientific study of women and men.

Karen Horney

Karen Horney was born in 1885, almost thirty years after Freud, and grew up under very different circumstances. Though it was unusual for a woman to become a physician, she was encouraged by her independent mother to attend medical school in Berlin, and later to seek training there in psychiatry and psychoanalysis.

Her training was in classic psychoanalytic theory, under two Freudian analysts, Karl Abraham and Hanns Sachs. Horney began her confrontation with the basic tenets of psychoanalysis in her first published paper, "The Technique of Psychoanalytic Therapy." "Psychoanalysis," she wrote, "can free a human being who has been tied hands and feet. It cannot give him new arms or legs. Psychoanalysis, however, has shown us that much that we have regarded as constitutional merely represents a blockage of growth, a blockage which can be lifted."[1] While not doubting the importance of the unconscious and of early childhood experiences, she thought that the person could be understood only by considering also his or her interaction with the present environment. Constitutional factors were not fixed and unilateral determinants, but were possibilities which would be shaped by this reciprocal interaction. Thus Horney defined her approach as *holistic,* a view of the person as a dynamic whole, in contrast to the nineteenth-century psychoanalytic theory which tended to view the person as a mechanistic system of parts whose operations were relatively independent of other variables.

Having shifted her philosophical base away from biological determinism, Horney began to develop her interest in feminine psychology. Between 1923 and 1935, she published a series of papers in which she critically examined Freud's theories of the libido and the psychosexual stages of development as they were alleged to affect women (Horney, 1973). In Horney's later work, these formulations became incorporated into a psychology of the whole person regardless of sex which showed how human growth, or its obstruction,

[1] In Kelman (1967), p. 167.

came about through the intimate interplay of the person and the changing environment.

Horney's method of investigation, like that of Freud and Deutsch, was based on clinical observation of patients. From the data of such observations, hypotheses might be formed, which could then be tested in further practice. She insisted that the explanatory statements of psychoanalysis be confirmed by actual observation in behavior. This rigorous attitude was an important factor in her critical approach to Freud's ideas about women. For example, in a discussion of his hypothesis of penis envy she cautioned that it is an hypothesis, not a fact. Furthermore, the claim that it is a primary factor in the early lives not only of neurotic females but of all females is unsubstantiated by data. "Unfortunately little or nothing is known of psychically healthy women, or of women under different cultural conditions" (1973, p. 216).

An important reason for the dearth of knowledge about women, Horney said, was the male bias of psychoanalytic observers. In "The Flight From Womanhood" Horney supported the point that in our civilization all its institutions were dominated by men. The concept "human being" was identified with the concept "man." The psychology of women evolved from a male point of view. Its alleged objectivity was inevitably colored by man's relation with woman. Woman, too, from a historical position of weakness, had adapted herself to man's desires and then had come to believe that the adaptation was her true self. It would be very difficult, then, for any individual, male or female, to become free of this bias.

In this paper, written one year after Freud's first paper on the psychology of women, Horney expressed the belief that the masculine bias of psychoanalysis reflected an earlier time when only masculine development was considered and when the evolution of women was measured by masculine standards. To show this influence in the existing analytic picture of feminine development, she compared the ideas that young boys have of girls with analytic ideas of feminine development (1973, pp. 57–48):

The boy's ideas	Analytic ideas of feminine development
Naïve assumption that girls as well as boys possess a penis.	For both sexes it is only the male genital which plays any part.
Realization of the absence of the penis.	Sad discovery of the absence of the penis.

The boy's ideas	Analytic ideas of feminine development
Idea that the girl is a castrated, mutilated boy.	Belief of the girl that she once possessed a penis and lost it by castration.
Belief that the girl has suffered punishment which also threatens him.	Castration is conceived of as the infliction of punishment.
The girl is regarded as inferior.	The girl regards herself as inferior. Penis envy.
The boy is unable to imagine how the girl can ever get over this loss or envy.	The girl never gets over the sense of deficiency and inferiority and has constantly to master afresh her desire to be a man.
The boy dreads her envy.	The girl desires throughout life to avenge herself on the man for possessing something she lacks.

Such a "remarkable parallelism," she proposed, might be an expression of the fact that observation of feminine development had been made from a male point of view.

Horney then re-examined the Freudian concepts of penis envy, the masculinity complex, and basic inferiority feelings in women. She did not deny the prevalence of these qualities in women. She argued, however, against the importance that Freud ascribed to them in the case of women and his designation of such traits to women only. While a young girl might openly display penis envy, this was not necessarily a manifestation of a deep instinctual need which would persist into adulthood and color her whole life. Furthermore, the masculinity complex was not, as Freud had said, an unresolved form of penis envy, but rather a "flight from womanhood," occurring in some cases when the girl, forced to renounce her libidinal wishes toward the father, abandons the feminine role altogether. Adopting a masculine attitude, she uses the "fiction of maleness" to escape from the female role and the guilt it holds as a result of the libidinous wishes. But the penalty must be feelings of inadequacy and inferiority. Deviating from her norm to that of the male, she must apply to herself values and pretensions that are biologically foreign to her, and must inevitably see herself as inadequate.

At this point, Horney added a further interpretation of the flight from womanhood. Historically, the relationship between the sexes has been similar to that between master and slave. The male does not need to remind himself of this difference in power; the female can never forget it. This difference might account for the inattention to this factor by male analysts. In addition, the girl is exposed from birth to the suggestion of her inferiority. Such an effect would surely reinforce her masculinity complex, and move her to envy the role of one who has all the power that she lacks. To make matters more difficult, the woman has few ways to compensate for this depreciation of herself and her role. Motherhood is now often a burden and a handicap. In our masculine civilization, all the professions are dominated by men. Since women are barred from accomplishment in the outside world, they have a factual basis for their feelings of inferiority. Thus could the flight from womanhood be reinforced by the actual social subordination of women; it could then be understood as an interaction of psychic and social factors.

Nor is it only women who consciously or unconsciously envy the attributes of the other sex. Horney drew attention to the intense envy in boys of the events of motherhood: pregnancy, childbirth, and the act of suckling, as well as of the breasts themselves. The sense of this clear biological superiority of the woman is so strong that the recognition of it must be kept from consciousness. Thus it is early repressed, and is kept repressed by transforming it into its more palatable opposite: a conviction of her inferiority, fed by a need to depreciate her, as if the denial of her worth would magically negate what he knew to be true. The fact that the femininity complex in males is seen less frequently than is its counterpart in females, Horney said, is because males have more opportunity for achievement in the world of work and creative activity than females have. Thus the great creative productivity of males can be seen as a compensation for their inability to create life. This view is quite different from Freud's idea that all the masculine achievements of civilization are a result of the requirement for the modification and rechanneling of the basic sexual energy, the libido.

Horney presented one of her strongest arguments for a consideration of cultural factors as major influences in the psychology of women in "The Problem of Feminine Masochism," published in 1935. Deutsch had already published her views on masochism in women, which had grown out of Freud's idea that clitoral sexuality had to be suppressed in the interest of the primacy of the vagina in mature femininity. Both Freud and Deutsch assumed a biologically determined relationship between femininity and masochism. Deutsch believed it was a basic drive in the mental life of women. It represented a directing inward toward oneself the active-aggressive drives associated with clitoral sexuality, a renunciation which occurred when the girl discovered the inadequacy of her organ compared to the male's. The events of sex and reproduction, with their potential for pain and suffering, could provide masochistic satisfaction. Since classical psychoanalytic theory held that general behavior patterns were modeled on sexual behavior patterns, it followed that women, masochistic in their attitudes toward sex and reproduction, would also reveal such trends in their nonsexual approach to life. Therefore masochism was normal for women, who would manifest it much more frequently than would men. In men, in fact, it was a manifestation of feminine qualities.

Horney's argument with this view was not whether a masochistic derivation of pleasure from pain is found more often in women than in men; rather, she doubted that its occurrence was psychobiologically necessary. While it might be observed in many neurotic women, she was unconvinced that most women would lastingly be driven to seek suffering as a consequence of the early genital trauma. "A living organism, when hit by some traumatic event adapts itself to the new situation" (1973, p. 221). The one-sidedness of the prevailing views, she said, came about because of the exclusion of cultural and social factors from the picture. As an example, she noted that Russian peasant women during the Tsarist regime had sought beatings from their husbands as proof of love. But lest one take this as evidence of innate masochism in women, one must note the emergence of the modern Soviet woman, who would hardly view beatings as signs of love. "The change has occurred in the patterns of culture rather than in the particular woman" (1973, p. 224).

Insisting upon the necessity for careful investigation, Horney suggested that cross-cultural research would show whether such traits as masochism were in fact inherent in the feminine personality. For example, anthropologists could examine different cultures for observable masochistic attitudes: inhibition of assertiveness, seeing onself as weak and helpless and expecting advantages on account of this, becoming emotionally dependent on the other sex, tending to be self-sacrificing and submissive, and using weakness and helplessness to subdue the other sex.

All of these attitudes came out in psychoanalysis with masochistic women, and because of their ubiquity in Western society, had been used as evidence of biological causation. But here, as she had with penis envy, Horney pointed to cultural factors as causative agents, and said that she would expect these masochistic behaviors to appear in any culture which included for women:

blocking of outlets for expansiveness and sexuality;
restrictions on the number of children, when childbearing is the
    measure of a woman's value;

estimation of women as inferior to men;

economic dependence of women on men;

restriction of women to roles that are built on emotional bonds such as family, religion, and charitable works;

surplus of marriageable women, facilitating emotional dependence on men and sexual competition with other women.

When these elements are present, Horney pointed out, then there appear ideologies about the "nature" of women, such as that she is weak, emotional, and poorly suited for autonomous and independent activity. Such ideologies serve to reconcile women to their subordinate role, to identify it with their hope of fulfillment, and to define it as desirable. Strengthening the influence of such beliefs is the practice of men in choosing women who have such traits. If she is to be chosen, she must conform to the image believed to be the true nature of woman. Given the powerful influence of such factors, and their prevalence in our culture as well as others, few women can escape becoming masochistic to some degree, without any contribution by anatomical factors. Beyond admitting the masochistic potential of woman's traditional role in sex and childbearing, any other assertion of an inevitable relation of her constitution to masochism is only hypothetical.

After coming to the United States, Horney continued to write on feminine psychology and to sharpen the differences between her ideas and those of Freud and his followers. In 1934 she published "The Overvaluation of Love," in which she analyzed what she saw as a very common problem among women, particularly the more able and gifted ones. Social conditioning taught the woman the importance of modeling herself after the patriarchal ideal of womanhood, to become a woman whose only desire is to love a man and to be loved by him, to admire and to serve him, and to adapt herself to him. Such an arrangement was a source of self-esteem for the male, but for the female, though it spared her the anxieties associated with the use of other abilities, and with the need for self-assertion when faced with criticism and rivalry, it meant diminished self-esteem and lack of confidence. The conflict was not for the woman whose only desire was to lavish devotion on a man, but for the one who, within a social system which held to that ideal, wanted to follow a vocation, pursue a special interest, or develop an independent personality. Such women often became ill, and were unable to function well in either sphere, that of work or that of love. Horney commented that they often sensed their difficulties as arising out of their own personalities in accordance with what Freudian theory would have interpreted as the masculinity complex.

In the course of her work with several such women, Horney

began to feel that the core problem was an overvaluation of love relationships, of men, and of sex, to the extent that a heterosexual relationship was the most valuable thing in life. If they could not have this, then everything else in life seemed flat and stale, and they felt themselves to be not normal. They depreciated their real gifts, in what Horney called a "falsification of values" (1973, p. 187). Contributing to the problem was the difficulty for women of achieving gratification other than through their relationships with men. While this area of their lives was invested with such importance, they felt intense rivalry with other women. This rivalry was both a cause and an effect. As a cause, it had begun early in life when the girl had "lost out" to another female, the mother or perhaps an older sister, in the competition for the father's love. The threat to her security and her self-esteem, and the resulting anxiety, motivated her need to prove her feminine potency and her normality. Because of its unrealistic quality and its self-depreciatory content, it could not be satisfied, and at the same time, its domination of the personality interfered with growth in other directions. As an effect, the woman's need for love and recognition was so great that other women could be seen only as rivals who might deprive her of what was so precious.

Although Horney based her understanding of this peculiarly feminine conflict on her analysis of neurotic women, she remarked that the type occurs frequently, in a less exaggerated form, among middle-class intellectual women. Its ubiquity was caused by the narrow sphere of women's lives and the contingency of women's self-esteem on the success of their relationships with men. Given these social factors, even slight difficulties in early development would be enough to drive women toward this type of womanhood.

The ideas that Horney formulated during her years of interest in female psychology became part of her general theory of the whole person, first presented in *The Neurotic Personality of Our Time*, (1937). She had rejected Freud's libido theory, with its emphasis on biological instincts and drives, and its pessimistic view of man as a driven creature at odds with himself and his world. Instead, she saw the child as born with a potential for growth, for self-actualization which could be facilitated by a healthful environment.

The basic principle motivating human behavior was not the instinctual dyad of sex and aggression, but the need for security. The child whose emotional needs were regularly and consistently met would experience a harmonious development, in the course of which his or her own capacities would unfold. The insecure child, sensing the world as a hostile place, would develop a feeling of basic anxiety, of isolation and helplessness. To cope with these feelings, the individual in the course of growth would develop various strategies for dealing with other persons. In general these strategies, motivated by the person's anxious needs, fell into three categories: moving toward people, moving away from people, and moving against people. In the normal person, these ways of relating are balanced and integrated in the personality, and are not in conflict with each other. The insecure person, however, is driven to exaggerate one or the other of these adaptations, becoming over-compliant and docile, over-withdrawn and isolated, or over-aggressive. Each of these "solutions" to the problem of anxiety is unsatisfying because it restricts the person's growth and engenders self-hate and impoverished relations with others.

By the time Horney wrote her last book, *Neurosis and Human Growth* (1950), she had broken completely with the Freudian school of psychoanalysis. Against the Freudian view of man as a creature born to conflict, whose best accomplishments in love and creativity were at the cost of renunciation of his basic instincts, she set her own vision of the person, whose best energies are affirmative strivings toward knowledge, toward developing spiritual powers and moral courage, toward achievements in all areas, toward the full use of intellect and imagination. "Albert Schweitzer uses the terms 'optimistic' and 'pessimistic' in the sense of 'world and life affirmation' and 'world and life negation.' Freud's philosophy, in this deep sense, is a pessimistic one. Ours, with all its cognizance of the tragic element in neurosis, is an optimistic one" (p. 378).

Clara Thompson

Born in Rhode Island in 1893, Clara Thompson planned to become a medical missionary. She abandoned this goal before going to medical school at Johns Hopkins, where she became interested in psychiatry and psychoanalysis. Between 1928 and 1933, she underwent psychoanalysis with Sandor Ferenczi, a Hungarian member of Freud's inner circle, who had already begun to move away from Freudian orthodoxy. In addition to Ferenczi, those who influenced Thompson most were Karen Horney and Harry Stack Sullivan. Sullivan, educated in the humanist tradition of American psychology, rejected the classical mechanistic view of human personality in favor of an interpersonal approach which saw the nature of the person's relationships with others as central to adjustment and well-being.

Interpersonal Psychoanalysis (1964) is a collection of most of Thompson's papers. It includes six papers on the psychology of women and an unfinished manuscript consisting of seven chapters of a book which she was working on at the time of her death, *Problems of Womanhood.*

The basic difference between Freudian psychoanalysis and interpersonal psychoanalysis is in their different views of personality development. Freud's instinct theory of the libido, the basic sexual energy, pictured development as a grim struggle against the primacy of savage instincts. Out of this battle emerged man's character, his conscience, and his creativity. The interpersonal school assumed as the basic drive the need to grow and to master one's environment. This meant learning the pattern of one's culture, its speech, customs, and taboos. The human becomes a product not of the renunciation of libidinal urges but of interactions with significant persons around him or her. Humans are the least instinct-dominated of all animals, and psychoanalysis should be concerned with the social forces which dominate human behavior.

The central feature of early childhood development was not the successful negotiation of libidinal stages but the formation of the self and the emergence of an identity separate from that of the mother. The child goes through a series of stages, involving varying and increasingly mature kinds of interactions with others. In infancy, the most important relationship is with the mother. Through their interaction he learns of his separateness and establishes a basis for communion and empathy with others. In childhood and the juvenile era, the beginnings of cooperation and competition develop through playing with others. Sex is not an important component of the child's growth. During preadolescence, the normal child learns to care about the happiness of others and to form close bonds with peers. Only in adolescence does sex begin to become important. It is not a problem in itself. It is the cultural attitudes about sex that make this a hazardous time, since the social restrictions make it difficult for the adolescent to gratify sexual urges. Maturity is achieved when the person is able successfully to form a durable and intimate relationship with another person. Thus personality development is a process of acculturation, and it is not dominated by the requirement to repress and to transform the sexual energy.

In "Cultural Pressures in the Psychology of Women" (1942) Thompson responded to Freud's view of female personality as an inevitable result of her original biological inferiority. She showed how penis envy and all its derived personality traits—jealousy, feelings of inferiority, weak superego, prematurely arrested development, and rigidity—could be explained by a theory of cultural causation, as adaptations to the lives women lead in Western society. The penis, she said, is a symbol of privilege in a patriarchal society, and it is this privilege that women envy in men. Women do not, as Freud thought, want a penis for themselves. Penis envy in the Freudian sense is not universal, and is not found in normal women. Jealousy and envy are traits characteristic of a competitive culture, which implies comparison of one group with another usually to the disadvantage of one of them. The restricted opportunities available for women, and the limitations placed on her development and her independence, are real bases for envy which have nothing to do with neurosis. Likewise, women's feelings of inferiority are a reflection of their real position in the society and not of a biological lack as Freud thought. Women's weaker superego, or the lack of internalized standards, is typical of those whose security depends on the approval of a powerful person or group. The Victorian girl, for example, protected and dependent on her father, had insufficient opportunity to develop a mind of her own. It would have been dangerous had she done so because it would have interfered with her adaptation to her future husband. The weak person must adopt the ideology of the strong one in order to survive.

Freud had further pointed out that women lose their ability to grow emotionally and intellectually earlier than men do, and that they become rigid in their beliefs and attitudes. The woman of thirty, he said, seemed inaccessible to influence for the future, while a man of that age was at the beginning of his growth to peak maturity. Thompson countered that as long as a woman's sole achievement was in marriage and motherhood, her career was made or lost by age thirty. In Freud's time, as well as in the mid-twentieth century, a woman of thirty had no future. Yet psychoanalysis itself held that in order for therapy to be successful, actual opportunities for further development must exist. This alone would explain the cessation of growth in women, and their greater rigidity, if in fact these could be demonstrated to affect women more than men. In reality, stunted and rigid men of thirty were not scarce. Given unfortunate life situations or lack of training, a narrowed outlook and early rigidity were predictable for anyone regardless of sex.

Thompson did not dispute Freud's observations of his women patients. What she did argue with was the inadequacy of his interpretation of those observations, resulting from two errors in Freud's thinking. First, he saw female development from a masculine point of view. The woman was the negative of the man, and her childbearing function was a compensation for the missing penis. Was not, Thompson asked, this function important in its own right? Second, Freud studied women only in his own culture and believed that what he saw in them was universally true for women. Freud was analyzing not "natural" women but women in a patriarchal society. Assumption of women's inferiority was a prevalent attitude accepted by both sexes as a biologic fact. Men would not only have an interest in believing this because of its obvious advantage to them, but would share with women the difficulty of freeing themselves from an idea which was part of their earliest training and permeated the whole society.

Thompson also considered some alternate explanations for the masculinity complex which Freud thought to be a refusal of the woman to accept her "castration." The culture, she said, invites masculinity in women. As women move out of the old sheltered role in a restless search for a better life, they tend to adopt the behavior of those who are already successful. Having no models of their own, they copy men because the world rewards masculine behavior. In a male domain, created and maintained by men, the so-called masculine traits of decisiveness and daring lead to greater achievement than do gentleness and submissiveness. When women behave this way, it is not necessarily a sign of pathological character development.

In a later paper on working women, Thompson (1953) returned to the problem of woman's conflict between being the way she is and feeling that she must adopt male values and behavior in order to be able to achieve anything of importance in the world outside the home. She cautioned against believing that one must behave like men in order to succeed. Women must find their place in the social order without feeling that they must compete with men in a system created by men. When women wanted to become free, they took as their blueprint the masculine pattern, as there was no other. Perhaps it would be better if women found their own pattern, remembering that the competitive race for success does not enrich the lives of those trapped in it. Tentatively, she suggested that women might lead in bringing about a change in the cultural attitude toward competition.

Thompson also drew attention to the effects of attitudes toward female sexuality on woman's self-perception and self-esteem. In 1950, she presented a paper which examined two derogatory attitudes: that women's sexual needs were unimportant and that women's genitals were inferior. The first arose because women did not have obvious evidence of erotic excitement as men did, and because the prevailing morality, a residual of Victorianism, encouraged a denial of pleasure in the sexual act. Woman was not supposed to be erotic, but she must participate in sex at any time. Since man must have his satisfaction, the wife must be available whether she participates actively or not. Thompson felt that such derogation of her sexuality generalized to a devaluing of herself as a person. If a woman's sexual needs and interests were relatively slight, then the male could use her as an instrument for his pleasure and gratification without much concern for her feelings. Given the puritanical flavor of attitudes toward the body and sexuality, woman, being invested as standard-bearer of morality and virtue, could least of all risk censure by expressing interest or making demands in the sexual area of her life.

The genitals themselves, being contiguous to the excretory organs, shared in the minds of many their classification as unclean. The odor associated with the female genitalia and their role in the production of the menses further contributed to the negative regard in which they were held. Striving for cleanliness is part of the basic training of children in our society. This can lead to a derogation of women's sexual anatomy, not only because of the connection with excretion and the menses, but because of its role in intercourse. Man in the sex act gets rid of his secretion; woman receives it into her body. If she has been conditioned to think of bodily secretions as unclean, this would increase her feeling of her own unacceptability. One woman patient, for example, felt that she could never marry because she would be unable to keep herself clean at all times for her husband. Before a date she would take special care to be sure that her genitals were clean and dry. She was able to overcome this obsessional derogation of her body when she began having sexual relations and learned that the normal lubrication of her vagina contributed to the sexual pleasure of herself and her partner.

Thompson's paper at this symposium was followed by discussion by other participants. One of these was Frieda Fromm-Reichman, a prominent analyst of the period. She expanded upon Thompson's analysis by suggesting that the derogation of female sexuality extended to include her natural creativity, her ability to create life (1950). Such a distortion originated, she suggested, in man's primary fear and envy of women's procreative ability. Woman, needing the protection and security offered by the male, had to deal somehow with his aversive reaction to her power. Consequently she developed the strategy of denying the pleasurable aspects of and her pride in pregnancy and childbirth by stressing the pain, discomforts, and negative side effects. This depreciation of the quality and meaning of her creative processes, in the service of her greater need to please man, spread to include her whole self, since the two aspects were so intimately involved.

What Thompson and Fromm-Reichman were rejecting was the notion that woman, her body, and her functions were inferior. They felt that woman's concurrence and her own depreciation of herself and her sex was a result of the social roles that man wanted her to play. Thus Freud was describing women who were the result of these social conditions, while Thompson and Fromm-Reichman emphasized that these social conditions were the cause of women's behavior.

An example of how the lack of opportunity for development and economic dependence force women to be docile and subservient is one of Thompson's own cases described in "Problems of Womanhood" (1964). The patient was a fifty-year-old woman who had been married for many years to a "mean, parsimonious, hypocritically religious" man of whom she was terrified. She had four children, the youngest fourteen, and all of them were emotionally disturbed. This woman came to Thompson in a panic, the type that one sees when "the awareness of an unlived life dawns on a person." She had no education beyond high school, and no training. What could she do? "People sometimes come to analysis for miracles. One must first face and come to terms with the fact that one can never make up for the lost years. One can only hope to live from now on" (p. 343). In this case, the woman was able to muster the strength to leave her husband, support herself doing odd jobs, take courses in college, and finally get a job working with handicapped children. But to strike out at this age, to take the terrible risks of loneliness and failure, are too threatening to most women who find themselves trapped in such a situation. Nothing in their social conditioning suggests to them that they can take control of their own lives, and for many, it is indeed too late.

The feminine personality was predictable from woman's role in the culture. Those characteristics which Freud considered to be specifically female and biologically determined, Thompson concluded, "can be explained as developments arising in and growing out of Western woman's historic situation of underprivilege, restriction of development, insincere attitude toward the sexual nature, and social and economic dependency. The basic nature of woman is still unknown" (p. 242).

Alfred Adler

Alfred Adler was born in Vienna in 1870. By 1895, he had begun to practice general medicine. Adler had already become interested in psychopathology through his own practice and through reading the works of Charcot and others. After Freud published *Interpretation of Dreams* in 1900, the two met, and Adler became one of the charter members of the Vienna Psychoanalytic Society. By 1911, it became apparent that Adler's views were at odds with Freud's, and the disagreement culminated in Adler's resignation from the Society. Adler believed that Freud's insistence upon strict adherence to his views was an infringement on freedom of scientific investigation, and he began work on a new approach to personality, which came to be known as Individual Psychology.

Adler's Individual Psychology differed in a number of important ways from Freudian psychoanalysis. He rejected Freud's assumption that behavior is motivated by biologically determined instinctual urges that are primarily sexual in nature. Adler believed that the human is primarily a social being motivated by social interests and relating to others through cooperation in work for the common interest. The individual acquires a style of life which is identified by his or her interactions with others. Adler was the first of Freud's circle to deviate in this important way. He must be considered the forerunner of the later emerging emphasis on the interpersonal context of behavior, brought out in the work of Horney, Thompson, and Sullivan.

Another contribution of Adler's was his attention to the person as a unique individual. Each person strives toward certain goals that will enhance the self, and these strivings direct behavior. Far from being a product of the renunciation of instinctual urges, the individual instead creates her or his own life by the actions performed. Emphasis is on what the person does in the immediate situation and on its meaning in terms of goals that are implicit in the unique personality.

Perhaps most important, Adler reinstated conscious thought processes to the role of greatest importance. Where Freud had presented the pessimistic view of the human as being at the mercy of unconscious forces which had their pathological roots in the events of early childhood, Adler taught that people are ordinarily aware of why they do what they do. He said that most of us know what our goals are and what our limitations are in striving for them. Furthermore, we can plan our behavior knowing what it will mean for the realization of our selves.

Adler's theory of personality directly influenced his ideas about women. The basic concepts of his theory were: fictional goals, inferiority feelings, superiority strivings, social interest, style of life, and the creative self (Hall and Lindzey, 1970).

Adler believed that individuals are motivated more by their expectations of the future than by their experiences of the past. Thus they develop *fictional goals*, which are beliefs about present or future events. These beliefs have a regulatory effect on behavior, and cause the person to behave consistently in situations relating to the belief. For example, the person might hold to such ideas as "every man for himself," "honesty is the best policy," or a belief in a life after death which will reward the virtuous and punish the wicked. It is reasonable to assume that such beliefs would have an effect on the person's behavior. Here, Adler seems to be recognizing the importance of a personal ideology which serves as a general guide for behavior. These beliefs consist of goals toward which the person strives in her or his attempt to maintain consistency between behavior and belief. This tenet of Adler's system was in total opposition to Freud's emphasis on the past with its deterministic grip on the future. Even if the goal did not in fact exist, Adler held the belief in its reality would motivate behavior, just as surely as if it were real.

Early in his medical career Adler became interested in the idea of organ inferiority, the tendency of a person's illness to focus on a certain organ system. He noted that sometimes the afflicted one attempts to make up for such an inferiority by developing unusual strength in that particular area of functioning. For example, a person who had a muscular weakness from childhood might exercise especial diligence and become a skilled ballet dancer. Adler later broadened the concept of inferiority as a motivating force to include not only biological but psychological sources. In normal persons, *feelings of inferiority* were part of the experience of everyone, issuing from the universal helplessness of the infant. Thus behavior was motivated by a need to overcome this basic inferiority, to attain ever greater development and growth of the self.

The innate principle that Adler thought was basic to human growth was a *striving for superiority*. By this he meant not dominance, leadership, or an important position in society, but a striving toward completion of the self and toward an actualization of the best that one could be given one's goals and the exigencies of one's life. It is this striving that carries the person from one stage of development to the next. The neurotic may strive for power, or for other selfish goals, but the normal person strives for goals that are in the service of social interests. It was in this connection that Adler introduced the concept of "masculine protest" or an overcompensation that both women and men may show when they feel inadequate. The compensatory behavior takes the form of an exaggeration of masculine qualities.

By *social interest* Adler meant the individual human's investment of self in the interests of the larger society. Thus it includes the willingness of the individual to cooperate with others to achieve common goals, to form interpersonal relations and to identify with the group. Alone, the person was weak; social interest was a compensation for the impotence of the individual. Adler saw this characteristic as an innate disposition which, like other potentials of the person, would fully develop with proper care and guidance. It was in this spirit that Adler stressed the need for improved educational practices and attention to the problems of childhood behavior.

Style of life was an Adlerian concept which accounted for the uniqueness of the individual. It was a manifestation of the particular inferiorities that the person felt, and the nature of her or his compensatory superiority strivings. Formed early in life, the life style was a unifying holistic principle whereby the person could order experiences assimilating those that fit and ignoring others. For example, the intellectual has a life style that includes reading, solitude, participation in cultural affairs, and so on. Other available experiences, such as sports, might be alien to such a person's life style. The life style developed in accordance with the person's goals. Though elements of it might be common to many, its overall quality was special, unique to the individual.

Finally, Adler introduced the concept of the *creative self,* which integrated all the other concepts of his personality theory. He developed this notion later than the others, and it took precedence over them as a more sophisticated concept that accounted for the consistency and the unity of personality. The creative self became for Adler the active principle of life. It was the intermediary between stimuli impinging upon the individual from the outside and the responses made to them. It was the amalgam which combined inherited attributes and environmental events, and from them determined the goals of the person's striving and the means of attaining them.

Adler's theory of personality, in contrast to Freud's, was an affirmative statement of trust in human potential and of one's ability to choose, to order, and to influence the course of one's life. Thus it restored a certain freedom and dignity to personhood, and held out the hope that humankind could fashion the good life for the individual and for the society. Like Horney, Adler was optimistic.

Adler's ideas about women followed directly and logically from his theory of personality. In fact, the key concepts of his theory seem unusually fitting as useful explanations of some aspects of the so-called feminine personality. For Adler, the only biological fact of any importance was the helplessness of the human infant. From this condition issued universal feelings of inferiority which motivated the compensatory striving for power. These strivings, when accompanied by social interest and common sense, all attributes of the normal human, were channeled into achievement behavior directed toward a goal. If the child were dealt with intelligently and sympathetically, the healthy personality would develop naturally, because of the innate capacity to do so. If the child's inferiority feelings persisted, because of parental failure to encourage compensatory striving, or if the child were neglected or permitted to become self-ish and spoiled, then she or he would fail to develop adequate coping power and would find "erroneous" solutions to life's problems. Adler believed that the system of socializing children into roles of dominance and submission based on sex had all the potential for inducing bad solutions in the form of neuroses and character distortions.

Adler's specific comment on women appeared as a chapter called "Sex" in his book *Understanding Human Nature* (1927), two years after the first of Freud's three papers on female personality. Contrasting the two works, one would never suspect that Adler had ever been influenced by Freud.

"All our institutions, our traditional attitudes, our laws, our morals, our customs, give evidence of the fact that they are determined and maintained by privileged males for the glory of male domination" (p. 123). All of these influence the child from its earliest days in the nursery. The boy is forced into an unnatural requirement for domination, a behavioral pattern which depreciates the female sex. The girl, in addition to the feelings of inferiority shared with all young children, has the added consciousness of her sexual subordination. The twin fallacies of the superiority of the male and the inferiority of the female erode the erotic and social relationships between the sexes, and result inevitably in hostility and suspicion at the expense of comradeship, trust, and candor.

Adler believed that the girl loses self-confidence as she continually experiences prejudices against women. She is routinely thwarted in acting out a basic drive for power and superiority common to all humans. Her sex category determines the way she is treated by society, and that treatment must cause disturbance in her psychic development. "The whole history of civilization . . . shows us that the pressure exerted upon women, and the inhibitions to which she must submit today, are not to be borne by any human being; they always give rise to revolt" (p. 134).

As evidence that the female's diminution of self-esteem is conditioned early in life, Adler cited research showing that daughters in families where the mother was the sole breadwinner were more talented and capable than girls in families where the mother's role was subordinate to the father's. Because of the model of competency presented by the mother, they failed to develop negative concepts of themselves as women.

Adler called attention to the division of descriptive concepts along sex lines, whereby "masculine" means worthwhile, powerful, and capable, and "feminine" means obedient, servile, and subordinate. Traits valued by society are masculine, and those less valued are feminine. Whatever pertains to women appears inferior, so that both women and men depreciate the female sex.

The psychic life of women, Adler said, is deeply affected by the imposition of this additional ascribed inferiority. Many girls and women find compensation in certain privileges accorded to them because of their sex such as special courtesies and exemptions from some kinds of obligations. While these may seem to elevate women, it puts them in a position which has been designed by men for the advantage of men.

The almost universal dissatisfaction with the feminine role may manifest itself, Adler thought, in three ways, all of which are distortions away from healthy personality. The first type develops in an active "masculine" direction. In this case the woman seeks to compensate for her inferior status by revolting against it. This is the "masculine protest" which both males and females adopt when they feel inferior. They are trying to purge themselves of the dreaded weakness of femininity. Adler seemed to think that given the situation, such a protest in women was predictable. Since there were only two socially approved types, the ideal woman and the ideal man, desertion of the female role could only appear masculine. "This does not appear as the result of some mysterious secretion, but because, in the given time and place, there is no other possibility" (p. 134). The second kind of rebellion appears in the woman who over-identifies with the feminine role, cloaking herself in resignation, humility, and obedience. She adjusts everywhere because of her docility, but is so helpless and weak that she accomplishes nothing. She develops neurotic symptoms, showing clearly how her "training" has made her sick. A third woman may accept the condemnation of inferiority and of subordination, and feel convinced that these sentences on women are just. She believes that men are entitled to their position of privilege, and that only they can do the important things in life. Her indirect way of revolting takes revenge by shifting all responsibility onto the male, as if to say, "Since only you are competent, you must do everything."

One can see certain similarities between Adler's first two types and Freud's women who developed neurotic solutions to their penis envy, but only the behavioral styles are similar. Adler refused to consider a constitutional determinant at all. He saw all these forms of protest as the result of man's privilege and woman's powerlessness and not a result of biology. While men were also hurt by their social conditioning for dominance, Adler implied that women could be expected to suffer more because as children they had to bear a double load of inferiority feelings from their status as child and their identity as female. Adler believed that it was normal for all humans to strive for superiority and that women who did so should not be considered deviant.

Adler's understanding of the factors underlying female behavior and personality led him to conclusions which were strongly supportive of the prevailing feminist positions on social reform. He deplored the competitive pressures of the educational process, which forced boys to prove their masculinity and taught girls to be victims. He thought that the prejudices against women, and the emphasis on roles, pushed many girls toward marriage as an "emergency exit out of life," and led to marital problems and increased tensions between the sexes. He deplored the inequality of sexual standards. "A subordination of one individual to another in sexual relationships is just as unbearable as in the life of nations" (p. 145).

Margaret Mead

Margaret Mead was born in 1901. Her father was a professor at the University of Pennsylvania, and both her mother and her paternal grandmother had been teachers. In Mead's autobiography, *Blackberry Winter* (1972), she attributes her attraction to intellectual interests to her father. But it was the two women, her grandmother and her mother, who most influenced her early life. Her grandmother, she wrote, was "the most decisive influence in my life" (p. 45). She had attended college when it was still unusual for a woman to do so, had married, had a child, and continued with her career in education. She had advanced ideas about child rearing and education, and, in fact, taught the young Margaret at home until she was ready for high school. Margaret's mother was an ardent supporter of social and political causes, including feminism and woman suffrage. With her large family, however, she had little opportunity to realize her talents and abilities. "In my life," Mead wrote, "I realized every one of her unrealized ambitions" (p. 29). With such models as these in her early years, Mead grew up with "no reason to doubt that brains were suitable for a woman. . . . I learned that the mind is not sex-typed" (p. 54).

Her interest in anthropology began at Barnard College, where Mead took a course with the famed anthropologist Franz Boas. She attended graduate school at Columbia and continued to work with Boas, who persuaded her to do her doctoral dissertation on adolescent girls to determine whether the troubles of adolescents were tied to the culture or if they were inherent in the psychobiology of youth.

Mead had learned from her training respect for all people and their various ways of life. Primitive people were not savages or bar-barians; they were people whose culture had developed and persisted "without script," that is, without written language or history. Any language or culture was as valuable as any other, and a primitive lan-guage or art could be as complex and elaborate as a civilized one.

For nine months Mead lived with the Samoans, observing, inter-viewing, and testing young girls. From this work came her first book, *Coming of Age in Samoa,* which became a best seller soon after its publication in 1932. This book included a chapter on the "deviant," in which Mead described girls whose temperament had a certain in-tensity of response which made them different from the placid per-sonality she came to expect of Samoan girls. The relationship be-tween temperament, sex, and deviance in different cultures became increasingly interesting to her, and by 1931 she was ready to look more closely at the way culture shapes the personalities of men and women. She wanted to develop a new approach to the old question of innate sex differences, because "until one had got out of the way the problem of the effects of cultural stylization on feminine and masculine personalities, it seemed to be futile to raise questions about biologically-given sex differences" (1972, p. 196). With this in mind, she began during the early 1930s her studies of three primi-tive societies in New Guinea: the Arapesh, the Mundugumor, and the Tchambuli. The result of this was the now-classic book *Sex and Temperament in Three Primitive Societies* (1935).

In the Arapesh tribe, both men and women exhibited "mater-nal," nurturant behavior and were equally concerned with the care of children. Child betrothal was practiced, and small boys learned to assist with the feeding and care of their small wives-to-be. Life cen-tered on making things grow: animals, plants, and children. Members of both sexes learned to be cooperative, unaggressive, and responsive to the needs of others. Aggression against the rights of others met with serious disapproval. Even so, a few men and women were known to be aggressive. The others took pains to avoid provok-ing them, as the one who aroused anger in another was even more guilty than the one who got angry. The model personality for both sexes was built on traits considered feminine in our society. Mead found the Arapesh rather uninteresting at the time, because they yielded little that was helpful to her question of how cultural pre-scriptions of sex-linked behavior affected the personalities of men and women. For the Arapesh, the prescriptions were one and the same.

The Mundugumor were different from the Arapesh in every possible way. Both sexes were ruthless, aggressive, and strongly sex-ual, and the maternal, nurturing aspects of personality were barely apparent. The cultural shaping of personality was very strong, and both women and men were expected to conform to a single model. Rivalrous and exploitative, they were rejecting and, by Western standards, cruel to their children. Women wanted sons and men wanted daughters, and babies of the wrong sex were tossed alive into the river. Not only did Mead loathe the Mundugumor culture, but again she felt that her central problem was not advanced by her contact with them. She was still missing the cultural contrast in sex training that she was looking for.

Finally, the Tchambuli provided the missing piece that made possible a new interpretation of the earlier data. Among these lake-dwellers, the roles and characteristics of the men and women were the reverse of those considered appropriate in our society. The women took charge of all important business and domestic affairs. They worked in large cooperative groups carrying their individual fireplaces about with them and setting them down whenever there was work to be done. The little girls, like their mothers, were competent. Mead remarked in 1972, that it was the only culture she had seen in which it was the girls who were the upcoming ones, curious, exploratory, and free. The men spent most of their time in ceremonial houses on the lake, carving, painting, and gossiping, and working out their rivalries with each other. The small boys learned this male way of life at an early age.

It was during this period that Mead began to develop her ideas about the cultural standardization of temperament, and the role of social conditioning that selected certain characteristics to reinforce and neglected or punished others. That these were not necessarily based on sex was apparent from the unisex models of the Arapesh and the Mundugumor. Such models, however, applied to ways of expressing feeling, to permissible manifestations of basic drives. The fact that these were independent of sex did not mean that the sexes were otherwise not differentiated. Beliefs about them, rituals and occupations assigned to them, were different. All cultures distinguished roles based on biological sex. But personality could be ascribed, and humans as groups could learn ways of being, on the basis of their membership in the group, or their membership in some category, such as sex.

Mead therefore concluded that human behavior expressed in personality characteristics is malleable beyond anything previously suspected. The differences between individuals who are members of different cultures are almost entirely attributable to differences in conditioning, and the form of this conditioning is determined by the culture. "Standardized personality differences between the sexes are of this order, cultural creations to which each generation, male and female, is trained to conform" (p. 280).

This emphasis upon the power of culture in shaping personality did not mean a complete denial of constitutionally determined individual differences. Mead's position was not the extreme environmentalist position of the psychologist John B. Watson (1924). Watson's notion that the infant was a *tabula rasa,* a blank tablet, upon which personality would be inscribed by experience suggested a homogeneity of potential totally responsive to social conditioning. Mead saw the same range of temperamental variation in all the groups. The culturally selected normative personality was an overlay through which one could still perceive the idiosyncratic character even though it was attenuated by the imposition of the cultural personality. What happened was that the culture selected some aspects of the possible range of individual temperamental variation, either for everyone or for all members of the same category, such as sex, age, or race. For example, if warfare is a highly valued activity in a society, then all male children are expected to suppress any display of fear. The traits required for the occupation of males become identified as male personality; traits which may naturally be strong components of some individual personalities are developed as the norm for all, as key elements of a masculine personality. Likewise, Mead observed, if great importance is attached to the role of nurturing children by women, then the culture selects the trait of nurturance (even though the strength of it varies in individual women), reinforces it, and defines it as an essential component of feminine personality.

In societies where personality types are specialized by sex, that is, where certain ways of being and behaving are held to be appropriate for one sex and not the other, then conditions favor the appearance of the deviant—the man or woman who temperamentally is unable to conform to the prescribed norms and behaviorally is more like the other sex. Such a maladaptive adjustment appears when the society has decreed an approved personality that is rigidly limited to one sex and considered unnatural for the other. As Mead pointed out, in societies such as our own and the Tchambuli where such sex-typing of personality is the rule, the appearance of deviants is inevitable. She found a compelling example of this among an American Indian group, which insisted that the ability to withstand any danger or hardship was a masculine characteristic, and small boys were relentlessly prohibited from crying, clinging, playing with younger children, or showing any sign of fear. Boys who did these things inspired the fear that they would turn out to be, not real men, but *berdaches,* transvestites who went about with the women and did women's work. The presence of the *berdaches* was a constant threat to parents, causing them to obsessively reinforce in their boys the behaviors identified with masculinity.

Later we shall see that women have more leeway in our society with regard to expression of personality than men have. Thus one would expect a greater tendency to see norm-violating men as deviant, with greater tolerance of women who behave in atypical ways. That this can be true among primitive people also was shown by another anthropologist, Oscar Lewis, who described "manly-hearted" women in a Blackfoot tribe in Canada (1941). Whereas the ideal woman was submissive, reserved, and obedient, the manly-hearted women were aggressive, independent, ambitious, and boldly sexual. They owned property, took part in religious rituals, and chose their own mates. In a male-dominated culture, these women were clearly deviant, but in a special, favored way. Manly-heartedness was associated with having been a favored child who had been given special privileges such as playing with boys and assuming a leadership role. Being deviants from cultural norms, such women were strong enough to break away from sex-role restrictions, to capitalize on their assets, and to take the place they wanted in society. They went from favored child to favored woman—a rare model indeed in the patterns of culture.

What about the relations between the sexes in societies with rigid sex role dichotomies? Even for one who has incorporated the model personality for one's sex there are repercussions. For example, if dominance and self-assertion are prescribed for males, the male having such characteristics requires submissiveness in others for reassurance of his own distinctiveness. When he encounters a woman who is as dominant as he is, doubt of his own manhood is set up in his mind. This is why, Mead said, that the man who conforms most closely to the masculine norm is the most suspicious and hostile towards deviating women. The male's conviction of his own sex membership depends upon the non-occurrence of "his" traits in the other sex.

Her observations of these primitive groups, and the theoretical concepts relating cultural conditioning to sex-linked personality types, led Mead at that time, forty years ago, to a far-reaching proposal for the socialization of children. She observed that there are three possible courses for societies to take in developing the personalities of their children. The first is to specialize personality based on sex, as the Tchambuli did, and as most Western societies do. The second is to value a personality type that is indifferent to sex, a unisex model, as she found among the Arapesh and the Mundugumor. Either of these, however, results in unconforming persons being labeled as deviants, and thus cause unhappiness for some of its members.

There is a third way which Mead thought would reflect greater respect for individual freedom and dignity. The society could make room for the development of many different kinds of temperamental endowments. It could actively build upon the different potentials which it tries to train out of some individuals and to encourage and insist upon in others. Beneath the superficial category of sex the same potentialities exist, recurring in every generation. But they cannot develop if the society defines them as inappropriate for the person. For example, if only males can make music, then the musical aptitude of the most talented woman will never be cultivated. The temperamental variations which appear in both sexes could be encouraged, so that the differences among the individuals in the society would be *real* differences, not artificially created ones. Such a society would abandon attempts to make boys aggressive and girls passive, or to make all children aggressive. It would instead permit the development of the boy who is nurturant and the girl who is stimulated by fighting against obstacles. No skill or talent would go unrecognized because the child who had it was of the wrong sex. No child would be shaped to one pattern of behavior, for there would be many patterns, with each individual allowed to grow into the one that was most congenial to her or his innate temperament. Thus would the fabric of society lose its arbitrary character, and become a place where every human gift would be valued.

From our perspective today we recognize in such ideas contemporary values of individual freedom and self-actualization which, however ideal, are still far from being the usual experience for most people. Historically, some avenues of development have been open to some persons and not to others, as a function of sex.[2] The removal of barriers and the "letting be" as far as personality is concerned would allow for the fullest development of individual potential. Such a plan would not obliterate sex differences, nor would it simply promote a model whereby boys and girls were conditioned to the same pattern. Rather, individual differences, regardless of sex, would become manifest, and sexual category would no longer be a determinant of personality, except to the extent that the contribution of biological sex differences, as yet unknown, would have its effect.

Mead's prophetic vision is reflected today in the goals of some members of our society. Stimulated by the feminist movement and

---

[2] The same may be said of other categorical variables, such as race or age.

counterculture values, it is now more possible for the male to renounce the old *macho* attitudes and values, and for the female to insist upon her right to be any way she wishes. If temperament is no
longer standardized along sex lines, then we can expect to see more
women exhibiting temperamental attributes heretofore called
masculine, and more men who are free to manifest aspects of personality which an earlier age called feminine. If this comes about,
one would expect it to be accompanied by changes in roles and institutions. For example, children might be cared for by nurturant,
expressive men, and laws might be made by competent, determined
women. At the present time, the impetus for change seems to be
stronger among women than among men. This is understandable if
one remembers that men, more surely than women, have had to ex-
punge from their natures every hint of the other sex. Given the low
esteem in which women and their traits have historically been held,
it will take a major reappraisal of values for men, whether collectively or individually, to partake of their "feminine" selves, and to
permit their sons to play with dolls if they wish. As for institutions,
such as government, education, business, and the family, they could
be maintained by persons who were temperamentally suited to fill
the required roles, regardless of sex.

Recently, Mead returned again to the issue in a critique of
Freud's last paper on the psychology of women (1974). Discounting
the penis-envy concept as hopelessly culture bound, she points out
that the possibility of biologically determined psychological sex differences cannot be totally dismissed until more information is available. Since it is only very recently in human history that women's
reproductive functions have been modified, with fewer pregnancies,
legal abortions, medical deliveries, and artifical feeding of infants, it
is not possible to know what effects these and other such interven-
tions will have on such ancient biological facts of a woman's life.
Mead suggests that it would be surprising if millions of years of
cyclic changes and other features associated with childbearing did
not have some effect on female personality. "The rhythms of human
development, patterned during a million years, are ignored at our
peril, and understood, give us wisdom" (p. 105). While this may
sound like a softening of her earlier position on the malleability of
personality, it is really a wise reminder of how little we know, and a
caution against making interpretations that may be tinged with prejudice and wishful thinking at the expense of objectivity and truth.

The views of Horney, Thompson, Adler, and Mead are unified
by the recognition that women's personalities are not necessarily determined by their biological functions. Their behavior and personal-

ity have been shaped, as men's have, by *both* their bodies and their cultural assignments. Each theorist emphasized the crucial importance of the social roles of women and the attitudes toward women for the development of women's psychology. They saw the effects also of the disparate valuing of the sexes and their respective attributes and achievements. They represent the appearance of a new way of looking at human behavior, and point out new paths in the search for understanding of human personality. They are our bridge between the past of myths and misunderstandings, and newly emerging knowledge that better informs our thinking about ourselves.

Sexual dimorphism, biology, and behavior

4

Therefore, the primacy of the embryonic female morphology forces us to reverse long-held concepts on the nature of sexual differentiation. Embryologically speaking, it is correct to say that the penis is an exaggerated clitoris, the scrotum is derived from the labia majora, the original libido is feminine, etc. The reverse is true only for the birds and reptiles. For all mammals, modern embryology calls for an Adam-out-of-Eve myth!

—Mary Jane Sherfey, *The Nature and Evolution of Female Sexuality,* 1972

The hypothetical models of female personality and the explanations of female behavior discussed in the preceding chapters were essentially based upon personal and cultural beliefs or upon observations by psychoanalysts and behaviorally oriented investigators who viewed women and theorized about them within the context of their own cultural and professional background. Such views were of necessity formulated from the viewers' experiences with women, both personal and professional, interpreted within the prevailing cultural milieu, and generated by the interaction of that milieu's wisdom with the experiences and ideologies of the observers. These views have varied widely and have included the invocation of mythical or supernatural explanations, the assumption of basic biological determinants, and the argument that personalities and behaviors labeled masculine and feminine are produced not by biological sex but rather by social expectations and conditioning.

The fact that humans differentiate into two sexes, female and male and that this differentiation has both biological and behavioral components is universally observable. However, the origins, manifestations, and effects of these have only recently begun to be understood. In order to evaluate theoretical explanations of female personality and behavior, one must consider the phenomenon of sexual differentiation itself, the influences which bring it about, and the extent to which it can be shown to affect sexual identification and sexually differentiated behavior.

The conventional wisdom that the sex of the individual is determined once and for all at conception, the union of an ovum and a sperm cell, has been shown in recent decades to be an inaccurate simplification. After conception certain intrauterine events occur which normally permit an unequivocal sex assignment at birth following which myriad sequences of related events begin to impinge upon the infant, shaping the course of its development toward a differentiated sexual identity. The sexual identity of the individual is the end of a process of sexual differentiation which begins at conception, proceeds along a course determined by intrauterine influences, and continues after birth in accordance with the socialization practices of the culture into which the child is born.

Sexual differentiation is a process which begins and ends with sexual dimorphism, that is, the separation of the sexes into two sexually different morphologic and psychologic forms. Both biosexual and psychosexual dimorphism are usually invariant for humans. That is, with certain exceptions, humans differentiate structurally and functionally into one sex or the other. In all societies they also differentiate a psychosexual or gender identity which is the individual's identification of herself or himself as a member of one sex category and not the other. This identification is usually followed by the subsequent adoption of the feminine or masculine sexual role according to the prevailing cultural definitions. The results of biosexual dimorphism, essentially finished at birth, are the same for all human groups. Their members are biologically either male or female.

Psychosexual dimorphism, or the experientially based gender identity, is also universal and is reinforced by associated behavioral and role assignments. These do not take the same form among all humans. The Tchambuli, for example, prescribed behaviors and roles for females and males which were the reverse of those traditionally observed in Western society. Though sex-linked assignments may vary from one society to another, all capitalize upon the principles of biosexual and psychosexual dimorphism, assigning sexually dimorphic role behavior to their members, and proscribing some behaviors which they define as incongruent with the sex assignment of the person. The principle of sexual dimorphism, then, and its underlying determinants, has far-reaching consequences for the individual and for society.

Determinants of Sexual Differentiation

The determinants of sexual differentiation fall into two categories and are roughly chronological. First, genetic and hormonal determinants bring about the biological differentiation of the embryo into a male or a female, causing the fetal gonad to differentiate into either a testis or an ovary, influencing the development of the sex-appropriate set of internal reproductive structures, and causing the embryonic genital tissue to differentiate into either male or female external genitalia. Second are influences beginning at birth and culminating in the formation of gender identity, the person's knowledge of and identification with her or his psychosexual category. According to some researchers, this outcome is contingent primarily upon the infant's sex of assignment and sex of rearing; that is, the designation at birth of the child as a member of one sex or the other, and its perception and treatment by others congruent with sexually defined cultural patterns that are appropriate to the sex of assignment (Money and Ehrhardt, 1972). Other research suggests that the mammalian brain itself is affected by the influence of prenatal hormones so that certain behaviors are more likely to be displayed by one sex than the other (Beach, 1970; Ward, 1972). The former observation is based upon clinical studies of human subjects, while the latter comes mostly from studies of subhuman primates. Obviously both these lines of thinking have important implications for theories of female and male development.

Normally, the biological and social determinants are congruent with each other. For example, the biological female will be assigned the sexual category of female at birth, will be reared as a female, and will differentiate a female gender identity. Occasionally, however, genetic and hormonal anomalies occur which place the person in a gray area between sexual categories. These cases have been instructive in revealing more about the relative effects of the biological and social determinants of gender identity.

In addition to prenatal biological determinants of sexual differentiation and postnatal cultural effects on gender identity are the further differentiating events of puberty with its distinctive body changes and of the menstrual cycle of the female. These developments are also under genetic and hormonal control, and their programs are laid down before birth. By the time they occur in the life cycle, however, gender identity has been firmly established. In the normal course, their appearance simply confirms what the child already knows: for the girl, that she is becoming a woman; for the boy, that he is becoming a man. In the woman, the menstrual cycle terminates during the climacterium with the ebbing influence of her sexual hormones. The hormonal variations of the cycle and its cessation in menopause have also given rise to controversial interpretations of their importance in the psychology of women.

Genetic determinants

All cells of the human body with the exception of one type normally have twenty-three pairs of chromosomes of which one member of each pair was contributed by the father, the other by the mother. Twenty-two of these pairs, the *autosomes,* carry genes which determine the various features of the individual. The remaining pair are the sex chromosomes, which are designated XX in the female and XY in the male. It is these chromosomes which carry the genetic material responsible for the genetic sex of the individual. The germ cells, the ova and the sperm, are the exceptions. Produced by the ovaries and the testes, these cells when mature have twenty-three chromosomes, including an X in the ovum and either an X or a Y in the sperm. When conception occurs, the resulting zygote, the fertilized ovum, has its full complement of chromosomes and may be designated 46,XX or 46,XY as the case may be. If the ovum is fertilized by an X-bearing sperm the offspring will be female; by a Y-bearing sperm, male. Thus it is the father who determines the genetic sex of the child. The X chromosome is one of the largest of all the chromosomes, whereas the Y is often the smallest, carrying practically no genetic material. It does, however, have one important function. The Y chromosome causes the embryonic gonad to differentiate into a testis instead of an ovary.

Technically, the genetic determination of sex, mediated by the Y chromosome, affects only the gonads—the testes and the ovaries. All other sexual differentiation is under hormonal control. If a Y-chromosome is present in the human zygote, the embryonic gonad will differentiate as a testis. If the Y is absent, it will differentiate as an ovary. In other words it is not the second X which turns the gonad into an ovary; it is the absence of Y. In the presence of Y, the critical period for the differentiation of the gonad into a testis is the seventh week after conception. If it does not occur at this time, the gonad will differentiate into an ovary. This illustrates an important principle of human embryonic development: for the differentiation of a male, something must be added. At the genetic level, this something is the Y-chromosome. In the absence of Y, the embryo will differentiate as a female. We shall see later that this principle is a precursor to a parallel principle governing hormonal influences on sexual differentiation.

It sometimes happens that in the process of cell division culminating in the mature ovum or sperm, the X or Y chromosome may be lost, or the cell may have one or more extra X's or Y's. If a zygote has such a chromosomal anomaly, the resulting individual will be a genetic variant from the normal XX female or XY male. Several such variants resulting from lost or supernumerary sex chromosomes have been identified. Two of these are 45,XO, Turner's syndrome, and 47,XXY, Klinefelter's syndrome. These variants best exemplify the principle that the absence of Y, rather than the presence of the second X, results in female differentiation. Conversely, if Y is present, the result will be a male.

The child with Turner's syndrome has only one sex chromosome, an X, which may have been provided either by her father or her mother. She appears at birth as a normal female with female genitalia; therefore she is assigned and reared as a female. She is without gonads, which has two important effects related to the absence of ovarian function. The ovaries produce ova and female sex hormones, which bring about the body changes at puberty, the secondary sex characteristics of breast development, body hair, and female body form, and also initiate and regulate the menstrual cycle. Without ovaries, the Turner's girl is sterile though she may have a normal uterus and thus can menstruate if provided with female sex hormones at puberty. She tends to be short in stature, usually under five feet. For this reason, the administration of estrogen is often delayed until she is sixteen or seventeen years old to permit her to grow as tall as she can, since estrogen tends to inhibit the growth of the long bones of the body. Under these circumstances, she will have a late puberty, and will be late in developing the female secondary sex characteristics, depending upon when her hormonal deficiency is corrected. The significant fact is that Turner's girls and women are unequivocally female, even though their body cells have only one X-chromosome. Without the missing chromosome, be it X or Y, no gonads are present. But because Y is absent, the body differentiates as a female. (The absence of sex hormones is also significant for this differentiation, and will be discussed in the next section). In addition, Turner's girls differentiate a female psychosexual identity, and have especially strong "feminine" interest patterns and behavior (Ehrhardt, Greenberg, and Money, 1970). The implications of this finding will be discussed later.

The individual with Klinefelter's syndrome has both the double X of the normal female and the XY of the normal male. However, he differentiates as a male with testes, a penis, and a scrotum, though the penis may be small, and the testes undersized and sterile. The body type is clearly masculine, however, though psychosexual identity problems are not infrequent (Money, 1972a). The presence of the Y chromosome in this case mediates a male differentiation in spite of the two X's. Variants of Klinefelter's may have more than two X's, but will still differentiate as males because of the single Y.

Thus the crucial genetic determinant is the Y chromosome. Its presence or absence starts the process of sexual differentiation of the embryo along a male or female line of development.

Hormonal determinants

After the genetic effects on biological sexual differentiation, the most important determinants are hormonal, directly affecting the differentiation of the internal system and the external genitalia (Fig. 4.1). The primitive gonad is unimorphic, that is, it is undifferentiated as to sex. Structurally, it consists of two parts, the inner part, or medulla, and the outer part, or cortex. If the genetic program calls for the gonad to become a testis, it is the medulla which proliferates, while the cortex becomes vestigial. If the gonad becomes an ovary, the cortex proliferates and the medulla regresses. While the testis begins to differentiate in the seventh week, the ovary begins much later around the twelfth week. This early differentiation of the testis allows it to begin secreting the hormones critical to the continued development of a male fetus with male internal reproductive structures and male external genitalia.

The human fetus is equipped with the primordia of both male and female internal reproductive structures. These are, respectively, the wolffian and mullerian ducts. In male development, the wolffian ducts differentiate into the vas deferens, the seminal vesicles, and the ejaculatory ducts. In the female the mullerian ducts differentiate into the uterus, the fallopian tubes or oviducts, and the upper part of the vagina. In the usual course, one or the other of these systems develops and the other becomes vestigial. Thus each sex carries in its body leftover remnants of the other. The decisive factor in determining which of these two systems will develop is the role of the secretions from the fetal testes.

The fetal testes secrete two hormones which promote the further development of the fetus in a male direction. One of these substances has the effect of inhibiting the development of the mullerian system which otherwise would grow into a uterus, oviducts, and vagina. This substance is called simply "mullerian inhibiting substance" after its only known function.

The other secretion of the fetal testes is the androgenic hormone testosterone. The androgenic hormones of which testosterone is the most potent are referred to as the male sex hormones because of their importance in male biological and sexual development. At this stage, testosterone promotes the development of the wolffian

SEXUAL DIFFERENTIATION IN THE HUMAN FETUS

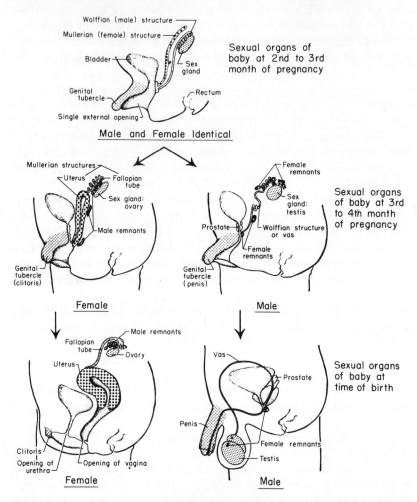

Figure 4.1 The three stages in the differentiation of the sexual system, internal and external. (Reprinted from Money, J. and Ehrhardt, A., *Man and Woman, Boy and Girl* [Baltimore: Johns Hopkins University Press, 1972], by permission of author.)

system into the male reproductive structures. Thus the suppression of the female duct system is complemented by the elaboration of the male duct system. These two systems are the only basically dimorphic structures of the human embryonic tract. The gonads and genitalia are all unimorphic in the beginning, later differentiating into either female or male structures.

In the absence of testes or of these fetal testicular products, the mullerian system will develop and the wolffian system will become vestigial. The presence of ovaries or of ovarian hormones is not necessary for development of the mullerian system into the internal reproductive apparatus of the female. In other words, in the XX embryo, there is no counterpart to the mullerian inhibiting substance secreted by the fetal testes. If the fetal gonads, be they testes or ovaries, are removed before the critical period when one or the other of these systems becomes prepotent, then the mullerian system will develop, and the wolffian system will degenerate, regardless of genetic sex.

Rarely, the testes of a male embryo will fail to produce the mullerian inhibitor. Such a situation will result in a male who is normal in all respects, except that he has a uterus and oviducts in addition to the usual male internal accessories. These extra organs can be removed surgically. The principle here, as with the Y chromosome, is that in the absence of the fetal testicular hormones, the differentiation of the internal reproductive organs will be female. This is true whether that "absence" is the result of surgical or chemical castration, or of non-secretion of the material if the gonads are ovaries. In the female no wolffian inhibitor is present, and that system will degenerate just because there is no testosterone to promote its development.

The external male and female genitalia develop from common embryonic structures; thus they are unimorphic in the beginning. Before the eighth week of gestation, these structures are undifferentiated, and have the potential to develop in either a male or a female direction (Fig. 4.2). At this stage they consist of a genital tubercle which is situated above the urogenital groove. On each side of this groove are urethral folds beside which are labioscrotal swellings. In the female, the genital tubercle becomes the clitoris, the urethral folds become the labia minora (minor lips), and the labioscrotal swellings become the labia majora (major lips). In the male, the genital tubercle becomes the body and the glans, or tip, of the penis, the urethral folds fuse around the urethra, and the labioscrotal swellings fuse to form the scrotum.

The differentiation of these structures as either male or female has been shown to be a function of the presence or absence of androgenic hormones. In the absence of these hormones, principally testosterone, they will develop into female genitalia regardless of genetic sex or sex of gonads.

Numerous experiments on rats, rabbits, and other mammals have confirmed that differentiation of the internal reproductive structures and the external genitalia is under the hormonal control

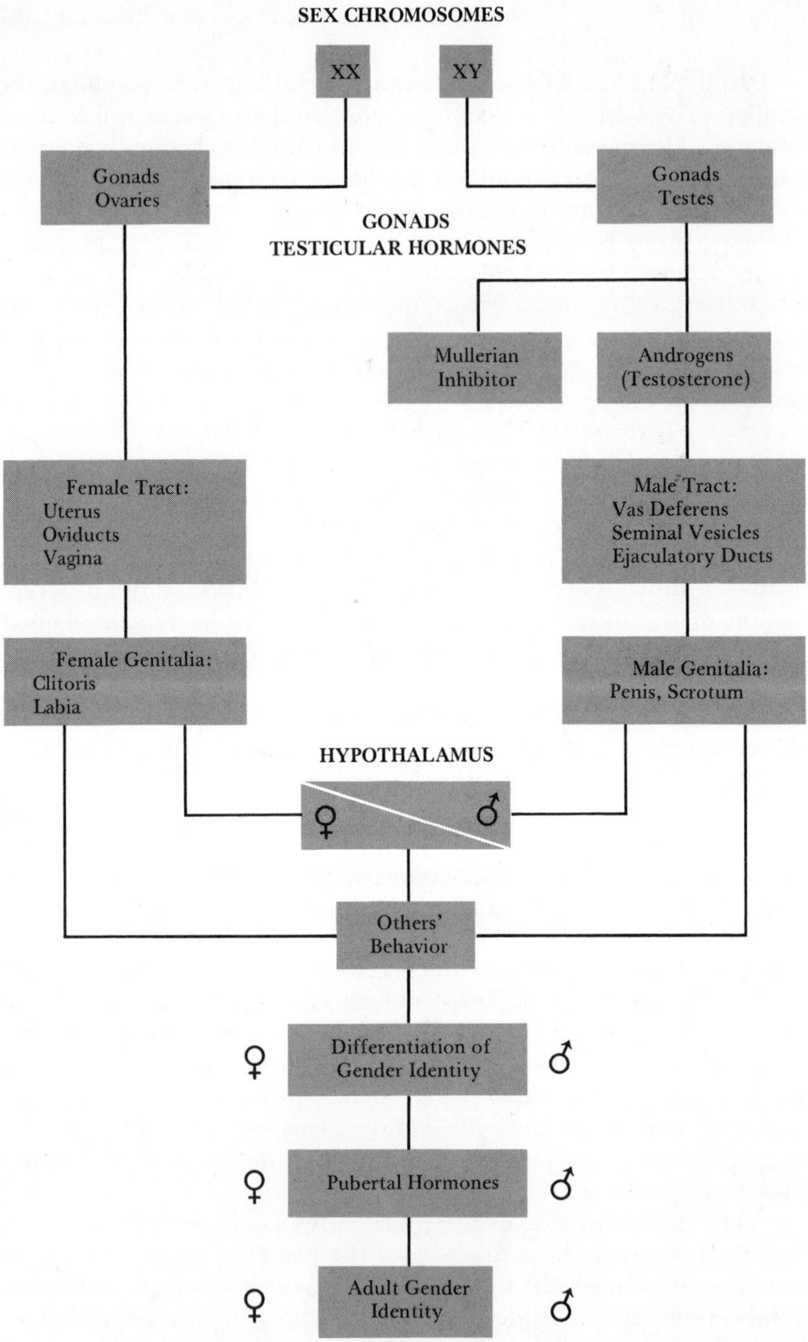

Figure 4.2 Process of sexual differentiation in humans. In the absence of testicular hormones the differentiation will proceed innately in the female direction.

of functioning testes (Jost, 1972). If the testes are removed from male embryos before these structures begin to differentiate as male, complete feminization of their development will ensue. Removal of ovaries from the female embryo has no effect upon female differentiation. Estrogen and progesterone, the female sex hormones produced by the ovaries, are not involved in the sexual differentiation of the female *in utero*.

These observations, that female sexual differentiation proceeds innately if no gonads are present, regardless of genetic sex, has led several researchers to conclude that nature's basic form is female (Money and Ehrhardt, 1972; Sherfey, 1972). Male development is a deviation from the basic female pattern: "We must accept as a fundamental fact that the mammalian sexual organs begin existence as anatomically and physiologically female structures with all the potentialities for development in the female growth pattern. If the genetic code then so dictates, these female structures are transformed into male sexual organs by the action of fetal androgens" (Sherfey, 1972, pp. 47–48).

The validity of the principle that sexual differentiation is mediated by the action of testicular hormones has been amply demonstrated in experimental studies on animals (Money, 1965). In humans, the effects have been studied primarily on hermaphrodites,[1] individuals born with ambiguous biological sex or with external genitalia and other characteristics which are the reverse of the genetic sex. Examples of the conditions which result respectively in the feminization of males and the masculinization of females will be described to elucidate the principle in humans.

The first condition is the androgen insensitivity syndrome, also called the testicular feminizing syndrome. In this case, a genetic male (46,XY) is born with female genitalia, and subsequently develops a female morphology with female secondary sex characteristics in puberty, although functioning testes are present, producing the characteristic male hormones described earlier. The condition results from a recessive genetic defect which renders the body's cells insensitive to the androgenic hormones provided by the fetal testes, so that all the structures that are dependent upon these hormones, primarily testosterone, for their normal male development differentiate as female. The functioning testes actually feminize the body at puberty, since estrogen, which is normally produced by the testes in small quantities, has full play to promote the development of the secondary sex characteristics typical of normal females. Such individ-

---

[1] Named after Hermaphroditus, child of the Greek gods Hermes and Aphrodite, who became united with the nymph Salmacis in a single body.

uals may grow up as females, unrecognized as genetic and gonadal males until failure of appearance of the menses or discovery of the testes in the groin reveal the problem. The wolffian system, also dependent upon androgens for its differentiation, remains vestigial. The individual, in appearance a normal female, does not have a uterus and oviducts, however, because though the body was insensitive to the fetal androgens, it was not insensitive to the mullerian inhibiting substance. Therefore, the differentiation of the mullerian system was inhibited as in a normal male. Such persons are usually assigned and reared as females, and develop a female psychosexual identity in spite of the discrepancy between their morphology and their genetic or gonadal sex (Money and Ehrhardt, 1972). They cannot be successfully corrected as males, since their bodies cannot utilize the androgens which are necessary for masculinization at puberty; that is, the development of secondary sex characteristics such as male body form, deepening of the voice, and the growth of beard and body hair. Since their bodies are unable to respond to androgens, they develop as if no androgens were present, that is, as if they had no testes. Without androgens, the body follows the female line of development.

The role of androgens in masculinizing the fetus is demonstrated in genetic females who have the adrenogenital syndrome. This condition is the result of a recessive genetic defect which causes the adrenal glands to malfunction beginning about the twelfth week of fetal life (Money and Ehrhardt, 1972). The adrenals, two of the body's endocrine glands, are located on the kidneys. Their cortex or outer layers produces cortisol, a hormone which is necessary to life. In persons, male or female, afflicted with the adrenogenital syndrome, the adrenals are unable to produce the correct amount of cortisol. Instead, they produce large quantities of substances which are precursors to the synthesis of cortisol, and these substances are androgenic hormones. In most cases these hormones enter the bloodstream too late in fetal life to bring about development of the wolffian system in females, and the development of the mullerian system is unaffected, so that the internal reproductive structures are usually normal. The main effect is masculinization of the external genitalia, so that in extreme cases the female infant is born with a penis and an empty scrotum. In less extreme cases, the clitoris is enlarged and the labia partly fused. Since the cortisol deficit can be life-threatening, the disorder is usually recognized at birth or soon after, and the adrenal malfunction is treated with cortisone, a synthetic hormone which the body converts into cortisol. In some cases, the genitalia can be modified to the female form by surgery, and fertility and biological motherhood are possible. Others are not recognized as females, are assigned as boys and develop a male psychosexual identity. At puberty, however, the ovarian hormones will induce feminization of the body, and menstrual bleeding can occur through the urethra. These events can be treated hormonally to maintain the male identification, though suppression of the menses requires removal of the ovaries and the uterus.

A similar masculinization of the female genitalia was found to occur in a few infants whose mothers had been administered certain hormones during their pregnancy in order to prevent miscarriage. These hormones, called progestins, are synthetic substitutes for progesterone, one of the female sex hormones which helps to maintain pregnancy. When they were first used for this purpose in the 1950s it was not known that, because of their chemical relation to androgen, they had the potential of having masculinizing effects on the fetus. Because of a timing effect, the internal organs were not affected, and since the excess masculinizing hormones were present only before birth and not after, no further hormone treatment was required. Rarely, masculinization of the genitals was complete, and the child was assigned and reared as a boy. In such cases, the problem of feminization at puberty would be the same as for the adrenogenital syndrome, and would be handled in the same way (Money and Ehrhardt, 1972).

The significance of such cases is twofold. The first is to demonstrate the effects of androgens on sexual differentiation of the body, elucidating the principle that without these hormones the fetus will differentiate as a female regardless of genetic sex. The development of male morphology depends upon their presence in body tissues capable of responding to them.

The second is that they provide the opportunity to study in humans the effect of such hormonal anomalies on behavior. Do the sex hormones circulating in the fetal bloodstream, affecting at certain critical periods the differentiation of the sexual-reproductive system, affect also the development of the central nervous system, predetermining certain differences in male and female behavior?

Data relevant to this question come from two sources: experimental studies of mammals other than humans in which prenatal hormones were manipulated by the experimenter to see the later effects on behavior; and longitudinal studies of humans with the hormonal anomalies described above. These studies provide a basis for understanding behavioral dimorphism, the extent to which biological influences program the individual to behave differentially in accordance with biological sex, and, in humans, their significance for psychosexual dimorphism, the differentiation of gender identity.

Sex Hormones and Behavior

Experimental studies

Experimental studies of the effects of the gonadal hormones on behavior have used a variety of species, among them the rhesus monkey (Goy, 1970), beagle dog (Beach, 1970), hamster (Swanson, 1971), and rat (Ward, 1972). These studies use such techniques as removal of the gonads (castration) *in utero*, in infancy, and in adulthood to see the effects on behavior of deprivation of the gonadal hormones; administering opposite-sex hormones to young and mature animals; and treating pregnant animals with testosterone to observe the behavioral effects on the masculinized daughters. The focus of such studies is usually upon mating, maternal, and play behavior because they are most readily identified as sex-linked in subhuman mammals. In general, it has been shown that gonadal hormones organize the nervous system so that certain behaviors will be dimorphically differentiated according to sex. For example, in a study using rhesus monkeys, hermaphroditic females were produced by administering androgen to their pregnant mothers. The social behavior of these masculinized females was then compared to a control group of normal females. The effect of the androgen was not confined to the genitals. The treated monkeys exhibited behavior more typical of males of that species: they threatened, initiated play, and engaged in rough-and-tumble play more often than the controls did. When placed with an untreated female, the hermaphrodites more often attempted to mount, showing pelvic thrusting and phallic erection. Their behavior as well as their genitals had been affected by the early exposure of their neural tissues to androgen (Young *et al.,* 1965).

Another study involved the effects on behavior of masculinization of female beagles *in utero.* When they grew up, their social and sexual behavior toward a bitch in heat was like that of normal males, although the effect was stronger if they continued to be treated with androgen after birth. Pattern of urination was also affected. Like normal males, they lifted a hind leg and urinated more frequently than females did.

Effects of deprivation of gonadal hormones on male mammals have been extensively studied. Hamsters, castrated shortly after birth and given ovarian transplants, displayed cyclic female mating behavior when placed as adults with normal males (Swanson, 1970), and the sexual behavior of neonatally castrated male rats can be manipulated in either a female or male direction by the administration of female or male sex hormones (Grady and Young, 1965).

The difficulties of drawing conclusions from the extensive literature on hormonal effects on brain and behavior in subhuman mammals were pointed out in a review of the research (Money and Ehrhardt, 1972). In any such experimental study, results will depend upon such important variables as sex, species, age when treated, nature of the treatment, and the behavior under investigation to mention only a few. Furthermore, although it is routine to assume that the behavior of lower animals is much more closely tied to innate factors than is the behavior of humans, the fact that animal behavior also is affected by experience is often neglected. For example, lordosis is the position assumed by the female rat (and many other mammals as well) preparatory to receiving the male in sexual intercourse. This response is usually inhibited in androgen-treated females. When females rats who had been masculinized with androgen neonatally were placed with males for extended periods, however, they displayed an increase of lordotic behavior as a function of experience (Clemens *et al.*, 1970).

The conclusion, however, that fetal androgens exercise an effect upon the central nervous system of mammals is strongly supported by research. Various investigators have identified the hypothalamus as the brain area which is affected (Money, 1972a). The hypothalamus has an important regulatory effect on the vital functions of the body. It controls the activity of the pituitary gland at the base of the brain, which in turn directs the release of gonadal hormones from the ovaries and the testes. In lower mammalian species, the sexual-reproductive activity of the female becomes cyclical at maturity. The estrous cycle, as it is called, determines when the female is fertile and willing to mate. This cyclicity is a function of the hormonal regulation of the hypothalamus and is a primary disposition of estrous species. That is, the cyclicity proceeds innately in the female and is destroyed in the male by the action of androgen on the hypothalamus. The critical period at which this occurs varies in different species, being either fetal or immediately postnatal. In any case, the effect is permanent and irreversible in estrous species.

Human female sexual behavior is not regulated by any such mechanism. The menstrual cycle of humans and other primates is related to reproduction and not to sexual receptivity *per se*. The sparse data on the effects of androgen on the menstrual cycle of primates are from studies of masculinized monkeys or human females with the adrenogenital syndrome. Menstruation was delayed in some, but not all, of the observed cases, but the results are equivocal (Money and Erhardt, 1972). It is clear, however, that the menstrual cyclicity of the human female is not definitively suppressed, as is the estrous cycle of lower mammals, by androgen acting on the hypothalamus.

The findings emerging from such research indicate that certain classes of behavior mediated by the hypothalamus follow the same principle of dimorphic sexual differentiation as observed in the male and female reproductive organs. As it has been succinctly put, "add something to obtain a male" (Money, 1972a, p. 568). The something is androgen, inhibiting the development of the innate female structures and, in lower mammals, female sexual patterns, and promoting the development of masculine counterparts. The strength of this inhibition varies across species. For the rat, it is very strong. With humans, however, it is another story.

Human studies

To study the effects of gonadal hormones on human behavior one must look to errors of nature or of human beings. Studies of girls masculinized *in utero* were conducted over a period of several years. In some case the masculinization had been induced by the administration of progestin during pregnancy, in an attempt to prevent spontaneous abortion. Others resulted from the adrenogenital syndrome described above, caused by excessive production of androgen-like hormones by the adrenal cortex during the critical period in which the genitalia were differentiating. For both groups, it was assumed that the masculinizing hormones were present at the critical period for brain organization, thus offering an opportunity to study the effects, if any, of androgen on the female human brain, and upon subsequent behavior (Money and Ehrhardt, 1972).

One of these studies compared twenty-five fetally androgenized girls, ranging in age from four to sixteen, with twenty-five normal girls who were matched with them for age, IQ, socioeconomic level, and race. The androgenized group consisted of ten with the progestin-induced syndrome and fifteen with the adrenogenital syndrome. All had been given early corrective surgery if needed, and the latter group had received cortisone therapy. All had been reared as girls. The subjects in both groups and their mothers were interviewed on standard topics relevant to the research, and the sex-role preferences of the girls were tested.

The results of this study indicated that the androgenized girls were more likely than the normal girls to display certain characteristics called collectively "tomboyism." Both they and their mothers identified them as tomboys, a status of which the girls were proud. However, they were not necessarily dissatisfied with being a girl, though some were ambivalent as to whether it was better to be a boy or a girl. None wished to change her sex.

Their tomboyism consisted of several elements of behavior and preference which distinguished them from the normal group. They had a high level of physical energy expenditure in vigorous outdoor activity and boys' sports. Unlike the androgenized female monkeys, however, they were not more aggressive in the sense of being hostile or threatening toward others. Their preference in clothing and hairstyles was for utility rather than for personal adornment, and they related little interest in doll-playing or baby-sitting. They were less involved in rehearsals for motherhood which seem to appeal to many girls, and were more likely to express the intention of having a nondomestic career, or of combining a career with a family.

Reported childhood sexual activity did not differ for the two groups, in that neither the androgenized girls nor the normal girls manifested much sexual behavior. Whereas the masculinized female monkeys exhibited sexual behavior which was closer to the male pattern, the androgenized girls were not observably affected. They had adopted the cultural norms to the same extent that the normal girls had. As adolescents, however, they were slower to develop romantic interest in boys and dating. Their erotic interests were entirely heterosexual. There was no indication that their exposure to fetal androgens had affected their sexual orientation.

The results of this study led to the hypothesis that the tomboyism displayed by these girls was an effect of the masculinization of the fetal brain. These researchers suggested that the effect may apply to neural pathways that mediate dominance assertion, manifested in high energy expenditure, and in the inhibition of pathways that would eventually serve the development of caretaking behavior. Those paths mediating eroticism were apparently not affected. There was an important difference between the results of such studies on humans and on lower species. The sex-linked behavior of lower mammals may be reversed by adding or removing androgen to the fetal environment. No such automatic effect occurs in humans, and any prenatally affected dispositions, such as the ones observed in these girls, can readily be incorporated into the postnatally developed psychosexual identity (Money and Ehrhardt, 1972).

To reinforce this point, and to put the study in proper perspective, several other observations should be made. If fetal androgen has an effect on the brains of lower species, facilitating the later differentiation of certain kinds of behavior along sexually dimorphic lines, then it is likely that it has some degree of effect on human brains as well. Studies of humans, however, do not support the conclusion that human role behavior is sexually dimorphic, that some behaviors such as competitive sports are "masculine" and others such as caretaking are "feminine" and that the brain is programmed before birth to facilitate the appearance of one kind and not the other, depending on the sex of the person. The elements of tomboyism, for example, are very common, even normative (and certainly normal) for American girls. Such behaviors are acceptable alternatives for girls. While the girls in Money and Ehrhardt's sample had interests which were closer to the masculine stereotype than to the conventional feminine model, their psychosexual identity was unequivocally female. If they had displayed a high level of erotic interest in other girls, similar to that displayed by adolescent boys, or if they had identified with the male sex and had wished to change their sex as transsexuals do, then the effect of the fetal androgenization would be more impressive.

The evidence indicates, then, that prenatal androgen affects the central nervous system of mammals at a critical period when some pathways of the brain are organizing along sexually dimorphic lines, thus facilitating the development of some behaviors that are more likely to be manifested by males of many species, such as dominance and sexual approach. In humans, the effects of prenatal gonadal hormones are much less observable in behavior, and by themselves do not bring about the differentiation of human behavior along sex lines.

Though societies may prescribe different roles for males and females, the *content* of these roles may differ from one group to another, as we saw in Chapter 3. Such boundaries on behavior are artificial, however, since no absolute dichotomy of behavior by sex exists. There are only four behavioral invariates that are related to sex: males impregnate, and females menstruate, gestate, and lactate (Money, 1972b). All other criteria of sexual dimorphism of behavior are either derivatives of these, or are optional according to time and place.

So, to the question, do fetal gonadal hormones directly affect the sexual differentiation of human behavior in later life, we can say that it is possible that they do, but that the effect may not be very important. The critical factors for the differentiation of human behavior and of human gender identity, the knowledge of who and what one is sexually, are those which impinge on the individual beginning at birth, which inform her and him by thousands of acts and subtle ways, of their membership in one sexual category or the other.

Gender Identity

We need now to look at some evidence for the overwhelming importance in humans of the sex of assignment and rearing on the behavior and on the formation of gender identity. To do so, one studies individuals who because of natural or human error required sex reassignment and who were subsequently reared in accordance with that reassignment (Money and Ehrhardt, 1972). Such cases include genetic male infants who were assigned and reared as girls after loss of the penis, or owing to malformation of the penis; and genetic females with the adrenogenital syndrome, some of whom were assigned and reared as boys and some as girls. These studies show the plasticity of human gender identity, and its relative independence, under certain circumstances, of biological determinants of sex differentiation.

The first case involved a normal male infant, an identical twin, who lost his penis at age seven months in a circumcision accident. At age seventeen months the decision was made to reassign him as a girl, and a few months later genital reconstruction as a female was begun. The plan included hormonal therapy with estrogen at puberty. This case is especially interesting because the patient had an identical twin brother, thus providing an ideal situation for observation of differential childrearing practices based on sex. The mother, no doubt more sensitive than normal to the innuendos of developing a feminine identity in a child who had begun life as a boy, consistently promoted the child's initiation into a feminine life style. Hair, clothing, toys, and training in domesticity and preparation for motherhood all became part of the conversion to being a girl. The mother was especially aware that she was consciously trying to introduce sexual differentiation between the boy twin and his new sister: ". . . of course, I've tried to teach her not to be rough . . . she doesn't seem to be as rough as him . . . of course, I discouraged that" (p. 122). By the time this child was in school her behavior as a little girl was in remarkable contrast to the "little boy" behavior of her twin brother.

In the second case of reassignment of a genetic male infant, the baby was born with a penis about the size of a clitoris, with no urinary canal. The scrotum was partly fused and contained two testes. The decision was made to reassign the child when he was seventeen months, and treatment similar to the first case was begun. In this case, the child had an older brother to whom explanation had to be made, and whose changed behavior to his new sister could be observed. He began, according to the father, to exhibit a much more protective attitude toward her, and to treat her more gently than he had when she was his brother. The parents both began to report that the child was becoming "feminine," and they were able to verbalize the difference in their treatment of her. The father no longer wrestled with her, but held her more and danced with her, while the mother encouraged her in imitative housekeeping activity. By the time the child was three, she was asking for a doll and Cinderella slippers for Christmas. Presumably, her transformation to female gender was complete.

These studies are interesting for two reasons. First, they show the extent to which gender identity can be acquired independent of the sex of genes and fetal hormones, and how sexually differentiated behavior can be shaped in accordance with cultural definition. Second, they demonstrate vividly the differential treatment of sons and daughters along the lines approved for each by the culture.

In another series of studies, the subjects were matched pairs of hermaphrodites, all genetic females with ovaries who at birth had masculinized external genitalia owing to the adrenogenital syndrome. Each pair consisted of individuals with the same genetic and gonadal sex, but one was assigned as a girl, the other as a boy. Although reassignment of these cases was made at varying ages, their medical biographies all included surgical and hormonal corrections so that subsequent physical development would proceed in harmony with assigned sex. These cases, like the first two, differentiated gender identities in accordance with their sex of assignment.

The significance of this research lies in the finding that, where chromosomes and gonads are discordant with the sex of assignment and rearing, which are the results of decisions made by the caretakers of the child, the latter determinants will prevail. "To use the Pygmalion allegory, one may begin with the same clay and fashion a god or a goddess" (p. 152). If the corrections are made early and the parents have resolved their ambiguity as to whether they are raising a son or a daughter, then it is predictable that the child will differentiate a gender identity which accords with her or his assigned sex. "The evidence of human hermaphroditism makes abundantly clear that nature has ordained a major part of human gender-identity differentiation to be accomplished in the postnatal period" (Money and Ehrhardt, 1972, p. 18).

Most agree that the differentiation begins during the second year of life and is virtually complete by age five or six (Brown and Lynn, 1966; Money and Ehrhardt, 1972). Gender identity is imprinted during a critical period between eighteen months and three years, and after this period an elective change is not only rare, but, if attempted, may result in psychosexual difficulties for the child (Money and Ehrhardt, 1972).

The differentiation of gender identity is less likely to cause problems for girls. Just as in embryonic development, it seems that postnatally, also, the course of females runs more smoothly. Deviations of gender identity from the expected biological bases are far more frequent among males. Such incongruities as transsexualism, the individual's conviction that he is trapped in the wrong-sexed body, and transvestitism, a compulsive need to wear clothing associated with the other sex, occur at least four and perhaps as many as ten times more often in the adult male population (Bermant, 1972). While nature is more likely to make such errors with males, gender identity differentiation of the brain after birth is conceptually similar to the differentiation of the internal reproductive structures (Money and Ehrhardt, 1972). Just as both male and female structures exist in the embryo, either one capable of becoming dominant or vestigial depending on the hormonal environment, so could the brain be capable of differentiating either a male or female gender identity depending on early environmental processes. From myriad cues the child differentiates a dominant gender identity of male or female, and the other recedes in importance without vanishing altogether. Typically girls have greater latitude than boys in gender identification and the display of gender-related behavior— for example, tomboyism, whereas boys' identification is more narrowly and rigidly prescribed. For males, it is more critical to repress the feminine traces. Thus the boy's developmental task is made more difficult, and the outcome less certainly consistent with the templates of nature and culture.

Puberty: Physical and Hormonal Changes

Puberty is the developmental period between childhood and maturity during which hormonal events regulated by the hypothalamus bring about a rapid acceleration of growth, the appearance of the secondary sex characteristics, and the maturation of the sexual-reproductive system in both sexes. While there is a great deal of variation in the age at which these events occur, in general girls begin their growth spurt a year or two ahead of boys and reach physical maturity earlier. Early physical signs of puberty include the increase in rate of growth, budding of the breasts, and appearance of pubic hair. These may begin to appear as early as the ninth year in some girls, though the average age is around eleven (Tanner, 1970). Later developments include the maturing of feminine body contours, its fat distribution and muscle-fat ratio distinguishing it from the male, a slight increase in skin pigmentation, and deepening of the voice. The ovaries and uterus increase in size, and the menarche, the first appearance of uterine bleeding which is the onset of the menses, occurs. Menarche is a late event in puberty, occurring usually after the peak of the growth spurt has passed. Even then, reproductive maturity may come later, as the first menstrual periods are often infertile and irregular. Here again, however, individual variability is the rule, and menarche as well as fertility may occur in normal girls from the twelfth to the seventeenth year.

Male development during puberty includes, in addition to the growth spurt, the appearance of pubic, body, and facial hair, deepening of the voice, and the maturation of the reproductive system. The testes, penis, and internal reproductive structures enlarge rapidly. Sperm production begins, and the first seminal ejaculation occurs about a year after the acceleration of penis growth (Tanner, 1970).

The timing of puberty is a function of the hypothalamus, a brain structure which, among other things, stimulates the pituitary gland to secrete hormones that regulate the activity of the ovaries in the female, and the testes in the male (Fig. 4.3). Beginning before puberty, the action of the hypothalamus of the female becomes cyclic with respect to the pituitary and its relation with the gonads but remains non-cyclic in the male. The potential for cyclicity in the mammalian brain is apparently innate, being preserved in the female and demolished in the male by the action of fetal androgens. In other words, the hypothalamus is programmed *in utero* to become cyclic or non-cyclic in puberty, depending on the presence of fetal androgens.

During childhood both sexes secrete small amounts of both estrogen and androgen. The girl's androgen and the boy's estrogen come chiefly from the adrenal cortex. In late childhood the pituitary increases its secretion of certain hormones which cause the ovaries and the testes to sharply increase their production of estrogen and androgen (mostly testosterone), respectively. At about this time, the pituitary and ovarian secretions in the female take on their cyclic pattern which becomes the basis later for the menstrual cycle. In the male no such cycle is known.

The onset of puberty cannot be dated exactly, since the changes in hormone levels and the resultant physical changes develop gradually over several years. Usually, the beginning of breast development and the growth of pubic hair precede the first menstruation. In Western countries the age of menarche has progressively decreased over the past several decades, probably owing to better nutrition and health care. In the United States the average age is about thirteen.

Rarely, tumors or lesions of the hypothalamus or gonads will cause an excessive production of hormones in young children, resulting in precocious sexual and reproductive development. When

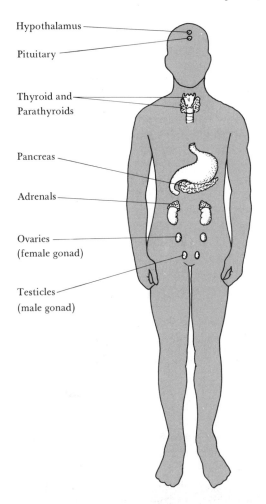

Hypothalamus

Pituitary

Thyroid and
Parathyroids

Pancreas

Adrenals

Ovaries
(female gonad)

Testicles
(male gonad)

Figure 4.3   Location of the hypothalamus and endoctrine
glands in the human.

this happens to a female child, the result is early breast development
and menarche, sometimes at the age of five or six years. Pregnancy
can occur in such cases. An example was Lina Medina, a Peruvian
child, who gave birth by Caesarian section to a six-and-one-half
pound male infant at the age of five and a half years. This birth, on
May 15, 1939, received much publicity, and was attended by several
physicians from the United States. Lina was reported to have menstruated from the age of three.

Menarche and the Menstrual Cycle

Those biological events which are in women's repertoire exclusively—menstruation, pregnancy, childbirth—have inspired myth and ritual for millennia. In particular, menarche and menstruation have mobilized man's fears of the evil powers of women, and it has not been uncommon in human history for women to be "put away" at such times, and to be severely restricted in their contacts with men, animals, food, and utensils. In Borneo, for example, one tribe confines girls in dark cells raised on piles, sometimes for many months. When they reach womanhood, they are brought out and shown the sun, the earth, the water, and flowers as if they were newly born. Two common rules seem to apply in nonliterate societies: the menarcheal girl must not touch the earth or see the sun. "The general effect of these rules is to keep her suspended, so to say, between heaven and earth. Whether enveloped in her hammock and slung up to the roof, as in South America, or raised above the ground in a dark and narrow cage, as in New Ireland, she may be considered to be out of the way of doing mischief, since, being shut off both from the earth and from the sun, she can poison neither of these great sources of life by her deadly contagion" (Frazer, 1951, p. 702).

Societies all over the world, both nonliterate and civilized, have believed in the power of the menstruating woman to pollute and to contaminate. A South African cattle-rearing tribe believed that their cattle would die if they passed over ground where even a drop of menstrual blood had fallen. To prevent such a calamity, the women of the village had special paths they must use in order to avoid the ground in the middle of the village where the cattle stood or lay down.

Such beliefs persist today in certain parts of the country. For example, one male student told about an episode which occurred during a visit he made to some relatives in the mountain country of eastern Kentucky. The mother of the family was hard at work in the kitchen "putting up" vegetables. The student was talking to her when her daughter entered the room. The mother shook her apron at her, telling her not to come near the food "in that condition." As the daughter ran from the room, two of the mason jars, filled with hot vegetables, exploded, thus confirming forever the mother's belief in the power of a woman in her period! Learning the facts of woman's biology has relieved us of most of the power and the stigma of such accounts.

Once established, the menstrual cycle in human females is a periodic interval of approximately twenty-eight days, though it may normally vary from twenty-five to thirty-four days, depending on the individual. The period of uterine bleeding is usually from three to seven days for most women.

The entire cycle is controlled by an elaborate feedback system involving the hypothalamus, the anterior lobe of the pituitary and its hormones, and the ovaries and their hormones. The hypothalamus monitors the level of the ovarian hormones in the bloodstream. Early in the cycle, counting the onset of the menses as day one, the estrogen level is at its lowest (Fig. 4.4). During these few days the endometrium, or lining of the uterus, is shed in the typical menstrual flow. Subsequently, in response to the low estrogen level, the hypothalamus signals the pituitary gland to release FSH (follicle stimulating hormone), which stimulates the maturation of one of the ova-containing ovarian follicles and also the increased production of estrogen by the ovary. As the level of estrogen increases, the endometrium begins to build up in preparation to receive the zygote if fertilization occurs. Ovulation, the rupture of the mature ovum from its follicle, occurs approximately fourteen days before the onset of the

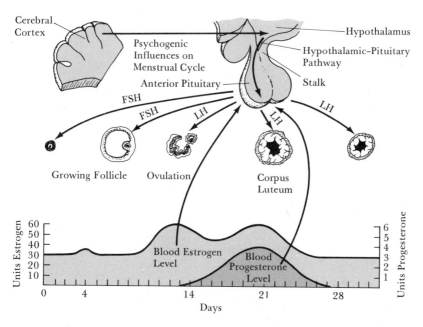

Figure 4.4 Ovulation during the menstrual cycle. (Reproduced, with permission, from Benson, R. C., *Handbook of Obstetrics and Gynecology*, 5th ed. [Los Altos, Calif.: Lange Medical Publications, 1974].)

next period. At this time, the level of circulating estrogen in the blood is at its peak. Responding to this high level of estrogen, the pituitary releases LH (luteinizing hormone) which moves into the bloodstream to the ruptured follicle, causing it to develop into a glandular structure called the corpus luteum. The corpus luteum produces both estrogen and progesterone, the "pregnancy hormone," which together stimulate the glands of the endometrium further to prepare for the nourishment of the zygote, if it appears.

If fertilization does not occur, the pituitary ceases production of FSH and LH, and the corpus luteum becomes inactive and withers away. The subsequent gradual drop in estrogen level triggers the shedding of the endometrial proliferation, consisting of blood, mucus, and tissues, which is the menstrual discharge. In turn, the low estrogen level signals the hypothalamus to stimulate the pituitary to begin again its production of FSH, and the next cycle is under way.

Dysfunctions Associated with the Menstrual Cycle

The biological events associated with reproduction are surely of great importance in the lives of women. Even those who never experience pregnancy and motherhood are reminded of their potential every month for some thirty years. The salience of menstruation, and the frequency of its occurrence, mean that any dysfunction, whether physical or psychogenic, will provoke concern and even dread, to say nothing of the physical discomfort sometimes experienced. Disorders of menstruation, until recently poorly understood, have variously been held to be a manifestation of hysteria, hypochondriasis, stress, rejection of femininity, or the natural inferiority of the female. "Women," said the eighteenth-century Italian writer Ferdinando Galiani, in *Dialogue sur les Femmes,* "only have intervals of health in the course of a continual disease." Although some women do experience discomfort associated with their menstrual periods, this morbid diagnosis hardly fits most women.

There are three major kinds of menstrual dysfunction: dysmenorrhea or painful menstruation (cramps), amenorrhea or the absence of menstruation, and the premenstrual syndrome, a phrase used to describe a variety of symptoms experienced by some women during the few days before the onset of the menses.

Dysmenorrhea, or cramps, is a well-defined clinical entity which occurs in about fifty percent of women at some time in their lives. The pain is reported in the pelvic area, and is caused by spasmodic contractions of the uterus. Usually, the pain is absent during the first periods, and it seldom persists after the birth of the first child or past the age of twenty-five (Lennane & Lennane, 1973). The cause of "childbirth cures" is not known. Dysmenorrhea has been found to be dependent on the occurrence of ovulation, and is usually removed or relieved by the suppression of ovulation with estrogen.

Primary amenorrhea means that the woman has never menstruated. In secondary, or functional, amenorrhea, menstruation has once begun but then ceased, or is very irregular. In either case, the condition may be caused by a variety of factors: congenital (absent ovaries, uterus, or vagina); physical (diabetes, trauma); or hormonal (diseases of the ovary, pituitary, or adrenal glands). It is not unusual for menstruation to cease as a reaction to emotional stress or drastic environmental change. In one study, twenty-five percent of a group of sixty-four American girls training in Israel developed amenorrhea of three months' duration (Shanan et al., 1965).

Premenstrual syndrome is a loosely defined collection of symptoms associated with the premenstrual period. The symptoms include swelling of body tissues and weight gain owing to water retention, emotional irritability, depression, feelings of anxiety and tension, and headache. Some women experience considerable distress from one or more of these symptoms each month, and others never experience them at all. The incidence of premenstrual symptoms varies from twenty-five to one hundred percent of women, depending upon how they are defined and the population studied. Although large numbers of women spontaneously report awareness of the imminence of their period because of characteristic symptoms, the concept of a premenstrual syndrome itself is highly ambiguous, and there is no clear-cut agreement on causative factors. Over 150 symptoms have been associated with the menstrual cycle (Moos, 1969). The only common denominator to such symptoms is that when they do occur, they do so at regular intervals (Sutherland and Stewart, 1965). Explanations of the phenomena usually implicate hormonal activity, such as estrogen-progesterone imbalance, alterations of adrenal cortical functioning, sodium and water retention due to hormone changes, and so on. If the syndrome itself is not well established or clearly defined, identification of causative factors is a difficult enterprise (Parlee, 1973).

Behavior and the Menstrual Cycle

The preceding discussion of menstrual dysfunctions raises two related questions. Do psychological factors cause or contribute to menstrual disorders? What effect does the physiological phenomenon of the cycle have on behavior?

It is almost certain that the various symptoms associated with menstruation have a basis in physical factors; the view that such problems are "all in the mind" can no longer be held seriously by anyone. Even so, menstrual discomforts continue to be regarded as psychogenic, as symptoms of emotional problems, rejection of the feminine role, or the result of a faulty outlook on life. The persistence of such notions among physicians is well documented. "The belief in psychogenesis, once reached, is remarkably persistent. The dependence of dysmenorrhea on ovulation, for example, was first demonstrated in 1940. There has been no corresponding demonstration of any dependence of ovulation on 'failure to adapt to the feminine role' . . . but thirty years later, standard gynecology textbooks still emphasize a psychogenic cause" (Lennane and Lennane, 1973).

On the other hand, environmental events affect emotions, and emotions affect the body. The result is an interaction of the soma and the psyche, each dependent upon the other to such an extent that, for these phenomena, it may be fruitless to search for the cause in one or the other. It has been shown, for example, that manipulation of the social setting can affect hormonal levels and cycles. In one study the menstrual cycle of women living together in college dormitories became synchronized in the course of the academic year (McClintock, 1971).

The question of the effect of the menstrual cycle on behavior also has no definitive answer. Numerous studies have reported correlations between the premenstrual phase of the cycle and such behaviors as crimes of violence, suicide, admission to psychiatric wards, and accidents (Dalton, 1964). However, most of these studies have methodological problems. The time of a behavioral act, such as commission of a crime, is readily identifiable, but information as to the phase of the woman's cycle at that time is less reliable (Parlee, 1973). For example, one study found that two-thirds of violent crimes committed by women occurred in the premenstrual week, but does not say specifically how the phase of the cycle was determined (Morton *et al.*, 1953). Another example correlated the test performance of schoolgirls with their menstrual cycle. Twenty-seven percent declined in test performance during the premenstrual period. However, seventeen percent increased premenstrually, and fifty-six percent did not change (Dalton, 1960). Obviously, this is not impressive evidence linking hormone levels to school performance.

A review of the research on the premenstrual syndrome draws conclusions which apply to the present status of knowledge about the relationship between the menstrual cycle and behavior (Parlee, 1973). Summarized, these conclusions are:

1. The existence of a class of behaviors which fluctuate with the phases of the menstrual cycle has not been demonstrated.
2. Studies of cyclic behavior in adult females cannot be evaluated without comparison studies of possible cyclic changes in the behavior of nonmenstruating persons, males or females.
3. Considering the prevalence of cultural beliefs and attitudes about menstruation and its effects, a distinction should be made between what subjects report about their behavior and what they actually do. This distinction is important for examining the relative influences of social and physiological factors in interpreting research data.
4. Investigators who propose a physiological explanation for hormone-behavior relationships should clarify both the nature of the assumptions underlying their explanations, and the specific kinds of behaviors that the explanations account for.

A recent study of premenstrual effects on fifty normal women brings the issue into perspective:

> The premenstrual mood change appears to be of the same order as afternoon lassitude, hurt feelings, or Monday morning blues. The anxiety . . . is dramatically different in magnitude from that found in psychiatric disorders. . . . [F]or most women, the premenstrual hormonal changes impose little psychological burden. Women readily cope with premenstrual mood changes, and are sometimes not even aware of them (Golub, 1973, pp. 8–9).

The Climacterium

As women age, they enter the developmental period of the climacterium, when ovarian function gradually declines and finally ceases. An important event of this period is the menopause, the cessation of menstruation. The psychological events associated with this period are discussed in Chapter 11. Here the concern is only with those aspects of it that are sexually dimorphic, that is, where the course of events is different for women and men. The differences are in two related areas, hormonal and reproductive.

Estrogen and progesterone secretion begins to decline as ovarian functioning decreases, beginning gradually in the fourth decade and progressing more rapidly in the fifth and sixth. As the ovaries cease to respond to the pituitary hormone FSH, ovulation ceases to occur. With the greatly reduced output of estrogen and progesterone, the periodicity of the menstrual cycle disappears and eventually the woman becomes infertile. Both the cessation of menstruation and the decline of ovarian function, including ovulation, develop gradually in most women. Typically, a woman in her late forties will begin to experience missed periods or diminished flow over several months until finally the cycle no longer occurs. The eventual decrease in estrogen production to about one-sixth its earlier level is associated with physical changes in the body as well as with such symptoms as the hot flush. Among the effects on the body are the thinning of the vaginal tissues, reduced lubrication in the vagina, loss of hair, and loss of muscle tone with consequent drooping and flabbiness of the breasts and other tissues. The hot flush is a brief episode of feelings of warmth and flushing, accompanied by perspiration. Its frequency and duration are quite variable. Some women report great discomfort and others none at all. Other symptoms reported by women at this time include vertigo (dizziness), insomnia, headaches, tingling sensations, and anxiety. As in the premenstrual syndrome, the range and variability of these symptoms is so great that no well-defined menopausal syndrome exists. The body changes and the hot flush are predictable, however, being less dependent on personality and cultural beliefs and attitudes about how one ought to feel at such a time. Many of the unpleasant and deleterious side effects of the menopause are reduced or eliminated by the exogenous administration of synthetic estrogen to replace the deficit caused by ovarian atrophy.

The virtual cessation of estrogen production by the ovaries brings about a drastic change in the hypothalamus-pituitary-ovary equilibrium which was maintained by the feedback mechanism discussed earlier. The final result is the absence of modulated periodicity: the menstrual cycle is extinct. If the postmenopausal woman takes estrogen daily, some endometrial buildup will occur. If she stops taking it for a few days, vaginal bleeding may result as the endometrium responds to the decrease in estrogen. This "withdrawal" bleeding is not a true period, however. The administration of synthetic estrogen does not bring about ovulation or restore fertility.

The male does not experience any event analagous to the menopause although certain psychological symptoms of middle-aged males have been referred to as the male climacterium. These are mostly affective and behavioral, however, such as changes in self-concept, mood swings, and abrupt changes in personality or life style, events which may reflect reactions to the perception of the aging process but not to any rapid change in gonadal functioning. Sperm production is affected only slightly by pituitary hormones, and the male theoretically remains fertile throughout his life span. The production of testosterone undergoes a gradual, continuous decline with aging; thus, the physiological mechanism is quite different from that of women. Male potency, the sexual capacity to sustain erection, declines with age but this is not directly related to spermatogenesis.

The biological fate of male and female differs in another important respect. Sexual differentiation extends to include different life expectancies throughout the life cycle, from conception to death. The importance of this statistical difference for the psychology of women, and its meaning, will be discussed in later chapters.

The Sex Ratio

The fact that humans are sexually dimorphic makes possible the collection of some interesting data on the relative prevalence of males and females at any particular age. The *sex ratio* is a statistic which is conventionally expressed as the ratio of males to females, times 100. The *primary* sex ratio, then, is an estimate of the number of male conceptuses per 100 females. Since many zygotes and early embryoes do not survive, the primary sex ratio must be inferred from the fact that sex ratios of the stillborn in the first four months have been variously observed as 200–400; that is, such a fetus is two to four times more likely to be male (Lerner, 1968). Given even this enormous loss of males *in utero,* the *secondary* sex ratio, at the time of birth, is still 106 for live white babies in the United States. The *tertiary* sex ratio, which may be taken at any specified time after birth, shows a steady decline with age. For example (Lerner, 1968):

Table 4.1   Sex ratios

Age	Sex ratio: secondary
Birth (live)	106

Age	Sex ratio: tertiary
18 years	100
50 years	95
57 years	90
67 years	70
87 years	50
100 years plus	21

Furthermore, of the fifty-nine causes of death relevant to both sexes and listed by the U.S. Census, only two show a higher rate for females: diabetes and pernicious anemia. Thus, there is little reason to doubt the observation that females have a biological advantage.

The various hypotheses advanced in explanation of these phenomena can be found elsewhere (Lerner, 1968). The pertinent generalization is that the male is more vulnerable than the female at all ages. Given this, the expectation is that his survival is more closely tied to the adequacy of the environment. Even so, other factors being equal, he is at greater risk than the female at all ages.

The emergence of sex differences

5

It makes no difference whether pink is for girls and blue for boys, emotionality for girls and rationality for boys, or the other way round. What does make a difference is that a difference is made. . . . . It is the bifurcation by sex that is the fundamental fact.

—Jessie Bernard, *Women and the Public Interest,* 1971

Sex is probably the most important category to which humans can be assigned, and it is the only one other than race which is invariant except in rare instances. Certainly the sex of the unborn and the new-born infant is a matter of great importance to the parents. Much speculation is evoked by interest in the sex of the infant *in utero,* giving rise to all kinds of predictive attempts based on signs of one sort or another. If the baby is carried high, it's a boy; if the mother suffers more from nausea this time than last, the sex of the baby will be different; a small weight suspended on a string held over the mother's abdomen will move in a circle if it's a girl, back and forth if it's a boy. Since even a random prediction would be correct about half the time, successful predictions by such signs probably occur frequently enough to insure their persistence in the popular culture. Reliable tests based on examination of cells in a sample of amniotic fluid are rarely made since there is usually no compelling reason from the physician's view to learn the baby's sex in advance.

In any case, interest in the sexual category of the fetus or neo-nate runs high. Why is this characteristic of the person so important? Perhaps nothing else so surely attests to the sexually dimorphic nature of human experience; sex is important because it is one major determinant of who and what the baby will be, and the kinds of life experiences it will have.

The question of whether males and females are different psychologically, and if so, what are the differences and their determinants, is presently eliciting much comment from both scientists and non-scientists. Widely held beliefs based both on myths and on research are being challenged. In this chapter we shall consider the nature, extent, and importance of observable sex differences in infancy and childhood, and some explanations for their development.

Throughout the discussion the term "sex difference" means a difference in the average performance of females and males in a given area of behavior. For example, a sex difference in spelling ability means that the average performance of one sex is higher than the average performance of the other. The performance of individuals of each sex varies around the average for that sex so that some persons in the high group score lower than some persons in the low group. The two sexes overlap in this way on all human intellectual and behavioral characteristics.

Infancy

Few aspects of human development are so impressive as the growth and individuation of the infant during the first year of life. Observing the relatively helpless, supine, and asocial neonate[1] whose behavioral repertoire consists of a small collection of unlearned responses, one is awed by the transformation a few months later into a mobile, curious, imitative, and socially responsive young person who often wields a Promethean power to shape the behavior of others and to manipulate the environment. As a function of maturation and interaction with the contingencies of the environment, the infant's behavior becomes increasingly diversified, differentiated, and complex. Do certain aspects of this behavior become differentiated along sexually dimorphic lines in infancy? Do boys and girls differ behaviorally from birth?

Physical development

Although few of us would have much confidence in our ability to identify the sex of each diaper-clad occupant of cribs in a nursery for neonates, there do exist biological sex differences in infancy in addition to those discussed in the last chapter. Girls are developmentally older at birth than boys are. Even though the gestation period is slightly shorter for girls, their skeletal maturation,[2] mea-

---

[1] The *neonatal period* is usually defined as the first month of life and is part of *infancy*, the first year or two of life. These terms are loosely used to designate newborn infants and babies who have not acquired language.

[2] Skeletal maturation or bone age is the most useful measure of physical maturity (Tanner, 1970).

sured by the shape and degree of ossification or hardening of the bones, is four to six weeks advanced compared to boys. It has been suggested that the central nervous system of girls is also precociously developed giving them a greater readiness to function (Kagan, 1972).

Boys tend to be heavier and longer at birth than girls are, and this difference is maintained through childhood. They also have a greater lung capacity and, beginning soon after birth, a higher caloric intake.

Another important biological sex difference is found in the viability of females compared to males. The female manifests fewer defects and has a demonstrably greater capacity to maintain life. In the last chapter we observed the dramatic decline in the sex ratio beginning before birth. The prenatal death rate from miscarriages and stillbirths is considerably higher for males, and almost 33 percent more boys than girls die in the first year of life in the United States (Garai and Scheinfeld, 1968).

An analysis of sex differences in physical, psychological, and neurological development of 15,000 children in the first year of life found the male to be at a significant disadvantage on all scales except one (see Table 5.1).

In the summary of the first year of life for this large sample, the sex difference in abnormalities was highly significant. Of 248 possible abnormalities, 65 percent had a higher incidence among males, while only 26.6 percent had a higher incidence among females. Although male babies had the advantage of a heavier birth weight, their neonatal condition was poorer, and they did less well in performance all through early childhood.

Studies of premature infants at a large New York hospital found that while boys and girls were about equal in incidence and severity of neonatal complications, the boys at 13½ months were in-

Table 5.1   Performance in first year of life (N = 15,000)*

Performance measures	Percent abnormal	
	Male	Female
8-month mental	7.9	6.8
8-month fine motor	15.0	11.0
8-month gross motor	15.7	12.7
8-month social emotional	7.7	9.4
8-month final diagnosis	15.5	12.5
12-month neurological	8.9	7.8

* From data in Singer *et al.*, 1968.

ferior on mental and motor tests (Braine *et al.*, 1966). The same male infants at age 30 months had a higher incidence compared to the girls of neurological abnormalities and significantly lower IQs (Cutler *et al.*, 1965).

The biological advantage of the female persisting through the lifespan has been attributed in part to the fact that she has two X-chromosomes, one from her mother and one from her father. Since the X-chromosome is larger and carries more genes than the Y, the girl can benefit from a greater variety of genetic material. Also, certain disorders[3] can be carried by genes on the X-chromosomes and will affect the individual unless they are offset by normal genes on a second X-chromosome. Thus the girl has a better chance of escaping such sex-linked disorders. The possibility of an immunological incompatibility between some male fetuses and their mothers may be related to productions controlled by the genes on the Y-chromosome (Singer *et al.*, 1968). This would explain the spontaneous abortion of greater numbers of male fetuses. Such an effect might cause non-lethal damage to the male fetus with mental and physical effects later in life.

Neonatal behavior

In general, it is reasonable to assume that the earlier a behavior occurs the more probable that it reflects the biological heritage, shared by the individual with other members of the species. This is one compelling reason for studying the infant, in whom one might expect to find precursors of later behaviors in their pure forms uncontaminated by knowledge of consequences, ulterior motives, or other descriptors of the loss of innocence. For studies of sex differences, especially since numerous examples have been held to exist in childhood and maturity, we wish to know such things as: How early do such differences or their precursors manifest themselves? To what extent do they arise from innate factors? How does such a substratum interact with subsequent environmental events to produce the increasing divergence observable both in roles and in personality traits which develop across the life span?

An important problem in studying the responses of very young infants for clues to etiology or sequelae of behavior is that in the neonate especially the behavioral repertoire is relatively small and its components are often not discriminately linked to specific eliciting stimuli. The neonate can sleep, cry, suck, flex arms and legs, move head and eyes, grasp, and respond to stimulation of its various

---

[3] Examples are hemophilia, the "bleeder's disease," and red-green color blindness.

senses. But a given response may be undifferentiated with regard to a stimulus. For example, crying may occur in response to hunger, discomfort, loud noise, loss of support, or no discernible cause. Because of these characteristics of the response repertoire, studies of neonatal sex differences have dealt mostly with sensorimotor reactions such as activity level or pain threshold and spontaneously emitted behaviors such as crying.

The most frequently cited sex differences in neonates include the finding that girls have greater tactile sensitivity (Bell and Costello, 1964) and lower pain thresholds (Lippsett and Levy, 1959), and boys move about more (Bell, 1960). However, a recent review of the literature on sex differences in infancy points out that such differences upon close inspection turn out to be unsubstantiated (Shepherd and Peterson, 1973). For example, one study revealed problems in both methodology and interpretation of results. It was found that girl neonates were more responsive to blanket removal and air jet to abdomen. However, the blanket-removal procedure was abandoned because uniformity across trials could not be achieved and test-retest instability resulted; and the observer reliability in the air-jet response study was too low for credible results. This same study measured male and female neonatal thresholds to pressure of nylon thread to the heel, and found that chubby babies tend to have higher thresholds to tactile stimulation, regardless of sex (Bell and Costello, 1964).

In another study the experimenters studied thresholds for electric shock to the toe in baby boys and girls aged twenty-four, forty-eight, seventy-two and ninety-six hours. Only at age seventy-two hours were the girls significantly more sensitive, and the overlap for the sexes was 25 percent (Lippsett and Levy, 1959). In a study of male infants only, a high activity level seemed to be associated with birth trauma. Since more boys have birth complications, it was speculated that neonatal hyperactivity would be more frequent in boys (Bell, 1960). The evidence for such a difference is not conclusive, however, and in any case it would not apply to differences in activity levels in normal neonates.

Studies involving 36 comparisons of neonates revealed that 6 favored boys (a subjective judgment as to desirablity of the direction of the difference), 7 favored girls, and 23 comparisons revealed no differences. Furthermore, where differences were found, sex differences in specific behaviors sometimes favored girls, sometimes boys; the overlap varied between 7 percent and 43 percent (Shepherd and Peterson, 1973).

Although the literature on neonatal sex differences in behavior indicates that reliable results clearly attributable to sex have not been demonstrated, one cannot conclude that such differences do not exist. They may yet be revealed by methodological improvements yielding more consistent results. Of greater importance is the reminder that some innate properties, such as the hypothalamic effect discussed in the last chapter, do not become manifest until later in life. The nonspecific responses characteristic of the neonate could mask traits which appear more clearly as behavior becomes refined in the older child. Maturation has an organizing effect upon behavior, revealing individual and group differences which may well have an innate component, previously obscured by the diffuse quality of neonatal behavior.

Older babies, still relatively free of the restraints and modifications which experience will teach them later, have a larger repertoire of behavior. It is more differentiated; its components are more reliably linked to stimulating conditions and are therefore more easily observed and measured. Consequently there is a sizeable body of literature on the developmental behavior of infants in the first and second years of life. Two areas which are important for understanding the emergence of sex differences are the development of cognitive and intellectual abilities, and the development of social and affective behavior.

Cognitive development

Cognition is the process by which the individual acquires knowledge about an object or an event. It includes perceiving, recognizing, judging, and sensing—the ways of knowing. The efficiency and level of the acquisition of knowledge are usually measured in older children and adults by the use of tests which require language. Studies of infant cognition, of what and how babies "know," have begun to appear only in the last decade, with the development of new techniques which provide insights into what and how babies learn.

In spite of the persistent belief that babies differ along sex lines—for example, that girl babies vocalize more and boy babies are more active—sex differences in cognitive functions in the first two years of life have not been demonstrated (Maccoby and Jacklin, 1974). Measurements of intellectual ability, learning, and memory do not differ on the average for boys and girls. However, patterns of performances are different for the two sexes, as is the consistency (thus the predictability) of the measures as the infants get older. A longitudinal study of 180 white, first-born infants, 91 boys and 89 girls, each of whom was tested in the laboratory at four, eight, thirteen, and twenty-seven months offers some evidence concerning these patterns (Kagan, 1971). One of the behaviors for which different patterns were observed for boys and girls was vocalization, the infant's response when aroused or excited by an unusual or discrepant stimulus.

The infant, in the third or fourth month, has developed schemata for recurring events in its life. A schema is a cognitive representation of an experience or an event. For example, the baby has a schema for the human face, or for its own room or crib. In everyday language, the baby "recognizes" its mother, or "knows" when it is put down on a strange bed. A strange face or bed is a discrepant event. Such a discrepant event in the life of an infant may provoke a variety of reactions, such as crying, fussing, smiling, or vocalization (a short burst of positive vocal activity), reflecting a state of arousal or excitement. It is this last reaction which concerns us now.

Stimuli presented to the infants included slides of human faces and taped auditory speech sequences. Sex differences were found in the significance of the vocalizations of boys and girls to these stimuli. The boys' vocalizations seemed part of a general restlessness, which included motoric behavior such as twisting and moving about. The girls, on the other hand, were responding to excitement generated by the attempt to assimilate an interesting, or discrepant, event. This special state of arousal was more closely related to vocalization for girls than for boys. Also, measures of attentiveness and subsequent vocalization were more closely related for girls. The girl who listened attentively to an auditory stimulus was more likely to vocalize when it ended. No such relation was found for boys (Kagan, 1971).

The finding that girls are more likely to vocalize as a function of an arousal state does not mean that vocalization indicates a general excitability factor in girls. Rather, it seemed to be specific to events, such as the strange faces and voices that were discrepant from earlier learned schemata. But why would girls who were most attentive to a discrepant stimulus be most likely to vocalize, and why would this tendency be more predictable across time for girls? There are two alternative hypotheses. One relies on the possible early sex difference in central nervous system maturity and organization discussed earlier, while the other proposes a difference in maternal behavior toward daughters (Kagan, 1971). Of course, these explanations are not mutually exclusive; an interaction between the two is possible.

The first hypothesis relates the patterns of the girls' attentiveness and vocalization to the maturity of their central nervous system development. The language function, for most individuals, is located in the left cerebral hemisphere, which gradually achieves dominance with the progress of cerebral asymmetry that occurs as a function of age. If this dominance were achieved earlier in girls, it would explain their earlier development of speech functions, specifically in this case the vocalization response to a stimulus with arousal effects.

The second hypothesis is that mothers are responsible for the relation between arousal and vocalization in girls. This explanation is based on the assumption that mothers have different conceptions of the ideal boy and the ideal girl and that the latter includes the expectation of proficiency in language skills whereas the former includes more emphasis on physical development and motor skills. Mothers of daughters, then, would spend more time in reciprocal vocalization with them, thus connecting vocal responses to human faces and states of excitement; whereas mothers of sons would engage in more motor play with them and display less excited vocal reactions. It is important to point out here that the absolute amount of vocalization was not different for the two sexes; rather, it was the significance of the vocalization that differed, as it related more to arousal state in girls and more to a general restlessness in boys.

Related to these findings is some evidence that, for the infant girl, auditory stimuli, such as a mother's vocalization or even her own, might have a greater reward value than for the infant boy. In one study ten- and fourteen-week-old girls learned to visually fixate one of two circles when the reinforcing stimulus was a soft tone, but not when it was a red circle. The opposite effect held for the fourteen-week-old boys, while neither affected the ten-week-old boys (Watson, 1969).

Data on early sex differences in patterning of cognitive abilities suggests that both hypotheses have some merit—that the special link between vocalization and excitement in infant girls may jointly reflect both central nervous system organization and special caretaking practices toward daughters (Kagan, 1971).

Though absolute sex differences in cognitive abilities in infancy have not been reliably established, one variable which interacts with sex to produce different effects for boys and girls from early life is social class. That is, social class has a greater relation to the cognitive development of girls than it has to boys.

The positive relationship between social class and intelligence as measured by IQ tests has been recognized since the early days of intelligence testing, and is one of the most stable findings in psychology. Although the trend of the correlation is the same for boys and for girls, the correlation for girls is higher. For example, a study of Hawaiian children examined the relation between IQ and certain measures of parental ability and socioeconomic status. At twenty months, 8 out of 10 correlations of the girls' IQs with these parental and environmental variables were higher than the boys' correlations at the same age (Werner, 1969). In the longitudinal study of infants described earlier, such cognitive measures as visual attention, increases in vocalization, vocabulary, and ability to identify embedded figures were all more clearly linked for girls, to parental social class (Kagan, 1971). Why should social class have a greater effect on the cognitive development of girls than of boys? Two possible explanations have been put forth (Kagan, 1972).

First, maternal behavior differs by class toward boys and girls. Social class has less effect on maternal behavior toward sons than toward daughters. Mothers of all classes have in common the belief that sons should be independent, self-sufficient, and achieving, and they behave in ways that facilitate the development of such behaviors in them. Greater variability occurs across social classes in maternal behavior with daughters. Upper-middle-class mothers have greater faith in their ability to affect their daughters' destinies, and spend more time talking to and entertaining them (Rothbart, 1971). Also, these mothers were much more concerned with the learning of task competence by their daughters than were the lower-class mothers. No comparable class difference was found for sons.

The second hypothesis is less tenable. It relies on the alleged lesser variability of girls; that is, that fewer of them display extreme behavior. For example, if the intellectual capacity of girls is less variable, that is, fewer of them testing very high or very low, then differences in training or experience across social classes would be expected to show an effect. Differences in treatment would be more noticeable in a more homogeneous group. However, the notion that girls are less variable on dimensions of cognitive abilities than boys are has not held up to careful examination of the research (Maccoby and Jacklin, 1974).

An alternative hypothesis relies both on the real differences across social class in mothers' treatment of babies regardless of sex, and on the hypothesized differences in cognitive development and maturation rate of boys and girls in infancy, a phenomenon which is ignored in the alternatives presented above. It seems reasonable that, if girls' cognitive structures are advanced compared to boys' in infancy, then the learning of girls would be more efficient and less equivocal during this period of rapid change. Thus girls' cognitive development would more accurately reflect differential treatment and stimulation across social class because of a greater readiness, on a neurological basis, to learn from experience. This explanation avoids the unproven hypothesis of a significant differential treatment of infants by sex across social class. It also avoids reliance upon a tortuous generalization of greater variability in boys, which, while it may be observable on some biological variables for large samples, hardly accounts for observations made on such samples as typically characterize the infant research.

To be more specific, suppose we assume that maternal reinforcement for cognitive performance does not differ significantly for male and female infants within a social class, although such maternal behaviors may indeed differ between social classes. Now, if females are more mature developmentally from birth onward through early childhood, one would expect them to assimilate more readily whatever stimulation the environment offers, whereas boys would not show such effects until later. Given that upper-middle-class mothers offer more intellectual stimulation to their infants, it follows that females would reflect this earlier than males would. Males of a given age, then, would show fewer effects across social class than females in infancy; such effects would be manifest later, as the cognitive development of the infant males became more responsive to the differential stimulation offered by mothers of different social classes.

Social and affective behavior

The earliest manifestations of affect, or emotional response, in infants are crying, including fretfulness and irritability, and smiling to social stimulation. Studies based on naturalistic observation of infants in their homes tend to report that boys sleep less than girls and cry more during the first three months (Moss, 1967). The sex difference in irritable crying diminishes, however, as a function of age, and later crying in older babies is more likely to be a reaction to fear, anxiety induced by separation, or some other exogenous event.

There is an interesting difference in maternal response to crying of boy and girl babies at three weeks and three months. Mothers were more likely to respond to irritability in girl babies at both ages, whereas at three weeks maternal contact did not vary with irritability of boy babies; in fact, by three months, mothers were less likely to contact the more irritable boys (Moss, 1967). A learning-theory explanation for this seems plausible: mothers' contact response, contingent upon babies' response, is reinforced by girls more than by boys. That is, boys are less likely to quiet in response to handling. Of course, such a negative relationship may also reflect the mother's belief that boys should learn to endure discomfort, to rely less on comforting. Such a belief in the desirability of fostering toughness in boys could mediate maternal stoicism to their early wailing.

The so-called social smile appears in infants between two and eight weeks old. It is most often elicited by the human face and voice, and peaks in frequency around four months. There is no indication of a sex difference in readiness or frequency of smiling;

rather, smiling seems to be a function of temperament interacting with experience. One study revealed a tendency for smiling to be related to slow tempo and chubby body build in girls, but not boys. Also, smiling behavior was more stable for girls across time. Those who smiled more at thirteen months did so also at twenty-seven months. This relationship did not occur for boys (Kagan, 1971).

The data on susceptibility to fear arousal in male and female infants are indeterminate. How does one infer fearfulness in a preverbal infant? Typically, the behaviors include crying, "freezing," clinging to mother, or trying to reach her if separated. Are these reactions to fear-eliciting stimuli more typical of female than male infants? A few studies bear on this, and show the ambiguity of the results of the research. Thirteen-month-old girls separated from their mothers by a wire barrier tended to stand in the center of the barrier near where they were placed crying and motioning for help. Boys under the same conditions were more likely to go to the end of the barrier and try to get around it (Goldberg and Lewis, 1969). However, a replication of this experiment revealed no sex differences in the infant subjects as a response to separation from their mothers (Jacklin *et al.*, 1973). Another study considered reaction to separation in 67 babies of each sex at age eight months. The child was placed on the floor with a toy. When the child was involved with it, the mother, on signal, rose and left the room, closing the door behind her. The child was observed for two minutes. During this period, 52 percent of the girls and 47 percent of the boys continued to play happily with the toy. Of the remainder, half fretted somewhat but did not cry intensely, while the other half cried very hard during the mother's absence. No significant sex difference was observed for these various reactions (Kagan, 1971).

The study described earlier was based on obervation of the same babies at ages four, eight, thirteen, and twenty-seven months (Kagan, 1971). While absolute sex differences in irritability or fear did not occur within age groups, there were differences in the derivatives of these reactions when the infants were studied at twenty-seven months. Boys who had been most irritable at four months had lower vocabulary scores and less well-developed speech. Boys who were fearful at eight months were later more inhibited and apprehensive, staying closer to their mothers, than were the nonfearful controls. By contrast, girls who were irritable at four months became restless and active two-year-olds, and girls who were fearful at eight months were more verbal than the controls at twenty-seven months, and showed no need to stay close to their mothers. Thus irritability and distress seemed to have different meanings and different derivatives for the sexes. The crying, fearful boys became inhibited, shy two-year-olds; the same behaviors in four-month-old girls were predictive of verbal, outgoing, precocious two-year-olds. Mothers are likely to react differently to fearful boys than to fearful girls, and this may account for the later observed differences.

Dependency is an extensively researched behavioral concept which has been widely held to characterize females more than males (Mischel, 1970). To ask the question, Are infant girls more dependent than infant boys? points up a problem in evaluating the research on child development. Different observers may have quite different behaviors in mind when they are studying dependency in young children, so that the results may not be directly comparable to each other. For example, clinging, help-seeking, staying close to the mother, touching, wanting to be babied, crying in response to strangers, may all be part of a concept of dependency, but researchers may emphasize different aspects of it. Also, two hypothetical children might be equally dependent but one might manifest it by staying near the mother, the other by attention-getting behavior. In general, studies of dependency in young children have focused on proximity seeking, touching, and resistance to separation as indications of a child's need for reassurance in an anxiety-provoking situation.

When such studies use infants as subjects, they are usually conducted in a test situation in which the child's behavior and the mother-child interaction can be observed. Almost no studies include fathers. A recent review of studies of touching and proximity to parent and resistance to separation from parent included 22 studies of children aged three months to two years. Several of the studies measured more than one kind of behavior; for example, returning to the mother after removal from her lap, crying when she left the room, amount of time spent near her before leaving to explore. Two-thirds of the measures showed no sex differences. Of the rest, girls had higher scores in the dependency direction on five measures, while boys had higher scores on six (Maccoby and Jacklin, 1974). Clearly, for these kinds of infant dependence behaviors, the sexes are more alike than they are different.

Some studies have sought the precursors of sex differences in later life in mothers' affective behavior toward boy and girl babies. Attachment behavior was studied between mothers and their infants at ages twelve weeks, six months, and thirteen months. The researcher distinguished between two classes of attachment behavior: proximal and distal. Proximal behavior included physical contact, such as holding, kissing, touching, and caressing; distal behavior was contact other than physical, such as talking, smiling, and looking at each other. In these studies, mothers looked at and talked to their girl infants more from the earliest age. For the first six months they had more proximal contact with boy infants, perhaps because of their greater wakefulness. But after six months a reversal occurred, and girl babies had more of both proximal and distal contact with their mothers. By age thirteen months, the boys ventured farther from their mothers, stayed away longer, and returned to touch her less frequently. In the same situation, girls vocalized more, stayed closer, and touched their mothers more often (Lewis, 1972). The results appeared to show a stronger tendency for mothers of sons to encourage separation, exploration, and autonomy, while maintaining a closer interpersonal bond with daughters.

On factors such as warmth, nurturance, and acceptance, however, mothers evidently treat boy and girl babies about the same. Studies of parental warmth toward children, including 12 studies in which the children ranged in age from newborn to two years have been reviewed. Some of the studies measured more than one kind of parental behavior, such as affectionate touching, smiling at infant, and expression of positive attitude. Of 18 measures of such behavior, no sex difference was observed for 12. Of the remaining 6, 3 were in favor of girls and 3 of boys (Maccoby and Jacklin, 1974).

In infancy, then, the conclusion is that sex differences in social and affective behaviors, including irritability, smiling, fear and anxiety, and dependency, have not been demonstrated. In early infancy boys may be awake more and be more fretful, but this difference does not persist. The derivatives of early behavior may differ, however, for the two sexes; for example, fearful eight-month-old boys were fearful two-year-olds, but the same was not true for girls (Kagan, 1971). Perhaps because of different developmental timetables a given behavior may have a different meaning for boys and girls at the same age.

The Emergence of Sex Differences

We want to look now at that period in the life span which includes childhood and early adolescence. By this time the young person has formulated an identity, and is discernibly different in personality and behavior from all other persons. Contributions from the uniquely given biological features and the uniquely experienced environmental events are inextricably meshed by this time, and one can hope only to discern the relative importance of one or the other to the observed manifestations of behavior.

Physical development

Throughout childhood boys tend to be slightly taller and heavier than girls are. This situation changes dramatically around age eleven, when girls start the growth spurt which signals the onset of puberty a full two years, on the average, before boys. For a year or two, around age twelve to thirteen, girls are on the average taller and heavier than boys are. The differences in skeletal maturity that were present at birth continue until adulthood, with boys having about 80 percent of the skeletal age of girls at any given age (Tanner, 1970). Few other body differences are observable, except for the genitalia, during the prepubertal period. Girls have slightly more subcutaneous fat, a difference which begins to increase around age eight.

Probably because of differences in central nervous system maturity, girls develop motor skills a little earlier and achieve sphincter control before boys do. In a national study in Britain, 12.1 percent of boys over five were still wetting the bed, compared to 9.7 percent of girls, a highly significant difference in such a large sample (Pringle, Butler, and Davie, 1966).

For a given body size, girls and boys are similar in strength during childhood. Girls reach their maximum strength, measured by arm pull and arm thrust, around menarche, while the strength of boys accelerates rapidly from age thirteen to adulthood. Boys' greater lung capacity and caloric intake, which began at birth, and their higher basal metabolic rate prepare them to expend more energy and to burn up calories faster (Tanner, 1970).

These sex differences in physical development, like those of puberty described in the preceding chapters, are innately determined by biological factors. Within each sex, however, there is a wide range of individual differences in the ages at which the various events occur. The accelerated maturation of girls is observed also in the females of other primate species. Its biological significance is not at present obvious (Tanner, 1970).

Intellectual and cognitive abilities

A very large literature on sex differences in intellectual abilities has accumulated during the last five or six decades, since techniques and methodology for measuring them have been developed. As in other areas of psychological research, conclusive findings are not common, since different studies often yield dissimilar results owing to differences in characteristics of the sample, research methods, type of tests, definitions of concepts, and so on. Because of this characteristic of psychological research, it is possible to find support in the literature for a variety of positions on an issue. In the area of sex differences for any given characteristic one can find some studies that favor girls, some that favor boys, and some that find no difference. The most judicious conclusions must be based on complete surveys of the literature for a determination of where the weight of the evidence lies. In this section we are relying heavily on one recent such survey, *The Psychology of Sex Differences,* by Eleanor Maccoby and Carol Jacklin (1974).

In their examination of the literature since 1966 on intellectual and cognitive abilities, they found three areas where sex differences are fairly well established: verbal ability, mathematical ability, and spatial ability. The first favors girls, and the second and third favor boys. These three abilities, with others, are included in a global concept of mental ability, or intelligence. Verbal and mathematical ability are more closely related to general intelligence than is spatial ability, which is usually classified as a special ability, such as mechanical or artistic aptitude. Since intelligence is not a single measurable trait in an individual, the question of which sex is brighter is meaningless. Intelligence tests are made up of many items. If a test is heavily weighted with verbal items, then girls would be expected to score higher; if it is loaded with mathematical or spatial items, boys would do better. Most tests of general intelligence are constructed to eliminate such bias, so that sex differences are not expected to occur. However, of twenty-nine studies covering the age range we are interested in, Maccoby and Jacklin reported that ten favored girls, one favored boys, and the remainder found no difference. Even so, they conclude that sex differences in general intelligence have not been demonstrated, since those tests in which girls did better relied on verbal skills.

Verbal ability. Verbal ability is a generic term that includes vocabulary, speech fluency, understanding language, and reading achievement and comprehension. We have already seen that absolute differences between the sexes were not demonstrated before age two. Until very recently, it has been widely held that the sex difference in verbal ability began very early in life, and was well established in early childhood. However, data from a large number of studies dating from 1966 do not support such a belief (Maccoby and Jacklin, 1974). These studies, using standardized tests, do not reveal consistent results favoring girls until middle childhood, beginning around age ten or eleven. Throughout the school years girls outscore boys on tests of verbal skills.

We should emphasize that these results are based on tests of verbal ability. Few studies have measured the verbal behavior of children younger than three, although those that exist either find no difference or favor girls. While girls have a possible early advantage in the onset of speech and are ahead until about age three, boys do catch up. However, by middle childhood girls move ahead again and maintain their lead from then on. The magnitude of the girls' advantage varies, depending on the nature of the task and other variables. An exception to the equality that begins to prevail at age three is found in studies of underprivileged children, where the girls maintain their advantage longer. It is suggested that, because of male vulnerability, a poor environment will contain more boys with systemic damage, which would tend to lower the average performance for their group.

Mathematical ability. Tests of mathematical ability include arithmetic operations, mathematical reasoning, and achievement in the formal topics of mathematics, such as algebra and geometry. Unlike verbal ability, mathematical or quantitative ability cannot be systematically observed before the fourth year, when such skills as counting or number comparisons can be measured. From this time through the preschool years, no sex differences appear. However, as with verbal ability, girls in disadvantaged populations are ahead of boys. Most studies showed no sex differences before adolescence, though when they appear in late childhood, nine to thirteen years old, they tend to favor boys. After this age, boys move consistently ahead (Maccoby and Jacklin, 1974).

Spatial ability. Spatial ability is not simple to define, because it has been used to characterize performance on a wide variety of tasks. Usually it is held to mean the ability to see the relationships between shapes or objects or to visualize what a shape would look like if its orientation in space were changed. Tests for spatial ability use mazes, form matching, puzzles, copying block designs, or problems. Field dependence is a related cognitive characteristic which is considered to reflect mostly a spatial factor. It refers to a subject's ability to separate or disembed an element in a display from its field, or background. The most familiar task used to measure field dependence is the Embedded Figure Test (EFT), in which the subject tries to find a certain figure hidden in a complicated background or picture. Persons who do well on such tasks are said to be field-independent (Maccoby and Jacklin, 1974). Spatial tasks which do or do not involve disembedding tend to yield similar results in the research on sex differences. Very few studies find any sex differences during childhood. Some studies show that by age eight or nine boys begin moving ahead. From adolescence on, boys are ahead (Maccoby and Jacklin, 1974).

Concerning sex differences in intellectual and cognitive processes, three myths have persisted until recently. First, it was thought that girls were better than boys at rote learning and simple repetitive tasks, while boys were better at high-level cognitive processes. Second, many believed that boys were better than girls at analyzing and selecting elements needed for the solution of a problem. Third, it was believed that the intelligence of girls is more affected by heredity, of boys, by environment. However, studies show that girls and boys do not differ in any of these characteristics (Maccoby and Jacklin, 1974).

For those three areas where differences are found, it is now necessary to look at some of the explanations which have been advanced to account for them. These are of two kinds: those which emphasize innate, biological influences, and those which stress environmental or acquired influences.

Determinants of sex differences

Innate factors. Of the three areas in which sex differences have been fairly well established, spatial ability appears to be most likely to have an innate component. Evidence indicates that spatial ability is highly heritable. Since the two sexes differ on the average, it is probable that a genetic determinant for spatial ability is sex-linked, that is, that it is recessive and carried on the X-chromosome. This means that if a boy receives the trait on the X-chromosome from his mother, the effect would manifest itself, since there is no dominant factor on his Y-chromosome to counteract it (remember that the Y-chromosome carries very little genetic material). On the other hand, in order for a girl to manifest the trait, she would need to receive it from both parents, in the form of matching recessive genes. If she received it from only one, the dominant factor on the other X-chromosome would suppress it. The evidence for a genetic influence on spatial ability comes from studies of the ability in parents and children, which show that boys score more like their mothers, and girls like their fathers, on tests measuring this ability. This is understandable, since the boy receives his only X from his mother. If she manifests the trait, then he would be expected to show it also. The chances would be less for a girl to manifest such a sex-linked trait, since she would have to receive the genetic factor from both parents. If she did, however, then her ability should be more like her father's since if he carried the trait it would be manifest, whereas the mother might carry it in recessive form.

Some kinds of problems requiring mathematical ability have spatial characteristics. Because of this, there exists the possibility of a genetic component in the sex difference in mathematical ability. However, this relationship is by no means established. Mathematical problem-solving can also require verbal reasoning ability, as well as logical, analytical ability, all skills on which the sexes have not been shown to differ. A review of studies of mental abilities in twins found support for the heritability not only of spatial ability but also of verbal ability, though the latter is more heavily influenced than the former by educational and social factors (Vandenberg, 1968). There is, however, no evidence that the hereditary component of verbal ability is sex linked.

It should be stressed that evidence for a sex-linked genetic factor in a given ability does not mean that one sex has it and the other does not. With regard to spatial ability, the genetic mechanism described above would mean only that more males than females would be likely to manifest the trait. Further, spatial ability is not determined by a single gene, such that one either has it or does not. Numerous components enter into the manifestation of all human abilities, and one of these, of course, is opportunity for development.

Another suggestion of the role of biological influences in sex differences in mental abilities comes from research on cerebral dominance. The two hemispheres of the brain are somewhat specialized with regard to certain functions. Language and speech functions are localized in the left hemisphere, while spatial perception and the perception of nonverbal sounds are located in the right hemisphere. This lateralization of brain function develops as the child matures.

Evidence that lateralization develops earlier in girls comes from studies of dichotic listening (Kimura, 1967; Knox and Kimura, 1970). If different digits are presented at the same time to each ear through earphones, typically subjects will more accurately perceive the digit presented to the right ear. Since the right ear has more connections to the left hemisphere than to the right, the finding of right ear dominance means that the left hemisphere is handling the information. When this task was presented to five-, six-, seven-, and eight-year-old boys and girls, all the three older groups had achieved left-hemisphere dominance; of the five-year-olds, only the girls had done so. Now when nonlinguistic sounds, such as melodies or common household noises, were presented in the same fashion, the boys' performance was superior. Nonlinguistic sounds are mostly processed by the right hemisphere, which also mediates performance on spatial tasks in which males are normally superior.

The earlier elaboration of left hemisphere dominance in girls may facilitate their verbal development at the expense of the development of nonlinguistic capabilities (Kagan, 1971). The male, in whom cerebral dominance comes later, could be expected to manifest a more even cognitive development, with less pronounced difference in early childhood between language and non-language skills. This hypothesis suggests that a partial explanation for girls' less impressive spatial ability is based on benign neglect. Her early verbal competence causes her to continue to prefer that mode of expression and problem solving, even when there is no longer any biological reason for doing so. The question is an empirical one. The nature of the relationship, if any, between early language development and spatial ability needs investigation of the two sexes separately. If boys who mature verbally earlier had less spatial ability then boys who mature later, this would support the hypothesis. At the present time, the evidence is intriguing, but not yet convincing.

Environmental influence. The influence of the environment or culture on the psychology of women is dealt with in various connections throughout this book. At this point we are concerned only with its influence on intellectual abilities, especially those where females and males are somewhat different. To evaluate the extent to which cultural factors affect these abilities, one looks at results of cross-cultural comparisons. Since spatial ability appears to be the most likely of those we have discussed to have a sex-linked genetic component, it is interesting to consider its distribution by sex in other cultural groups.

Field independence, the ability to separate a form or object from its background, reflects primarily a spatial ability. Using the Embedded Figures Test, field independence was measured in the Temne of Sierra Leone, an African culture group, and in a group of Canadian Eskimo (Berry, 1966). The Eskimo showed greater field independence than the Temne, with no sex differences. Both Temne males and females were more field dependent, but the females were more so than the males. Two explanations exist for this interesting finding. First, field independence had survival value for the Eskimo whose environment was bleak with little variation or contrast. A group dependent upon hunting for subsistence would need to develop the ability to discriminate small differences in the visual field and to be able to orient themselves directionally with minimal cues. For ecological reasons, the Temne did not have this requirement, their setting being much more variegated, and their primary occupation, farming, required little skill to find their way around in the bush.

Second, the socialization practices of the two groups contrasted sharply with each other. The Temne emphasized severity of discipline and conformity. Wives and children were firmly controlled by the males. Eskimo children, on the other hand, received unconditional love and approval, were rarely punished, and were encouraged to assume responsibility. Both wives and children had a considerable degree of autonomy.

This study suggests the importance of both physical environment and socialization practices. The greater spatial ability as manifested in field independence of the Eskimo regardless of sex can be attributed to qualities in the physical environment which made a requirement of this ability. However, the absence of sex differences in the Eskimo, but their presence in the Temne, require further explanation. Here, the consensus seems to be that socialization practices that foster autonomy, independence, and relative freedom from parental domination also facilitate the development of field independence as a cognitive spatial ability (Kagan and Kogan, 1970). Where cultural and sex differences appear, they may reflect a difference in the distribution of power: parents versus children, male versus female. Among cultural groups in which power and dominance relationships are not an issue, spatial ability might be expected to be more evenly distributed in the population, and to be more heavily influenced by factors other than sex. In any case, cross-cultural evidence suggests that socialization practices have some effect on differences in spatial ability.

The manifestation of spatial ability, then, is multidetermined. Since the genetic factor is combined from several sources, its contribution is not all or nothing but a matter of degree. Such a factor can interact with the environmental and socialization factors to produce the level of spatial ability that the individual manifests. The contribution to spatial ability from several sources and not sex alone was brought out in an extensive review which concluded that the sex difference is of small magnitude with large within-sex variation (Kagan and Kogan, 1970). Here again, more meaningful results might be attained by studying the distribution of spatial abilities in girls and boys separately, and identifying those factors which are associated with, for example, high and low spatial ability in each sex independently.

Parental behaviors have a differential effect upon the development of mental abilities of boys and girls. While social class was a better predictor for girls than boys of IQ and other measures of cognitive development early in life, the reverse effect holds for the influence of early maternal behavior on the later intellectual development of the child. That is, the intellectual development of boys seems to be more susceptible to the emotional climate generated by the mother, whereas the girl's development is relatively independent of this relationship. One longitudinal study investigated the relationship between maternal behavior in the infant's first three years and the child's intelligence test scores from infancy to age eighteen. Maternal behaviors were ordered roughly along a love-hostility dimension, including positive evaluation of the child, expression of affection, and emotional involvement at one end, through achievement demand and intrusiveness, to perception of the child as a burden, punitiveness, and ignoring at the other end. For boys, early maternal love and acceptance were negatively correlated with IQ scores in infancy, but were positively related to high intellectual achievement later. On the other hand, girls' scores in infancy were positively related to maternal love and acceptance, but this influence diminished after three years, and then ceased to be significant. By the time the girls were teenagers, their mothers' behavior toward them as infants was unrelated to their mental development (Bayley, 1970).

Another study looked at affectional relationships in the family when the child was twenty-one months old, and subsequent intelligence test performance at age eighteen years. The girls' performance at age eighteen was significantly related to early close affectional ties between the father and the mother, and was independent of maternal affectional behavior toward them. Boys' scores on seven of the tests were positively related to their mothers' early affectional behavior, whereas the father-mother relationship had no effect (Honzik, 1967).

The relative independence of girls' intellectual achievement from maternal affectional behaviors is not easy to explain. It may be that mothers are less variable in the extent to which they have a close affectional relationship with daughters. This would have the effect of reducing the correlation between that measure and other variables. These data do not show the effect on children's intelligence test performance of a close affectional relationship with their fathers. What they do show is that the girls' performance was enhanced by a close relationship between father and mother. Several studies show that high achievement in girls is related to father identification and to above average masculinity scores (Hoffman, 1972). The more feminine the girl is and the more strongly identified with her mother, the less likely it is that she will be a high achiever. In general, the studies show that high achieving boys had warm, nurturant mothers. These findings suggest the hypothesis that a girl with a less nurturant mother and an affectionate father would establish a cross-sex identification which would mediate certain personality characteristics that facilitate achievement. For example, girls high in analytical ability tended to identify with their fathers (Bieri,

1960). The evidence for cross-sex typing as a correlate of intellectual abilities is stronger for females than for males (Maccoby, 1966).

The emergence of sex differences in intellectual and cognitive abilities around puberty is clearly demonstrated in only a few areas. For one of these, spatial ability, there is some evidence of a sex-linked genetic component which at most would mean a shift upward in the distribution of boys' scores on a test of the ability. While hereditary factors probably affect verbal and mathematical ability to some unknown extent, there is no evidence that these are sex-linked. Knowledge of the genetic transmission of specific abilities is very sparse, and at the present time it is impossible to separate out the genetic from the acquired. The question of why girls are favored in verbal ability and boys in mathematical ability from later childhood on is not answered in the literature. Although socialization and sex-typing of interests may account for part of the difference, it is simplistic to attribute all of it to learning by children that math is for boys and reading is for girls. Too many of them do not learn any such lesson. The point is that abilities and behavior patterns are not dimorphic for sex. For any human psychological trait there is great overlap between the sexes, and the differences within each sex are greater than are the differences between the sexes.

Social and affective behavior

Stereotypes about the ways that males and females are or ought to be as they interact with others in the social world are even more numerous and persistent than are those held to describe their intellectual differences. In our society females are supposed to inhibit aggression and sexual urges, to be passive, nurturant, attractive, and to maintain a poised and friendly posture with others. Males should be sexually aggressive, independent, and suppressive of strong emotions, especially anxiety (Kagan, 1964). Much research has been done in the areas of social and behavior differences between the sexes (Bardwick, 1971; Maccoby and Jacklin, 1974; Mischel, 1970; and Sherman, 1971. This discussion will concentrate on a few areas which seem especially important for the psychology of women, areas which not only have attracted much research attention but also have served as focal areas for strongly held beliefs about the differences between males and females. These areas are fearfulness and anxiety, dependency, nurturance and maternal behavior, and aggression.

Fearfulness and anxiety. Most of the research does not make a definitive distinction between fear and anxiety. At the physiological level, they are closely related to each other. Both describe an arousal state which includes body changes, such as increased heart and respiratory rates, trembling, muscle tension, and sweating. Studies of fearfulness in children usually refer to a specific object or situation, such as fear of strangers or fear of being left alone. Anxiety often means a more generalized state of arousal, sometimes with nonspecific causes. A highly unpleasant state, anxiety is sometimes described as a feeling of impending disaster or of threat to one's well-being or self-esteem. People differ in their readiness to experience anxiety. Some become anxious only rarely or in certain situations such as stage fright; others feel anxious most of the time. All persons at times experience both fear and anxiety. Those who have a generally fearful outlook on life, who are timid and hesitant in their approach to most situations, and who have frequent and intense anxiety are impaired in their psychological functioning. Research on sex difference in fearfulness and anxiety uses three basic methods: observation of subjects' behavior in certain situations, subjects' self-report of their feelings, and physiological measures.

Studies of children who have not learned to read and write have used reports of observations by parents and teacher rating scales. For example, one classic study had parents keep a diary for three weeks of all the occasions when their children showed fear. In another study two- to six-year-old children were asked to do "frightening" things: approach a large dog, walk on an elevated board, go into a dark place, or investigate a loud noise. In neither of these studies was there any difference in the frequency of fear responses of boys and girls. In the latter, however, the girls were seen as displaying a greater intensity of fear than the boys. In other words, those girls who were afraid were more afraid, according to the observers, than those boys who were afraid (Jersild and Holmes, 1935). More recent observational studies have not found consistent differences in fear or timidity for boys and girls (Maccoby and Jacklin, 1974).

With subjects who can read and write, the most frequently used method of assessing levels of fear and anxiety is some kind of self-report. Typically the subject is presented with a set of items which reflect fearful and anxious feelings and behavior, such as "I am nervous about being alone at night," or "I am afraid of dying." There are many such inventories to measure anxiety in both children and adults. Of 26 such studies on subjects aged six and over, 9 found no sex differences. Where differences were found, girls scored higher (Maccoby and Jacklin, 1974).

There are several possible explanations for these results. The first is that females are more fearful and anxious than males. But there are at least two reasons why this conclusion may not be valid. The first is the possibility that girls are more willing to admit to such feelings than boys are (Hill and Sarason, 1966). Related to this is also the possibility that some of the tests are weighted with items which are closer to the kinds of things that boys get anxious about, thus arousing their defenses more and eliciting negative answers. For example, an item such as "Are you afraid something might happen to your body?" might arouse castration fears in more boys than girls, but the boys' defensiveness about castration fears could cause them to respond in the negative. Another suggestion is that the tests might be weighted with items which are more likely to elicit anxiety responses from girls. Girls are constantly being warned about strange men, lonely places, and other possible risks of sexual molestation. Such warnings and the fear they generate could generalize to other men, such as the doctor, and to a variety of unusual settings. One 45-item test had 10 items which were believed to elicit such fears. Such a test would be biased in favor of higher scores for girls (Maccoby and Jacklin, 1974).

Some attempts have been made to learn about sex differences in anxiety by measuring the physiological responses of the body to induced fear. Subjects in the laboratory may be told that they are going to receive an electric shock or that they must take an important intelligence test. The body changes associated with anxiety are then measured. While some differences in physiological arousal have been reported, their relationship to fear states is not known (Duffy, 1962). Such measures are not strongly related to self-report measures; that is, subjects with the strongest body arousal do not necessarily make the highest scores on an anxiety inventory.

In conclusion, the research on fear and anxiety indicates that females report themselves as more anxious than males. While they may in fact be more susceptible to anxiety, it is also likely that greater willingness to admit feelings, and factors in the tests themselves, contribute to the feelings. Observational and physiological studies have not revealed sex differences in behavior or body changes.

Dependency. Infant studies of dependency behaviors such as seeking proximity with the mother, touching, and clinging, did not reveal sex differences. Studies of dependency in older children have dealt with a greater variety of behaviors, such as frequency of contact with teachers, help seeking, proximity to age-mates, and social interactions with adults and peers. Such studies usually rely upon observation, teacher or parent ratings, and self-report questionnaires. For example, three- and four-year-old children were given a puzzle that was too difficult for them to solve to observe their coping behavior. Boys were more likely to become emotional and disorganized, and more of them sought help with the problem. Girls asked for information, continued attempts to solve the problem alone, and sought contact with the experimenter (Zunich, 1964). It was interpreted that the girls were more dependent in this study. However, others pointed out that the girls' contact-seeking was a coping attempt rather than an escape from threat (Maccoby and Jacklin, 1974). A review of eight observational studies of children's dependency behavior with adults other than family revealed that five of them found no sex differences, while the rest were inconsistent (Maccoby and Jacklin, 1974).

Studies which use ratings as contrasted to direct observation of behavior more often find girls higher in dependency, leading these reviewers to caution against over-reliance on such measures. A culturally imposed bias to perceive girls as more dependent than boys could operate to influence ratings in that direction. For example, if a teacher is asked to rate each child in her class for dependency on a five-point scale, her cultural assumptions about dependency in girls and boys could bias her ratings so that the girls appeared more dependent than the boys. The fact that dependency is less pejorative as a descriptor of girls than of boys would tend to enhance this effect.

Studies of social interaction with peers and affiliative behavior have revealed some different trends for boys and girls. Boys have been found to have more extensive social interaction with age-mates, and to play in larger groups in middle childhood, while girls of similar age are more likely to have intense personal relationships with one or two close friends (Waldrop and Halverson, 1973). Further evidence that girls' friendships involve greater intimacy was found in a study of self-disclosure or the willingness to be open with others in a self-revealing encounter (Rivenbark, 1971). Both sexes were more self-disclosing to their best same-sex friends than to their best opposite-sex friends, but girls were more disclosing to both male and female friends than boys were. Also, girls disclosed more to their mothers than boys did to their fathers. In a related study, it was found that girls would permit more areas of their bodies to be touched by female and male friends, and by parents, than boys would (Jourard, 1968).

These studies support a generalization that girls are more interested in the personal qualities of relationships and are more comfortable with intimacy than boys are. Other research found girls more oriented toward the gentler aspects of interpersonal relations and less toward the active aggressive possibilities. Also, they became interested in boys at an earlier age than boys became interested in them, and cared more about their personal appearance (Maccoby, 1966).

Although varying in definitions of dependency, more studies find females to be higher on measures of dependency behavior (Mischel, 1970). A longitudinal study of 44 males and 45 females over a twenty-five-year period found that dependency was a stable dimension for females but not for males (Kagan and Moss, 1962). That is, girls who were considered to be dependent as children continued to be seen as dependent as they matured, while dependent boys did not necessarily grow up to be dependent men. It is reasonable to assume the cultural pressures operate differentially on the sexes with regard to dependency behavior. The experimental data suggest that one sex is not more emotionally dependent than the other during the first few years of life, but a continuation or persistence of dependent behavior is less likely to be tolerated in boys. If such behavior in girls is viewed more benignly by parents and reinforced later by males who are socialized to be helpful and to alleviate distress in females, then its continuity into maturity, such that those girls who were dependent grow into women who report themselves to be less self-sufficient and higher in need to be cared for, is not surprising.

While such findings propose different trends for the two sexes in various kinds of behavior commonly thought to reflect dependency, they cannot be interpreted as conclusive evidence for sex differences in dependency. The biggest problem in understanding the meaning of the research results was mentioned in the discussion of dependency in infants. Researchers in a general area of behavior, such as dependency, include different behaviors in their conceptualization, and use different methods for obtaining knowledge about the occurrence of such behaviors, with the result that inconsistencies and inconclusive results are common. Also, there is no consistent agreement on just what behaviors under what conditions constitute dependency. Whether a greater interest in intimacy in relationships is a sign of dependency is a matter of definition.

An example of terms being defined differently is the following: sometimes *attachment* is used to signify those behaviors that seek to maintain proximity and to resist separation, and *dependency* is reserved to mean physical dependency, as of the infant (Bowlby, 1969). The term *dependency* has negative connotations, implying that it is culturally undesirable and should be eliminated from the child's repertoire. Attachment behavior, by contrast, is natural and functional for humans. Its continuation into adult life does not necessarily imply psychological pathology. Separating attachment behavior from the dependency concept would allow for more precise definition and would rid the research and its interpretation of the negative meaning which dependency gives it.

This approach is of special interest to studies of sex differences. If *dependency,* including all the behaviors subsumed under it, has pejorative connotations and if more studies find girls dependent, then it follows that the pejorative connotations become associated with girls and their behavior. The statement, "girls are more dependent than boys," has a certain stigma for girls, because in our society "dependent" qualities are less valued than "independent" qualities in behavior. The illogic of this is apparent when one looks at the behaviors that are considered to reflect "dependency" in the research. Some of them, such as interest in the interpersonal qualities of relationships and greater willingness to be open and self-disclosing, are positively valued even though the dependency rubric has meanings which are not. Future researchers in this area might do well to look more closely at the twin problems of definitions and values which characterize the literature on dependency.

Nurturance and maternal behavior. "*Nurturance*" means a readiness to give care and comfort to others, especially to those whose condition manifests such a need: the young, the weak, the sick. Much maternal behavior is nurturant involving taking care of and ministering to the needs of infants and children. Women throughout the world have always been far more likely than men to perform such a role and to be perceived as more nurturant by nature than men are. To the question, "Which sex is observably more nurturant?" on the basis of actual behavior, the answer is obvious. The question whether females have a greater readiness to be nurturant, perhaps on a biological basis, is more difficult to answer. Because of the current interest in women's roles and questioning of the traditional assignment to women of child care, the research in this area of sex differences may be the most socially relevant of all. Do males ever display "maternal" behavior, and if so, under what conditions? Is it feasible to consider a restructuring of society to include male involvement in the care of children, or is there a fateful bias which would run counter to such a shift?

Animal studies of maternal behavior are more plentiful than human studies. Because of the biological relationships between humans and other mammals, it is important to learn the extent to which maternal behavior in animals is sex linked; that is, the extent to which it is inevitably linked to the female condition, by hormones or other innate mechanisms.

The development of maternal behavior in rats is partially under hormonal control, but it is also affected by experience. It was shown that virgin females treated with blood plasma from females who had just given birth would develop such maternal behaviors as nest-building and licking and retrieving pups in about half the time it took untreated virgin females. This study also found that pregnant rats increased their maternal behavior toward other pups, but that the increase did not appear if the ovaries were removed. But experience with the young was also a factor. Both males and virgin females, deprived of gonads, developed maternal behaviors after a few days if presented with a fresh litter of pups each day. This finding suggests that there is a base level of readiness to respond to young that is independent of hormonal control and can be elicited by the stimulus of contact with the young (Rosenblatt, 1969). Another study reported that the adult male's aggressiveness toward pups diminished after several fresh litters were supplied, and that nurturing behavior then appeared (Rosenberg et al., 1971).

The response of preadolescent rhesus monkeys to infants revealed that when young male-female pairs were presented with an infant, the females showed four times as much positive behavior toward it, including body contact, grooming and play, as the males did. The males, by contrast, showed ten times as much hostility to the infant (Chamov et al., 1967). In an earlier study if only a male was available, the infant persisted in its attempts to make body contact and eventually the male relented and held it for long periods (Harlow, 1962).

Child-care participation by males varies much among subhuman primate species. For example, one study described a high level of involvement with juvenile care among young male hamadryas baboons. In that group, males display nurturant behavior toward the young before they themselves are adult (Kummer, 1968). This child-care rehearsal seems to be preparatory for the male adult role, which includes a protective attitude toward his first consort, a juvenile female. His "maternal" behavior toward her seems to be a continuation of earlier practiced behaviors toward the very young of the group.

Such studies of other species indicate that maternal behavior is promoted to some degree by the sex hormones so that the females have a greater readiness to release such behavior when stimulated by the presence of young. Both sexes have the potential for appropriate child-care responses, however, and both virgin females and males can develop maternal behavior with continued exposure to infants, although in some species male aggressiveness toward the young competes with the development of more positive behavior. When adult males participate in the care of children, as in the hamadryas, the juvenile males also show interest in them.

In humans very little is known about sex differences in nurturing potential. In most societies little girls receive early training for the mother role. In Indonesia they become surrogate mothers for their infant siblings when they are still children themselves. In our society they have dolls to play with to imitate the rituals of their mothers as they care for real babies. Given such initiations beginning early in life, it is difficult to learn what the contribution of nature is. Certainly among humans both sexes are able to behave in nurturing ways toward the young. Given that some base level of potential exists for both, it may be that the behaviors are simply elicited and reinforced earlier and more consistently for girls. Does male aggressiveness inhibit nurturing behavior in humans? The only hint of an answer to this question comes from observations of the androgenized girls reviewed in the last chapter (Money and Ehrhardt, 1972). These girls were reported to be less interested in dolls than their normal sisters were. Their interest in dolls was not measured systematically, however, but was based on their mothers' report. Since the mothers knew that the daughters had been influenced by male hormones, their observations were likely to be affected. Furthermore, normal girls differ greatly in their interest in dolls and doll play. The reality of an innate repertoire of nurturing behaviors which young girls have and boys do not, or which is larger and more predictable in girls, has not been demonstrated.

A recent study provides a sequel to the research on nurturant behavior in childhood. Its findings challenge the often-repeated assertion that men are naturally uninterested and inept when exposed to newborn infants. Fathers and mothers of newborns were observed in the hospital. When the baby was brought in, the nurturant behavior, looking, holding, smiling, rocking, of each parent was observed. Except for smiling, fathers exhibited more such behavior than mothers did. When the parents were observed separately with the baby, fathers were at least as nurturant in their behavior as mothers were. The sample consisted of two groups of different backgrounds. The first group was well educated; and half the fathers had attended classes in childbirth and some had been present at their child's delivery. The second group observed was in a working-class hospital; the group was racially mixed. None of the fathers in this group had been present at his child's birth. Yet all displayed interest in their infants, and a high level of nurturant behavior (Parke and O'Leary, 1974).

Margaret Mead, writing about the distinctions that societies make between boys and girls, showed how cultural variations in early life style affect later feelings toward the nurturing role:

> girls as well as boys may spend most of their time with men, busying themselves with masculine activities and pastimes. Or the children may

spend most of their time with women. Then the boys also will learn to care for babies and cook, and they will go with their mothers and sisters to visit the newborn and mourn the dead. Later, all men will be left with a nostalgia for the childhood they shared with girls and women, but they will guard against it by renouncing all forms of tenderness, by speaking in loud, harsh voices, by making their stance aggressively masculine. . . . Or women may be left hungry for activity, . . . restless when they are confined to their homes, and chafing against their feminine tasks of tending the hearth and caring for the children. . . . (Mead and Heyman, 1965, p. 100).

Aggression. The term *aggression* is used to apply loosely to a collection of behaviors whose general intent is to threaten or hurt another individual. In animal studies it usually covers acts of physical threat or attack, while in human studies it can mean these as well as negativistic, hostile acts, quarreling, and verbal abuse. The conditions under which aggressive behavior will occur and the sanctions for and against it vary widely across species, individuals, and cultures. A given individual often is inconsistent from time to time in his aggressive behavior even under similar conditions. Therefore an examination of the sex differences in aggressive behavior must begin with an understanding that such behavior, like other classes of behavior, has many sources of variation, of which sex is only one.

The evidence is very persuasive that males are more aggressive than females are. This generalization is supported by a large body of research including studies of a variety of human cultures and animal species. Reviews of more than a hundred studies of human sex differences in aggression revealed that males were more aggressive beginning around age two (Oetzel, 1966; Maccoby and Jacklin, 1974). In a cross-cultural analysis of sex differences in the behavior of children aged three to eleven, it was found that boys engaged in more rough-and-tumble play than girls, were more verbally aggressive, and were likely to react to an attack with counteraggression (Whiting and Pope, 1973). These findings were based on combined samples from Kenya, Okinawa, India, the Philippines, Mexico, and the United States.

Evidence from primate studies echoes observations on humans. Male ground-dwelling Old World monkeys observed in their natural habitat engaged in much more rough-and-tumble play than females did (De Vore, 1965). Such play in monkeys is a rehearsal for the adult role of dominance-seeking and defense of the group. Young male macaques (monkeys) reacted more aggressively to attack than young females did (Harlow, 1962).

While there is considerable agreement that the sex differences in aggressive behavior found among mammalian species other than humans are largely produced by the action of male sex hormones on the nervous system (Hamburg and Lunde, 1966), explanations for such differences in humans are more divergent. The most popular hypothesis in recent years attributes the observed differences to differences in socialization pressures on the two sexes and suggests that active aggression is discouraged in girls, who learn to express it in alternative ways such as cattiness, or to repress it altogether in the interest of living up to a feminine ideal. According to this hypothesis the sex difference is more apparent than real. The underlying potential for aggressiveness is the same for both sexes, but its appearance is suppressed or attenuated in girls and allowed to become manifest in boys (Feshbach, 1970).

> the difference between boys and girls in aggression does not lie in the strength of aggressive drive but in the mode of behavior by which aggression is manifested. The evidence is compelling that boys are more physically aggressive than girls, yet a different pattern of results is obtained when more indirect, nonphysical forms of aggression are evaluated (Feshbach, 1970, p. 193).

The belief that girls use substitute methods for acting out their aggressive drives is based on a few studies which showed boys higher in physical aggression but not in verbal aggression (Bandura et al., 1961; MacIntyre, 1972). However, this finding has not in general been supported. Several studies have found boys to be higher in both physical and verbal aggression (Whiting and Pope, 1973; Sears et al., 1965; Hatfield et al., 1967). In one study a third child was introduced into established pairs of same-sex groups of six-to-seven-year-old children. During the first four minutes the girl pairs displayed more indirect types of aggression (ignoring, excluding) toward the newcomer whether the child was a boy or girl than the boy pairs did. However, the sex differences disappeared during the remainder of the observation (Feshbach, 1969).

When children observe a model who is making aggressive responses, boys produce more spontaneous imitations of the model's behavior than girls do (Bandura et al., 1966). But in one study when children were rewarded for remembering and imitating a model's aggressive acts, the girls and boys scored quite closely suggesting that girls know more about aggression than they exhibit (Bandura, 1965). However, even if girls' imitative aggressive behavior can be elicited at almost as high a level as boys if it is rewarded, other evidence indicates that girls are less likely than boys to add aggressive responses to their behavioral repertoire through observation. For example, when children were shown pairs of pictures, one showing a violent scene and the other a nonviolent one, girls less frequently remembered the violent one (Moore, 1966). Similarly, when shown aggressive scenes at various exposure times, girls required a longer time to recognize the scene. Such findings may be interpreted to mean that girls' potential for aggression is the same as boys' but that it is less likely to become manifest because of its suppression or attenuation in the socialization process. Relevant to this point is a longitudinal study which found aggression to be a more stable personality dimension for boys than for girls (Kagan and Moss, 1962). An aggressive three-year-old boy was likely to be an aggressive adolescent. This relationship of early to later aggressive behavior was not observed for girls.

The argument that sex differences in aggression are brought about by differential treatment of children rests upon the idea that aggression is an acceptable component of the masculine model in our society but is not desirable or appropriate when incorporated by females. It is thought that because of this differential valuing, parents reinforce or at least permit the display of aggression in boys and punish or discourage it in girls. This explanation for the observed sex differences in aggression has been challenged. A review of studies on parental permissiveness for aggression (Maccoby and Jacklin, 1974) revealed that there was no consistent evidence that parents were more tolerant of aggression in boys. There were some cross-sex effects, however. Fathers were especially severe in reprimanding sons for aggressive behavior, and were more permissive with daughters. Mothers, on the other hand, were more lenient with sons' aggression or insolence than with daughters'. On the whole, the evidence does not support the hypothesis that sex differences in aggression are primarily the result of socialization practices. But if girls' universally observed lower level of verbal and physical aggressive behavior is not altogether or mostly the result of social inhibitions, then what is its origin? One alternative explanation is that these differences between the sexes, variable and modifiable as they are, come from a biological substratum. Though not as potent a determinant for human behavior as for animal behavior, this substratum accounts for the consistency of the sex differences in aggression across cultures and human groups.

The contention that sex differences in aggression have a biological basis is centered on the following points: first of all, males are more aggressive than females in all societies for which evidence is available; second, the sex differences appear early in life, around age two to two and a half at a time when the available evidence indicates no differences in parental reward or punishment for aggressive behavior; third, similar sex differences are found in both human and subhuman species; and fourth, aggression is related to levels of sex hormones and can be changed by changing the levels of these hormones (Maccoby and Jacklin, 1974). We have already considered material relating to the first three of these points. Evidence for the last point comes mostly from animal studies of the relationship between the sex hormones and behavior (Lunde, 1973, and Money and Ehrhardt, 1972). A few examples are presented here to document the point and to make the connection between animal and human behavior.

As we saw in the last chapter, when pregnant females are administered male sex hormones, their female offspring show masculine patterns of behavior. For example, masculinized female rhesus monkeys engaged in more rough-and-tumble play than is usual for the young female of that species (Young, Goy, and Phoenix 1965). Such play is functionally related to later aggressiveness in animals, although no such relationship has been established for humans. In the "tomboy" syndrome of girls androgenized *in utero,* an increased level of such play was observed (Money and Ehrhardt, 1972). But the girls were not more aggressive in the sense of being antagonistic or hostile. The main component seemed to be an increased activity level with liking for vigorous outdoor play. In these studies, prenatal androgenization did not result in a higher level of threatening or assaultive acts toward others, the kind of aggression more frequently shown by boys.

The aggressive response of female monkeys treated with the male hormone testosterone from age 6½ months has been recorded (Joslyn, 1973). Three treated females and three untreated males were placed together and observed for thirty minutes a day during three time periods, at ages 5–9½ months, 13½–16 months, and 25–27½ months. Before the testosterone treatment of the females, the males were dominant and more aggressive than the females. After the treatment began, the females became more aggressive, and two of them attacked and subdued the two most dominant males. These two females maintained their dominance until the end of the study, long after the administration of testosterone was discontinued. Although the females became more aggressive vis-à-vis the males, their rough-and-tumble play did not increase; rather, the male rough-and-tumble play decreased from its earlier level. Thus the treatment of the female did not change *her* rough-and-tumble play, but did change that of her male playmate. A possible explanation for this is that the increase in aggression and dominance by the females had the effect of subduing the normal ebullience of the young males.

Some studies have shown correlations between levels of testosterone and aggression in males; that is, higher levels of testosterone have been found in more aggressive males, and vice versa. For example, one study revealed that male prisoners with higher testosterone levels had committed more violent crimes (Kreuz and Rose, 1972). On the other hand, there is some evidence that behavior affects testosterone level. When single male monkeys were placed with all-female groups, they immediately assumed the dominant role. Tested later, their testosterone level had risen to about four times its pre-experimental level. When these same males were placed separately with mixed-sex groups where the dominance hierarchy was already established and they had to assume a peripheral nondominant role, their testosterone levels dropped sharply (Rose *et al.*, 1972). Thus in males the relationship between testosterone and aggression can work both ways. High levels of aggression can be both an effect and a cause of elevated levels of testosterone.

What do these data mean for explanations of sex differences in aggression in humans? The sex differences are real, but they cannot be accounted for by placing the sole responsibility on differential socialization nor by deducing a proposition that testosterone rules all. Aggression, like spatial ability, is not something that males have and females do not have. There exist aggressive and unaggressive persons, and in-between variations, in both male and female populations. The suggestion from the data on sex differences in aggression is that a biological substratum exists which predisposes males to be more aggressive in situations which elicit such behavior. The threshold for aggressiveness in males seems to be lower so that under certain stimulus conditions aggressive behavior is more likely to appear. The empirically demonstrated link between male hormones and active aggression, and the physical superiority of males in build, strength, and muscle mass provide a biological basis for a readiness to behave aggressively.

Yet in humans it is obvious that much behavior is acquired. Specific aggressive acts are learned, and the inhibition of such acts is also learned. Boys are probably more primed to learn them and in some environments are less likely to be taught to inhibit, while the reverse may be true for girls. Again, cross-cultural studies are helpful in gaining perspective on the issue. Although children regardless of sex are reported to show aggressive behavior in most societies, each society has its own way of dealing with it (Whiting and Child, 1953). And children, again regardless of sex, reflect their culture's approach. As Margaret Mead showed, the Mundugumor reared aggressive, hostile children of both sexes. By contrast, today's Chinese children, reared in state-run nurseries, are taught cooperative behavior and are not punished physically (Sidel, 1973). Observers marvel at the absence of hostile and aggressive behavior in their play groups.

What Do We Know About Sex Differences?

The foregoing discussion of psychological differences between the sexes has presented current knowledge in areas where differences have been shown to exist, and in a few others, where the findings are not conclusive and where misconceptions are common. Sex differences in other areas, such as achievement, will be discussed in other contexts later on. In general, then, we can conclude that:

1. Behavioral differences between boy and girl neonates have not been demonstrated.

2. Absolute differences in cognitive ability and in social and affective behavior in the first two years have not been conclusively demonstrated. However, patterning of cognitive development is more consistent with age for girls, and is more strongly related to social class. Irritability and fearfulness are more consistent with age for boys. Mothers are equally warm, nurturing, and accepting of boy and girl babies.

3. Sex differences in cognitive abilities emerge in middle to late childhood. Girls have higher verbal abilities, and boys have higher mathematical and spatial abilities. Spatial ability is the only one of these which may have a sex-linked genetic component. Such a component would account for only a small part of the difference between males and females in spatial ability, since it has also been shown to be affected by environmental and socialization factors.

4. The evidence for sex differences in fearfulness, dependency, and nurturance is inconclusive. Teacher ratings and self-reports tend to show girls more fearful, but it is not known to what extent cultural expectations and girls' greater willingness to admit feelings affect these results. Girls seem to be more oriented toward intimacy in interpersonal relations, but they do not exhibit more of the behaviors usually included in definitions of dependency in the research. While girls are more often in a nurturant role, as in doll play, it is not known to what extent nurturant behavior is innate in females. Both males and females can display nurturant behavior. There is some evidence that early exposure of males to infants and child care enhances their nurturant behavior as they mature.

5. From early childhood, boys have a higher level of aggressive behavior than girls. This difference has been observed in other cultures as well as in animal species. It is probable that a hormonally induced pattern of readiness to respond aggressively, as well as other physical characteristics, contribute initially to this difference. Human behavior, however, is highly malleable, and within-sex and cross-cultural differences are significant also.

The next chapter will take up the role of society and socialization practices in the further development of sex differences and in the sexual differentiation of social roles. Meanwhile, the very nature of the sex-differences research itself has been attacked by sociologist Jessie Bernard in a provocative examination of the objectives and use of such research:

> . . . its latent function has been, in effect to rationalize and hence to legitimate the status quo, including of course its role structure, especially the inferior position of women. The inferiority of women was self-evident from the research (1973, p. 3).

The research in this chapter and the conclusions drawn from it do not in themselves suggest that females are inferior in any way. Bernard's argument is directed primarily to the importance attached to the evidence for biological factors in the components of aggression, broadly defined. These components include some that are valued in our society, such as strength, need for achievement and power, competitiveness, independence—in short, "the components of the archetypical *macho* variable, offensive aggressiveness (p. 5)." She suggests that a society of the future will need and value more those traits which today are called feminine, and which if applied to some of the great problems of society will help to bring about a more human environment for us all.

The biggest problem with research in the area of sex differences, however, is not altogether political. It is the risk of simplistic interpretations which reinforce stereotypes about both sexes and cause individuals to receive differential treatment on the basis of sex. For example, the difference in developmental maturity of boys and girls led one educator to suggest seriously that the legal age of school admission should be 3 to 8 months higher for boys than for girls (Pauley, 1951). More recently, a proposal to return to sexual segregation in schools was based on two points: one, that boys are at a disadvantage in the academic competition, and two, that boys through daily association with girls are stimulated to precocious sexual interest which further interferes with their school work (Gilder, 1973). Such suggestions based on interpretation of sex differences ignore the much greater variability within the sexes.

In any case, the resilience of the question of sex differences suggests not only that it is of profound human interest, but also that its answer can help to solve important human problems. But can it? Perhaps the best approach is still the response of the eighteenth-century British writer Samuel Johnson, who when asked who was smarter, man or woman, replied, "Which man—which woman?"

Growing up female

6

I adore being dressed in something frilly,
  When my date comes to get me at my place,
Out I go with my Joe or John or Billy
  Like a filly who is ready for the race.

When I have a brand new hairdo
  With my eyelashes all in curl
I float as the clouds on air do
  I enjoy being a girl.
                —from *Flower Drum Song,*
        Rodgers and Hammerstein, 1959*

I am young and I possess many buried qualities: I am young and strong and am liv-
ing a great adventure; I am still in the midst of it and can't grumble the whole day
long. I have been given a lot, a happy nature, a great deal of cheerfulness and
strength. Every day I feel that I am developing inwardly, that the liberation is draw-
ing nearer and how beautiful nature is, how good the people are about me, how inter-
esting this adventure is! Why, then, should I be in despair?
                —from *The Diary of a Young Girl,* Anne Frank, 1944

In India, a small Rajput girl plays at making bread. She builds herself a little hearth of three stones, pats and shapes her mud cakes,
and fries them in a pan. When they are done, she stacks them on a
dish, washes the pan, and sweeps up the floor where she has been
working, all her motions an exact replica of those she has seen her
mother use many times. Outside, her brother is "plowing" the
ground with a stick. He says, "burr," "burr," which is what his father
says as he walks behind the cattle (Minturn and Hitchcock, 1963).
    Across the world a behavioral scientist comes upon a small Sioux
girl sitting behind a tree. She is bent over a toy typewriter, and he

---

notices that both her lips and her fingernails are painted red. Nearby, a young boy is lassoing a tree-stump buffalo (Erikson, 1963).

Everyone who has observed children from about age three on has seen such imitations of and rehearsals for adult roles, little girls doing what women do, little boys practicing to be men. Such behavior is sex-typed, that is, it is behavior which is appropriate to the child's gender. All known societies prescribe certain behaviors for women, others for men, and these define not only sex roles but also concepts of masculinity and femininity. In Chapter 4 we saw that children learn their gender identity during their second year of life. By age three, they know what their sexual category is and also are able to classify others by sex. Subsequently they incorporate into their identities the preferences, interests, and behaviors that characterize the role of their sex in their society. Sex-role identification is the extension of gender identity, the internalized knowledge of one's sex, to include internalization of the role typical of one's sex in the society and the reactions and attributes characteristic of that role. It is distinguished from parental identification, which is the internalization of the personality characteristics of a parent and the development of reactions and behavior similar to those of the parent. The process by which sex-role identification and parental identification are acquired and the content of the socialization experiences which differentiate girls from boys are the subjects of this chapter.

How Children Learn

While there may be underlying biological predispositions for the acquisition of some sex-typed behaviors, we assume that the role of learning in a social context is far more important for developing sex-role identification. Given that the society has different sex-role models for males and females, how are these acquired by children? What factors facilitate or retard the identification with a sex role apparent so early in life? At the present time there is no consensual answer among learning theorists to these questions. Instead there are three major proposals to explain the learning of sex roles. The first emphasizes the role of *reinforcement* by rewards and punishments in establishing behavior. The second attaches importance to *modeling,* or imitating, the behavior of others. The third is a *cognitive-developmental* approach which stresses the child's growth of understanding both of her or his sexual identity and the content of the sex roles prescribed by the society.

These three explanatory concepts of how children learn sex

roles are not mutually exclusive. It is quite possible that all three contribute to the child's acquisition and performance of sex-typed behavior. Also, although we are discussing them as they apply to sex-typing, it should be understood that as causal principles they can apply equally to the learning of other social behaviors. There is no reason to believe that sex-typing is learned under any different conditions than are other complex behaviors.

Reinforcement

Behavior, including sex-typed behavior, can be acquired under conditions of reward and punishment. The term *reinforcement* is not easy to define, as it can be applied to a variety of events which may have little in common. For example: When a child learns not to use certain prohibited words because her mother spanks her for it, the spanking is the reinforcement. When a child appears before company clean, combed, and dressed up and is told that she looks very pretty, the phrase, "You look very pretty," is the reinforcement. When a child brings home her first report card with all *A*'s and is given a new bicycle, the bicycle is the reinforcement.

Even though the spanking, the praise, and the bicycle seem to have little in common, they all act as reinforcers to facilitate learning. Reinforcers are considered to be positive if they represent desirable goals, so that the child will repeat the behavior which resulted in the reward. They are considered to be negative if they have aversive effects on the child's behavior, so that she will refrain from the behavior in order to avoid the negative consequences.

An explanation of the acquisition of sex roles through reward and punishment would propose that as children try out various behaviors which are sex-typed, they are rewarded for those that are appropriate and punished for those that are not. While there is no doubt that reinforcement is very important in the acquisition of behavior, it is too simplistic to account, by itself, for children's learning of sex roles. The rate at which these roles are learned, and the scope of their content, require additional processes. Gender roles not only encompass broad areas of behavior but are often quite subtle as well: "It would be difficult to imagine that any kind of direct tuition could provide for the learning of such elaborate behavioral, attitudinal, and manneristic patterns as are subsumed under the rubrics of masculinity and femininity. Furthermore, these qualities are absorbed quite early and are highly resistant to modification" (Sears *et al.*, 1965, p. 171).

Modeling

The importance of modeling, or imitation, in the acquisition of sex-typed behavior has been brought out by most of the reviews in the area (Sears *et al.*, 1965; Bandura, 1969; Mischel, 1970). Learning by modeling is dependent upon observational and cognitive processes and can occur without any direct reinforcement. "People learn sex roles through their eyes and ears and by observing other persons and events and not merely from the consequences they get directly for their own overt behavior" (Mischel, 1970, p. 29). Such learning may occur from watching what other people do, observing the consequences of their behavior, attending to environmental events and to symbolic material such as stories and pictures. Through these processes the child develops the knowledge of her own sexual identity, and learns the concepts of male and female, including cultural stereotypes of masculinity and femininity.

The concept of modeling as a major process in the learning of sex-typed behavior implies that girls learn female role behavior by observing and imitating the behavior of other females. The hypotheses which come out of this proposal are several. First, because the mother is the most available, important, and rewarding female, she is most likely to become the role model, at least in the preschool years. Second, in selecting the mother's behavior to imitate, the girl will become more like her than like the father; and third, same-sex models in general will be imitated more than opposite-sex models because the child perceives them as more similar to herself. "It certainly seems likely that children are much more frequently rewarded for watching and imitating same-sex models (rather than cross-sex models), especially when the models display sex-typed behaviors. Boys do not learn baseball by watching girls and girls do not learn about fashions from observing boys (Mischel, 1970, p. 38)."

However, the importance of modeling in the learning of sex-typed behavior is controversial (Maccoby and Jacklin, 1974). If the first hypothesis, contiguity of mother, is correct, it would lead to the conclusion that both sexes early in life establish their primary identification with her through observing and modeling her. But other research has shown that, when exposed to several models, children will imitate the more dominant one. Likewise, other things being equal, they will imitate the more nurturant one. If the father is dominant, then both sexes should imitate him, and if the mother is nurturant, then both should imitate her. While this may actually be the case very often, it would not account for differences in acquisition of dominant or nurturant behavior by the two sexes.

Do very young girls learn sex-typed behavior by modeling their mothers and thus become like them? Available research does not support the hypothesis of parent-child similarity along a dimension of femininity or masculinity (Maccoby and Jacklin, 1974). A popular research technique for measuring sex-role identity and preferences in children is the IT scale. The child is given a card with a representation of a sexually ambiguous figure, asked to assign a sex to it, and to choose toys for it from objects or pictures associated with sex roles. Studies of sex-role similarities in parents and children have compared children's performance on this scale with measures of femininity and masculinity of parents, to ascertain like-sex and cross-sex identification in sex-typing of interests and preferences and so on. In one study the sex-typed choice patterns of first-grade girls were unrelated to the femininity of their mothers. Likewise, boys' responses were unrelated to their fathers' masculinity (Mussen and Rutherford, 1963).

While some studies show parent-child similarities on non–sex-typed dimensions of personality, such as values and attitudes, they fail to show that the child is more likely to resemble her or his mother than father (e.g., Troll et al., 1969). With regard to the kinds of behaviors usually subsumed under femininity and masculinity, there is no evidence that feminine mothers have feminine daughters.

Studies of direct observation of children's imitative behavior with parents are rare. One series of studies with children at various age levels (4–11, 4–5, and 3–6) investigated the relationship between parents' dominance and children's imitations. At none of the age levels did the children show a consistent tendency to imitate the same-sex parent (Heatherington, 1965).

The third hypothesis suggests that same-sex models in general will be imitated more than opposite-sex models because of their perceived similarity to the child. Again, the research does not demonstrate this to be the case. A review of twenty studies in which children were presented with models of both sexes revealed little consistent tendency for preschool children to select same-sex models. When shown models who were displaying affection, aggression, toy choices, aesthetic preferences, and other activities, the children's modeling was indiscriminate with regard to sex (Maccoby and Jacklin 1974).

The essential point here is that while children do learn through modeling, through observing and imitating the behavior of others, they do not limit their modeling in any systematic way to same-sex models. If they observe and imitate equally models of both sexes, then they acquire a repertory of behavior which includes both "masculine" and "feminine" components. These components, however, are not equally manifested in behavior. By the age of three or four, children's behavior does become sex-typed. Girls display lower levels of aggressive behavior than boys do, prefer to play with other girls, and choose play activities that are defined as sex-appropriate. If modeling is of minor importance for such an outcome, then what are the reasons for it? Two explanations which require that the distinction be made between *acquisition* and *performance* have been suggested (Maccoby and Jacklin, 1974). We have already seen that a wide range of behavior can be acquired by direct reinforcement and by modeling. Some of these become part of the patterns of consistently occurring behavior for a particular child, and others do not. They may be tried briefly and then dropped or never tried at all. For example, the little Rajput girl may be as well able as her brother to "plow" the ground with a stick, but she does not do it. What she does do is to employ her toy dishes to make bread. The selection of such behaviors for actual performance depends on the *necessary eliciting conditions,* and the *belief that the action is appropriate.* Both the little Rajput girl and the boy had observed their mother making bread and knew what to do with the toy dishes, but the dishes had been given to the girl, not to the boy. Also, on the basis of observation and various reinforcing conditions, the child knows what is appropriate to her or his own sex. This last factor brings us to the third explanation for the way children learn about sex-roles.

Cognitive-developmental theory

The cognitive view of the processes mediating the learning of sex roles states that sex-typed behavior is learned neither by the simple reinforcement of discrete acts nor by the imitation of the actions of same-sex people. Instead, the child develops rules or generalizations from what she observes, and then applies these over broad classes of behavior (Kohlberg, 1966). In the early stages of this learning, the rules may be oversimplified and inaccurate, and the child may be unable to take into account the exceptions she encounters. For example, a young child who does not know yet that gender is constant has induced a rule that all persons who wear dresses are girls. When she is shown a male model in male attire, she correctly identifies him as a boy. Shown the same model in a dress, she now identifies him as a girl in accordance with her rule. Similarly, a young woman who lived for a while on a houseboat near a small country town became the object of curiosity to a five-year-old native, who did not know any adult single women, let alone any who lived on a boat. "Where's your husband?" she asked over and over. "You gotta have a husband!"

The child's knowledge of what constitutes masculine or feminine roles or behavior must undergo change and revision as she matures and has a greater breadth of experience. Once she learns what her own sexual identity is, she then learns which other persons share that category with her. At the same time she is observing what all these persons, as well as those in the other category, have in common, within her experiential range. From these observations she learns what is appropriate to her sex, and begins to match her behavior to that sex-role standard.

These stages of identity development, learning of sexual categories, and formulation of rules about sex-typed behavior do not occur in any formal sequence. During the same time that her own gender identity is becoming firmly established, she is observing the similarities and differences in others which permit her to think of them in terms of categories with rules assigned to them. These rules are established and confirmed as a function of the consistency of her experience. Clearly the more rigidly sex-typed are the roles in the society, the stronger her confirmation of the rules will be. Presented with an anomaly, as in the case of the five-year-old above, she must recast her whole formulation concerning adult women, from "All adult women have husbands," to "Not all adult women have husbands," or, "Most, but not all, adult women have husbands."

The three most widely held theories, one emphasizing reinforcement, the second, modeling, and the third, cognitive development, explain the way that sex-typed behavior, and with it identification with a sex role, is learned. It is probable that all three processes are involved in the emergence of such behavior, in different degrees of importance, depending on the situation and the age of the child. Consider, for example, the four-year-old girl who gets "dressed up" for a brief appearance at her parents' party. She is willing to do this because of a history of reinforcement with praise, approval, and warm compliments from adults when she "looks pretty," a harbinger of things to come. She wears a long skirt like her mother's and helps to pass the hors d'oeuvres, modeling from her mother the appropriate ways that a female behaves as a hostess. At the same time, she can see that all the other women are dressed similarly, and she can observe their tone of voice, their gestures, and the kinds of things they talk about. From this experience and numerous others like it she forms generalizations about the state of being female in her world. All three kinds of learning are occurring, each facilitating the other, to organize the child's sex-role concepts and sex-typed behavior.

Development of Sex-Role Identification

Three aspects are involved in the process of developing sex-role identification. They are (1) sex-role preference or the perception of the role of one sex as more desirable than the other, (2) sex-role adoption or the display of sex-related behavior, and (3) sex-role identification or the incorporation into one's personality of the responses characteristic of a sex role (Lynn, 1959).

Sex-role preference is observed in both girls and boys beginning at about age three, and is well established by age five. Children younger than three are unlikely to show a preference for sex-related toys or activities or to attach a value to one sex role over the other. One study provided one-year-old boys and girls with a variety of toys in the presence of their mothers, including stuffed animals, a ferris wheel decorated with pink ribbons, and robots. Except for the boys' preference for the robots, no sex differences were found, and the mothers did not differ in their toy selections for girls and boys (Jacklin *et al.*, 1973). By age three, however, nursery-school children show sex-related preferences for toys and activities. Little girls are in the doll corner, dressing up and playing house; boys are outside, tumbling about and fighting, and playing with cars and trucks.

In middle childhood, however, an interesting phenomenon appears, and continues to differentiate the sexes into adulthood: a widespread preference by girls of the masculine role, and greater ambivalence in girls for clear-cut identification with the feminine role. In contrast, boys do not show a cross-sex role preference, and they are more likely to identify unequivocally with the masculine role. A study of toy preferences among four- to seven-year-olds found much greater variance among the girls; boys preferred boys' toys more than girls preferred girls' toys (Ward, 1968). A study of sex-role preference among five- and six-year-old boys and girls, using picture cards depicting various objects, figures, and activities associated with the masculine or feminine role further illustrated this phenomenon (Brown, 1956). A child figure of no discernible sex (IT) was given to the subjects who then made choices for it from among the items. The study found dichotomous sex-role preference in these young children, but girls twice as often as boys showed a mixed preference pattern. The tendency to strong opposite sex-role preference was more pronounced in girls, and boys showed a significantly greater preference for the masculine role than girls showed for the feminine role. For example, Table 6.1 shows that on paired items reflecting aspects of masculinity-femininity, from 71 to 91 percent of the boys chose the masculine alternative, while 40 to 69 percent of the girls chose the feminine alternative.

Furthermore, when subjects could show a preference for being male or female, only one boy in ten chose female, while one girl in three chose male. This finding of preference for the male role by both sexes has been widely replicated for age groups extending into adulthood. Results suggest that between 20 and 31 percent of adult women, compared to between 2.5 and 4 percent of adult men, recall a conscious desire to be the other sex (Brown, 1958; Sherman, 1971).

What factors contribute to this ubiquitous disenchantment with

Table 6.1 Percentages and differences of choices of boys and girls on the eight paired pictures section of the IT scale for children (Brown, 1956)

	Boys		Girls	
	Male choice %	Female choice %	Male choice %	Female choice %
Indian princess Indian chief	86	14	51	49
Trousers and shirt Dress	77	23	38	62
Sewing materials Airplane parts	88	12	60	40
Cosmetic articles Shaving articles	91	9	50	50
Mechanical tools Household objects	82	18	49	51
Men's shoes Women's shoes	76	24	34	66
Girls playing Boys playing	71	29	50	50
Building tools Baking articles	74	26	31	69
Totals: eight paired items	81	19	45	55

the condition of being female? Freud, of course, had a ready answer in the anatomical difference between the sexes, which he thought was clearly disadvantageous to the female and produced in her a profound envy of the male. Since the data do not support the concept of penis envy, one must look to sociocultural explanations. It is not improbable that girls early perceive the male role as invested with higher status and greater rewards:

> That our culture has been and still is masculine-centered and masculine-oriented is obvious. The superior position and privileged status of the male permeates nearly every aspect minor and major, of our social life. The gadgets and prizes in boxes of breakfast cereal, for example, commonly have a strong masculine rather than feminine appeal. And the most basic social institutions perpetuate this pattern of masculine aggrandizement (Brown, 1959, p. 235).

Another explanation for females' preference for the male role, however, is the fact that girls are freer to state a cross-sex preference. In addition, girls have much greater latitude to engage in a host of male activities, especially before adolescence. No onus is attached to tomboyish behavior; girls may wear pants and play softball, but no boy may wear dresses or play Barbie dolls with impunity. Thus the greater freedom girls have to display cross-sex preferences and behavior probably shows up in the research as a variable which interacts with actual preference to produce the most clear-cut results. But it is clear that the pressure is less great on girls to use sex-appropriate behavior.

The second aspect of sex-role development, sex-role adoption, identifies observable, sex-related behavior. In girls, the adoption of the feminine role appears to occur concomitantly with sex-role identification. That is, at about the same time that the little girl begins to exhibit sex-typed behavior, she also begins to internalize the female role and its attributes. There is some evidence that for boys these processes are sequential. For example, five- to seven-year-old girls perceived similarities between themselves and their mothers, whereas boys of the same age had not yet established a like identification with their fathers (Ward, 1969). One explanation for this is that the course of the identification process is different for the two sexes.

We have already seen how role adoption, the display of sex-typed behavior, is learned as a function of reinforcement, modeling, and the development of concepts about what is appropriate for one's sex. We are now going to consider a model for the development of sex-role identification. This formulation consists of hypotheses which have empirical support from the research in the area (Lynn, 1971). It rests upon the assumption that the learning process occurs under the same conditions that we have already described.

The first parental identification of both sexes is with the mother, who is the usual omnipresent caretaker. The boy, not the girl, must make a shift in identification with the appropriate sex role. This shift can be difficult, since his father is typically away much of the time, and the adults of his early social world are mostly women. Thus girls continue to elaborate their early parental identification because the behavior of their mothers is female role behavior. However, boys must learn to identify with a culturally defined model whose components may be less than clear to them for a very long time. Evidence suggests that both sexes identify more clearly with the mother throughout childhood, but males' identification with her is more likely to be revealed in personality variables that are not sex-typed. Sociability and preference for being with people as contrasted to being alone are two such examples. The girl learns her identification within a close interpersonal context, by imitating her mother as a model.

The boy has a more difficult problem. He has to define the goals of the masculine role, learn what its components are often by being told what they are not. Finally, he must abstract from this set of conditions principles which can guide a large number of behaviors. Because of the different conditions under which girls and boys learn their identifications, girls have fewer problems in learning their same-sex identifications and succeed more completely with less probability of an opposite-sex identification. Because of the more favorable conditions under which girls learn to be women, they are less anxious about sex-role identity than males are. Since girls are less often punished for boyish behavior than boys are for girlish behavior, they develop less hostility for males and male activity than males do for females and female activity.

Since the acquisition of feminine role behavior is learned under less stringent contingencies of punishment and reinforcement, girls are less rigidly identified with their role. When boys do surmount their difficulties and become firmly identified with the masculine role, they enjoy the status of being the dominant sex and the perquisites that attach to the status of maleness. Thus, males develop identity disturbances at a slower rate as they get older. Girls, on the other hand, grow up to discover the prejudices prevailing against them on all sides, learn that they occupy an inferior status, and become disenchanted. As we saw already, more of them than males show a preference for the role of the other. They may state this preference quite openly, as it is perfectly rational to feel envious of others whom one perceives as greatly favored in contrast to one's own oppressed condition. But preference is not identification; girls may prefer the male role but maintain a feminine identification. Thus, when there is a discrepancy between preference and identification, it tends to be as follows: Males show same-sex role preference (because the consequences of doing otherwise are too punishing) with covert opposite-sex identification; females show opposite-sex preference (which is permissible) with same-sex identification. To rephrase, when there is a discrepancy, it will take the form for both sexes of male role preference and feminine identification. Finally, because of the greater latitude for females in these matters, more of them will adopt aspects of the culturally defined male role than will males of the female role. As an example, the proportion of girls who plan to have careers is expected to be greater than the proportion of boys who prefer domesticity. Although, parenthetically, if the housewife's job were accorded wages and high status, we might see an increasing number of males taking an interest in it.

This model, while it fits with both systematic and informal observation, consists of a series of *generalizations* which attempt to conceptualize and to explain observable behavior. But no model relevant to human behavior can do more than account for trends and for widely validated observations which are typical for a significant proportion of the population. While this model seems to explain relevant socially reinforced phenomena in general, significant erosion of it has occurred recently. Data which formerly were not taken seriously are now considered to have the authority to modify and enrich theory. The next section explores an example of what happens when empiricists began testing the revealed wisdom of traditional theory.

Parental Identification in Adolescent Girls

Parental identification, the internalization of characteristics of a parent, interacts with sex-role identification in complex ways. Children may identify with their same-sex parent, with their opposite-sex parent, with both parents, or with neither. A parent may not be unequivocally feminine or masculine in her or his own sex-role identification, but may manifest attributes of each. A child may identify with some aspects of one parent and some of the other or may shift her identification as she moves into a different stage of her life cycle. Prediction of sex-role identification from parental identification, or vice versa, would depend upon an assessment of the interactions among the following elements: the strength of the identification with either or both parents, the extent to which the parents themselves are identified with typical sex roles, and parental reinforcement and modeling of sex-role identification. For example, a girl may develop a strong identification with a mother who is not very feminine; thus the girl's sex-role identification would not be feminine. She might identify with a feminine mother and be rewarded for typically feminine behavior by both parents, in which case one would expect an unequivocal feminine sex-role identification.

Freud's prototype theory of identification saw the girl resolving her Oedipal conflict by incorporating the mother, thus reducing her fear of losing the mother's love. For daughers, identification with the mother and with the female sex role was the normal course, and girls who deviated from it by identifying with the father, or with the masculine sex role, had adopted a neurotic solution which was incompatible with a healthy personality adjustment. As we saw in Chapter 2, this formulation does not lend itself gracefully to empirical testing of all its components. Even so, its effect continues to be seen in the assumption that a girl identifying with a feminine mother has the best chance for a healthy adjustment. Paradoxically, empirical studies have failed to find a positive relationship between maternal identification and personality adjustment in girls, though father identification has been related consistently to good adjustment in boys. In fact, several studies have found that when parents present sex-typical models for their daughters, those who identify with a masculine father have a better level of personal adjustment than do those who identify with a feminine mother (Heilbrun, 1968a). Another study of sex-role identification and level of personality functioning in late adolescent girls went as follows. Behaviors were categorized into four parental models: ascendant-dominant mother, ascendant-dominant father, retiring-passive mother, and retiring-passive father. The extent to which the girl attributed the behaviors to each parent and to herself identified the model and measured the strength of her identification with it. Composite profiles for the four identification groups revealed that girls identifying with ascendant-dominant fathers had the highest level of functioning, while those identifying with retiring-passive mothers had the lowest (Williams, 1973). This, of course, is diametrically opposite to a prediction based on Freudian theory.

Other attempts have been made to explain such anomalous findings by using the constructs of expressive and instrumental orientations, seen as the essence of feminine and masculine sex roles. The expressive person is sensitive to relationships, attitudes, and feelings, and rewards others by being solicitous, warm, and understanding. The instrumental person is goal-oriented seeing relationships as means of attaining ends. Being less sensitive to the immediate emotional responses of others, he learns to tolerate the hostility which his instrumental approach sometimes elicits. It should be obvious that these styles can coexist to varying degrees in individual behavior repertoires and that a mature and healthy personality would combine both, would be both sensitive and competent, though perhaps more one than the other. Thus, a masculine father though primarily instrumental could also behave in expressive, nurturant ways, especially toward his daughter. He could model for her both instrumental and expressive behavior, thus facilitating healthy personality functioning (Heilbrun, 1968a).

In a study of the strength of expressive and instrumental tendencies in masculine and feminine girls, groups of college undergraduates worked together on a project. After three hours, they rated each other on dimensions of expressive and instrumental behavior. Their sex-types were determined by a conventional masculinity-femininity scale and were compared to their expressive-instrumental ratings. Interestingly, both masculine and feminine girls were equally expressive, but the masculine girls were also instrumental, whereas the feminine girls were not. Further, when parental identifications were examined, 62 percent of the masculine girls were masculine-father identifiers, and 64 percent of the feminine girls were feminine-mother-identifiers (Heilbrun, 1968b).

Such intriguing findings support the idea that fathers can model both instrumental and expressive behaviors for their daughters, and that daughters who identify with such fathers and who adopt both kinds of styles will have more effective personalities than will those who, by identifying with feminine mothers, develop their expressive behaviors only.

Basically the *sex* of the parent model is not important. If the personality of the healthy person includes an integrated balance of both expressive and instrumental styles, then she or he could surely learn these competencies from a variety of people, unspecified as to sex. More men than women are likely to be instrumental because of the different role requirements in our society. More women are likely to be expressive for the same reason. Girls *can* learn the instrumental attitude from mothers, but they are less likely to.

Sex Typing and Socialization

All societies differentiate between the sexes through the assignment of different roles. They also promote different standards for females and males in various areas of behavior and personality. In our society, females are supposed to be unaggressive physically and sexually, nurturant and caring toward others, expressive and friendly, and attentive to their appearance. Males are expected to be physically and sexually assertive, independent, competent, and emotionally tough. The behavior thought to be appropriate for females is facilitative of interpersonal relations, while that expected of males is facilitative of solving problems. Such expectations make up sex-role standards and are inculcated in children by sex typing in the socialization process.

What this means is that the society through its institutions encourages the development of different behavior patterns for boys and girls owing to beliefs about the desirability of certain attributes in boys and others in girls. Thus the socialization process by which the child is trained both formally and informally to fit the requirements of the society differs in some ways for girls and boys. Society arranges for them to have different sets of experiences in preparation for the roles they will take up as adult members of the society.

There is a difference between sex typing and sex stereotyping. Sex typing is the prescription of different qualities, activities, and behaviors to females and males in the interest of socializing them for adult roles. Sex stereotyping is the promotion or expression of commonly held beliefs about sex differences or sex roles, sometimes to the point of caricature. Thus, a real girl is preoccupied with her looks, unambitious, loves animals (but is afraid of mice), and cries a lot. A real boy is fearless, noisy, insensitive, interested in sports and science, and resistant to bathing. Sex typing gives rise to stereotyping, the forming of loose generalizations about categories of people, failing to make discriminations among their infinite varieties.

Sex typing and its exaggeration in stereotyping have caused much concern in recent years and have attracted widespread attention from many quarters. Practices relevant to them in the socialization process have been examined, and a considerable body of literature has appeared which documents differential socialization for girls and boys, and in some cases, presents some unexpected results.

Parental influences

Do sex-role standards influence the child-rearing practices of parents? Is there a "double standard" for bringing up children which is promoted by the parents' perceptions of the child's sexual category and their beliefs about sex differences? That parents attribute different qualities to girls and boys from birth was documented in a study of parents' perceptions of their newborn infants. Although male and female infants did not differ in weight, length, or

Apgar scores,[1] daughters were significantly more likely than sons to be described as little, beautiful, delicate, weak, and as resembling their mothers. Boys were seen as firmer, more alert, stronger, and better coordinated. Father were much more extreme in their sex-typing than mothers, who tended to rate boys and girls closer together with respect to these qualities (Rubin *et al.,* 1974). Such labeling can be expected to influence expectations about future behavior of the child and also to guide the parents' behavior as they begin to interact with the child in the home.

A related study asked parents of six-year-olds how they believed the sexes to differ in behavior, and how they thought they *ought* to behave (Lambert *et al.,* 1971). Rating boys and girls on such items as "more helpful around the house," "more likely to be rough and boisterous at play," and "more likely to act scared," the parents described boys as rougher, noisier, more active, more competitive, and more likely to do dangerous things. Girls were more helpful, neater and cleaner, quieter and more reserved, more sensitive, and more easily upset and frightened. However, when asked which qualities they thought it important for children to have, they differed very little in their values for girls and boys. *Both* should be neat and clean, helpful in the house, able to take care of themselves, and thoughtful and considerate of others. Thus their socialization goals were much alike for both sexes, but they believed that they were starting from different points with different "material" to work with.

A recent review of the literature on differential socialization of girls and boys found surprisingly few differences in the ways that parents treat their children, in spite of widely held assumption to the contrary (Maccoby and Jacklin, 1974). However, there are some areas where differential effects are found. Parents provide sex-typed clothes and toys for children, and they discourage them, especially sons, from engaging in activities which they believe to be appropriate only for the other sex. Parental anxiety is elicited much more readily by a boy who wants to wear makeup and dresses than by a girl who wants to wear pants and play baseball.

Some surprises appear in the research. It is generally believed that one reason for boys' greater aggressiveness is that they are encouraged or rewarded for it while girls are not. The fact is that parents do not value aggression in either sex, and a major thrust of their socialization efforts is directed toward teaching children to inhibit aggressive responses. There is no evidence in the research that parents reinforce boys and not girls for aggressive behavior, or that

---

[1] The Apgar score refers to a group of physiological signs which indicates the infant's condition at birth.

they are more permissive of it in boys. Another area of childrearing, the encouragement of independence and autonomy, is also usually thought to distinguish parents of boys from parents of girls. But in the preschool years parents behave similarly in their reactions to independence seeking (or its opposite, dependency behavior) in girls and boys, with mothers showing some tendency to be more restrictive toward boys. However, as girls begin school, parents become more protective of them, and are more likely, for example, to walk home with them. Beginning around age seven, daughters begin to receive what is called "chaperonage," with adults checking on their whereabouts and accompanying them more than they tended to do with boys (Newson and Newson, 1968). But they are allowed to make their own decisions about where they want to go and what they want to do as often as boys are. The chaperoning seems to be less a fostering of dependency than an expression of concern about the danger that the child will be sexually molested, a risk to which very few parents of daughters are indifferent.

One area where parental behavior was different for the two sexes was in the administration of discipline. Boys were clearly found to receive more physical punishment than girls (Maccoby and Jacklin, 1974). One study provided an interesting explanation. The sequence of maternal acts leading up to punishment of the child was analyzed, and it was found that mothers tend to escalate their pressure on the child if their first request for compliance with a request is not obeyed. The mother then raises her voice, or removes the child if it is a dangerous situation, or spanks. Girls were more likely than boys to obey the first request, thus avoiding more spankings (Minton *et al.*, 1971). Also, it is likely that boys simply do more things that draw parental wrath. If boys are more aggressive, and parents are working to teach the child other ways to settle problems, then boys would come in for a greater share of parental punitiveness. In addition, parents do see boys as tougher and girls as more fragile, and thus might be less likely to restrain themselves when they feel the child needs to be punished.

Few studies bear on the ways that fathers treat children, or on differences in fathers' and mothers' treatment of boys and girls. But those that do so reveal some interesting cross-sex effects. In general, parents seem to be more permissive with children of the other sex, and more strict with children of their own sex. In the area of aggression, mothers tend to be more tolerant of angry behavior directed toward them by sons than by daughters; fathers react in the reverse (Rothbart and Maccoby, 1066). Fathers were much more repressive toward expression of anger by sons (Block, 1973). Fathers were also more likely to take their daughter's part in an argument with a guest, but if a son argued with a guest, fathers would take the guest's side (Lambert *et al.,* 1971).

Why should parents be more strict with children of their own sex and more lenient with children of the other sex? The father-son interaction may be a recapitulation of male dominance struggles. That is, the father is reacting to the son as a male who is challenging him, whereas a daughter is no such threat. The daughter, in fact, would benefit in this case from the probability that her father was socialized to be gentle with girls. As for mothers' greater tolerance for their sons, women are accustomed to use moderation in their re-actions to male threat, and perhaps this conditioning comes into play when they are confronted with boys' flouting of their authority. A challenge from another female could be more openly dealt with (Maccoby and Jacklin, 1974).

In general, where parents are concerned, it seems that boys re-ceive more socialization pressure than girls do. Their behavior is subject to more and stricter sanctions. While there are fewer dif-ferences in the ways that parents treat sons and daughters than was once thought, where differences do occur, with boys they are in the direction of greater coerciveness and less tolerance for violations of sex-role prescriptions. Apparently, it is more important for a boy to be all boy than for a girl to be all girl.

Other influences

As children grow, other sources of influence beyond home and family converge to strengthen sex-typing of the socialization process. Television, books, and school provide models for them, instructing them in how they ought to be and behave, informing them in count-less ways, often indirectly, of the values of the society and of its ex-pectations of them as females and males.

A popular educational television show for preschool children was widely acclaimed when it appeared in the early 1970s. But a feminist critique of the show found it pervasively sexist, portraying girls and women in traditional stereotypes (Bergman, 1974). Girls played with doll houses and trailed along after the boys; mothers (all the women were mothers) wore aprons and made tortillas. Watched regularly by millions of children, the show taught them not only the alphabet and the number system but also culturally approved sex roles.

A study of prize-winning children's picture books concluded that the females were dull and stereotyped, neat and passive, their status determined primarily by their relationship to males—*wife* of a king, *admirer* of an explorer, *helper* of a worker. Working mothers and divorced women did not exist. "The world of picture books never tells little girls that as women they might find fulfillment outside of their homes or through intellectual pursuits. Women in the books are excluded from the world of sports, politics, and science. Their future occupational world is presented as consisting primarily of glamour and service" (Weitzman *et al.*, 1972, p. 1146).

A popular line of children's books sold by the millions in supermarkets and drug stores includes a story of a small boy and girl fantasizing about the future (Vogel, 1968):

1. He will be a baker, an icing expert. She will be the baker's wife.
2. He will be a mailman, delivering surprise packages. She looks, listens, says nothing.
3. He will be an explorer in the jungle, and will bring back a lion. She will curl the lion's mane in her beauty shop for animals.
4. He will be a policeman. She will wear a disguise and be his helper.
5. He will be a doctor. She will be a nurse.
6. He will be a fireman. She will be rescued by him.
7. He will be a deep-sea diver. She will be a mermaid and serve him tea and ice cream.
8. He will be an artist. She will be a singer. As he paints, three of the four people watching him are females. As she sings, all her admirers are birds.
9. He will be an astronaut and go to the moon. She will be there, prepared to serve him moonburgers.

All nine of his fantasies have the potential to be realized. They are real occupations for which people are trained and paid. Of hers, only three seem to have even the slightest vocational potential: nurse, singer, and animal groomer. In the others, she marries him, helps him, and serves his food. And is a victim if the house catches on fire.

When boys and girls start school, they do not need to make any adjustments in their previously acquired perceptions of sex roles. A ten-year study of 554 stories in readers for elementary school revealed that men and boys continued to outnumber females in the new editions, and role stereotypes were if anything stronger. While more occupations for women appeared in the newer editions, they were still far from reflecting reality, especially where women were concerned (Graebner, 1972). An extensive study of nearly three thousand stories in over one hundred readers for grades one through six found the following sex ratios:

Boy-centered stories to girl-centered stories	5:2
Adult male main characters to adult female main characters	3:1

Male biographies to female biographies	6:1
Male animal to female animal stories	2:1
Male folk or fantasy stories to female folk or fantasy stories	4:1

These readers do much more than teach reading. Those traits valued as positive and desirable in our society are displayed by the protagonists most of whom are male. Boys are clever, brave, creative, and resourceful; girls are docile, kind, dependent, and self-abnegating. Fathers solve problems, and take the children (boys) hunting and fishing. Mothers are the perfect servants, disgruntled sometimes but always on call. "The reader mother is a limited, colorless, mindless creature. She wants nothing for herself you have to assume, since her needs are mentioned only once in this entire study when she treats herself to some earrings on a shopping trip" (*Women on Words and Images*, 1972, p. 26).

That exposure to sex-role learning is effective was demonstrated in a study of first- and second-grade boys and girls who were asked what they wanted to be when they grew up and what they thought they would really be when they grew up. In answer to the first question, boys mentioned eighteen different occupations, most frequently football player and policeman. Girls named only eight, most frequently nurse and teacher. One girl said she wanted to be a doctor. Answers to both questions reflected traditional sex-typed aspirations. The girl who wanted to be a doctor, when asked the second question, thought she might really be a sales clerk (Looft, 1971).

A recent study of major fields by sex at a large state university in the Southeast provided some interesting data on the later effects of sex typing of roles and of socialization practices relevant to career choice (Fisher, 1974). Majors with high female enrollment included Dance, Speech Communication (Theater), French, Nursing, Rehabilitation Counseling, and Early Childhood and Elementary Education. The only major in the College of Education which had fewer than 20 percent women was Administration and Supervision. Other majors with fewer than 20 percent female enrollment included Medicine, Political Science, and Engineering. All the others with low female enrollment were in the colleges of Natural Science and Business.

Thus the majors with highest female enrollment are those which imply roles of expressiveness, verbal skills, and nurturance of the young and the sick. However, the high proportion of females in these areas reflects not only their appeal for women but their lack of appeal for men. Such observations on young adults of both sexes show clearly the results of differential treatment and expectations applied earlier in the life span.

While it is easy to document institutional pressures for sex-typing of activities, interests, and roles, and the stereotypes that arise therefrom, their persistence and implications need to be considered also. Schools as institutions of society tend to support the status quo, and despite the idealism of their goals, they do not necessarily initiate innovations that will lead to social change. Schools in general are conservatories of the past, and they change in the wake of social change—they do not initiate it.

The authority structure of the school itself is a model for the larger society. The large majority of elementary teachers are female, but most principals are male. When children misbehave they are sent to the principal, the ultimate authority figure.

Children spend a very large amount of their time in the classroom interacting with each other and with their teachers. The teacher is the representative of the adult society. Does she behave differently toward boys and girls, and if so, what does this mean for the subsequent development of the child? A review of the few studies in this area supports an affirmative response to the first question. Boys were the recipients of more blame for disobedience than girls, but they also received more positive attention. Girls exceeded boys on disapproval for lack of knowledge. When teachers were asked to describe incidents in which they had rewarded creative behavior, of those mentioning sex, 74 percent involved boys, and 26 percent girls (Sears and Feldman, 1974).

Different experiences should have different effects. Boys have more difficulty adjusting to the requirements of the school situation for disciplined, conforming behavior, thus making greater demands on the teacher's attention. But attention, both positive and negative, can have reinforcing effects, can confirm feelings of importance, and encourage a certain resistiveness to authority which goes with motives for autonomy and independence. For girls, criticism for lack of knowledge (even though they make better grades) could have a negative effect upon self-esteem and undermine confidence in their ability and worth. Further, the "feminine" behaviors rewarded by teachers and schools seem to be just what girls do not need for future achievement. In addition, studies show that nonconformity with that role is associated with higher IQ, and that the girl whose IQ increases from ages six to ten is likely to be competitive, independent, and dominant (Baumrind, 1972).

It is unfortunate that personality qualities such as autonomy, assertiveness, competitiveness, and initiative have been consistently called masculine in the literature, while others such as conforming, dependent, passive, nurturant, and sensitive have been labeled feminine. It may be that more males are described by the former, and more females by the latter, so that it became expedient to use such terms, subsuming a whole array of characteristics under the words *masculine* and *feminine*. But such usage is not only sexist,[2] reinforcing the relationship between socially valued characteristics and males, it also encourages the notion that if girls are going to fulfill their potential, they must become more masculine. The emotional and value loading of the word *masculine* when applied to females may itself mediate resistance to permitting or encouraging the display of these traits in girls. Since sex itself is not a personality characteristic, should we not recast our formulations to consider what traits in what strengths combine in individuals tő effect a wide range of healthy personalities distinguished by many diversities not necessarily linked to sex?

Achievement: Conflict and Resolution

The finding that women do not attain to the level of their intellectual and creative potential echoes with a dreary sameness through the literature on achievement. In 1913, Castle undertook a statistical study of the thousand most eminent women of history but found that in all of recorded time there were not many women who could be called eminent by any reasonable criteria (Castle, 1913). A classic longitudinal study of gifted children begun in 1921 showed that the girls were more gifted artistically, and the seven most talented writers were girls. But when these gifted children grew up, all the eminent artists and writers among them were men (Terman *et al.,* 1947; 1959). As adults, almost half the men were professionals in high-level occupations. Only 11 percent of the women were in professions, mostly teaching. Many of the women had made their most notable achievement in their selection of a mate. Their husbands were the achievers.[3]

Many reasons have been advanced for this ubiquitous phenome-

[2] Prejudice or bias operating to favor one sex over the other; a discriminatory practice based on stereotypes; for example, the exclusion of women from certain roles, occupations, or activities because of beliefs about their physical and psychological attributes.

[3] It has been suggested both facetiously and seriously that one reason for the dearth of females among the achievers is that women don't have wives. Edwin H. Land, inventor of the Polaroid camera, said in an interview (Bello, 1959) that he found it important to work intensively for long hours when he was approaching a solution to a difficult problem. "You are handling so many variables at a barely conscious level that you can't afford to be interrupted. If you are, it may take a year to cover the same ground you could otherwise cover in sixty hours." For most married women, life is a history of interruptions. One of my older students told me that on weekends when everyone was at home, whatever *she* was doing was the least important of all the ongoing activities—she was the most interruptible. Even the dog knew it!

non. During the nineteenth century, spurred by the discoveries of Charles Darwin, many writers promoted the hypothesis of greater male variability in such attributes as intelligence and creativity (Shields, 1975). That is, more males are found at both the high and the low end of the ability spectrum. This doctrine explained both the finding that more men were in institutions for the mentally retarded and also the common observation that many more men were among the achievers, the eminent, and the creative. The hypothesis of greater male variability has not been seriously challenged as yet, though alternative explanations have gained more credence. The preponderance of males at the low end of the mental ability spectrum is well documented and is explicable on the basis of the greater male vulnerability to congenital defects and early brain trauma discussed in the last chapter. The difference at the upper end of the spectrum can be explained as a reflection of the differences between women's and men's lives—as a social artifact. Evidence of innate differences in variability in intelligence or creativity is lacking. The literature on sex differences in variability reveals that boys were more variable, that is, more scored very high and very low, on tests of spatial and numerical ability, but they were not more variable on measures of creativity (Maccoby and Jacklin, 1974). If as many girls as boys are creative in their youth, then the greater creativity of males in later life would have to be explained on grounds other than innate characteristics which would determine that men are more talented than women, or that more men than women are talented.

Genius is rare in any population. For its quality to become manifest, motivation, opportunity, training, and tools must be available. It seems reasonable to believe that such a combination has been more probable for males than for females in the history of civilization. For example, Anne, a seventeenth-century queen of England for whom life must have been more propitious than for the average woman at that time, had ten miscarriages and gave birth to five infants, only one of whom survived his first year, and he died at age eleven. One of her biographers tells us that "she took no interest in the art, the drama, or the literature of her day" (Yorke and Thomson, 1958). The twentieth-century British novelist Virginia Woolf, in *A Room Of One's Own*, imagined that Shakespeare had an equally talented sister named Judith. What would her fate have been? She was "not sent to school. She had no chance of learning grammar and logic, let alone of reading Virgil and Horace. She picked up a book now and then, one of her brother's perhaps, and read a few pages. But then her parents came in and told her to mend the stockings or mind the stew and not moon about with books and papers" (quoted in Rossi, 1973, p. 639). To escape an arranged marriage, Woolf thought, she would have run away to London as did her brother; but there, she would have been laughed at for her ambitions, and denied training in her craft. "No girl could have walked to London and stood at a stage door and forced her way into the presence of actor-managers without doing herself a violence and suffering an anguish . . ." (p. 641).

Observations of sex differences in high-level achievement reveal effects not causes, and cannot really answer the questions posed by woman's lesser productivity away from the home. "Very few women have ever had the opportunity to enter this world and fewer still have been admitted fully to it. For most of human history most women have spent most of their adult lives gestating, nursing, and caring for small children, these functions preempting their entire lives. They were ignored for all high-level purposes, shut out from the world that supplied the conditions of productivity. They are only now beginning to enter it and even yet there are many barriers" (Bernard, 1973).

This scenario of the fate of the capable woman has been documented in countless lives. In the past decade researchers have become attentive not only to discrimination and lack of opportunity as deterrents to female achievement, but also to elements in the socialization process which give rise to a number of interlocking hypotheses. While boys identify with a culturally defined masculine role, which includes an achievement yardstick by which they will be evaluated, girls identify with their mothers, most of whom have not achieved independently outside the home. Girls are more dependent upon the reward value of interpersonal relationships, thus they work for love and approval rather than for the intrinsic value of the achievement itself. Girls and women are assigned the social roles of providing nurture and compassion to other members of society, and the domestic setting is a natural stage for the display of these qualities. The prevalent mores are such that males do not like to compete with females. This provides negative consequences for girls who dare, such as loss of popularity and denial to them of social perquisites reserved for conforming women. Great difficulties lie in the path of the young woman with potential who decides to use it to the fullest. Not only will she encounter the remnants of sex discrimination, but the combination of the demands of a family and the demands of a career on time and energy are impossible for many, entailing at best the loss of a few years in her career development while babies are young. Confined to home for those years, her confidence in her ability diminishes. If she decides later to make a commitment away from home, she may be plagued by guilt and anxiety, and so settle for a role which is less demanding.

It has been suggested that contrasts between the experiences of females and males are rapidly diminishing along with a depolarization of sex roles (Winick, 1969). But if work roles are becoming disengaged from sex, little effect was noted in a study in which the responses of fifth-graders revealed their views of career and employment patterns, and of home and family responsibilities to be highly traditional. When given a list of jobs and asked whether men, women, or both should perform them, a majority of both sexes thought that bosses, taxi drivers, mayors, factory workers, and lawyers should be men, and that nurses and house cleaners should be women. Asked to indicate who does what around the house, they held that women wash dishes, cook, dust, scrub floors, and get up at night with a sick child. The men's list was shorter—they pay bills, fix things, and work in the yard. Career aspirations of the children also reflected traditional sex typing. The boys wanted to be engineers, professionals or sportsmen; the girls, teachers, nurses, and stewardesses. Only 6 percent said they would be a mother or housewife only. But when asked to describe how they would spend a typical day when they were grown up, most of the girls emphasized marriage and family life in their descriptions, while the boys overwhelmingly ignored it, focusing instead on details of job and career (Iglitzin, 1972). While it would be difficult to find evidence for a blurring of sex roles in these data, we may note that, while girls no more than boys took an innovative posture, more of them were willing to see jobs open to both sexes, could see both parents performing household tasks, and assigned similar personality traits to both sexes.

The task of answering the question What do I want to be? is probably less conflict-ridden for ten-year-old girls than for their older sisters who are closer to the time of choosing. The younger girl is still free to imagine the future in any way she likes. And if her statement of what she wants to be does not mesh with her vision of a typical day in her future as an adult, it is of no consequence. The contingencies and the payoffs of the choices she will make are still far from clear to her, and she can comfortably tolerate the ambiguities and contradictions in her fantasies.

Let us consider two revealing and touching examples, one from science, the other from literature. A ten-year-old girl in the above study said that she wanted to be an artist, or maybe a beautician. When asked to look into the future, and describe a typical day of her adult life, she wrote:

> I would start the morning after getting out of bed by eating breakfast. Then I would clean house. If I was done before lunch I would probably visit a friend. Then eat lunch. After lunch I would go shopping. Then I would come home and rest for a while. When my husband came home (if I was married) he would probably tell me how his day

went and I would tell him how mine went. If he was in a real good mood he would take me out to dinner. When we were done with dinner we would go to a movie. Then we would go home and go to bed (Iglitzin, 1972).

Where in this regimen is the painting of pictures or the dressing of hair? I suspect that the discontinuity lies in the available responses evoked by the questions. The question to a ten-year-old, What do you want to be, opens to her the whole spectrum of occupations observed by her thus far, and invites her to choose one. By this time she has a global idea from the media and from the various commentaries available to her of the activities associated with certain jobs, and she chooses on the basis of that knowledge. But when asked to visualize a typical day in her future, she falls back on her observations of what real women really do. What other data has she? We should not read into this a doom-saying prescience of little girls saying: I want to be Leonardo, but I will settle to be La Gioconda.

"A Child's Day" is a short story by contemporary novelist Jessamyn West, about a young girl who elected to stay home while her family went on a day's outing. She could hardly wait until they were gone so she could begin her private activities. She made lists of beautiful phrases from Shelley and of words from the dictionary and copied her own original poems in her notebook:

> I was lithe and had dreams;
> Now I am fat and have children.

As the day wore on, she gave up on the poetry and went into her mother's room where she took off her clothes and wrapped her body in her mother's black lace fascinator. Admiring her image in the mirror, she began thinking of him who was yet to come:

> She loaned him her eyes that he might see her, and to her flesh she gave this gift of his seeing. She raised her arms and slowly turned and her flesh was warm with his seeing. Somberly and quietly she turned and swayed and gravely touched now thigh, now breast, now cheek, and looked and looked with eyes she had given him.

She thought that she might be evil, might be faithless to the imaginary one, and she trembled with pity for him. Finally, having exhausted the possibilities of this drama, she looked into the mirror and said, "There is nothing I will not touch. I am Minta. I will know everything." Then she went into the kitchen and made the oyster soup for her family, who had returned after the long day.

One sees in Minta the fluctuations of mood and interest, the trying on of various selves, the intense narcissism which are part of the adolescent experience. But most striking is the passion for the uses of intelligence, for words and poetry. This passion is so strong that "they would enter her veins through her palms," giving way to a flood of romantic fantasy, conjuring the one who would come.

The motif of ambivalence and conflict in the development of identity and personality in the young woman has attracted considerable theoretical interest (Bardwick, 1971; Douvan, 1970; Mednick *et al.*, 1975). The culture prompts her very early to become sensitive to the responses of others, and to evaluate herself accordingly. She learns to be and to behave in ways that will maximize for her the powerful rewards of love, admiration, and approval. But to the extent that her self-esteem and sense of self become dependent upon such rewards, she is dependent upon the presence of significant others for their delivery, and she fails to develop internal criteria for an evaluation and definition of her self. Thus, she remains tentative in outline so that she may adapt more easily to the man she marries whose personality is as yet unknown. While such an adaptation to a future contingency does not necessarily lead to conflict, it does represent the deflection of considerable energy into the motivation to form affiliative relationships, within which her needs for positive response and affirmation of herself by others can be met.

At the same time however, middle-class girls as well as their brothers live in a society which values competence, mastery of skills, and achievement in the educational and vocational areas. To the extent that a girl is intellectually capable and has acquired these values, she can be expected to respond to early rewards for appropriate accomplishment by the development of a motive to achieve. Achievement by the young in our society is defined in terms of academic excellence, or mastery in a special interest area, such as music or sports. Since education is seen as crucial, and since all children go to school, successful achievement in that area is seen as highly desirable by parents and teachers and probably not less so for daughters than for sons. Now one can turn one's capabilities to, let us say, academic achievement for two possible reasons. While they are not mutually exclusive, they may have differential strength as motivators. They are the pleasure of doing something well for its own sake, achieving an internalized standard of excellence—in Keats's words, the fascination of what's difficult; or the approval, recognition, and benevolent warmth which the achievement brings from others. Thus the bright girl conditioned already to seek out the latter can work hard and do well in school in the service of her affiliative needs without experiencing conflict between the two modes of behavior.

But as she grows older, social pressure becomes very great to conform to a feminine image and to set for herself the eternal feminine goals of finding a mate and making a home. Now she is faced with a paradox because the feminine image does not include the display of intelligence, competence, and skill mastery, nor is it compatible with the high-level academic or vocational achievement. If she persists in manifesting these characteristics in the pursuit of such goals she may perceive herself and be perceived by others as unfeminine, and she may be unable to reconcile her achievement orientation with her interpersonal needs. Because successful achievement threatens to interfere with or to preclude successful affiliation leading to identity and performance as wife and mother, any serious contemplation of it as a major part of one's life style is productive of anxiety and avoidance. The threat consists of two major obstacles, the evidence for which is all around her. First, if her successful achievement is unfeminine, then men will not find her desirable, and second, high achievement calls for difficult preparation and sustained effort, which may require deferral of affiliative goals.

Achievement tends to be redefined for girls as they grow older with the most drastic change occurring during puberty. During their school years, the ways that girls can achieve are not drastically different from those for boys. A girl who makes good grades, takes a leadership role in school activities, and is acceptable to her peers is praised for achievement just as the boy is for doing the same things. During and after puberty, however, new patterns of behavior take on achievement meaning for girls. Social skills, physical attractiveness, and popularity all become goals to which most girls clearly aspire, and which, while they are still in school, are not inconsistent with academic or leadership goals. These goals, highly salient during the pubertal years, comprise in themselves an area of achievement concern with its own standard of excellence (Stein and Bailey, 1973). This development, combining with pressure to conform to feminine role definitions and low expectations for adult female achievement in male terms, effects for many developing women a redefinition of achievement with its own standards and goals, very different from those of men and of her own childhood. While noticeable striving may simply drop out of some females' repertoire, it may often be manifested in activities that are at least partially congruent with the feminine role. Such achievement behavior, while compatible with affiliative needs, is not simply a corollary to them but is itself a visible result of an internalized standard of excellence. While achievement is usually defined by what men do, many women may be just as strongly motivated to achieve different goals: interpersonal competence, an attractive, effective self, and, later, a harmonious, well-run household and healthy children, to mention just a few.

But the intellectually capable woman may not be able to smoothly deflect her achievement motive into this channel. She may perceive that she must make a choice or at best a compromise. And since social pressures and her own affiliative needs are important, her sensing of the consequences of competitive achievement may give rise to the motive to avoid success (Horner, 1970; 1974).

The motive to avoid success is a stable personality characteristic which develops early in life as part of the learning of standards of sex-role identity. The explanation for the motive is given by expectancy/value theory, which proposes that the strength and direction of one's behavior are determined by the belief or expectation one has about the probability and consequences of one's behavior and by the value which one places on these consequences. According to the theory anxiety is aroused when one expects negative consequences to ensue from certain actions. The anxiety then functions to inhibit the behavior expected to have negative consequences. Thus for women, if success is seen to have negative consequences, actions or behavior which are pertinent to it arouse anxiety which in turn inhibits them. The motive to avoid success, then, is a disposition of women to avoid behavior which will have negative consequences such as rejection or threat to one's feminine image.

Now it should be clear that the motive to avoid success is of variable potency in individuals, and may be absent altogether. It tended to be most important in bright women who had incorporated achievement as a value. If a woman does not desire to achieve and is incapable of doing so, then the behaviors leading to the inhibitory anxiety would not occur (Horner, 1974). A recent review of fear-of-success studies, however, reported that direct tests of the relationship between ability and fear of success do not support the theory (Mednick & Weissman, 1975). That is, one cannot conclude that the brighter the woman the more fearful she is of success.

More recent studies have examined the effects of mixed-sex competition on performance of women who are high or low in the motive to avoid success. Performance on achievement tasks was measured in a competitive mixed-sex situation, and compared to subsequent performance in a noncompetitive situation where achievement was relevant only to the task and to the subjects' internalized standards of accomplishment. Female subjects who were high in the motive to avoid success did significantly less well in the competitive than in the noncompetitive situation, while those who were low, and most of the men, did better in the competitive condition (Horner, 1974).

Thus a motive to avoid success, especially in competition with males, may be important in the personality dynamics of many bright young women. And for them it means that sights will be set shorter, potential will be unfulfilled, talents will be wasted, and society will be poorer. At the same time some capable women do not show a fear of success and proceed to display achievement and to compete on an equal basis with males. What could account for the difference in fear-of-success motivational strength in women? What developmental events might promote a high dependence on love and approval and a fear that noncomformity with sex-role standards will lead to their withdrawal?

One theory holds that the female child is not adequately encouraged for early independence striving and for the development of an identity separate from her mother (Hoffman, 1972). This theory and the data supporting it are highly relevant to findings both on achievement motivation and success-avoidance motivation in women. Freedom from crippling emotional dependence on the approval and good will of others and a sense of oneself as an autonomous person clearly underlie the kind of commitment and willingness to extend oneself to take risks that characterize the high achiever.

Independence and competence are personality characteristics laid down in childhood as a function of the child's experience with her caretakers and with her environment. Her optimum development occurs when the child has a secure emotional base in a warm, nurturant parent who permits exploration, encourages independent action, and is not too protective. Dependent orientation can result from parental behavior which threatens the child's security, such as neglect or rejection, and also from overprotectiveness and failure or delay in providing experiences which encourage independence striving. The development of a sense of self occurs as the child increasingly becomes able to perform independent acts, to do things for herself, and to experience herself as a competent person.

Some studies show that parents are more protective of girls and grant them independence at a later age than they do boys (Hoffman, 1972). Since children pick up attitudes of their caretakers, it is not unreasonable to infer from such findings that girls begin under these conditions to sense themselves as less able and as more fragile and thus more in need of support and reassurance from others. Such rewards then become necessary for security, and any threat of their loss is anxiety provoking.

Related to the development of autonomy and sense of self are studies showing that strong mother-feminine identification is maladaptive both for psychological well-being and for achievement. Thus the daughter who is able to separate early from her mother and to develop confidence in her own coping abilities may later be more willing to test herself and to risk negative consequences in the pursuit of a valued goal. Indeed, the Fels longitudinal study found that

"maternal hostility" was positively related to later achievement behavior in girls, while maternal protection and warmth related positively to boys' achievement (Kagan and Moss, 1962). This does not
mean that cold, rejecting mothers are good for girls. Rather, it is
likely that a mother-son interaction which is seen as perfectly normal
may be perceived as hostile when the child is female. This explanation reflects again the problem of comparing the sexes on some
dimension in which the norms for males and females are different.
It is highly probable that there is some optimum combination of
parental support, encouragement of independence, and gentle
disengagement which results in a self-confident, competent, non-
anxious person whose sex is incidental.

The Development of Competence in Girls

A study of socialization strategies and patterns of childrearing which
facilitate the development of competence and mature independence
revealed four patterns of parental authority (Baumrind, 1972):

1. The authoritative parent who exercises firm control and sets
   limits, but values autonomous self-will and recognizes the child's
   individuality. This parent encourages verbal give and take, so-
   licits the child's opinions, and gives reasons for policy decisions.
2. The authoritarian parent who values obedience, restricts autonomy, uses punitive control, and believes that the child should
   accept the parent's word as final authority.
3. The permissive parent, affirmative and accepting, presenting
   her or himself to the child as a resource to be used as the child
   wishes. The belief of this parent is that the child should be free
   of all restraints except those required for physical safety.
4. The harmonious parent, who has control but does not exercise
   it. The child seems to know intuitively what the parent would
   want, thus the parent does not need to direct or command.

The difference between the authoritative and the harmonious
parent may be more of degree than of kind. That is, the former may
represent a higher level of interaction between members of the family or simply more explicit presentation by the parent of what her or
his expectations are. It seems reasonable to believe that the harmonious style can be an evolution from the authoritative. That is, a
parent who was authoritative with a very young child can gradually
abandon explicit controls when the child has learned what the
parent's expectations are. In any case, neither the permissive nor the
authoritarian model of parental authority promotes instrumental

competence in girls because both shield and overprotect her, the one by placing no demands on her, the other by so structuring her life that she never learns to make her own decisions. With neither type of parent can she experience the anxiety of nonconformity because in the permissive situation nothing is defined as nonconforming and in the authoritarian setting nonconformity is not allowed. Thus, she has no opportunity to learn to handle such anxiety or to become desensitized to it. By contrast, in the harmonious and the authoritative families the child's personhood is valued and respected, and competent, autonomous behavior is not only sanctioned but expected. In the course of testing limits and trying out autonomous behavior the child inevitably experiences the anxiety that comes from violation of norms—but she also learns the nature of real consequences and can make rational choices from the range of alternatives.

What are specific ways in which instrumental competence can be developed in girls? To ask the question should not imply that girls need a different kind of preparation than boys need, but it does point up the possibility that more conscious attention may be required for such a result in girls, who are less likely than boys to be assisted in the acquisition of such skills by prevailing social pressures. Girls should be taught to compete in sports and other contests and to win and lose gracefully (Baumrind, 1972). Also, girls can learn to be assertive in defense of their persons and their rights as individuals. This does not mean an obnoxious insistence upon having one's own way all the time or a selfish disregard for others, but it does mean having a clarity of vision into the merits of a situation, so that one can rationally insist upon justice, and not need to fall back upon a plea for mercy. Finally, girls should be socialized to assert their individuality and to be independent of pressures either to conform or to rebel. The independent person does not display a mindless obedience to illegal authority or a conformity to irrelevant social norms, nor does she resist or violate them purely as a response to peer and other pressures to do so.

Instrumental competence is a drab phrase to describe the development of skills and powers which can enormously expand the experience and enrich life for all humans. John Stuart Mill, speaking more than a century ago of the benefits of the extension of full equality to women, said that for them it would mean the difference "between a life of subjection to the will of others, and a life of rational freedom. After the primary necessities of food and raiment, freedom is the strongest want of human nature. . ." (1973, p. 238). At the same time the American poet Walt Whitman had a vision of women who are

. . . not one jot less than I am
They are tann'd in the face by shining sun and blowing winds,
Their flesh has the old, divine suppleness and strength,
They know how to swim, row, ride, wrestle, shoot, run, strike, retreat,
    advance, resist, defend themselves,
They are ultimate in their own right. They are calm, clear, well
    possess'd of themselves (p. 117).

Surely, to be ultimate in one's own right is what instrumental competence is all about.

Values and Interests

The values and interests of females collectively are different in important, measurable ways from those of males in this society. Several
decades ago a scale to measure the strength of certain values in the
individual's personality was developed (Allport and Vernon, 1931).
Adopted from the earlier work of Spranger, a German philosopher,
the values are defined as follows:

theoretical: interest in the discovery of truth; a critical, rational,
    "intellectual" approach;
economic: emphasis on useful, practical things; a "hardheaded"
    approach;
esthetic: valuing form and harmony; enjoyment of grace, sym-
    metry, and fitness;
social: interest in helping people, in philanthropy; altruistic;
political: valuing personal power, influence, and renown;
religious: concern with the unity of experience; mystical; seeking
    to understand the universe as a whole.

Studies using this scale have consistently found large sex differences
in all the values. Women are much higher in esthetic, social, and
religious interests, while men show more strength in theoretical, economic, and political areas (see Figure 6.1). It is not difficult to see
the relationship between these values that women hold and the kinds
of work and activities that they usually do. But even when males and
females of similar ability are engaged in the same kind and level of
activity, their values and interests are different as are the personality
characteristics they bring to the situation.

One study investigated the abilities, interests, and values in
seven hundred girls and thirteen hundred boys taking a high-school
physics course in an attempt to shed some light on the matter of the
paucity of women in science and their relative lack of eminent ac-

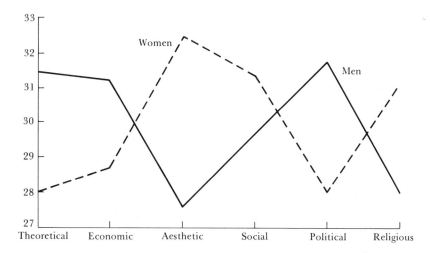

Figure 6.1 Composite psychographs of adult men and women on the Allport-Vernon study of values. (Allport and Vernon, 1931.)

complishment. Since physics is seen as a masculine subject and relatively few girls take it, one might expect that those who do would be more similar to males in their values and interests. But a comparison of Figure 6.1 with Figure 6.2 shows that the large sex differences in values observed in a general population were just as prominent for

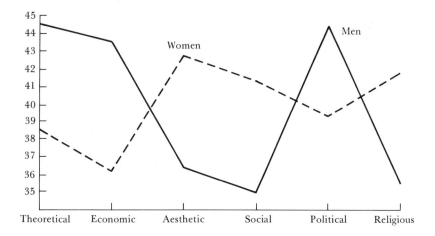

Figure 6.2 Mean scores of male and female high school physics students on the Allport, Vernon, and Lindzey study of values. (Allport, Vernon, and Lindzey, [1960]. Data from Walberg [1969].)

physics students almost four decades later (Walberg, 1969).[4] The girls scored higher than the boys on Esthetic, Social, and Religious, results implying, respectively, greater valuing of form and harmony, greater interest in people, and more concern with the unity of experience and with mysticism. The largest differences between the sexes were on Economic and Social values. The author thought that this difference might reflect the students' preoccupations during the last year of high school: boys' thought of making a living and girls' concern for homemaking and family life.

Furthermore, this highly selected sample of girls (their mean IQ was 118, significantly higher than the boys' 113) differed from the boys in their self-initiated scientific activities. They liked to participate in activities involving nature study and the applications of science to everyday life, like collecting insects or bird nests and learning about nutrition and how the body uses food. The boys were more likely to show interest in cosmic questions of time, space, gravity and to spend some time in scientific tinkering with machines and electronic equipment. Girls were more interested in the life sciences and their application, boys in abstract ideation and the physical manipulation of objects.

Medicine, another field which is atypical for women, might also be expected to attract persons with common values and interests, regardless of sex. But a study of seven consecutive classes of entering medical students found that the women differed from the men in ways similar to those observed in other studies of more typical samples (Cartwright, 1972). They saw themselves as more willing to express feelings, and to admit weaknesses, and less likely to endorse the extremes of dominant and aggressive behavior. On personality tests they were more responsible, more highly socialized, and more tolerant. They were more sensitive to relationship values, and more alert to moral and ethical issues. While the direction of all these variables seems typically linked to their sex, two were the opposite of a prediction based on sex: the women valued independence and individuality more highly than did their male colleagues. But the independence and nonconformity which probably facilitated their choice of an atypical career coexisted in their value system with concerns which have traditionally been more characteristic of women.

Thus the values and interests of women, even of those in atypical fields, distinguish them from men. These characteristics, as well as social prejudices and lack of opportunity, may have mitigated

---

[4] The score ranges on the ordinates of Figures 6.1 and 6.2 are different because a revised form of the instrument was used for the latter study.

against their emergence in any numbers among the eminent creators of civilization. In a study of creative scientists, thirteen distinguishing traits were found (Taylor and Barron, 1963). Another study of sex differences of physics students revealed that seven of those thirteen traits distinguished the males from the females in the samples (Walberg, 1969): 1. a high degree of autonomy and self-sufficiency; 2. a preference for manipulations involving things rather than people, a detached attitude in interpersonal relations; 3. a high degree of personal dominance, but a dislike for personally toned controversy; 4. a high degree of impulse control, with relatively little inclination to talkativeness, gregariousness, or impulsivity; 5. a liking for abstract thinking; 6. rejection of group pressures toward conformity; and 7. interest in trying oneself in uncertain circumstances in which one's own effort can be the deciding factor. To the extent that these traits distinguish not only creative scientists but also males, from females in scientific fields, there is a discontinuity, at least in science, between women's characteristic traits and values, and those distinguishing persons who become noted for creative achievement.

Finally, even male and female professors in universities have different values relating to their profession (Bernard, 1964). Women academics are more likely to show concern for developing students, for promoting scholarship, and for providing service to the institutions. Men are more concerned with academic prestige and institutional power.

Though interests and values sometimes change drastically during adolescence, they become fairly stable attributes of the person in adulthood. Learned under the conditions of experience and socialization, they influence behavior and contribute to its direction. Attempts to understand and to explain the differential roles and outcomes for females and males can be enriched by considering the differences in what is important to them, what they care about.

Familial and social processes shape the experience of a girl in ways that result in special outcomes for her. Identification with her own sex and with its characteristic role is learned early by most girls. Her socialization gives her perceptions and learnings that show her clearly where her "place" will be. As she matures, she may find that she has to make choices that boys do not need to, and that something of herself gets lost in the process. By adulthood the values and interests of women are very different from those of men, and while these interests are functional for the role women are socialized for, of themselves they may be inadequate for other kinds of achievement in the larger world.

It is surely not accidental that women occupy few positions of leadership and power in the society. Two major explanations have been advanced to account for this. One rests on the greater aggressiveness of the male which serves practically to insure that more men than women will seek those positions which carry with them some degree of power over others. If, as seems probable, male aggression has a biological base, then this explanation would suggest that male dominance is inevitable.

On close scrutiny, however, such a causal link between aggression and leadership or the exercise of influence in the society seems rather weak. Our society does not value overt aggression and tries to socialize it out of children of both sexes. The emerging ethos in political and business leadership seems to favor less reliance on the flagrant use of power or show of strength and more emphasis on leading others by defining mutual goals and by cooperative effort, a style of leadership which women might find more to their liking.

In a modern society most roles do not require either high levels of aggression or the ability to forcefully dominate others. Perhaps those that do will continue to be sought after by men more than women. In any case, an explanation based on the idea that men are naturally more aggressive fails to substantially account for the great differences in outcome for girls and boys.

The other major explanation lies in the different sets of experiences of the two sexes as they are socialized to be members of the society. These experiences, by which girls learn to be attractive and pleasing so that they can attract a husband and enter into a domestic and nurturing role, and by which boys learn that they must prepare themselves for positions commensurate with their abilities reflect old and stable needs and values of the society which do not give way easily to pressures for change.

However, as the needs of the society change, so do its values, and the exceptional and the unacceptable become commonplace and acceptable. Society no longer needs to prepare girls for a lifetime of domesticity, and other qualities in addition to those related to expressiveness can now be encouraged and valued. Girls can be socialized to be competent, and when they are both competent and expressive, instead of expressive only, they are psychologically healthier. While little is known about the effect of a comparable balance in males, it is conceivable that both competence and expressiveness, instead of competence only, would result in healthier personalities for them too. As girls and women acquire skills and competencies relevant to the many social roles heretofore held by males, their display of these will become commonplace and accepted, and many will acquire the confidence which, more than aggression, is necessary for leadership. When all conditions for the acquisition of competence and confidence become equal for girls and boys, then we shall see what the contribution of nature to woman's "place" really is.

Sexuality

7

*Just within the very recent past, a decided lifting of the ancient social injunctions
against the free expression of female sexuality has occurred. This unprecedented development is born of the scientific revolution, the product both of efficient contraceptives
and the new social equality and emotional honesty sweeping across the world. . . .*

—Mary Jane Sherfey, *The Nature and Evolution of Female Sexuality,* 1972

The sexual nature and experience of women is rich and complex.
It is often misunderstood and misinterpreted. Women themselves,
young and older, frequently display a lack of knowledge of their
own bodies and capacities for sexual experience which one is
tempted to characterize as a kind of developmental lag. On the other
hand, some women of all ages and of all times have without doubt
enjoyed the discovery and exploration of their own sexuality to the
fullest. In this area of human behavior, females have displayed
greater variability than males. That is, the range of such variables as
frequency of orgasmic response and reported interest in sexual activity is greater for females than for males. For example, it is not uncommon to find that an adult woman has never had an orgasm. At
the other extreme, some women have been known to have had as
many as fifty orgasms in an hour (Masters and Johnson, 1966). It is
probably safe to say that no physically intact adult male has not had
some form of orgasmic experience; nor, on the other hand, has any
male had fifty orgasms in an hour. While there may be in the annals
of human lore reports of exceptions to the above, the research supports the generalization of greater female variability.

Attitudes toward and beliefs about sexuality, as well as sexual
behavior itself, vary widely from culture to culture and from era to
era. Manners of manifesting the sexual drive and the forms and
meanings of its acting out are carefully prescribed and codified in
human societies. These prescriptions and codes are part of the social
learning of the members of a society, though much of the learning
of these is of an informal nature. In Western society, as in most

others, the behavior of women has been more carefully and rigidly defined and regulated than has the behavior of men. In the past, this has had the effect of obscuring the "true nature" of female sexuality. It is only within recent years that a relaxation of sexual codes and the undertaking of serious research into the matter have begun to inform us about the nature and potential of female sexuality.

At the present time we are witnessing an increasing acceptance of the idea of sexual equality and of the individual's right to seek her own personal modes of sexual expression and fulfillment. While these ideas are not new in human history, they are new as an emerging ethos of this generation. They have the potential for providing new insight into old problems of sex and sexual relationships, such as the role of biology in sexual activity, sexual response patterns, sexual behavior as a function of social norms, effects of psychological factors on sexual functions and dysfunctions, and variations from the conventional model of the heterosexual dyad.

While sex and sexuality have always been of interest and concern to humans,[1] the intense search for objective knowledge about them is a feature of contemporary science. Scientific disregard for the subject of sexual behavior reflected prevailing attitudes and mores during the last century especially, for that era generally held that discussion of the subject was taboo, except within a highly moralistic framework whose intention was to describe what was proper and acceptable. In such a climate, scientists and nonscientists alike were constrained by the code of silence and by a belief which rigorously defined both the style and the limits of sexual behavior.

Only Yesterday: The Victorian Context

It has been suggested that "our culture is gradually convalescing from a sexually debilitating disease: Victorianism" (Brecher, 1971, p. 367). It is no novelty to observe that the Victorian era was highly repressive of all aspects of sexuality, but the truly morbid flavor of the middle-class teachings of the times can best be savored by examination of the original sources. The prudery and propriety of the time were exemplified in books and articles on health and hygiene, and in pamphlets on religion and ethics (Haller and Haller, 1974). The prevailing message was chastity, continence, even in marriage, and self-control, which meant denial of sexual desires and avoidance of all temptation, especially for women.

---

[1] For analyses of sexuality in relation to culture, see Katchadourian and Lunde (1975), Marshall and Suggs (1971), and Ford and Beach (1951).

Since sexual intercourse was approved only for the purpose of procreation in the marriage relationship, young girls were admonished to avoid all sources of possible stimulation which might lead to the misstep that would ruin them for life. The worst of these was masturbation, the "solitary vice," which brought the threat of disease, mental derangement, and future childbirth complications. Romantic novels, dancing, and "unnatural" affection for other girls carried the seeds of disaster. They contributed to premature sexual development and introduced girls to impure thoughts and actions for which they would pay dearly later.

The young girl was advised to be passive in relations with males. She was to be courted and pursued, and perhaps caught in marriage, but without any contrivance on her part. Boldness and immodesty were equally deplored mainly because of their effect on the young male, who might lose control and make an improper advance. Male writers warned of the untrustworthiness of males where females were concerned. The tenor of these warnings suggested that male lust was barely held in check, and that it was up to the female to make sure that no provocative act of hers unleashed it.

Many women entered marriage quite ignorant of sex. In fact, one writer said that there were some women into whose minds the thought of sexual intercourse had never entered (Haller and Haller, 1974). The manuals, however, did not dispel such ignorance of the facts. Rather, the emphasis was on avoidance and restraint. Since men were considered naturally aggressive, it was up to the wife to maintain decorum in the marriage bed by her passivity and lack of passion. It was her duty to submit to her husband's embraces, but she must not react with desire or pleasure. Orgasm must be avoided because it interfered with conception, inducing a relaxation and weakness that could lead to barrenness.

Since intercourse was approved only for the purpose of procreation, separate bedrooms were advised to avoid temptation and to cut down on excessive stimulation of the male. The moral dictum which confined sex to reproduction was reinforced by the teaching that excessive ejaculations would have a debilitating effect on the male. On the other hand, reserves of seminal fluid in the conservative male would have a beneficent effect upon his mental activity and productivity.

The derogation of sex as an activity which should be engaged in as seldom as possible and enjoyed not at all by women was a residual of the ascetic doctrine of early Christianity. During the Victorian era, however, it became part of the value system of manners and morals which was supposed to set the middle class apart from such earthier citizens as immigrants and slum dwellers. The effect of such views, widely promulgated by physicians, preachers, and self-appointed moralists, was to generate a climate of attitudes about sexuality whose effects still characterize our "convalescence." We saw in Chapters 2 and 3 how this climate affected psychoanalytic views, especially of female sexuality, and the recognition of its derogatory consequences for women by such observers as Clara Thompson. As early as the turn of the century, however, others began to speak out in dramatic opposition to the approved wisdom, and in the course of time a few works appeared which attempted to introduce objectivity into the discussion and to place sexuality in perspective as an aspect of human behavior worthy of investigation. Sex research gradually became respectable, and information based upon systematic study of sexual phenomena became widely available.

The Study of Human Sexuality

Although the scientific study of sexual behavior began as a mid-twentieth century phenomenon, it has its origins in the turn of the century with the work of Havelock Ellis, an English physician whose *Studies in the Psychology of Sex* were published in six volumes between 1897 and 1910. Ellis's contributions went far beyond clinical study of patients, drawing upon anthropological and medical material, case studies and life histories. His vast collection of data from cultural groups all over the world showed the variability of sexual norms, and it introduced a new idea to the Western world: "Not everyone is like you". Although Ellis endured considerable vilification for his views, he argued for sex education, trial marriage, legal immunity for sexual acts of consenting adults, and removal of sanctions against sexual experimentation.

Emphasizing normal human sexuality, Ellis's findings startlingly presage many findings of contemporary research. Masturbation and other sexual responses appeared early in life and were common for both girls and boys. Women's sexuality reached its peak later than men's and continued strong late into life. The prevalent notion that women had little or no sex drive was a myth. The orgasm was similar for both men and women, but the multiple orgasm was common for women, whose pleasure was enhanced by prolongation of the sex act. Frigidity in women, a common phenomenon at that time, was the result of repression of sexuality in girlhood and male ignorance of female sexuality, particularly the importance of the clitoris.

Ellis was an advocate of sexual equality for women, and he worked for the reform of divorce laws and for the abolition of laws banning the promotion and sale of contraceptive devices. Shortly before his death in 1939—also the year of Freud's death—he expressed his delight that the Victorian attitudes against which he had battled for so long were beginning to change. "I cannot see now a girl walking along the street with her free air, her unswathed limbs, her gay and scanty raiment, without being conscious of a thrill of joy . . . that I am among people that are growing to be gracious and human."[2]

In 1926, a Dutch gynecologist, Theodoor van de Velde, published *Ideal Marriage,* which became one of the best-selling sex manuals of all time. In spite of its quaintly Victorian title, the book was concerned with showing this first post-Victorian generation how to develop and maintain enjoyable sexual relationships. Van de Velde had learned from his patients that love and affection were not enough to insure a good sexual adjustment in marriage. He therefore addressed what he saw as the two most common problems: first, the introduction of the virginal bride to the joys of sexual responsiveness by her loving and desirous (and presumably more experienced) husband; and second, the maintenance of enthusiasm, excitement, and novelty in sex over many long years of marriage. Van de Velde did not concentrate on one sex or the other, but rather was concerned about mutuality in the sex act. He emphasized the importance of the adequate arousal of the woman, and of her need for longer stimulation to achieve orgasm. Many women were capable of and wanted to have several orgasms; the sensitive male would be sure she was satisfied before he reached his climax. Both clitoral and oral-genital stimulation were described in detail. However, van de Velde saw these as acceptable and desirable in foreplay, in preparation for intercourse, but not as substitutes for penile-vaginal orgasm. Even so, he lifted them out of the catalog of perversions. Van de Velde was one of the first to give equal importance to the sexual satisfaction of the woman. If the husband climaxed first, and his wife was not yet satisfied, he should stimulate her genitals manually until she had an orgasm. If this did not work, it was *perfectly acceptable* for her to masturbate herself to her satisfaction. Van de Velde even quoted a Catholic treatise by a French cleric which sanctioned this radical advice.

Another student of female sexual response was Robert Dickinson, an American gynecologist, who with Lura Beam documented the continuing effects of Victorianism in *A Thousand Marriages* (1932), and *The Single Woman* (1934). Based on hundreds of detailed sexual histories of his patients, these books painted a dismal picture of women's sex life in marriage. Dickinson described the character-

[2] Quoted in Brecher (1971), p. 74.

istic coitus as brief and oriented toward male satisfaction. Without preliminaries, it occurred once or twice a week, lasted about five minutes, and ended when the male achieved orgasm. The woman submitted without excitement, expecting exactly what she got—nothing.

Dickinson did more than report histories. His classic *Atlas of Human Sexual Anatomy* (1933) contained detailed drawings of the vagina in various stages of sexual stimulation. He obtained the information by inserting a glass tube resembling a phallus into the vaginas of dozens of his patients. He observed the changes which occurred in both the vagina and the cervix as they stimulated themselves. By this process he was able to lay to rest at least one myth, that at the moment of orgasm the cervix opened and sucked up the deposit of semen. Such opening was very rare, and was not accompanied by any sucking action. Dickinson also pioneered the use of the electrical vibrator to help women learn to reach orgasm. Applied to the pubic area above the clitoris, this device gives erotic stimulation which leads to orgasm in many women who have previously been unable to experience it. Dickinson demonstrated the use of the vibrator to patients, who subsequently found themselves able to reach orgasm by masturbation or coitus.

Social changes following World War II eroded many traditional attitudes toward sex and sexuality, and research on the psychology and physiology of sexual response appeared in the arena of modern science. The most important studies for female sexuality were those of Alfred Kinsey *et al.* (1953) and William Masters and Virginia Johnson (1966; 1970).

Kinsey was an entomologist at Indiana University in the mid-thirties when he was selected to teach a course on sexual behavior. Discovering the paucity of scientific research in the field, Kinsey embarked upon the most extensive study of the sexual habits of white,[3] mostly middle-class Americans. Through personal interviews, he collected the sexual histories of more than five thousand males and more than five thousand females. The data from these samples are the basis for Kinsey's first book, *Sexual Behavior in the Human Male*, and his second, *Sexual Behavior in the Human Female*. These studies deal primarily with the frequency and variety of sexual outlets. Although questions have been raised about their validity and the degree to which they are representative of the sexual habits of the entire population, they continue to be the most complete and reliable sampling available (Brecher, 1971; Katchadourian and Lunde,

[3] The number of blacks interviewed was too small for statistical analysis (Katchadourian and Lunde, 1975).

1975). Their publication created a furor because of some of the findings, especially on the incidence of premarital sex and homosexuality. They also challenged some cherished myths about the sexual behavior of females.

The studies of Masters and Johnson differed in important ways from those of Kinsey. They were interested in the physiology of the sexual response from arousal through orgasm and back to the quiescent state. To learn what happens in the human body through the sexual response cycle, they used the method of direct observation of subjects in a laboratory setting. Their sample consisted of 694 males and females, white and black, ranging in age from eighteen to eighty-nine. As a result of this research, the book *Human Sexual Response* appeared in 1966.

Sexual Anatomy

The female sexual anatomy serves both sexual and reproductive functions. It consists of the external genitalia and the internal reproductive structures. Although all these structures belong to a single body system, the external genitalia are more closely associated with sexual activity, and the internal organs with procreation. The origin and sexual differentiation of this system was described in Chapter 4.

External genitalia

The external female genitalia include the *mons pubis;* the major and minor lips, called *labia;* the clitoris; and the vaginal opening, or introitus, which is flanked on each side by erectile tissue called the vestibular bulbs (Fig. 7.1).

The *mons pubis* or *mons veneris,* "mount of love," is the most visible of the external genitalia. It is a rounded area of fatty tissue which becomes covered with hair in the course of puberty.

Running back from the mons pubis and blending into the tissues in front of the anus are the major lips, two loose folds of skin whose outer surfaces also grow hair during puberty. The inner surfaces are smooth and hairless. The size and color of these labia vary with individuals and with age and parity. The minor lips are thinner and hairless and lie within the major lips, where they enclose the clitoris, the urethral opening, and the vaginal opening, as well as the duct endings of Bartholin's glands. They come together in a single fold over the clitoris, forming the prepuce, or hood, of the clitoris.

The clitoris is unique in the human body in that its sole function is sexual. It is homologous to the penis, although the penis also con-

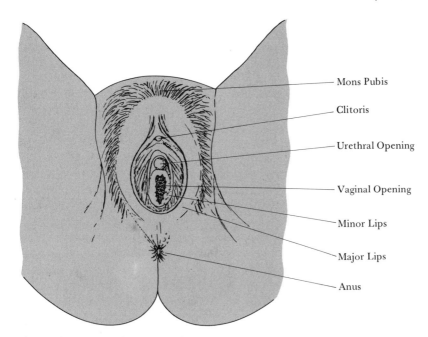

Figure 7.1   Female external genitalia.

tains the urethra through which pass urine and semen. In women, the urethra is a separate duct entirely. The clitoris consists of the glans, or tip, the shaft, and the crura, "legs", which attach it internally to the pelvic bone. The glans is the only part of the clitoris which is visible. It projects slightly from under the prepuce or hood, and it may be viewed with a mirror by parting the minor lips. Richly endowed with nerves, the clitoris is the most sexually sensitive part of the female body. Masturbation is more likely to involve areas over or around the clitoris than in the vagina. It was not an uncommon practice in Victorian times to excise the clitoris of young girls to prevent masturbation (Sherfey, 1973). This operation, a clitoridectomy, is rare today except as a radical procedure for cancer.

The urethral opening is the end of the urethra, the tube which carries urine from the urinary bladder. It is unrelated to the sexual reproductive system.

The vaginal opening or introitus is much larger than the urethral orifice, and is easily seen by parting the minor lips. This opening may be partially covered, or bridged, in young girls by the hymen,[4] a thin membrane which has no particular function but

[4] Hymen was the Greek God of marriage, son of Dionysus and Aphrodite.

around which has accrued considerable mythical and psychological significance. Though the size and shape of the hymen varies, it has an opening which permits the passage of menstrual blood and even the use of a tampon. An erect penis is usually too large to be admitted past the hymen without tearing it, a point which has given the hymen its particular niche in sexual folklore. As a consequence, many young women experience slight pain and bleeding when the hymen is torn during their first intercourse. This "evidence" of virginity has been highly prized in many socieites. However, the intact hymen is not a definitive sign of virginity, as hymenal ruptures can occur during normal childhood activities.

Bartholin's glands open between the edge of the hymen and the minor lips. While they secrete a scanty amount of fluid during sexual stimulation, the major source of vaginal lubrication is the wall of the vagina.

A detailed description of the male sexual reproductive system is beyond our scope. However, a diagram of the organs and structures is presented in Fig. 7.2 for reference.

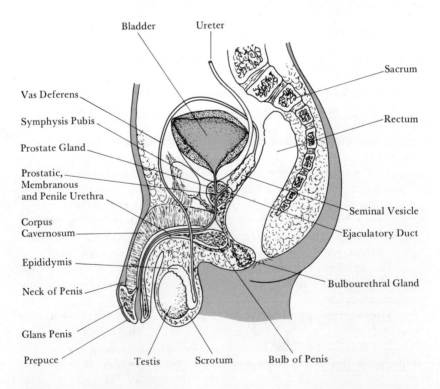

Figure 7.2 Male reproductive system.

Internal reproductive system

The internal reproductive organs include the ovaries, the two Fallopian tubes or oviducts, the uterus, and the vagina (Fig. 7.3).

The ovaries lie on either side of the uterus to which they are attached by ligaments. They have two major functions: the production of ova, and the manufacture of estrogen and progesterone, the female sex hormones.

The female child at birth has about four hundred thousand immature ova in her ovaries. During puberty, when the ovarian cycle begins, some of the ova begin to mature, and subsequently each month one ovum ruptures the thin wall of its follicle and leaves the ovary. The ovum is captured by the ovarian end of the Fallopian tube. The tubes are not connected to the ovaries but have projections which appear to close about the ovary during ovulation.

The ovum is moved through the tube by hairlike cilia. If it meets spermatozoa, it may become fertilized, subsequently moving on through the tube and into the uterus, where it either implants if fertile, or is flushed out during menstruation.

The uterus is about three inches long, and is normally held in place by ligaments and tipped forward, its cervix or neck protruding into the vagina. It is very muscular and elastic, expanding greatly

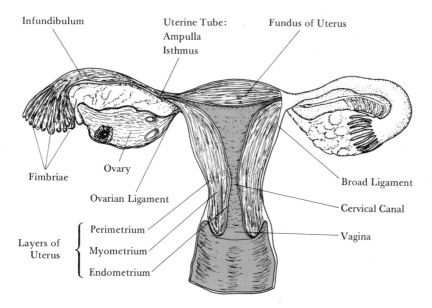

Figure 7.3   Female internal reproductive structures.

during pregnancy. Its function is to shelter and to nourish the developing fetus.

Of all the internal structures, the vagina is the most involved in sexuality. It receives the penis and its deposit of semen. It serves also as the tract through which pass the menstrual blood and the baby at birth. Slanting downward and forward, it is about four inches long and is usually a collapsed tube. Its walls are muscular and are lined with a mucous skin similar to the inside of the mouth. The vagina itself is rather poorly equipped with nerve endings, and thus is relatively insensitive, especially its upper two-thirds. The area surrounding the introitus is, however, very sensitive.

The size and condition of the vagina have been the subject of evaluative appraisal and commentary in the popular culture. Since the vagina of the adult female can expand to permit the passage of a baby, it can accommodate the largest penis; thus no mature vagina is too small for sexual intercourse. It is possible that a muscular spasm, vaginismus, will prevent penetration in a tense and anxious woman. Such an event is psychogenic in nature and unrelated to the size of the penis or the vagina. In the premenopausal woman, the vagina develops its own lubrication when she is sexually excited. After menopause, the walls of the vagina become more delicate and thin, and lose their lubrication efficiency. This condition results from the gradual cessation of estrogen production by the ovaries and can be treated by exogenous lubrication or by estrogen replacement therapy. The vaginal opening may become larger and looser after childbirth. However, the contraction of the opening is to some extent under the voluntary control of the woman. That is, she can tighten or relax it at will, much as one shuts off the flow of urine. Further, the muscles controlling this phenomenon can be developed by exercises, and such exercise has been shown to be related to the development of orgasmic potency (Masters and Johnson, 1970).

Physiology of Sexual Response

We now move to a consideration of the physiological processes of the woman's body during sexual experience. For much of what follows we are indebted to the *nonpareil* studies of Masters and Johnson (1966).

Sexual response may be elicited by a wide variety of stimuli, and stimuli which may be arousing to some individuals may be neutral or aversive to others. As the individual matures, her responses become selective and are likely to be elicited by direct stimulation of parts of the body and by erotic situations. Though arousal can involve all the sensory modalities, touch is probably the most important in women, followed by vision and fantasy.

Certain areas of the body thought to be especially sensitive to sexual arousal are called erogenous zones. In women these include the clitoris, the minor lips, the breasts, the mouth, and the inner thighs. However, almost any area of the body can have erotic potential since individual preferences differ. Probably most important is a sensitivity for the other's wishes and preferences.

The observations of Masters and Johnson led to a description of the sexual response cycle in both sexes which include four phases: excitation, plateau, orgasm, and resolution. Reactions of the sex organs and other body reactions during each of these are summarized in Tables 7.1 and 7.2. Two points should be emphasized regarding these data. First, the sequences and timing of reactions are generalizations based upon observations of a large sample; individual variations from these data are to be expected. For example,

Table 7.1   Reactions of sex organs during sexual response cycle*

Male	Female
Excitement phase	
Penile erection	Vaginal lubrication
Elevation of scrotum	Thickening of vaginal wall
Testicular size increase	Ballooning of top ⅔ of vagina
	Clitoral tumescence
Plateau phase	
Cowper's gland secretes	Orgasmic platform develops
Testicular tumescence	Uterine and cervical elevation
Full testicular elevation	"Sex-skin" coloration
	Bartholin's gland secretes
Orgasmic phase	
Contraction of vas deferens, seminal vesicles, ejaculatory duct, and prostate	Uterus contracts from fundus down
Contractions of penile urethra, 5–8 times at 0.8-second intervals	Contractions of orgasmic platform 8–18 times at 0.8-second intervals
	Rectal and urethral sphincter contracts for some subjects
Resolution phase	
Loss of pelvic vasocongestion	May return to orgasm
Loss of erection (may be entire or partial; some subjects capable of continued intercourse)	Slow loss of pelvic vaso-congestion and orgasmic platform
	Return of clitoris to normal position

* Adapted from Beach, F. A., ed., *Sex and Behavior*, New York, John Wiley and Sons, 1965, by permission of editor.

many sexual experiences do not culminate in orgasm, or an individual may return from near-orgasm to plateau several times in one cycle. A cycle may be as brief as a few minutes or last for hours. Second, the phases are not discrete, except perhaps for the orgasm; plateau, for example, is an extension of excitement during which the maintenance of sexual tension leads to orgasm.

Several characteristic features develop during the female cycle. The first sign of excitement is the appearance of vaginal fluid, which becomes more copious as the cycle progresses. This exudate actually comes through the vaginal walls owing to the vasocongestion which develops in the pelvic area. The congestion, which is an accumulation of blood and fluids, pushes fluids into the tissues, and results in the "wetness" which lubricates the vagina. This pelvic vasocongestion is the single most important factor underlying the female sexual response cycle.

In the excitement phase, the upper two-thirds of the vagina begin to balloon out, and as the phase is prolonged the cervix and uterus lift away from their usual position. Further, the lower vagina and labia begin to thicken as the tissues become engorged, and, in the plateau stage, this part of the vagina develops the *orgasmic platform*, the congested walls in which the rhythmic contractions of orgasm are most manifest.

The glans and shaft of the clitoris also become engorged under stimulation. During the plateau stage shortly before orgasm the shaft of the clitoris increases in diameter and decreases in length, to such an extent that the clitoris retracts under the hood, and its glans is no longer visible or in direct contact with any stimulating agent. Penile thrusting, however, exercises a "pulling" effect on the hood, moving it in such a way that the stimulation of the clitoris continues indirectly. Most women find direct stimulation of the clitoris undesirable owing to its extreme sensitivity.

In general, women reach the orgasmic stage of arousal more slowly than men do because greater pelvic congestion is necessary prior to orgasm. In a heterosexual situation the male must be willing and able to continue to stimulate her until she reaches orgasm.

The orgasm is a neuromuscular discharge which occurs with appropriate stimulation and massive buildup of pelvic vasocongestion. It is characterized in women by a sequence of rhythmic contractions of the orgasmic platform, of the uterus, and in some women, of the rectal and urethral sphincters. These contractions, timed at about 0.8-second intervals, may vary in number and in intensity for different women and for different experiences.

The difference between the male and female resolution phases accounts for some women's ability to experience several orgasms

Table 7.2   Body responses during the sexual cycle*

Male	Female
	Excitement phase
Nipple erection	Nipple erection
	Sex flush
	Plateau phase
Sex flush	Skeletal muscle tension
Skeletal muscle tension	Hyperventilation
Hyperventilation	Rapid heartbeat
Rapid heartbeat	
	Orgasmic phase
Specific muscle contractions	Specific muscle contraction
Hyperventilation	Hyperventilation
Rapid heartbeat	Rapid heartbeat
	Resolution phase
Perspiration	Perspiration
Hyperventilation	Hyperventilation
Decreasing heartbeat	Decreasing heartbeat

* Adapted from Beach, F. A., ed., *Sex and Behavior*, New York, John Wiley and Sons, 1965, by permission of editor.

during the course of one experience. The male normally has only one.[5] Following orgasm, the clitoris emerges from its retracted position, and begins to lose its tumescence, or erection. The orgasmic platform also begins to subside. Decongestion of the female pelvic structures proceeds at a much slower rate than does detumescence of the penis which rapidly loses its erection after ejaculation. Vasocongestion underlies the capacity for orgasm, so as long as this condition exists, the female may continue to experience multiple orgasms. If the woman does not have an orgasm after prolonged stimulation, the congestion may be a source of discomfort for several hours.

Factors relating to orgasm

Several physiological factors affect the experience of orgasm. The most important is stimulation. Prolonged physical stimulation of the labial and clitoral area is necessary for many women to reach

[5] The length of the male's refractory period during which renewal of response is impossible varies with age, length of time since last intercourse, alcohol consumption, and other variables. The capacity for a quick succession of erections and orgasms in the male is usually lost after thirty.

orgasm. Following orgasm, further stimulation may result in prolonging the pelvic vasocongestion, making more orgasms possible.[6]

Masters and Johnson found that most women in their study who were multiorgasmic would be satisfied with three to five orgasms. Women who had much greater numbers of orgasms in succession usually did so by masturbation or by the use of an electric vibrator. The latter was most productive since the fatigue factor was less important. In general, the number of orgasms and the intensity of the orgasmic experience was highly related to the duration and the efficiency of stimulation regardless of the source.

A second finding was that age and childbearing history are related to orgasmic potency for women. In general, women reach their peak of sexual activity later than most men do. The physiological consequences of pregnancy enhance the orgasmic potential of the woman. In the course of pregnancy an elaboration of the system of blood vessels supplying the pelvic area occurs, and this system continues to be available after the woman has given birth. Consequently, the capability for vasocongestion increases, thus increasing the potential for orgasm.

Although the findings are sometimes contradictory, the weight of evidence indicates that the sex drive in women is greater during the luteal or premenstrual phase of the cycle. This finding persists in spite of evidence that most experience heightened feelings of well-being during the ovulatory phase when the estrogen level is highest, and that a majority report some symptomatology characteristic of the premenstrual syndrome during the luteal phase (Golub, 1973). The increased interest in sex during this period is a function of the vasocongestion and edema of the lower abdomen and pelvic area prior to the onset of menses (Sherfey, 1973). There is, however, considerable individual variation among women as to when they are most interested in sex, and it is likely that situational factors contribute more to this variability than phases of the menstrual cycle do.

Theories of orgasm

Freud proposed two types of female orgasm, the clitoral and the vaginal. The clitoral orgasm, resulting from stimulation of the clitoral area as commonly practiced in childhood masturbation, would give way, Freud thought, to the vaginal orgasm, which characterized

---

[6] For a highly detailed and technical account of female eroticism and response and the mechanisms underlying them, see Sherfey (1973).

the sexually mature woman. If this shift did not occur, the woman was sexually immature and technically frigid. The notion that women experience two kinds of orgasm has persisted until quite recently. For example, a recent study of twenty-seven gynecology textbooks revealed that of the four which indexed orgasm, three said that the vaginal orgasm was characteristic of the mature woman (Scully and Bart, 1973). An essay on "The Clitorid Woman" referred to her as the perfect sexual partner, passionate and conforming, but said that these traits "do not necessarily give her the vaginal orgasm which is the ultimate, and she may even be frigid" (Meyer, 1966).

The studies of Masters and Johnson led them to conclude that physiologically there is only one type of orgasm. The physiology of the orgasm triggered by a neuromuscular discharge and including rhythmic contractions of the orgasmic platform and related pelvic structures is always the same regardless of which parts of the body are being stimulated or who the partner is. Orgasmic experiences can vary greatly, depending upon a host of factors. But these differences are psychological. The physiological basis remains the same.

An extensive investigation of the anatomical and physiological bases of erotic responses in the female corroborated the single-type theory of orgasm. Because of the extreme sensitivity of the clitoral glans and the relative insensitivity of the vagina, penile or other intravaginal stimulation affects the clitoris, the minor lips, and the lower vagina as an inseparable functional unit with the clitoral glans being the indispensable initiator of the orgasmic reaction. It is a physical impossibility to separate the clitoral from the vaginal orgasms as demanded by psychoanalytic theory (Sherfey, 1973).

The issue continues to be debated, however. Another theory suggests that the vaginal contractions, an essential component of orgasm according to Masters and Johnson, are not necessarily present in all orgasms. A triple model of orgasmic experience has been presented. The first is the "vulval" orgasm, the kind observed by Masters and Johnson. The second is the "uterine" orgasm, characterized by a gasping type of breathing followed by a forceful exhalation. The result, as in the first type, is sexual gratification. This kind of orgasm is brought about by repetitive displacement of the uterus owing to the physical impact of the penis causing it to stimulate the peritoneum, the tissue covering the abdominal organs. The third type is a blend of the first two (Singer and Singer, 1972).

Another theory of the female orgasm suggested that some women are vaginally oriented and some are clitorally oriented. While the clitoral orgasm resembles the kind described by Masters and Johnson, the vaginal orgasm, on the other hand, seems to be more like Helene Deutsch's description of the ideal orgasm of the mature woman: subjectively, a happy, warm, contented feeling, without the convulsive quality of the clitoral orgasm (Fisher, 1973).

The fact that agreement has not been reached on the question of what constitutes an orgasm exemplifies a certain elusive quality surrounding many aspects of female sexuality. Regarding orgasm, the problem lies primarily in the differing subjective reports of women as they describe the experience. Since women have no ejaculation, which signals orgasm in the male, it is not possible to know on a descriptive level whether two women are describing the same physiological event when they describe their orgasms. Some women describe very satisfying orgasms which do not include vaginal contractions. Exactly what these are at a physiological level is not known.

The view which has the strongest empirical base of support is that of Masters and Johnson, whose single-type theory of female orgasm is based upon direct observation of the physiological responses of sexually stimulated females. Furthermore, the subjective reports of the women in their study taken in interviews immediately following the orgasmic experience are consistent with Masters and Johnson's objective description of the physiological events. From reports of 487 women, they were able to describe three stages of the orgasmic process.

The first stage, the onset of orgasm, is identified with a sensation of suspension or stoppage. At the same time or immediately after, there is an intense sensual awareness in the clitoral area which radiates into the pelvis. Paralleling this is a loss in sensory acuity; the compelling quality of the imminent event diminishes awareness of everything else.

The second stage, a sensation of suffusing warmth beginning in the pelvic area and spreading throughout the body, was experienced by almost all the women.

By the third stage, the women consistently described a feeling of involuntary contraction in the vagina followed by a throbbing sensation in the pelvis, sometimes spreading to the whole body and becoming combined with a sense of the pulse or heartbeat. This stage of the orgasm as reported by the women was correlated with the contractions of the orgasmic platform as objectively observed by the researchers.

Proponents of theories which propose two or more kinds of orgasm might argue that Masters and Johnson defined orgasms as only those events characterized by contractions of the vaginal barrel. In that case, the subjective reports of the women who experienced that type of orgasm would of course tally with the recorded physiological data. Other culminations of the response cycle which might be quite satisfying and conclusive as a sexual event to some women would not fit the "contraction" definition, and thus would not be called orgasm. If the orgasm is qualitatively different from the earlier stages of the cycle, however, one would expect physiological changes to underlie the difference. So far, the other kinds of orgasms described in the literature have not been shown to have physiological correlates.

Sexual Behavior

The term "sexual behavior" is deceptively simple. As many psychologists understand it, behavior is what one does, those acts which are observable, in contrast to processes which are not observable, such as mood states, thoughts, and feelings. Sexual behavior is behavior that is related to the arousal and gratification of sexual feelings. Narrowly defined, it means the activity done by people to achieve orgasm. This simple definition has problems because an almost infinite variety of behavior can be potentially sexually stimulating, and a great deal of behavior which is clearly sexual does not culminate in orgasm. Most of the research on human sexual behavior has restricted the focus of investigation to a few selected behaviors which account for most of the ways that humans reach orgasm. For example, Kinsey collected data in six categories of behavior: heterosexual intercourse, heterosexual petting, homosexual relations, masturbation, nocturnal sex dreams, and sexual contact with animals. A later study by the Playboy Foundation included those areas plus oral-genital sex, anal intercourse, sadism, and masochism (Hunt, 1974). These last four can be subsumed, of course, under either hetero- or homosexual behavior. The discussion here will be much more limited.

Development of sexuality

The biological capability to experience sexual arousal and to reach orgasm is present in infants, and it is widely recognized that at least some infants under one or two years do exhibit behavior that is clearly sexual in nature. Kinsey described what appeared to be sexual activity culminating in orgasm for both sexes very early in life (1948; 1953). While we cannot know what the subjective experience of such activity is in the preverbal child, the physical signs are the same as those exhibited by adults, including bringing the genitals in contact with an object, such as a doll or pillow, rhythmic thrusting movements of the pelvis, rapid breathing, increase in body tension,

loss of sensory acuity, and sudden release of tension followed by relaxation. While the emergence of such sexual behavior occurs at
variable times, with infant orgasm being infrequently reported by
parents who may overlook evidence of sexuality, there is no reason
to doubt its pervasiveness in the very young.

Whether sex differences exist in infant sexuality or even in observable behavior that appears to be sexual is not known. Clearly reliable data would be difficult to obtain. Male infants have erections
frequently beginning soon after birth, but whether these have any
erotic significance is questionable. Although erections are the most
visible sign of sexual arousal in older males, their appearance in very
young males is probably reflexive, that is, occurring independently
of higher brain centers that mediate thought and feelings. Kinsey
believed, however, that a majority of boys were capable of orgasm by
age four. No comparable estimate was made for girls, though Kinsey
included in his study of sexual behavior in females a graphic account, provided by a mother, of her three-year-old daughter's masturbation to orgasm (1953, pp. 104–5).

Sex play and genital exploration are very common in children
after the age of two or three. Kinsey found an interesting sex difference in the incidence of sociosexual play as contrasted to self-mas-
turbation in children aged five to thirteen. As Figures 7.4 and 7.5
show, girls were more likely to be engaging in sex play with others at
age five, and maintained a fairly constant level of such activity until
age nine, when the percentage begins to decline. The percentage of
boys engaging in sociosexual play increased fourfold from age five
to age twelve, when it peaked at 39 percent compared to 10 percent
for girls of the same age. Obviously, these data should be viewed

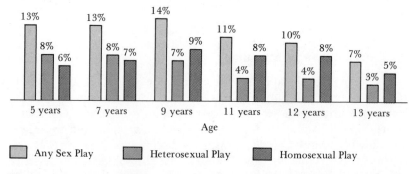

Figure 7.4   Percentages of prepubescent girls who had engaged in
sociosexual play. (From A. C. Kinsey *et al.*, *Sexual Behavior in the
Human Female* [Philadelphia: Saunders, 1953], p. 129. Courtesy of
the Institute for Sex Research.)

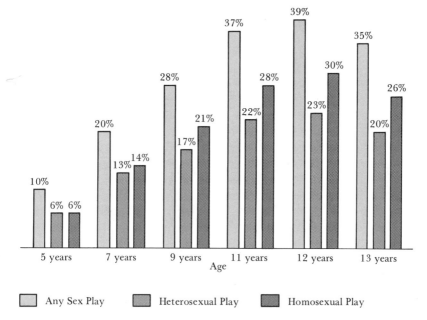

Figure 7.5 Percentages of prepubescent boys who had engaged in sociosexual play. (From A. C. Kinsey *et al., Sexual Behavior in the Human Male* [Philadelphia: Saunders, 1948], p. 162. Courtesy of the Institute for Sex Research.)

with some caution, as they are primarily based on the recollections of adult subjects. Further, both the memory of the behavior and the behavior itself are subject to cultural pressures, affecting adults' perceptions of themselves as children, as well as their childhood perceptions of their own behavior in a social milieu.

The most common sociosexual activity for both sexes in childhood is the exhibiting and handling of genitals. Most of this in prepubertal years is homosexual in context, although 30 percent of the women in Kinsey's sample and 40 percent of the men recalled heterosexual play before puberty. Homosexual play was unlikely to persist after puberty, though Kinsey found that the adult homosexuals in his sample had discovered their sex preference in the course of childhood homosexual play.

Although infants and young children often discover the pleasures of genital stimulation and engage in masturbatory activity on a sporadic, nonsystematic basis, deliberate masturbation becomes prevalent in prepuberty or the early pubertal years. Kinsey's data indicated that a higher percent of girls than boys between the ages of five to ten had masturbated to orgasm. After that age there was a slow but steady increase in the percent of females who had ever masturbated, reaching a peak of 62 percent by age forty-five. Women continued to discover and to practice masturbation well into middle age. By contrast, the percent of males who had masturbated increased rapidly after age ten or twelve, reaching a peak at age twenty when 92 percent of males had masturbated to orgasm. The salience of masturbation for females in the Kinsey sample was indicated by the fact that 85 percent had reached their first orgasm through masturbation, compared to 70 percent of the males.

The Playboy survey provides some interesting comparisons with Kinsey's data on masturbation. For the total samples of males and females over eighteen, 93 and 63 percent respectively reported that they had ever masturbated to orgasm, an increase of only 1 percent over the Kinsey samples. However, the incidence of masturbation to orgasm by the age of thirteen was much higher for both sexes than Kinsey found, as shown in Figure 7.6.

How real this increase in masturbation to orgasm is for children under thirteen is problematic. Again, the figures are based on adults' memories of their early behavior, and while they may represent a genuine shift toward an earlier breaking through of parental and social barriers of disapproval, they may also reflect in part a relaxation of the taboos against admitting such behavior, or even an enhancement of the self-image through such admission (Hunt, 1974).

The sexual development of females begins in infancy with the potential of experiencing sexual arousal, sometimes to orgasm. Since such behavior is not approved by the culture, and is not frequently reported, the real nature and extent of infantile sexuality is not known. Girls as well as boys display an early curiosity about their own and others' bodies, and self and mutual exploration, both het-

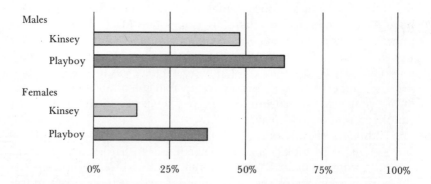

Figure 7.6 Ever masturbated to orgasm by the age of 13. (From *Playboy*, 21 [February 1974].)

erosexual and homosexual, are common. More girls than boys engage in sociosexual play up to age 5. The increase in masturbation for both girls and boys, but especially for girls, probably reflects a softening of Victorian sanctions against the practice, as well as a greater willingness to be open about one's early sexual activities.

The sexual revolution?

The Playboy Foundation survey of adult sexual behavior in the United States population makes it possible to compare recent data with the Kinsey data and to examine changes in premarital, marital, and extra- or postmarital sexual behavior which have occurred in the last two decades. While the general shift is toward a higher incidence of all kinds of heterosexual activity and more permissive attitudes toward homosexuality and variety in the sexual act, the change has been more dramatic among women than men.

Probably the most significant change is in the reported incidence of premarital coitus. The increase, especially among females, from the older to the younger age groups, has accelerated within the last fifteen years (see Table 7.3).

By contrast, in the Kinsey sample, only a third of the women had had premarital coitus by age 25, consistent with the Playboy findings for the 45–54 age groups. The increase was striking enough to lead to the conclusion that in another five or ten years, premarital coitus will be an all but universal experience for the young in our society (Hunt, 1974).

While sex before marriage seems to have become the norm, it has not become more casual for those under 25, nor are the young more promiscuous, according to the more recent survey. Of those females who had had premarital coitus, both the Kinsey and Playboy surveys found that approximately half had had only one partner— the man they expected to marry. Both older and younger males in the Playboy sample had had an average of six premarital partners. Kinsey did not give data on premarital partners of males.

Sexual liberation has affected the marital relations of people of

Table 7.3 Percent of respondents who ever had premarital coitus, by age* (*Total Married Sample*)

Percent	Under 25	25–34	35–44	45–54	55 and up
Males	95	92	86	89	84
Females	81	65	41	36	31

* Reprinted from Hunt, 1973.

all ages in the United States. At every age group, the frequency of coitus has increased from the Kinsey to the Playboy survey. (Table 7.4).

Nine-tenths of the wives in the Playboy survey said that their coital experiences in the past year had been generally or very pleasurable. Among women who had been married fifteen years, the number who always or nearly always had orgasm increased from 45 percent (Kinsey) to 53 percent (Playboy), while the number who seldom or never did so dropped from 28 percent (Kinsey) to 15 percent (Playboy).

One of the most striking findings in the Playboy survey was the increase in duration of coitus among married couples. Kinsey had estimated that about three-quarters of married males reached orgasm in two minutes or less after intromission. Today, according to the Playboy data, the median duration is about ten minutes for all couples, ranging from thirteen minutes for the youngest age group to ten for those 55 and over.

The Playboy survey also found a strong correlation between marital success and sexual pleasure. The large majority who rated their marriages very close also found coitus very pleasurable, whereas three out of five women and two out of five men who rated their marriages not close found marital coitus not pleasant.

The Playboy study also noted that the increase in frequency and satisfaction among married couples was caused by freer attitudes, better birth-control methods, and the influx of information relevant to obtaining sexual satisfaction. The women's liberation

Table 7.4 Comparison of Kinsey and *Playboy* respondents on frequency of marital intercourse: median weekly frequency of marital intercourse*

1938–49 (adapted from Kinsey)		1972 (Playboy survey)	
Age	Frequency	Age	Frequency
16–25	2.5	18–24	3.0
26–35	2.0	25–34	2.5
36–45	1.5	35–44	2.0
46–55	.9	45–54	1.0
56–60	.5	55 and up	1.0

* Reprinted from Hunt, 1973.

movement is credited, also, with getting rid of the image of women as passive and uninterested in sex.

Sexual liberation seems to have had the least impact on the incidence of extramarital relations. The only groups in which more subjects had had at least one extramarital experience were the under–twenty-five married and divorced, both males and females. Males in this category increased from 27 to 32 percent, and females from 8 to 24 percent. Paralleling the premarital statistics, the rate of increase is much greater for females than for males, suggesting that liberated attitudes and better contraception have made more of a difference for women than for men. The figures on mate-swapping and group sex, which Kinsey did not collect, indicate that only about 2 percent had ever engaged in mate swapping, and 2 percent of men and less than one percent of women had ever had sex with other partners in the presence of the spouse.

Divorced women in the Playboy sample were much more active than those in Kinsey's sample. The median frequency for the sexually active was almost twice a week, almost as high as for divorced men and four times higher than the divorcees in the Kinsey sample. Also, only a tenth of the divorced women in the Playboy sample were sexually inactive, compared to a third of Kinsey's younger postmarital group and the majority of those older than the mid-40's.

Are we experiencing a sexual revolution? The major changes reflected in the two surveys we have been discussing are in increased incidence of sexual activity in the premarital period, within the marriage relationship, and among the divorced. Inhibitions in sexual behavior have relaxed, more information is available, and the fear of pregnancy is reduced. The changes have occurred within the existing cultural framework:

> there has been no chaotic and anarchic dissolution of standards, but, rather, a major shift toward somewhat different . . . standards that remain integrated with existing social values and within the institutions of love, marriage, and the family (Hunt, October 1973, p. 207).

Experiencing sex

How do women feel about sex? At the beginning of this chapter we commented on the great variability among women in sexual experience and satisfaction. Later we noted an elusive quality to the available information on the female orgasm. Both these observations are pertinent to the question in that they show why there is no definitive answer. To paraphrase Samuel Johnson, "Which woman? What kind of sex?"

The sexual behavior of women is changing so rapidly that all generalizations about it must be suspect. Earlier writers were quite sure that women had a lower sex drive than men, that their capacity for arousal was lower, that they engaged in sex mostly to satisfy men, and that they could adjust quite comfortably to a life without any sex at all. In view of the recent investigations into the physiology of sex and into sexual behavior showing women's biological potential and behavioral response in an environmental context, it is evident that any conclusive statements about female sexuality would be premature.

We can, however, consider the variability of sexual experience and some of the factors affecting it. Masturbation, for example, is begun early and practiced regularly by some girls and women. Others never even think of it. Many women enjoy sex greatly and are orgasmic from their first experience. Others grow old without ever having experienced an orgasm. Many nonorgasmic women nonetheless take great pleasure in their sexual relations. Others resent it as one more chore or see it as an exploitation of their bodies.

If we assume that women do not differ greatly in their biological capacity for sexual arousal and orgasm, then we must conclude that the variability in women's sexual experience is primarily caused by extraneous factors: experience and opportunity, and sociocultural attitudes toward sex.

Several writers agree that an important factor in female eroticism, particularly orgasm, is experience (Bardwick, 1971; Kaplan, 1975; Kinsey, 1953). Simply stated, women can learn to have orgasms. The ability to do so is latent in all females and responds to cultivation. Once a woman achieves arousal to orgasm by any means, masturbation, petting, or intercourse, it should be easier for her to do so again under similar circumstances. As she learns more about the responsiveness of her body, she becomes more adept at stimulating and facilitating it. With practice she becomes less inhibited and less fearful, and more willing to "let go," to give herself over to the experience. The role of experience is supported by Kinsey's finding that sexual activity reached its peak in women at about age thirty and continued over the next decade.[7] The Playboy sample showed that, compared to single women, the number of married women who reported that all their sexual intercourse resulted in orgasm was about 20 percent greater. Likewise, the number reporting that *none* of their sexual intercourse resulted in orgasm was about 10 percent. Since it is reasonable to assume that married women in general have

[7] The male sample was already close to its maximum in the youngest group, the fifteen- to twenty-year-olds.

more experience with coitus than single women do, these findings are consistent with the notion that experience is a good teacher.

Sociocultural attitudes toward sex and the body and the extent to which the individual woman has incorporated them into her own attitudes and value system clearly have an effect upon her sexual responsiveness. Leah Schaefer studied the sexual experiences of thirty married, college-educated women in New York City. The recollections of their childhood sexual explorations uniformly included reactions of shame and guilt and need for secrecy. The repressiveness characteristic of the Victorian attitudes discussed earlier pervaded the teachings and admonitions they received about masturbation, petting, and intercourse. Enjoyable sexual experiences before marriage were exceptional, owing to the fear and guilt surrounding them. Even so, twenty-three of the thirty had premarital intercourse. They engaged in their first act of coitus not because of sexual desire but because of a wish to lose their virginity, to "get it over with," or out of curiosity. Only 3 of this group had orgasm in their first coitus. Of the 7 who remained virgins until marriage, none had orgasm in their first coitus. While this is evidence for the experience factor discussed above, most of these women also felt a need to "hold back," a fear of the loss of control which orgasm meant to them, and a continuing feeling of shame and guilt, that something was wrong with what they were doing (Brecher, 1971).

This awareness of the partner and what he thinks of her, and anxiety about his attitudes toward her sexuality also affect the sexual experience. For example, a female student of mine wrote, "The first time I had an orgasm I didn't know what was happening to me. It was like a series of spasms that I couldn't control . . . it just happened. I was very embarrassed. My boyfriend looked at me like I was some kind of a whore. From then on I felt I had to control it."

Certain attitudes are more typical of unmarried college women who are coitally orgasmic than of those who are not. The orgasmic women had less conflict with parents, especially fathers, and believed that they themselves would be no more restrictive with their daughters than with their sons. They also rated themselves freer of sexual inhibitions, became more aroused from petting, and were more satisfied with their capacity for sexual arousal. They felt that their sex drives were about equal with their partners', and they were more likely to initiate sexual activity (Shope, 1975).

Investigation of some correlates of coital response which differentiated orgasmic from nonorgasmic unmarried college women revealed that the two groups were about equal in amount of sexual experience, length of experience, number of partners, masturbatory history, and experiences of different techniques in intercourse. The dimensions on which they differed significantly are presented in Table 7.5.

While the orgasmic women reported more total coital contacts,

Table 7.5 Some correlates of coital orgasm adequacy among unmarried women*

		Percent of subjects	
Dimension	Response	Orgasmic (N = 50)	Nonorgasmic (N = 40)
Number of times subject estimated she had engaged in coitus	15	20	5
	16–40	14	40
	41–80	20	27½
	81–130	14	7½
	131	32	20
Usual degree of arousal from coitus	None/little	0	2½
	Some	2	12½
	Much	16	47½
	Very much	82	37½
Usual enjoyment of coitus	None/little	0	10
	Some	2	15
	Much	10	35
	Very much	88	40
Amount of time woman felt that she must "give in" to male pressure for coitus	Never	74	32½
	Sometimes	24	20
	Often	0	25
	Usually	2	22½
Desire for a continuation of sexual activity following coitus	Never	8	35
	Sometimes	32	37½
	Often	36	5
	Usually	24	22½
Amount subject is disturbed by outside noises	None/little	62	15
	Some	22	30
	Much/very much	16	55
Subject's rating of her degree of sexual inhibition	None/little	62	18
	Some	32	40
	Much/very much	6	42
Best coital position	Man over woman	34	62½
	Woman over man	2	5
	All equal	44	20
	Other	10	2½
	Only tried one	10	10

* Excerpted from Shope, D. F., *Interpersonal Sexuality*, 1975, by permission of author.

the numbers in both groups who reported 41 or more were not very different from each other. Although there may have been an experiential effect, greater weight was given to the attitudinal differences which distinguished the two groups. As one would expect, high levels of arousal and enjoyment characterized the orgasmic group. But three out of four of the nonorgasmic group enjoyed coitus much or very much. Plainly, the coital experience had dimensions of pleasure even in the absence of orgasm.

Willing involvement in the sexual act was much more characteristic of the orgasmic group. Giving in to male pressure was rare for them, in contrast to the nonorgasmic group. This mutuality of interest, along with the previously noted belief in the equality of their sex drive with their partner's, suggests a certain freedom of action, of autonomous consent in the relationship.

The desire for sexual activity to continue after coitus was typical of the orgasmic group, while only about a fourth of the nonorgasmic group expressed such a wish. Probably different motivations affected the two groups in their responses to this question. Many sexually experienced women can have multiple orgasms. For this reason, the orgasmic women might have wanted to continue their highly pleasurable experience, while the nonorgasmic women who expressed a desire to continue might have felt frustration at the termination of the encounter before their own orgasmic relief has occurred. Those in the orgasmic group who did not express a wish to continue said they were "too tired" after the experience, while those in the nonorgasmic group were more likely to see coitus as an activity to be "gotten over with."

Focusing on the sexual experience was much more characteristic for the orgasmic group. Most of them were not disturbed by outside noises whereas over half the nonorgasmic group were. Again, the extent to which one can abandon the self, and shut out interference from other sources including the conscience is a correlate of responsiveness in the sexual experience.

Most of the orgasmic women rated themselves as uninhibited in their sexual expression. This probably reflects a global evaluation by the women of their general interest and willingness to participate in sexual activities. That they judged themselves to be uninhibited, however, does not necessarily mean that their freedom from inhibition was a cause of their orgasmic ability. The fact that they were orgasmic could have caused them to see themselves as less inhibited.

Orgasmic women were only half as likely to prefer the man-over-woman position in coitus, compared to the nonorgasmic group. Their general satisfaction with their sexual experience led many of them to report that all coital positions were equally preferable. This suggests a willingness to experiment, and an openness to the possibilities of the experience.

Clinical evidence strongly suggests that women who are typically orgasmic in coitus have certain attitudes which mediate their sexual responsiveness. Such women value their sexuality for its own sake. They are interested and seek actively to satisfy themselves. Sexual interaction in and of itself is positively valued. Many nonorgasmic women who enjoy sexual interaction focus less on the purely sexual aspects of coitus, and are less likely to engage in sex for the sake of sex. Their reaction is global, to the totality of the situation, to its setting, its timing, its romantic overtones, and to the closeness, warmth, and sharing experienced with the partner. While orgasmic women are likely to appreciate these too, they may be less dependent upon them for their own sexual gratification.

Sexuality has become a much-discussed and researched topic in recent years, and a gratifying sex life has become the norm sought after by everyone. Failure to reach this goal is now defined by many as a problem. In this climate, a new discipline has emerged, the study of sexual dysfunctions, and a new therapy has been developed to help people overcome them.

Sexual Dysfunction

Sexual dysfunction is the inability of the individual to function adequately in terms of sexual arousal, orgasm, or specifically coital situations. Until recently the sexual problems of women were subsumed under the general label of "frigidity." Hardly understood, they were thought to be symptomatic of neurosis or other psychopathology and to require lengthy treatment such as psychoanalysis for the identification and resolution of the underlying problem. Such a traditional approach persisted in spite of the absence of a demonstrated relationship between the treatment and the alleviation of the sexual problem. Rarely were sexual dysfunctions of women treated as problems in and of themselves. Rather, they were seen within the context of the woman's intrapsychic conflicts or as part of a complex of problems within the marriage relationship. The relative lack of attention to problems of sexual adequacy is attributable to several sources, all applicable to women and some to men as well. First, until recently, the prevailing mores were incompatible with sex research. The level of knowledge about sexual response and behavior was simply inadequate to support effective treatment. Second, cultural taboos prevented open discussion of sexual problems even with physicians and other therapists. Third, women's sexual needs were not considered to be of major importance to her adjustment and well-being, and women themselves were led to think that their submission to the male and identification with his satisfaction were the important components of their own sexuality.

Social changes in mores and values have substantially undermined the last two obstacles, and research has provided an empirical basis for eliminating the first. The major research in this area and development of treatment methods and procedures was done by Masters and Johnson following their earlier studies of human sexual response. An important recent contribution is Helen Singer Kaplan's *The New Sex Therapy* published in 1974. Her approach extends from the work of Masters and Johnson. Kaplan's work is the primary source for this section.

The sexual dysfunctions of women are of three kinds: general sexual dysfunction, orgasmic dysfunction, and vaginismus. After describing each of these briefly, we shall consider the etiology, the psychological origins of sexual dysfunctions, and the principles of therapy which are being used to correct them.

General sexual dysfunction

General sexual dysfunction is what most people have in mind when they use the word "frigidity." The woman who is generally nonresponsive describes herself as being devoid of sexual feelings. She experiences little or no erotic pleasure from sexually oriented stimulation. Genital vasocongestion and lubrication, the physiological accompaniment of arousal in the female, develop either minimally or not at all. Women with this type of dysfunction vary in their reaction to coitus. Some consider it a tedious ordeal; others find it frightening or disgusting. A third group can appreciate the positive experiences of physical contact with a loved one even though erotic arousal does not occur.

Primary and *secondary* types of general sexual dysfunction can be distinguished. The woman with a primary general dysfunction has never been sexually aroused with any partner. The woman with a secondary general dysfunction has been responsive at some time with someone, but is not with her present partner.

Orgasmic dysfunction

Orgasmic dysfunction refers specifically to the inability to experience the orgasmic component of the sexual response cycle. The dysfunction is primary if the woman has never experienced orgasm. It is secondary if she had been orgasmic in the past but no longer is.

In addition to this distinction there is another which is dependent upon the circumstances. The dysfunction is *absolute* if the woman cannot achieve orgasm in coitus or with any other kind of stimulation. It is *situational* if she can reach orgasm under some circumstances but not others.

The women with orgasmic dysfunction may have a strong sex drive, become readily aroused, and develop vasocongestion and lubrication. It is the orgasm itself, the neuromuscular discharge, which is inhibited. Inability to reach orgasm is the most common and the most quixotic of the sexual dysfunctions. Some women seem to have a very high threshold for the triggering of the neural mechanisms involved in orgasms. That is, they require prolonged, continuous stimulation of the clitoral area before they are "ready." Such women will clearly be nonorgasmic in a penile-vaginal intercourse situation of a few minutes' duration. Others readily have orgasms by masturbation or with the use of a vibrator, but cannot in the presence of another person.

Achieving orgasm is not a criterion of sexual competence or normality in women. Nor is orgasmic dysfunction necessarily a symptom of pathology. Orgasm is basically a physical response which occurs under stimulating conditions which are variable for individual women. While almost all women[8] are physically able to have orgasms, many who do not are not unduly disturbed. Many women experience pleasure and gratification in the sex act even in the absence of orgasm (Shope, 1975).

Vaginismus

Vaginismus is a relatively rare condition in which the muscles surrounding the vaginal entrance close tightly whenever any attempt is made to introduce anything into the vagina. Attempts to achieve coitus are painful and frustrating failures, and even physical examinations involving vaginal penetration are impossible without anesthesia. Women with vaginismus are often extremely fearful of coital or other penetration, and develop high levels of anxiety under such circumstances.

Vaginismus is not always associated with sexual inhibition or orgasmic dysfunction. Some women with vaginismus are sexually responsive and orgasmic even though they cannot tolerate coital intercourse. The inability to have coitus still can be a serious problem and can have devastating psychological effects both on the woman and on her partner. The unpleasant consequences of attempting

---

[8] For exceptions related to physical causes, see Kaplan (1974).

coitus can set up an avoidance reaction in the woman which results in a complete disruption of her sexual adjustment, especially if it is dependent upon a coital relationship.

Etiology of Sexual Dysfunction

A very large number of factors have been implicated as contributors to sexual dysfunctions in women. Physical factors, such as debilitating illness or neurological or endocrinological disorders, can interfere with sexual response, but these account for a very small percentage of female sexual dysfunctions. The great majority are caused by psychological factors (Masters and Johnson, 1970). Many of these causative factors are nonspecific in their effects. That is, they are general factors which can result in any of the sexual dysfunctions. Childhood and marital history, trauma, and attitudes about sex do not seem to differentiate unresponsive, nonorgasmic, and vaginismic women from each other. It is the way that women individually adapt to and react to these multiple determinants that produces the different symptoms.

Three kinds of variables are contributors to the sexual dysfunctions in general: intrapsychic, dyadic, and situational. Traditional therapies such as psychoanalysis tended to lay most of the blame on the first; the new therapies, while not ignoring the intrapsychic, are more likely to focus on the other two.

Intrapsychic factors

Intrapsychic factors are those which arise from conflicts often on an unconscious level within the individual. Deep ambivalence about sex; shame, guilt, and fear can set up negative contingencies which produce avoidance of sexual encounters, defenses against sexual feelings or opening oneself to spontaneous participation. Such feelings are residuals of childhood experiences and conditioning. Repressive teaching about sexuality, harsh punishment for masturbation or exploratory activity, fearsome stories about the horrors of childbirth, or an incorporation of the evaluation of sex as bad or sinful can set up powerful inhibitions to the enjoyment of sexual activity.

Inhibition of responsiveness because of fear of loss of control affects some women. An anxious, insecure woman may be so concerned about monitoring her performance and so guarded in her participation that she cannot risk abandoning herself to her feelings. With its diminution of sensory acuity and of consciousness, orgasm is the triumph of the senses over mind and will. The implications of being out of control are quite threatening to some women.

Resentment, distrust, or fear of men can result in inhibition of sexual pleasure in coitus. Such feeling can emanate from many sources. Harsh treatment by the father, sexual brutality or other trauma related to males, experiences leading to expectation of exploitation or rejection, or to conflict over the dominance-submission dimension in the sexual act may promote a pervasive attitude toward men which is not conducive to enjoyment of coital sex.

Psychoanalysis attributed frigidity in women to unresolved penis envy. Some women do experience envy toward men, as well as fear and anger, because of cultural injunctions which force women into dependent, submissive roles. This can set up strong role conflict in some women who accept the cultural prescription on a conscious level and at the same time suppress the hostility it engenders which they cannot express because of fear of rejection.

Dyadic factors

Dyadic factors in the sexual dysfunctions are those which characterize the relationship between the two persons. It is widely believed that compared to men, women tie their sexuality more closely to the quality of the relationship and their feelings about it. The male's arousal and ability to have orgasm seem to be less dependent upon relationship factors and to be more affected by the urgency of his sexual needs at the time. While the point is controversial, clinical experience supports the observation that women are much more likely to complain about the context in which sex occurs than men are. They are bothered more by negative qualities in the relationship, including transient ones such as a recent argument, hurt feelings, or the manner of approach. It is quite common to hear a wife say, "We had been fighting all afternoon, and I was really upset. Then when we went to bed he wanted to have sex, exactly as if nothing had happened!" This is not to say that men are insensitive to the quality of the relationship, but rather that women's responsiveness may be more contingent upon it. The role of cultural conditioning is important, though the extent of its influence is unknown.

Women vary greatly in their preferences where lovers are concerned. Some are completely unable to respond to anyone but their husbands; others are orgasmic only with lovers. Some want to be pursued and captured by a dominant, strongly desirous man; others enjoy seducing and arousing a less-than-bold partner.

Under the best of circumstances a woman may be unable to respond if her partner is inept, too hasty, or unaware of her needs.

Some men do not know enough about female sexuality to be good lovers. And some women are too reticent to communicate their needs and wishes to their partner.

Situational factors

Sexual dysfunction can be caused by factors in the immediate sexual situation. The most common of these is inadequate stimulation. Although some women are aroused very quickly and easily to orgasm, many women require extended stimulation before they are ready to have an orgasm. Most males, particularly younger ones, are readily aroused and able to ejaculate in a few minutes or less. If his ejaculation signals the end of the sexual experience, the woman may not even have been aroused. Often the sexual encounter is initiated by and is completely controlled by the male who may simply be guided by his own desires.

Women vary in the kind of stimulation they find most pleasureable. Rhythmic friction of the clitoral area, but not directly on the clitoris, caressing of the breasts, the labia, and other parts of the body are all erotically exciting for most women. The communication of her wishes and feelings helps the partner to meet her sexual needs.

It is probably more difficult for a man than for a woman to know how the other is progressing in the sexual act. Not only is the male arousal state manifest in the erection, but he is often less reticent about the active pursuit of his pleasure. If a woman is silent, or fails to assume responsibility for her own pleasure, he may simply take it for granted that she is having the same kind of experience that he is.

Having been socialized to be nurturing and solicitous of others, many women are more concerned about their partner's pleasure than about their own. They refrain from making demands because they do not wish to alienate him, interfere with his enjoyment, or wear him out. The fear of displeasing him is basically a fear of rejection, and the insecure woman may choose compliance and passivity rather than take the risk that he will seek someone who is sexually more responsive than she is. While the underlying dynamic in this sort of situation is intrapsychic rather than situational, it mediates what transpires in the situation, particularly with regard to the woman's willingness to be assertive in the service of her own sexual needs.

There are numerous situational factors which may cause a normal woman to be sexually unresponsive even if the relationship is generally satisfying. If she is worried or anxious about anything, the effect can be inhibitory. A sick child, a visiting mother-in-law in the next bedroom, noises in the hallway, fear of pregnancy, or if the relationship is illicit, fear of discovery and guilt feelings—all these can be inhibitory. Alcohol, tobacco, and body odors can be offensive.

In spite of everything, however, most women are responsive at least some of the time. For those who are not, new therapies are directed not only at the general causes of sexual dysfunctions, but at specific factors which are immediately related to the symptom: general lack of response, inability to reach orgasm, and vaginismus.

Treatment of Sexual Dysfunction

The new therapies for treatment of sexual dysfunction differ from conventional approaches in several important ways. First, the dysfunction itself is seen as the problem. By contrast, a psychoanalytic approach would see the dysfunction as a symptom whose cause must be discovered in the deeper layers of the psyche and dealt with. Only then would the symptom yield. The new therapies, while not neglectful of underlying problems or pathologies, are based on the recognition that many persons who have sexual problems are otherwise normal in every way. Second, the goals of sex therapy are limited to relief of the sexual dysfunction. The initial aim of the therapy is directed at the immediate causes of the problem. More distant possible causative agents, such as childhood events, are dealt with only if they are directly related to the impairment of the individual's sexual functioning. Third, sex therapy employs prescribed tasks and exercises which the client and her partner carry out when they are alone. They are given specific instructions as to what to do in their lovemaking in order to achieve the desired results. Traditional treatment takes place in the therapist's office and rarely includes direct intervention in the client's life or the assignment of tasks.

These basic differences are not uniformly observed by all sex therapists. Many innovations in procedure and technique have been introduced since Masters and Johnson described their model in 1970. Helen Kaplan, whose approach we are describing here, considers sex therapy to be a form of psychotherapy. Although the goal is limited to removal of the sexual problem, the treatment also takes into account both the deeper and the immediate causes. Thus etiological factors such as those we have just discussed are not ignored even if they are nonspecific to the dysfunction and vary greatly among persons with the same symptom. Kaplan views sex therapy as "a task-centered form of crisis intervention" (p. 199) within which conflicts can rapidly be solved.

Treatment of general sexual dysfunction is directed primarily to the creation of a nondemanding, relaxed, and sensuous atmosphere in which sexual responsiveness develops. Communication with the partner about her sexual feelings and wishes is encouraged, and certain experiences are prescribed which reduce sexual anxiety and facilitate the unfolding of sexual feeling. These are, in sequence, the sensate focus, genital stimulation, and nondemand coitus. Sensate focus requires that the couple refrain from intercourse for a while, limiting their erotic activity to touching and caressing each other's bodies. Freed from the pressure of having to respond, the woman can relax and abandon herself to her own sensations as she focuses on the feelings evoked by her partner's nondemanding attention to her body. This experience, repeated over a period of time if necessary, often is successful in producing erotic arousal in the woman. When this happens, genital stimulation, again nondemanding and noncoital, is begun. In response to the woman's arousal, and without any pressure to produce an orgasm, intercourse is the next step. The woman is encouraged to focus her attention on her vaginal sensations with the aim of heightening sensory awareness. The experience is in her control, the goal being to bring out her responsiveness. Therefore, the partner must be willing to suspend his own drive to satisfy his needs in the interest of pleasuring the woman. The exercises have two advantages: they are designed for the erotic pleasure of the woman, and they relieve her of any pressure to respond. Because of this nondemand quality, they do not mobilize that anxiety previously associated with sexual activity (Kaplan, 1974).

This treatment is frequently successful in producing sexual arousal in the nonresponsive woman. Orgasm may or may not result from the process. If it does not, then the failure to have an orgasm is treated as orgasmic dysfunction, the inhibition of the orgasmic component of her sexual-response cycle.

Kaplan conceptualizes the inhibition of orgasm as an over-control of what is basically a reflex function by means of an involuntary ceasing of the response when the premonitory sensations appear. The treatment includes both psychotherapy which fosters awareness of the conflicts causing her to stop at a point just before orgasm, and exercises which show her how to eliminate the blocking of the response. The procedures are different for the woman who does not have orgasm at all and for the woman who has orgasm under some conditions but not others. For the first kind of problem, the exercises are a combination of eliminating tension, encouraging adequate stimulation by masturbation or use of a vibrator if necessary, and teaching the woman to use such aids as fantasy and muscular contractions. Some women are unable to have orgasm in coitus because

they require more clitoral stimulation than penile-vaginal intercourse provides. Inability to have an orgasm through coitus alone is
extremely common. However, such women were formerly seen as
frigid or sick, because it was thought that only the vaginal orgasm
was achieved by mature, healthy women, whereas the need for clitoral stimulation for orgasm to occur was an immature persistence of
childhood sexuality. According to Kaplan, some women with high
orgasmic thresholds cannot reach orgasm in coitus because coitus
alone can never provide the stimulation they need. In such cases,
anxiety about her failure is dispelled by counseling, and the woman
and her partner are reassured that clitoral stimulation to orgasm is
completely normal and in no way inferior to coital orgasm. They are
shown ways to maximize clitoral stimulation during coitus by both
manual and postural variations.

The treatment of vaginismus is less complicated than the treatment of the other sexual dysfunctions. Vaginismus is an involuntary
conditioned response which originates in fear of penetration of the
vagina. Its treatment has two elements: alleviating the fear and de-
conditioning the response. The woman is given reassurance and
support in addition to an explanation of her vaginismus and its
probable origins, and she is instructed in the procedure which she
will use at home to gradually eliminate the muscular contraction
which closes the vagina. Basically this involves dilating the vagina in
gradual increments by inserting, for example, a finger or a tampon.
When the woman can tolerate this without anxiety, further dilation
is begun. In some cases, a graduate catheter is used, beginning with
a very thin tube and progressing gradually to each next-larger size.
It is most important that the desensitization proceed at a sufficiently
slow and relaxed pace that anxiety is not aroused. At no time should
the procedure be repellent or frightening to the woman.

Do the new sex therapies work? Compared to the use of traditional therapy, such as psychoanalysis, other kinds of psychotherapy,
or psychiatrically based treatment, the results are impressive. Both
Masters and Johnson and Kaplan report that almost all persons they
have treated are either cured or improved. Masters and Johnson reported an overall cure rate of 80 percent with their two-week treatment regimen, and a five year relapse rate of only 5 percent. While
not reporting overall percentages, Kaplan agreed with Masters and
Johnson that the treatment is close to 100 percent effective for
vaginismus and that the great majority of nonresponsive or nonorgasmic women can be helped by these short-term methods developed specifically for the treatment of the sexual dysfunction. Sex
therapy is not a panacea, however. The best results are obtained
with psychologically healthy people whose relationship with their sex

partner is basically sound and rewarding. Kaplan is careful to describe the conditions under which failure to improve or adverse reactions can occur.

Sexual dysfunctions of males can be of importance to women, just as the dysfunctions of women can be important to their male partners. The male sexual dysfunctions of impotence and premature ejaculation and their treatment are dealt with in detail in both Masters and Johnson (1970) and Kaplan (1974).

Homosexuality

The term *homosexual* simply means a sexual preference for one's own sex. Homosexual behavior has been observed throughout history across most cultures. It has variously been regarded as a sin, a crime, a mental disorder, and a life style. There is no single known cause for homosexual preferences; in fact, the assumption that there is such a cause implies that homosexual behavior is symptomatic of an illness.

Responding to pressure both from professional mental-health workers and from homosexuals themselves who do not see themselves as mentally ill, the American Psychiatric Association in December, 1973, decided to remove homosexuality from its status as a mental disorder. Further, many states and other countries, such as West Germany, England, and France, have decriminalized homosexual acts between consenting adults.

Female homosexuals are often called lesbians. The word comes from Lesbos, the Greek island home of Sappho, a sixth-century B.C. poet who wrote love lyrics to her young female students. The sexual activities of lesbians may include all kinds of sexual behaviors observed among any human group: kissing, caressing, oral-genital stimulation, breast stimulation, mutual masturbation and so on. Simulated coitus, with one woman lying on top of another, is relatively uncommon, as is the use of an artificial phallus, or dildo (Katchadourian and Lunde, 1975).

Lesbian women do not fit any stereotypes of personality or appearance. A lesbian may adopt a masculine or feminine role similar to traditional roles of males and females in marital relationships. The "butch" or "dyke," for example, may wear male clothes and take a protective stance toward the "femme," who appears more conventionally feminine in dress and mannerisms. Younger lesbians are less likely to adopt such stereotypical roles.

The liberation of sexual attitudes from old prejudices and misconceptions has resulted in increasing acceptance of homosexuality in both sexes. Kinsey found that about one-tenth of his sample expressed tolerance for homosexuality, whereas in the Playboy survey, one-half of the respondents thought that homosexuality should be legal and agreed with the statement "There is some homosexuality in all of us." The gay liberation movement has encouraged many homosexuals to identify themselves. Its basic goal is to free its constituents from social, legal, and economic sanctions against them and their life styles so that they may receive the same treatment accorded to other members of society. Members of the lesbian contingent of the feminist movement see themselves as subject to dual discrimination, both as women and as lesbians. This group believes that women will never have true freedom and equality until they are totally independent of men, sexually as well as in every other way.

In view of the changing social climate, one might expect the incidence of homosexuality to increase. But this does not appear to be the case. While the data are less than completely reliable, Kinsey (1953) and Hunt (1974) found remarkably similar incidences of homosexuality in their samples. About one in five single women and one in ten married women eventually have some homosexual experience. It is extremely difficult to make any definitive statements about the incidence of homosexuality since, as Kinsey pointed out, people cannot be placed in two discrete categories, heterosexual and homosexual. Homosexual experiences in childhood are quite common, and among girls in the thirteen-to-nineteen age range, about 6 percent have one or more homosexual experiences (Sorenson, 1973). The incidence of exclusive homosexuality among women is estimated to be between 0.5 and 1 percent of the adult female population (Katchadourian and Lunde, 1975). This is about one-third the incidence among males.

Individuals may have only a few homosexual experiences in an otherwise heterosexual life. Others may be bisexual, equally interested in sexual activity with partners of both sexes. Some engage in homosexual behavior only under conditions of deprivation, as in prison or other sexually segregated situations. Except for persons who are exclusively homosexual, the question of who is and who is not has no meaningful answer. In fact, the question itself is probably meaningless.

Because of the protean nature of the phenomenon of homosexuality, theories of its etiology and psychological correlates are for the most part quite unsatisfactory. Notions about causative factors in early childhood and in unresolved neurotic conflicts came mostly from studies of patient populations conducted when it was widely believed that homosexuality was an aberration properly classified among the mental disorders (Rosen, 1974). It is only in the last few years that the view has emerged that homosexuality is not a discrete clinical entity, like alcoholism or appendicitis. Furthermore, studies of nonpatient populations have shown that homosexuals are not necessarily emotionally disturbed. Rather, they exhibit the same range and kinds of psychological disorders as heterosexuals do. If a higher incidence of such disorders occurs among homosexuals, a common-sense explanation would rely on the obvious effects of societal stigma, persecution, and discrimination which in the past have driven the homosexual into concealment and secrecy, often alienating her or him from family and society.

"We have begun to question whether homosexuality is really a psychologic illness or merely a way of life for much of our population" (Auerbach, 1968, p. 170). Contemporary psychological studies of lesbianism indicate that the only difference between lesbian women and others is their choice of lover. Lesbian women do not have a higher rate of psychological disorders than heterosexual women have. A recent psychological study of twenty-six members of the Daughters of Bilitis, a lesbian organization, found no significant difference between the lesbians and heterosexuals (Rosen, 1974). Their psychological test results varied in the same ways as in all normal groups, and the overall pattern was normal with respect to psychological functioning.

The psychology of lesbians is not a special category in the psychology of women. Nor is the sexuality of lesbians different, except in the sex of the partner. The sexual-response cycle and the range of sexual behavior do not distinguish lesbians from heterosexual women, nor do their sexual problems. Homosexual couples are now appearing for sex therapy with the same kinds of problems that heterosexual couples have.

Birth control 8

Men and women have always longed both for fertility and sterility, each at its appointed time and in its chosen circumstances. This has been a universal aim, whether people have always been conscious of it or not.
—Norman Himes, The Medical History of Contraception, 1963

The shift from the Victorian moral position that held sex to be a duty in the service of procreation to the evaluation of sex as an intrinsically rewarding activity quite independent of procreation was made possible by technological advances which separated sex from its biological consequences. Although the motivation to achieve and to maintain pregnancy has traditionally been reinforced by both social and personal needs, compelling social trends and related value shifts have undermined the reproductive aim of sexual behavior and reduced the number of children that women will have, as well as the number of women who will have children. Coexisting in the past and in the present with the desire to realize fertility potential is the opposing desire to limit or control it, to make it contingent upon individual choice rather than biological chance. The development of methods and devices which prevent or terminate pregnancy have freed sexuality from reproduction. They can now be viewed as quite separate aspects of a woman's life to a far greater extent than ever before.

Although the worship of fertility is the basis for most if not all of the oldest known religions, attempts to limit fertility, to control and space births, are as old as history itself and are documented for the last four thousand years. Women in any known society have never had as many children as they theoretically could. Under favorable conditions the greatest number of children that a woman could produce during her reproductive life is about twenty. But the total maternity ratio, the average number of live births per woman past 45, even in nonindustrial societies, rarely is greater than 5 or 6 (Wood and Suitters, 1970). In the United States the number of births per woman declined from 7.0 in 1800 to 2.3 in 1971. Thus it is appropriate to consider some of the values that are served by birth control, and the rewards to the individual and to society that accrue as a result of the limitation of fertility.

Values of Birth Control

Although explosive population growth has been only recently defined as a problem, it is not difficult to identify factors mediating attempts to control births by those living in earlier times on a less crowded planet. These could have included the availability of food, land, and other resources; the difficulty of migrating with a large family; and the desire to avoid illegitimate children. Also, uncontrolled fertility could mean that an individual woman would be either pregnant or lactating all the time, thus reducing her availability for sexual purposes. The Egyptians saw the avoidance of pregnancy as a way for women to retain their youth and beauty, and four millennia later, Jane Austen, the British novelist, approved of the late marriage of a niece, writing, "You will be quite young in constitution, spirits, figure, and countenance, since confinement and nursing make women grow old" (in Wood and Suitters, 1970, p. 104).

Contemporary values which support birth control reflect both individual needs and social pressures. The recognition of women as individuals and their increasing participation in nondomestic activities mitigate against large families and a lifelong dedication to serving them. Children extract a very high price in time, effort, and money, and though most women still expect to experience the role of mother, few are interested in spending all of their adult life caring for young children. The emergence of such values as egalitarian male-female relationships, sexual adjustment, and the quality of life is compatible with the desire for few or no children. The woman's right to control her own body and to enjoy her sexuality without fear of pregnancy are dependent upon reliable methods of birth control. Sexual adjustment in a relationship is easier to achieve in a situation uncomplicated by pregnancy or fear of it.

Successive pregnancies close together are associated with health problems for both mother and child. The ability to space pregnancies permits consideration of the woman's general condition, as well as health factors such as diabetes, heart disease, or psychiatric conditions, which could be aggravated by pregnancy. Statistically, family size is related to child health as well as intellectual level and later achievement, all of which are related to standards of living. Control of a family's size allows its economic condition to be given consideration and permits greater flexibility in choices pertaining to quality and style of life.

Another advantage of birth control is the reduction of risk of transmitting genetic disorders to children. Huntington's chorea, cystic fibrosis, and certain anemias are examples of genetically transmitted disorders which married adults might not wish to chance in offspring.

Social pressures favor limitation of family size and avoidance of unplanned pregnancies. Since the worldwide population crisis has given priority status to curbing the birth rate, large families have come into disfavor. Responsible fertility control is seen as the only way to solve the population problem, and in most societies this control must still be left up to individuals.

The prevention of pregnancy among the unmarried continues to be regarded as desirable in our society. While such pregnancies are more easily terminated today and are viewed with greater tolerance whether terminated or not, they still are rarely planned or wanted and often involve many problems and much personal distress.

Though the human fertility rate has not yet been brought under control, a developing technology is providing the scientific basis to make such control possible on a broad social basis. Birth control, however, is still very much an individual matter. Its management is not only an important social issue but a crucial determinant in the lives of women.

Methods of Birth Control

The methods of birth control currently available and in use fall into four categories: abstinence, sterilization, contraception, and abortion.

Abstinence

Abstinence for birth control means refraining from heterosexual genital intercourse in order to avoid the risk of pregnancy. Sexual abstinence has historically been advocated for a variety of reasons, most of them related to religion or character development. The notion that abstinence was correlated with sanctity seems to have been a Christian invention. St. Paul, for example, spoke very plainly in an Epistle to the Corinthians:

It is good for a man not to touch a woman . . .

For I would that all men were even as I myself . . .

. . . he that standeth steadfast in his heart, having no necessity, but
hath power over his own will, and hath so decreed in his heart that
he will keep his virgin, doeth well (I Corinthians 7: 1, 7, 37).

Proof of victory of the spirit over the body was the major motive for
abstention from sexual intercourse during most of the Christian era
until the nineteenth century, when physical health of the male was
added to its benefits. Conservation of semen meant conservation of
energy, and life would thereby be lengthened and debilitating diseases warded off. Sexual abstinence in marriage continued to be
widely advocated all during the nineteenth century, primarily in the
service of moral and health beliefs. Its practice as a method of birth
control was publicly advocated by Thomas Malthus (1766–1834),
who proposed it as a solution to the crisis he foresaw of population
outstripping the ability of earth to support it. Though his solution
was never taken seriously, his concern with the problem of population was an important factor in changing attitudes about contraception. Today, abstinence in preference to other methods of birth control continues to be practiced for religious, moral, or health reasons,
or when no other method is available.

In the narrow sense of our definition, it is clear that abstinence
as a method of birth control does not necessarily mean total abstention from sexual activity. Nocturnal (involuntary) orgasm, petting to
orgasm, self- or mutual masturbation, and oral-genital stimulation
are all sexual outlets used by persons who are abstaining from genital intercourse because of the risk of pregnancy.

Two widely used methods of birth control which require partial
abstinence are the rhythm method and *coitus interruptus*. The rhythm
method relies upon abstaining from coitus during the woman's fertile period. As a general rule an ovum is released from the ovary
about fourteen days before the onset of the next menses, but this is
highly variable. It is generally accepted that the ovum lives for about
twenty-four hours after ovulation if it is not fertilized. Sperm can
survive for approximately forty-eight hours once they reach the
uterus. Theoretically, then, a woman can become pregnant only during about three days per cycle. Abstaining from intercourse during
this period has long been a favorite method of birth control by individuals who felt they must eschew chemical or mechanical methods
because of their religious beliefs. Unfortunately, it is difficult to determine accurately the fertile period since women vary in their menstrual schedules and an individual herself may vary considerably

from month to month. Two-thirds of women are sufficiently irregular that the use of calendar rhythm alone offers too little protection from the risk of conception. This is especially true of adolescents who commonly experience irregularity for the first few years of their menstrual history, and of women who have just given birth and whose periods are not reestablished on a regular basis. Further, if a woman is lactating she may not menstruate at all.

A slight additonal safeguard relies upon the maintenance of a temperature chart during the monthly cycle. At the time of ovulation there is a slight drop in body temperature followed by a rise of half a degree or more, which persists until just before the onset of the next menses (McCary, 1973). One problem is that the change in temperature is not remarkable in some women. Another is the necessity for preparing a chart and for taking and recording the temperature, all requiring planning and resources which are not available for many women. At any rate, the effectiveness of calendar and thermal rhythm for birth control is quite low (McCary, 1973).

Coitus interruptus is one of the oldest and most widely used methods of birth control, as well as one of the least effective. It is correct to consider it a form of abstinence only in that the male abstains from ejaculating into the vagina by withdrawing the penis just before ejaculation occurs. Many couples use this technique successfully over a long period of time. Members of the nineteenth-century Oneida colony, a commune in upstate New York, trained themselves in its use not only for birth control but for the prolongation of sexual pleasure for both sexes. Failure results if the man does not withdraw in time, if the secretion of the Cowper's glands[1] contains sperm—which can be the case even if ejaculation does not occur— if he has an early partial ejaculation, or if he ejaculates near enough to the vulva that the motile sperm can find their way into the vagina.

Neither abstinence in the narrow sense that we have defined it nor coitus interruptus as methods of birth control need have deleterious effects upon the female since these do not preclude the female orgasm. If the male is practiced in the use of coitus interruptus and can delay his climax until the woman has had as many orgasms as she wishes to have, then his ejaculation outside instead of inside the vagina may not be of great consequence to her. The psychological effects of such methods are more likely to come from lack of confidence with the resulting fear and anxiety, thus spoiling her pleasure as well as interfering with her capacity to have orgasm.

---

[1] Cowper's glands are the male counterpart to the Bartholin's glands of the female.

Sterilization

Sterilization is a procedure, usually surgical, by which a person is made sterile, that is, unable to reproduce. Women have been sterilized by X-irradiation of the ovaries or by intrauterine application of radium, but the obvious hazards of such methods mean that they are highly unlikely to be used for sterilization today. In women, sterilization may be effected by removal of the ovaries or the uterus, or by interruption of the Fallopian tubes, the last being the most common when the goal is sterilization and not treatment for a gynecological disorder (see Fig. 7.3).

There are several methods of sterilization. *Oophorectomy,* or removal of the ovaries, brings ovulation and the ovarian cycle to a permanent halt, thus inducing premature menopause in the younger woman, unless she is treated exogenously with estrogen. *Hysterectomy* involves the removal of the uterus and sometimes the ovaries and uterine tubes as well. As a sterilization method, hysterectomy is most often performed at caesarian section. An advantage of hysterectomy is that it removes the risk of uterine cancer. It also means the cessation of the menses, but if the ovaries are left intact the supply of estrogen is unaffected and menopausal symptoms would not occur any sooner than they would have otherwise. Removal of the ovaries or the uterus or both is a major surgical procedure, usually involving an abdominal incision, and requiring several days' hospitalization followed by two or three weeks of recuperation.

Tubal sterilization is accomplished by interrupting the uterine tubes to prevent the passage and union of sperm and ova. While over one hundred variations of this method are used (Overstreet, 1970), most of them may be subsumed under three types. *Tubal ligation,* or *salpingectomy,* is a major surgical procedure in which the tubes are cut, a section is removed, and the ends are tied off. *Laparoscopic sterilization* is a more recently developed technique which is becoming quite popular. Two small incisions are made in the abdomen, one to admit the laparascope (an instrument for visualizing the area), the other for the passage of an electrical instrument which cuts the tubes and cauterizes their ends. This procedure leaves no scars, is relatively inexpensive, and requires only a few hours' hospitalization. It is less likely to be reversible than the ligation method and seems to have a lower failure rate (McCary, 1973). *Reversible sterilization,* by placing small clips on the tubes, offers an option to the woman who may not wish to chance an irrevocable decision. The surgery involved in placing or removing the clips is minor and can be performed on an outpatient basis.

Tubal sterilization has an analog in the male of vasectomy, a procedure in which two small incisions are made in the scrotum and the sperm-carrying ducts, the vas deferens, are cut, sectioned, and tied (see Fig. 7.2). Since no abdominal surgery is required, a vasectomy is simpler and safer than tubal methods for the female are.

Psychological effects of sterilization. For many women the reproductive system with its manifestations of menstruation and pregnancy is inextricably related to their self-concept, their identity as women, and their concept of youthful femininity. To the extent that this is so, any violation of the system resulting in the visible cessation of its functions would have the potential for producing undesirable psychological side effects. For example, with the reappearance of uterine bleeding in postmenopausal women who were started on estrogen replacement therapy some women experienced an elevation of spirits at this sign of "rejuvenation," though others found it a nuisance (Kaufman, 1967). Body systems and organs can be invested with a meaning that is far beyond their biological function, and for women the reproductive system is probably the best example, being that which defines them as women, making motherhood possible, a source of both pain and pleasure to themselves and others, and a potent variable in the transactions between the sexes.

One approaches the research on psychological effects of sterilization with caution for several reasons. It is not always possible to separate the noncontraception effects of the surgery itself from the psychological impact, if any, of sterility. When a woman develops symptoms of emotional disturbance following sterilization it is not always discernible whether her symptoms were caused by the surgery or by her knowledge of her sterilization, or whether they would have occurred anyway in the absence of either. Many of the studies are on small samples, and in addition there are the usual difficulties of definition of terms and lack of precision in psychiatric diagnosis. Also, differential effects would logically be expected between surgery performed at the woman's request and involuntary sterilization for medical reasons, or between, for example, tubal sterilization and hysterectomy, since the former is less traumatic physically and includes the possibility of reversal. Also, hysterectomies are often performed because of cancerous or precancerous conditions, whereas tubal sterilization is most often an elective procedure. If the hysterectomy was related to the threat of cancer, the woman's psychological reaction would be expected to reflect not only her sterilization but also the life-threatening reason for it.

A variety of symptoms following surgical contraceptions have been reported (Rodgers and Ziegler, 1973). Among them are depression, pregnancy fantasies, false pregnancy, and sexual dysfunction. Negative emotional impact, however, is highly individual and is a function of a number of variables such as the woman's emotional stability, her mate's attitude, the size of her family, her understanding of the procedure, and whether or not the operation is elective. One group of women who had had a hysterectomy had marked differences in response to the operation. Some regretted the termination of the menstrual function, seeing it as a way of getting rid of body waste; others were concerned about sexual activity, believing themselves to be tender and vulnerable inside. Of importance is the fact that no general response characterized this group. Since any changes that occurred were in no way uniform for all individuals, no basis exists for generalization (Drellich and Bieber, 1958).

Because of the paucity of general findings on the psychological effects of sterilization, attempts to understand or predict such effects must focus on the individual and on the factors that are relevant to her particular case. An example of the interrelatedness of such factors was the experience of a twenty-eight-year-old woman who was married and had two children, a boy aged seven and a girl aged five. She had been under treatment for a year for menstrual problems, including irregularity and heavy flow, when her physician advised her to have a hysterectomy and "get it over with." She related this to her husband, who agreed, whereupon she had the surgery and was hospitalized for about a week. A month or two later, she began feeling anxious and depressed. She believed that her interest in sex, which had always been high, was diminished, and that she was no longer attractive to her husband. She became obsessed with the idea of having an affair, of actively seeking out someone just to have intercourse with—not to satisfy her sexual needs, but to prove that she could attract a man. Although she was relieved of her menstrual problems, she said that she "missed her periods," and wished she had them back. When questioned, she did not know whether only her uterus had been removed, or her tubes and ovaries as well.

In this case, while the woman and her husband had agreed to the doctor's advice, the procedure and its implications had not been adequately described to her. Even if the presence of a uterus has little or nothing to do with sexual pleasure, on a psychological level she equated it with her identity as woman and felt bereft when it was gone. Its meaning, and its loss, had brought out old insecurities which had been dormant within the context of a favorable life situation. Also, the irrevocability of the decision to terminate her reproductive capacity with its cyclical reminder of her sexual identity created anxiety and the feelings of depression which often accompany loss of something of value to the individual. Her age was a factor in that termination of the menstrual cycle would be expected to have a different meaning to a twenty-eight-year-old than to a woman in the climacterium or older. She did not understand the role of ovarian function in introducing the climacterium. If the ovaries had indeed been removed, she should have known this so that she could seek hormonal replacement treatment. It turned out that in this case they had not, but that fact had not been explained to her either before or after the surgery. She required several months of psychotherapy in order to free herself of the psychological aftereffects of her sterilization.

Negative effects have been observed more often following hysterectomy than after tubal sterilization. One study contrasted twelve hysterectomy patients with ten tubal-ligation patients. Both groups had had elective surgery for contraceptive purposes only, but psychological reaction was much more favorable in the latter group. Even so, 20 percent of the tubal-ligation group and 75 percent of the hysterectomy group were rated as having a "poor outcome," suggesting that more attention should be paid to preparation of the patients and to the possibility of such sequelae (Barglow *et al.*, 1965). Since this was a small sample consisting mostly of low-income black women seen at a public clinic, no generalizations can be made. The findings are merely suggestive, but they are consistent with a common-sense expectation that the tubal procedure would result in fewer problems.

A review of the literature concluded that no adequate data are available on severity of emotional response to surgical contraception, the majority of subjects are satisfied with the results of their surgery, and there is no compelling evidence to indicate widespread negative emotional sequelae to the procedures (Rodgers and Ziegler, 1973).

Contraception

Contraception may be defined as the use of substances or devices whose purpose is to prevent pregnancy resulting from coitus between fertile partners. Although the "discovery" of sperm did not occur until the seventeenth century, an Egyptian papyrus dated 1850 B.C. described three methods of birth control all of them involving introduction into the vagina of substances which might have retarded the motility of sperm or had a spermicidal effect, such as honey, sodium carbonate, and a paste made of crocodile dung. The use of lint or wool tampons soaked in herbs, wine, and a variety of bark or leaf distillations was recommended by Egyptian writers as early as the sixteenth century B.C., a method which continued to be used in Western society as late as the nineteenth century. Soranos of Ephesus, a Greek physician of the second century A.D., presented a long list of vaginal barriers, such as various oils and tampons, and suggested that people should refrain from intercourse when conception was likely. Unfortunately for those who took his advice, he thought the fertile period was around the time of menstruation (Wood and Suitters, 1970).

During the Middle Ages and subsequently, contraception came to be viewed as a sin, and advice on methods could not be openly promulgated unless one wanted to risk swift punishment. Many tracts were written containing advice on how to conceive, and how to avoid errors which presumably would result in failure. A thirteenth-century Dominican bishop, Albert the Great, wrote about reproduction and the causes of failure to conceive. Mistakes included failure to achieve simultaneous orgasm, and errors of position. If the woman lay on top, the semen would flow out, thus preventing conception. Other female behaviors, such as rising after intercourse, jumping, sneezing, or urinating, would dislodge the semen and interfere with conception. The attention given to such mistakes suggests that these were deliberate methods used to prevent conception (Wood and Suitters, 1970).

Although the origin of the condom, or penile sheath, is lost in antiquity, it apparently was first described by Fallopius, a sixteenth-century physician whose interest in female anatomy resulted in the uterine tubes being designated by his name. Fallopius described a linen condom to prevent syphilis, and by the early eighteenth century condoms of gut were available. The major use of the condom was to protect the male from infection, although Casanova attributed some of his fame as a lover to his considerate use of it to avoid pregnancy for his partner.

Casanova is also credited with the use both of a gold ball in the vagina to block the passage of sperm, and of a hollowed-out half lemon placed over the cervix. During the 1870s commercial devices to cover the cervix began to appear. Annie Besant, a follower of Malthus, sent private circulars to women describing the "womb veil," a rubber cap on a flexible ring to be inserted into the vagina over the cervix.

During the nineteenth century gynecologists began to prescribe an incredible assortment of items for introduction into the vaginas and uteri of their female patients to enhance fertility, prop up "fallen" or prolapsed wombs, and cure a variety of female complaints all attributed to the reproductive system. One popular device was the so-called stem pessary, which had over a hundred variations. The basic design was something like a long-stemmed mushroom, such that when inserted, the flat disclike part remained in the vagina covering the cervix while the stem went through the cervix into the uterus. In accordance with the eccentric gynecology of the time, these devices continued to be advertised and prescribed both to cure infertility and to prevent pregnancy well into the twentieth century.

A German physician named Graefenberg is usually credited with the invention in the early 1920s of an entirely intrauterine device to prevent pregnancy, although centuries earlier Arab travelers and oriental farmers were known to introduce pebbles into the uteri of their camels and other animals to prevent unwanted conceptions. Graefenberg's device was a coiled ring made variously of gut, silver, or gold. The precursor of today's popular IUD's, the metal varieties had to be abandoned because they often caused uterine infections.

For thousands of years humans have searched for a reliable, reversible contraceptive that could be taken orally. Apparently contraception was not forbidden in early Jewish law, and herbal drinks were given on occasion by rabbis to women who for one reason or another ought not to become pregnant. A fifteenth-century Spanish story, *La Celestina,* describes contraceptive potions issued by Celestina, a midwife, abortionist, and "something of a witch," and Daniel Defoe wrote in 1727 of women who took "purgations, potions, and poisons" to avoid childbearing (Wood and Suitters, 1970). But an effective oral contraceptive had to wait until science developed an adequate understanding of the female reproductive system, its hormonal regulation, and the hormones themselves.

The search for the perfect contraceptive continues. Those substances and devices that are available, their effects on women, and the trend of continuing research are the topics of the next section.

Oral contraceptives. The clue to the development of oral contraceptives was the fact that during pregnancy a woman does not ovulate owing to the large quantity of progesterone in her blood. This hormone is secreted by the corpus luteum, the ovarian structure which develops from the site vacated by the ovum as it erupts from its follicle. During the 1930s progesterone was isolated from the ovarian tissues which produce it, and a decade later it was shown to inhibit ovulation in rabbits. However, extraction of the natural hormone from female animals was prohibitively expensive, and serious development of its use on humans did not begin until the 1950s following the discovery that progesterone could be derived from certain plants. Subsequently progesterone was synthesized in the laboratory and a number of related products collectively called progestagens, all resembling progesterone in their actions on the body, became available in large quantities. Early experimental trials with these substances confirmed that some were indeed powerful inhibitors of ovulation, but that they gave poor control over the menstrual cycle with irregular, unpredictable bleeding. Combination of the synthetic progestagen with a synthetic estrogen, however, relieved this problem, and in 1956 such a combination was successfully tested in controlled studies on Puerto Rican and Haitian women. Thus began the era of "the Pill." In less than two decades the development and production of oral contraceptives became a huge pharmaceutical industry, and the Pill in one form or another became the most widely prescribed method of fertility control in the United States (Garcia, 1970).

Several dozen varieties of the oral contraceptive are presently available, most of them consisting of a combination of synthetic estrogen and progestagen in varying strengths and dosages. Basically, the Pill acts by imitating the state of pregnancy. The ingestion of the hormones normally secreted in large quantities during pregnancy causes the pituitary gland to inhibit its production of FSH, the hormone that promotes the maturation of the ovum in its ovarian follicle. Thus no ova mature, and fertilization cannot occur. Also, the hormones have an effect on the intrauterine surface, modifying it so that implantation of a fertilized ovum is less likely to occur; in addition, they cause the mucous plug of the cervix to become more resistant to the invasion of the uterus by sperm.

Typically, a woman takes the Pill for twenty consecutive days, beginning on the fifth day following the onset of her menstrual period. Normally her next period will begin about three days after she takes the last dose. This regimen thus effects a twenty-eight-day menstrual cycle which is highly predictable for most, but not all, women taking the Pill.

Many variants of the basic concept of endocrinological control of fertility have been developed, and others are being tried experimentally. One example is the so-called mini-pill, consisting of a very small amount of progestagen and no estrogen. Taken daily, it does not affect ovulation or menstruation, but it makes the cervical mucus thick and sticky, rather than thin and watery as it normally is during the ovulatory period, thus preventing the passage of sperm into the uterus. The advantages of this method are in the elimination of the undesirable side effects associated with the estrogen content of the conventional pills, and in the daily schedule, which avoids the necessity for counting days and thus reducing the possibility of forgetting.

Another variant is the "morning-after" pill, involving the administration of large amounts of estrogen for several days following possible exposure to pregnancy to prevent implantation of the zygote in the uterus. This treatment is not used routinely for contraceptive purposes because of negative side effects associated with the high estrogen level.

Research trends in hormonal contraceptive development are aimed at convenience, safety, reliability, and feasibility for large-scale fertility control programs (*Population Council Annual Report,* 1973 and 1974). Among methods currently in experimental trial are: progestagen compounds that can be injected, providing slow and constant release of the hormones over a long period of time; implants under the skin of plastic rods containing progestagens, also for long-term release; vaginal rings and contraceptive arm bracelets made of plastic incorporated with progestagens to be gradually absorbed through the skin; a monthly pill to bring about the menstrual discharge by suppressing the corpus luteum function, thus eliminating the progesterone base necessary for preparation of the endometrium for implantation; and post-coital pills to be used on a regular basis to prevent sperm penetration of the cervical mucus. Hormonal compounds to arrest sperm production or to prevent sperm maturation in males are being tested in clinical trials; however, the only male contraceptive device in widespread use is the condom. That contraception continues to be woman's work is indicated by the 1974 report of the Population Council, showing that of ten new methods being tested, nine are for women and only one is for men.

Reactions to oral contraceptives. Women who begin taking the oral contraceptive pill almost always report physical changes and frequently psychological changes as well. The nature and extent of these changes are dependent upon a number of factors. First, the pills contain synthetic estrogen and progestagen in amounts considerably higher than those produced by normal ovarian function, thus producing symptoms associated with elevated levels of these hormones. Commonly reported physical symptoms include increased breast size with soreness and tenderness, water retention and weight gain, headaches, nausea, vaginal discharge, more regular menstrual cycles, and improvement of acne. Second, types of pills vary in the relative amounts of estrogen and progestagen they contain. Considerable evidence indicates that the gonadal hormones influence mood states in women, although the results are far from definitive (Janowsky and Davis, 1970). In general, high estrogen compounds have been associated with positive mood effects, while high progestagen compounds are more likely to have depressive effects (Grant and Pryse-Davis, 1968). These data fit with observations that many women who are not taking the Pill report feelings of well-being during the ovulatory part of their cycle when estrogen levels are high, and depression and other negative effects during the premenstruum when endocrine levels are low. Third, the individual physical and psychological status of the woman herself can be expected not only to interact with Pill-induced changes, but also to determine her perception and tolerance of them and her reactions to them.

While the oral contraceptive pill is the most effective contraception product currently available, it is not without physical risk. Its most serious side effect, attributed to the estrogen content, is the increase of coagulatory action of the blood, thus increasing the possibility of thromboembolic (clotting) disorders. Recent studies in the United States and the United Kingdom reveal that the risk of a thrombotic stroke is about nine times greater for women taking the pill. This risk is greater in white women than black, and greater for cigarette smokers than for nonsmokers. However, the probability that any given woman will develop thromboembolic disorder is small. Of every one million women taking the Pill, about one hundred will be admitted to the hospital, and about five will die each year from a thrombotic stroke attributable to the preparation (Vessey, 1973).

Psychosomatic and psychological reactions to the Pill have been assessed through tests and interviews used to evaluate personality and attitudes toward the body before and three months after beginning the use of oral contraceptives. The women reported three kinds of body changes: normal, unusual, and beneficent. Normal changes were those expected because of the high hormone levels, including breast soreness, weight gain, and the others mentioned above. These changes tended to be reported by psychologically normal women, who acknowledged them with normal levels of anxiety or hostility. Unusual changes were the opposite of the expected drug effects, and included smaller breasts, irregularity of menstrual cycle, and more acne. Women reporting these kinds of changes were characterized by passivity, difficulty in expressing anger, and feelings of being used in the sexual relationship. Beneficent body changes were increased energy, reduced appetite, and weight loss. Women who experienced such changes had a high degree of dependency upon the sexual partner for self-esteem, and such positive changes were seen by them as enhancing their value to the partner (Bardwick, 1973).

The subjects in this study also reported on psychological changes subsequent to Pill use. Some of these changes were: feeling less feminine and attractive, increase in depression and anxiety, and decreased interest in sex and frequency of orgasm. Such negative changes were reported by both psychologically healthy and less healthy subjects. The healthier women were expressing appropriate levels of anxiety and resentment as they perceived normal body changes resulting from their responsibility for contraception. The passive women who had unusual changes seemed to be somatically expressing their anger, an indirect form of hostility toward those who might be responsible for their unpleasant symptoms. Dependent women with a high fear of pregnancy were most likely to report positive psychological changes with anxiety reduction and enhancement of self-esteem. Thus the preexisting personality of the woman interacted with hormonally induced effects to determine to some extent both psychic and somatic consequences of Pill use. Other variables are also important. The woman's relationship with her partner, her feelings about the sexual use of her body, her motives for avoiding pregnancy—these and other dynamic factors must affect her reactions to the use of any contraceptive, let alone one with such telling effect upon her entire reproductive system (Bardwick, 1973).

Intrauterine contraceptive devices (IUD'S). IUD's are small devices either plastic or metal which are inserted into the uterus by a physician. They are believed to act in some way to prevent implantation of the zygote in the wall of the uterus. The IUD remains permanently in the uterus until the woman wishes to become pregnant at which time a doctor can remove it.

Since the IUD is a foreign object, the uterus may attempt to reject it at first. About 10 percent of all IUD's are expelled in the first year, though 40 percent of these will be retained on a second insertion (Westoff and Westoff, 1971). Some women experience cramps and bleeding after insertion, a reaction which usually disappears after a few days or weeks. IUD's have become very popular in the past ten years especially among women who cannot take oral contraceptives because of negative side effects. They are inexpensive, require no attention, and have no common side effects other than those mentioned. However, they are not as reliable in preventing pregnancy as oral contraceptives are. About 2 percent of women with IUD's in place become pregnant in the first year of use. After that the risk is less.

A serious but uncommon risk with the IUD is infection from perforation of the uterus. In fewer than one in ten thousand cases, performation occurs when the device is inserted into the uterus. Although this is a rare event, it can be fatal. Obviously, the skill of the physician is important in reducing or eliminating such a risk.

New types of IUD's continue to appear. Several of these use the IUD as a carrier for an antifertility agent, such as progestagen or copper. One of them, the Copper T, is now widely used in other countries, including India, where it is the major method in a national family-planning program (*Population Council Annual Report,* 1974). The Copper T is smaller and causes fewer side effects than the older IUD's. The action of the copper is effective for two years, at which time the device must be replaced. There is currently no evidence that the minute amount of copper released into the uterus does any harm to the body.

The diaphragm. The diaphragm is a shallow cup made of thin rubber on a flexible ring, designed to fit over the cervix to prevent the passage of sperm into the uterus. Fitted and prescribed by a physician, it is used with a spermicidal cream or jelly which also provides lubrication. It must be inserted shortly before intercourse and left in for six to twelve hours after in order for the jelly to be effective.

While in principle the diaphragm and spermicide combination is highly effective, in practice it has a failure rate of 5 to 20 percent. There are several reasons for this. Unless advance plans have been made, the woman must interrupt the love-making to insert the diaphragm. One is often tempted not to use it. The diaphragm may be inserted incorrectly, or it may slip during intercourse. Correctly fitted and used, however, the diaphragm is a reliable contraceptive device with no negative physical side effects.

Other contraceptives. A few contraceptives are available without a physician's prescription. These include the condom, chemical methods, and douches.

The condom, or penile sheath, is made of thin rubber or sheep intestine. About 7½ inches long, it is slipped over the erect penis before penetration. It works on the simple principle of containing the seminal fluid so that none of it gets into the vagina. There are several possibilities for failure, however. The condom may be defective; it may break during use; or it may slip off after ejaculation when the penis becomes flaccid or is withdrawn from the vagina. The condom may be inspected before use by blowing air into it. If seminal fluid spills into the vagina owing to breakage or slipping off, contraceptive cream or jelly should be inserted into the vagina immediately. If this is not available, a water douche can be used.

Correctly used, an intact condom is highly effective. It is the most widely used contraceptive in the United States, and the only one used by men. Also, it is the best method, other than abstinence, to prevent the spread of venereal diseases.

Chemical methods of preventing conception are spermicidal

creams, jellies, and foams. They must be introduced into the vagina a few minutes before ejaculation occurs, and the process repeated if intercourse continues. These substances, while better than nothing, are among the least reliable of the contraceptives, with a failure rate of about 25 percent.

Douches can be used to flush seminal fluid out of the vagina immediately after ejaculation occurs. Water alone, or combined with vinegar or a commercial preparation, is a harmless vaginal wash, but mostly ineffective as a contraceptive. Although water is toxic to sperm, the douche often fails to reach them because they move so rapidly into the cervix. Studies on the effectiveness of douches as a regular means of contraception report a failure rate of about 35 percent

Abortion

Abortion is the practice of terminating unwanted pregnancies. A Chinese medical text described a method for inducing abortion by mercury five thousand years ago, and Egyptian papyri of the same era describe other techniques. Abortion was common among the Greeks and Romans both for population control and for the preservation of feminine beauty. Greek philosophers favored family limitation for eugenic reasons, and Aristotle spoke frankly to the matter:

> If it should happen among married people that a woman, who already had the prescribed number of children, became pregnant, then before she felt life, the child should be driven from her (Taussig, 1936, p. 32).

Presaging contemporary concern with the ethical issues of abortion, Aristotle believed that it should be permitted before the soul entered the fetus, but not after. Since this event was thought to occur at forty days for the male and eighty days for the female, abortion would be restricted to to the first forty days. Methods included abortifacient drugs, instrumental interference, and intrauterine injections. Drug-soaked tampons and pessaries made of metal or wood were also commonly used (Bates and Zawadski, 1964).

The practice of induced abortion has been found among nonliterate people all over the world. Methods include the ingestion of supposed abortifacient drugs and herbs, violent exercise, and if these are not effective, beating or stamping on the abdomen. Mechanical means such as an "abortion stick" are also common. Used by a primitive Hawaiian group, the stick is a curved piece of wood about twelve inches in length and one inch in diameter, coming to a sharp point. The handle is carved in the form of the head of an island god.

In Western society, the development of moral and legal sanctions against the practice of abortion is traceable through the corpus of Jewish law and the position of early Christian theologians. The Old Testament contains only one reference to it, stating that a fine may be levied "if men strive together, and hurt a woman with child, so that her fruit depart," but she herself survives. But if she were fatally injured, then those responsible had to "give life for life." (Exodus 21: 22–23). The Talmud ruled that the unborn child might be destroyed to save the mother's life. These two references sum up the classic Jewish view: abortion was permissible only to save the mother's life; otherwise, destruction of the unborn child was a serious offense, but not murder (Jakobovits, 1973). Christian theologians almost from the beginning denounced abortion for any reason whatsoever. Sanchez, a sixteenth-century Italian, allowed that a rape victim could attempt to get rid of her attacker's semen, but this right was terminated at the moment when the semen achieved "peaceful possession" of the victim's uterus (Means, 1970).

Since effective contraception has only recently become available, it is safe to say that abortion has historically been the most widely practiced method of birth control. The history of abortion is the history of women's attempts, for whatever reasons, to avoid bearing unwanted children and to have some measure of control over their reproductive function. During the colonial period in the United States, the sanctions against abortion were mostly religious and moral, involving strong social taboos. In the nineteenth century, as an independent body of American law developed, most of the states passed laws making abortion a criminal offense unless to save the life of the mother (David, 1973). These laws became unconstitutional by a Supreme Court decision on January 22, 1973. Before then, it was estimated that over one million abortions were induced in the United States each year, and that one in every five pregnancies was terminated by abortion (Smith, 1973). There is no reason to doubt that these figures have increased significantly since then.

Abortion means the termination of a pregnancy before the fetus is viable, that is, before it can survive outside the uterus. It is generally held that a fetus is nonviable prior to the beginning of the seventh month, although there is considerable variation in the definition of viability (David, 1973). Several medical methods are in use for the induction of abortion, depending upon length of the pregnancy and preference of the physician.

Methods of abortion. The vacuum suction method is now the most commonly used medical technique for the termination of pregnancy up to twelve weeks. The cervix is dilated under local or general anesthesia and a sterile tube attached to a vacuum aspirator is inserted into the uterus. The fetal tissue is withdrawn, the whole procedure taking only a few minutes. This procedure is usually done on an outpatient basis, as hospitalization is not required.

A relatively new related practice is the removal of the uterine contents before pregnancy is confirmed. Menstrual extraction, as it is called, is not abortive in the strict sense of the word, though its use is to the same purpose. It requires the use of the suction technique by a physician if the woman's period is overdue and she has reason to believe she is pregnant.

Dilation and curettage (D and C) is an older method for removing contents from the uterus. Under anesthesia, the patient's cervix is dilated and the curette, a metal loop shaped like a small spoon on a long handle, is inserted into the uterus and used to scrape its walls to remove tissue. Some doctors who are familiar with it continue to use it for abortion, although the suction method is generally held to be preferable because it is faster, safer, and involves less physical trauma to the uterus. Dilation and curettage requires hospitalization for a day or two.

The usual method for inducing abortion during the second trimester is by saline injection, also a hospital procedure. A hypodermic needle is passed through the abdomen and the uterine wall into the amniotic sac, and a quantity of amniotic fluid is withdrawn. A like quantity of saline solution is then injected into the sac, killing the fetus and inducing labor in a few hours. The fetus is then expelled much the same as in a normal delivery.

A hysterotomy may be performed if for some reason the other methods are contraindicated or if a tubal sterilization is also planned. This operation is actually the same as a caesarian section. The uterus is surgically opened and the fetus removed. This is considered major surgery and usually involves a few days of hospitalization.

At the present time, no chemical abortifacients are in general use in the United States. The prostaglandins, a group of naturally occurring fatty-acid derivatives found in many body tissues, have the effect of producing uterine contractions resulting in expulsion of the fetus. They are administered intravenously or directly into the uterus, a procedure requiring several hours. Since their use requires hospitalization and a lengthy procedure, they have no advantage over the suction method in early pregnancies. Their only advantage so far in their development is that they make a nonsurgical abortion possible in the second trimester of pregnancy.

Psychological effects of abortion. Do women typically experience negative psychological effects as a result of having an abortion? Examination of the literature on the after effects of abortion reveals an almost complete turnabout of medical and psychiatric opinion on this question. Prior to this decade it was difficult to find a psychiatric authority who did not believe that the experience of abortion left serious psychological scars on the woman's psyche, especially depression and guilt. A few years later the emerging research on post-abortion psychological effects is almost unanimous in proclaiming them negligible. Several factors appear to be important in bringing about this change.

First, the climate of belief about abortion and its relation to woman's role has changed. One typical psychiatric attitude is that since woman's main role on earth is to conceive, deliver, and raise children, it was to be expected that "when the function is interfered with, we see all sorts of emotional disorder" (Bolter, 1962). As long as doctors and women themselves believed that their main role was defined by their reproductive function, that is, "A woman is a uterus surrounded by a supporting organism" (Galdston, 1958), then the logical extension of this belief led to a prediction of distressing consequences to interference with it. The emergence of different views which valued women's freedom to define their roles in any way they chose forced a revision in thinking about women which required a changed attitude toward abortion.

Second, it is only since the legalization of abortion in this country that carefully controlled research studies on the psychological sequelae have appeared. Earlier opinion tended to be based on a few case studies or on uncontrolled clinical observation, the resultant data being used to buttress arguments based on the particular belief of the reporter—a marriage of ideology and evidence which may constitute revealed truth to the believer but is hardly science. Objective research directed to this question has generally contradicted psychiatric belief in the emotional-trauma theory of abortion.

Third, the legalization of abortion and its widespread acceptance and availability have largely moved it out of the class of behaviors for which one should, in the traditional view, feel guilty and be punished. Prior to the 1973 decision, a woman living in a state with a liberal abortion law could have a safe legal abortion if a psychiatrist would certify that the continuance of the pregnancy was detrimental to her mental health. Since that time, however, large numbers of women have had legal abortions simply because they did not wish to have a child, regardless of the reasons for such a wish. This removal of abortion from the influence of religious and quasiscientific beliefs permits its effects to be more accurately measured.

The question of whether abortion would have the negative psychological aftereffects which had been attributed to it was the subject of a study (Fingerer, 1973). Tests measuring anxiety and depression were administered to groups of persons as follows: group 1a, numbering 324 women who came to a clinic for an abortion during a three-week period; group 1b, numbering 177 of the women in group 1a who returned questionnaires after their abortions; group 2, consisting of 207 men and women who accompanied group 1a to the clinic; group 3, consisting of male and female postdoctoral students in psychoanalytic training programs; and group 4, made up of female graduate and undergraduate psychology students who were asked to role-play either the abortion patient or one accompanying her to the clinic. Groups 1a and 1b were instructed to respond to the tests in accordance with how they felt on the day of the abortion and again afterwards. Groups 2, 3, and 4 were asked to project themselves into the abortion patient's position and respond as they thought she felt. According to the results, the women who were the abortion patients reported less anxiety and depression than did any of the subjects who were predicting how they would feel. The postdoctoral psychoanalytic group predicted the highest scores for anxiety and depression; the lowest scores came from the responses of the women themselves, after the abortion. In contrast to psychoanalytically oriented predictions of psychological distress associated with abortion, the women themselves reported only a transient mild depression which was not above expectation for any minor surgical procedure. "The psychological aftereffects of abortion seem to reside in psychoanalytic theory and societal myths" (Fingerer, 1973).

Another recent study reported on the characteristics of 154 unselected women who contacted a "problem pregnancy" counseling service, and on the subsequent adjustment of about two-thirds of those who obtained abortions. Interviews were conducted before the abortion and in a follow-up contact between one and two years following the abortion. The interviews were structured to elicit social and psychiatric information pertinent to the patients' adjustments. A year or more after their abortion, 90 percent of the women interviewed reported no negative psychological consequences. In addition, three-fourths of them recalled no negative reaction immediately following the abortion. In contrast, many of them reported feelings of relief and satisfaction, and 94 percent were satisfied with their decision. The small number who had regrets felt that they had been influenced by others. Thus the study did not support the belief that women frequently experience guilt and depression following abortion. The few women who did report depression experienced it as mild and self-limiting, not requiring professional help or impairing functioning (Smith, 1973).

Other studies confirm that psychologically healthy women do not usually suffer adverse effects from the experience of abortion.

To the contrary, the termination of an unwanted pregnancy with its concomitant stress alleviates the emotional distress accompanying such a condition. Abortion per se, however, does not necessarily modify a preexisting psychiatric condition. Women with the most severe symptoms before an abortion are likely to show the most severe symptoms later. The abortion is simply an intervening event with no specific causal effect (Sarvis and Rodman, 1973).

The availability of safe means for limiting fertility and the legal right to use them are probably more important than any other agents of change during the long course of women's history. All the evidence indicates that healthy women are in no way harmed by being able to choose whether or not they wish to have a child. Since the widespread use of reliable contraception and the availability of abortion are still less than a generation old, the full effects of chosen motherhood as a matter of course on women and on whole societies will be more apparent in the future. In the meantime, most women want to experience, at least once, woman's oldest role. The events leading up to the role of mother and their psychological effects are the subject of the next chapter.

Pregnancy, childbirth, and breast-feeding

9

It cannot be argued that childbirth is both an unbearable pain and a bearable pain, both a situation from which all women naturally shrink in dread and a situation towards which all women move readily and happily, both as a danger to be avoided and a consummation devoutly to be desired. At least one aspect must be regarded as learned, and it seems simpler, in the light of present knowledge to assume that women's attitudes towards childbearing and men's attitudes towards childbearing have complex and contradictory elements in them. . . .

——Margaret Mead, *Male and Female,* 1949

The capacity of women to bring forth young and to nourish them from their own bodies has always had a profoundly impressive effect upon attitudes toward them as well as upon women's own perceptions of themselves and their roles. Whether worshipped as goddess, symbol of regeneration and the earth's own fecundity, or viewed with facile sentimentality as God's special creation for the protective, all-forgiving care of the young, woman as childbearer has preoccupied artists, mythmakers, and philosophers of all cultures. While her power to excite desire and to satisfy men sexually has been variously valued, causing her to be treasured in some times and burned at the stake in others, her ability to reproduce has inspired men to create goddesses in her image and to imbue her with great power for good as well as for evil. Only in recent times has the fertility of women begun to be negatively valued as pressures increase to limit growth of the numbers of people on earth. It remains to be seen how this entirely contemporary devaluing of woman's primary biological function will affect her future status. Clearly the role of woman is changing rapidly in response to demands for equal opportunity to participate in all the goods and activities of the society, but this change will be accelerated by pressures on women to limit to one or two the number of children they have or to refrain from having any at all.

Concern about population growth has generated interest in factors that influence family size. Advances in birth-control technology and the increasing availability of information and family-planning services have only recently provided alternatives to the traditional destiny of women ordained by reproductive capacity. But visions of a brave new world made possible by technology have had to be tempered on more than one front by the sobering recognition that traditional behaviors which come to be seen as hostile to broad social interests may continue in spite of the recommendations of social planners. The availability of the technological means to avoid or to safely terminate pregnancy, for example, does not necesarily lead quickly to results in all affected segments of the population. Reproductive behavior, because of its unmatched importance in the life of the species and of the individual, is a function of accretions of values, beliefs, and attitudes which powerfully affect the ways it will be played out or modified. A change in extrinsic mitigating circumstances inevitably meets resistance from covert motivations which may be difficult to identify or to change. The experience of the woman in all societies has always included the bearing and rearing of children, and thus her performance of and identification with these functions has shaped her concept of herself as a woman and as a human being and has determined in a real sense her value, whether she lived in a palace, a harem, or the slave quarters of a plantation.

Motivations for Having Children

There is a strong and widespread desire for children among couples in the United States. One study revealed that the average number of children wanted was between three and four. Only 2 percent of the population wanted one child or none, compared to estimates of 6 to 11 percent favoring childlessness during the Depression (Pohlman, 1970). Since children are no longer an economic asset but a drain on family finances and since they have other important negative consequences such as loss of freedom and worry and concern for parents, the motivation for having them must be very strong.

Understanding of variations in fertility rates and in cultural and historical trends is facilitated by examination of the possible *value* of children to parents, particularly to women. A theoretical model for studying such variations included the value of children as one of its elements (Hoffman and Hoffman, 1973). In this system the ways in which children are valued are related to psychological needs that are influenced by the society and thus are subject to cultural variation. The values all have the potential of being satisfied by some aspect of parenthood, though alternative means of satisfying them are possible.

Especially for the woman, having a child is seen as conferring upon her adult status and identity. Becoming a mother implies that one is no longer a child. The responsibility for new life is expected to elicit mature and conscientious behavior, more characteristic of the adult than of the child one was. A new identity emerges: one is now Mother, which is more than just a name. This identity implies a whole new and lasting set of duties, commitments, and values, not the least of which is a new sense of being important, of being truly necessary to another person.

Children are often valued as an expansion of the self, as permitting oneself a kind of immortality. Two persons become three, or five or more, providing a bridge to the future by which one's physical and psychological characteristics can continue beyond the evanescent self.

Values associated with morality encourage the production of children in some groups. Catholics, for example, are enjoined against the use of birth control on religious grounds and tend to want more children than Protestants do (Rainwater, 1965). The Judeo-Christian tradition clearly viewed having children as a moral duty and barrenness as a curse. Altruistic needs are served by the sacrifices required by parenthood. Lack of interest in having children is often seen as selfish, a sign of unwillingness to share one's time or goods, whereas the willingness to endure the difficulties, suffering, and sacrifice involved are seen by some as evidence of strength of character, integrity, and other cherished values of American society.

Children make a family and thus supply primary group ties through which affiliative needs can be met. They can add stimulation, novelty, and fun to a household. As they grow and change they provide a continuing challenge to parents who want to experience them and to understand them. The expectation of a new baby is fraught with mystery and anticipation. "Each one is different," mothers say. Studies of the values of having children find that parents related feelings of joy, and describe their children as a source of happiness to them.

Parents of all social classes report feelings of creativity, accomplishment, and competence from the experience of having and rearing children. A woman with several young children may have few other ways to demonstrate competence and to win recognition;

thus the observable results of her skills in this area can give her a deserved feeling of achievement. For the mother especially, having one or more children gives her a degree of power, the ability to command service or concessions from others that she would otherwise not have. Children are also seen as a chance to have an effect on the world, particularly by persons who are otherwise powerless. For persons who are disadvantaged in the population because of race or social class, or for women of all classes, a baby holds forth the chance of making a difference. Having a baby is something one *can* do.

The economic value of children varies greatly from one society to another. In developing countries with rural, subsistence economies, children provide valuable work when they are young, and later they give care to aged parents. In the United States, however, the economic value of children is very low, as in all industrialized countries with higher standards of living, child labor laws, and compulsory education.

Given these values associated with having children, is it possible to predict a person's or a group's desire for children? There are four motivational variables whose relative strengths are determinants of the desire to have or not to have a child: alternative sources of the value, costs, barriers, and facilitators (Hoffman and Hoffman, 1973). Alternatives are other means besides children for actualization of a value. For the woman, a career and the independent life style it affords can serve many of the same values associated with having children. The availability of such alternatives could be expected to affect the number of women desiring children, as well as the number of children desired by individual women. Costs pertain to how much one must give up or sacrifice in order to obtain the values associated with having a child. For example, freedom of activity and flexibility of one's personal schedule are drastically reduced when one has small children. Barriers and facilitators are the factors which realistically lower or raise the probability that the value can be realized by having children. For example, the prevailing belief that having more than two children is inconsistent with genuine concern for the future of humankind is a barrier, while the desire of one's parents for a grandchild is a facilitator.

Even though alternative sources of gratification are increasingly available for women, and the costs and barriers seem to outweigh the facilitators, there is no evidence that even a high-status, interesting career is a completely adequate substitute for having children. A study of graduate women at Yale found that the majority wanted three or more children, and 82 percent of the women in the law and medical schools wanted at least three (Levine, 1968). Even though the seventies brought a dramatic shift in family size aspirations of college women, most still planned to have children. A study of a national sample of freshman women revealed that 58 percent felt that raising a family was an "essential" or a "very important" personal objective (Wilson, 1974).

The reproductive events leading up to motherhood not only define the major experiential differences between women and men, but because of the dramatic and compelling nature of both their biological and psychological effects, they have a profound impact on any woman who experiences them. Men themselves have never been indifferent to the procreative power of women, reacting not only with wonderment and envy, but even with vicarious participation, taking on the very identity of woman as she moves through the reproductive process. In the next section we shall review the biological sequence leading to advent of a new life, and then consider some psychological and behavioral factors that are relevant to pregnancy, childbirth, and breast-feeding.

Pregnancy

The average duration of human pregnancy is 266 days, or nine months, although premature birth is not uncommon, and much longer pregnancies have been recorded.[1] Obstetricians think of pregnancies in terms of trimesters, or three-month periods. Each trimester has its characteristic features in terms of both the experiences of the mother and the development of the fetus. Our discussion will focus primarily on the experiences of the mother.

The first sign of pregnancy is usually a missed menstrual period, an event which is unlikely to be viewed with equanimity by any woman, whether joyous or distressed at its possible meaning. Failure to menstruate can be caused by other factors, however, such as psychological stress or malnutrition. Also, it is not uncommon for cyclic bleeding to persist during the first months of pregnancy, so that presence or absence of the menses is not always a reliable indicator. By the eighth week, the pregnant woman will begin to have other signs. Responding to greatly increased levels of estrogen, the breasts become somewhat enlarged and tender, and the woman experiences feelings of fullness and tingling with increased nipple sensitivity. "Morning sickness" or nausea, sometimes accompanied by vomiting, occurs in about 75 percent of pregnant women during the

---

[1] The length of a pregnancy sometimes has legal implications if a child is born when the husband has been away more than nine months. The longest pregnancy upheld as legitimate in this country was 355 days (Katchadourian and Lunde, 1975).

first six to eight weeks. Although this symptom has been widely held to be psychogenic, the present tendency is to view it as a physical consequence of hormonal changes, inasmuch as it also occurs in women receiving estrogen therapy and is a common side effect of the oral contraceptives containing estrogen. Other signs of pregnancy in the first weeks are increased frequency of urination, unusual sleepiness or fatigue, and deeper pigmentation of the nipples.

Having missed a period, many women wish to know as soon as possible whether or not they are pregnant, especially if they are contemplating an abortion. Endocrine tests have been developed which can accurately diagnose pregnancy from two to six weeks after the first missed period. The most popular of these is the agglutination test which relies upon the presence in the pregnant woman's urine of a hormone secreted by villi protruding from the implanted fertilized ovum. A sample of urine is mixed with chemicals. If agglutination (clumping) occurs the woman is not pregnant. This test will detect pregnancy two weeks after the first missed period with about 97 percent accuracy. The oral administration of progesterone is also used as a pregnancy test. If the woman is not pregnant, she will begin a period a few days after the progesterone treatment. If no period begins, then she is assumed to be pregnant.

A physician can usually diagnose pregnancy by examination at about the sixth week. By this time the uterus has increased slightly in size and the cervix has softened considerably. The physician will look for "Hegar's sign," a soft consistency of the area between the cervix and the uterus, which can be felt on pelvic examination. Even without endocrine tests, these changes together with some or all of those previously mentioned in a sexually active woman are usually considered as rather firm evidence of pregnancy.

Very early in the first trimester, the placenta, the organ which supports the life of the fetus, begins to develop from both fetal and maternal tissue. Sometimes called the afterbirth, it is a large, flat mass of vascular tissue which is connected to the fetus by the umbilical cord. The placenta mediates, in a sense, between the fetus and the mother. Through it pass oxygen, nutrients, and waste materials, as well as certain antibodies, drugs, and other materials which may be beneficial or harmful to the child *in utero*. The placenta has effects upon the mother too. It functions as an endocrine gland, producing a variety of hormones all during the pregnancy. One of these is human chorionic gonadotropin (HCG) which assists in the maintenance of the pregnancy by stimulating the continued production of progesterone during the first trimester. The placenta itself secretes large quantities of progesterone and estrogen until just before the onset of labor. The sudden decline in the level of these hormones is believed to cause labor to begin. Other hormones produced by the placenta prepare the mammary glands for *lactation,* the process of secreting milk. These hormones also inhibit the pituitary gland from releasing the actual milk-forming chemical until it is needed.

Miscarriage, or spontaneous abortion, is most likely to occur during the first trimester. An estimated 10 to 15 percent of all pregnancies end in miscarriage, and most of these happen before the fourteenth week. Although miscarriage may be caused by physical · trauma or by illness of the mother, in most cases the reasons are not known. About half of all miscarried fetuses are defective in some way.

The second trimester brings abundant evidence to the woman of the dramatic changes in her body as a result of her pregnancy. Confirmation of the pregnancy can now be made by physical signs alone. The physician can monitor the fetal heartbeat, and both can feel the movements of the fetus, which by the end of the sixth month, is about fourteen inches long and weighs about two pounds. The waistline of the pregnant woman thickens, and her abdomen begins to protrude; she is recognizably pregnant. Many women experience this period as the best time of their pregnancy. Most of the earlier symptoms have ameliorated or disappeared, and the woman is usually quite able to continue with her normal activities, barring complications. Many women experience feelings of serenity and well-being during this time, probably as a combination of attitude toward their condition and their high estrogen level.

Certain hereditary and biochemical defects of the fetus can now be detected during the second trimester of pregnancy by a procedure called amniocentesis. Fetal cells are obtained by tapping the fluid in the sac surrounding the fetus. These cells are cultured, and from them information can be derived on the child's chromosomes and cell biochemistry. The test has been used successfully to diagnose Down's syndrome, adrenogenital syndrome, and Tay-Sachs' disease,[2] among others. The value of amniocentesis in genetic counseling was demonstrated in one study of fifteen women with a 25-percent risk of delivering a child with Tay-Sachs' disease. Six cases of the disease were diagnosed; five were confirmed in the fetus after therapeutic abortion, the other after birth (O'Brien *et al.,* 1971). In another study of one hundred fifty pregnant women the test showed that the fetuses of fourteen had chromosonal disorders. Abortion was requested by thirteen of the women, and in each case the diag-

---

[2] Tay-Sachs' is a fatal hereditary blood disease found almost exclusively among Jewish people.

nosis was confirmed by the abortus. The fourteenth woman delivered a child with Down's syndrome (Nahum, 1970).

During the last three months the fetus grows very rapidly and is quite active, kicking, twisting, and turning, its vigorous movements sometimes interfering with the mother's sleep. Weight gain can be a problem during this trimester, when appetite increases and activity level usually slows. A weight gain of about twenty pounds is considered optimum for a full-term pregnancy, though many women may gain more or less than this and be perfectly healthy. The baby at birth accounts for about a third of this weight. Two or three more pounds will be lost at birth with the placenta and the amniotic fluid. The remainder results from enlargement of the uterus and breasts, and from retained fat and fluids.

About 7 percent of babies born in the United States are premature. Prematurity is a function of the weight of the baby, not of the length of the pregnancy. An infant weighing less than five and a half pounds at birth is considered premature. The less the infant weighs, the poorer its chances for survival. Babies who weigh less than four pounds at birth often develop fatal respiratory difficulties. In addition, premature babies who survive are more likely to have congenital disorders such as mental retardation and brain damage.

During the seventh month most babies move into a head-down position in the uterus. This is the most common birth position and is the most free from complications. A few remain upright in the so-called breach position, and some turn sideways in their orientation to the birth canal. Both these last positions can result in more difficult deliveries. But about 97 percent of full-term babies have turned to the head-first position.

Childbirth

Labor and birth are subjects of widely varying beliefs, attitudes, and practices around the world. Although our discussion of the reproductive events in women's lives is primarily from the perspective of our own society, we should be aware that these experiences are patterned in very different ways in other societies. An appreciation of this basic fact can give perspective on our own practices and show the effects of social forces on the conduct of these natural biological events. For this reason we shall briefly consider some attitudes and practices in other parts of the world before describing the typical biological sequence as most women in our society experience it.

Cross-cultural attitudes and practices

Patterns of behavior have been related to birth in nonliterate and traditional cultures, using both medical and anthropological sources (Newton and Newton, 1972). First, the attitudes surrounding the birth experience, such as privacy and sexual implications, achievement connotations, "dirty" or defiling effects, and the attitudes toward birth as a painful illness or as a normal process were examined. Second, practices in the conduct of labor and birth which result in different sorts of experiences for the mother were studied.

While all the cultures placed great importance on the phenomenon of birth, they varied greatly in their attitudes toward specific aspects of it. For example, the Navaho were very much interested and very open in their observance of birth, moving freely in and out of the hogan where a baby was being born and partaking of food and drink provided there. Others, such as the Cuna of Panama, surrounded birth with secrecy, concealing facts about it from children as long as possible, preventing them even from seeing animals during labor or birth.

In contrast to our own society, where the birth is often seen as an accomplishment of the obstetrician, the Ila of Northern Rhodesia shout praises of the woman who has given birth. Her husband and male relations give her gifts and congratulate her. Other groups feel that birth is a "dirty" process which defiles and contaminates both the woman and those who come in contact with her. For example, among the Kadu Gollas of India the laboring woman is isolated in a hut and is impure then and for three months after delivery. She and the child may not go home until permitted to do so by the deity.

People in many parts of the world view childbirth as a normal and even casual procedure, experienced with little apparent discomfort. Others combine an expectation of intense pain with strong social sanctions against crying out since such a display brings disgrace on the woman. The Aranda of Australia report pain only at the onset of labor, but make "little fuss" during the rest of the process.

There is also a great variety of practices in the conduct of labor. Food and drink may be prohibited or freely given to the woman in labor. She may be required to lie down or to stay in one place, or encouraged to walk about and actively exercise. While most births are social acts, occurring in the presence of others, a few are unattended by any other person. In almost all nonliterate groups, birth is women's business, and men are excluded. The delivery itself occurs in many different positions. In contrast to the usual supine position familiar to Americans, a survey of seventy-six non-European societies found that sixty-two used upright positions of kneeling, sitting, squatting, or standing, or combinations of these (Newton and Newton, 1972).

In looking at other ways of feeling and behaving, we can perceive and react to our own ways more clearly. Our society's attitudes and practices about childbirth are changing rapidly, and some of the changes reflect lessons learned from people from other cultures. The process of labor and birth, however, follows a biological sequence which is the typical experience for American women today.

Labor and birth

The onset of labor is triggered by hormonal changes resulting in the disinhibition of oxytocin, a pituitary hormone which is believed to initiate the contractions of labor and delivery. The entire process of childbirth, called *parturition,* occurs in three stages. The first stage begins with the earliest signs of labor and ends with the full dilation of the cervix. As a woman approaches the end of her pregnancy, she may experience back pains and irregular contractions of the uterus. Many a woman has gone to the hospital with such "false labor," only to return home and wait another few days or weeks. Several signs suggest that labor is imminent: regular uterine contractions at intervals of fifteen or twenty minutes, lasting about thirty seconds, mild and rhythmic in the beginning, and later increasing in frequency, intensity, and duration; the expulsion of the cervical plug, which appears as blood-tinged mucus; and the rupture of the amniotic membrane, or "bag of waters," which produces a clear fluid from the vagina.

By the time the cervix is fully dilated, which may be twelve to sixteen hours for first births, the woman is experiencing contractions every three to four minutes each lasting for about a minute. The powerful muscular walls of the uterus push the baby downward toward the birth canal. At about this time the woman is likely to be taken to the delivery room.

The second stage of labor begins with the full dilation of the cervix and concludes with the expulsion of the fetus from the mother's body. Powerful uterine contractions stimulated by the pituitary hormone continue to move the baby along the birth canal until its head is visible at the vaginal opening. In order to accommodate the passage of the infant's head and shoulders, which are the largest parts of its body, the opening of the vagina must stretch tremendously. In order to avoid tearing of the tissue between the vagina and rectum, the physician may perform an *episiotomy,* a surgical slit which is stitched after the birth and heals within a few days. Also during this period the mother is now instructed to push, or to bear down, to facilitate the emergence of the baby from her body. Once the head and shoulders are born, the rest of the body appears quickly. When respiration and independent blood circulation have been established in the infant, the umbilical cord is cut and clamped.

The third stage of labor consists of the delivery of the placenta, which separates from the uterine wall and moves out of the vagina a few minutes following the birth of the baby. Muscular contractions shrink the uterus and facilitate the detachment of the placenta. If an episiotomy was performed, it is now repaired with catgut stitches. This incision heals rapidly, after a few days of mild discomfort and itching.

Lactation

The first secretions of the breasts are not milk but *colostrum,* a protein-rich liquid which is present soon after parturition and meets the baby's nutrient needs, if breastfed, for the first two to four days of life. Colostrum is also thought to give the baby protection from certain infectious diseases for the first few months of life. The production of milk is induced by *prolactin,* a pituitary hormone, and within a few days the ducts in the breasts become engorged with milk. Oxytocin, the same hormone involved in uterine contractions, brings about the "letdown" response of the milk when the nipple is stimulated by the baby's sucking.

Postpartum amenorrhea (absence of menses) tends to be prolonged in breastfeeding women giving rise to the notion that conception is thus inhibited. While statistically the lactating woman is less likely to become pregnant, breastfeeding is an unreliable method of birth control. The first postpartum ovulation will occur before the first menstruation. If she is not using effective contraception when this happens, the nursing mother may become pregnant before she experiences her first postpartum menstruation. Women who are breastfeeding are generally advised not to take oral contraceptives containing estrogen because of the hormone's inhibitory effect on lactation, and because of the possible effects on the infant of ingesting it with the mother's milk.

Effects of Maternal Behaviors

Can the emotions and behavior of a pregnant woman have an effect upon her unborn child? A few years ago such a suggestion would have been dismissed as an old wives' tale, but contemporary research responds with a qualified affirmative. Several studies have found a relationship between the mother's emotional state during pregnancy and the infant's well-being and progress during the first few months of life. One study investigated the psychological adjustment during pregnancy of 177 women and found that among the multigravidae (women who had given birth before) those expressing more fears for themselves and their babies, and more tension, depression, and withdrawal, had babies who weighed less at birth and had a lower Apgar score than did those women not so affected (Erickson, 1965).

A Japanese study reported on maternal emotional characteristics and body-weight gain of infants in the early neonatal period (Murai and Sato, 1971). Babies whose mothers had scored high on tests of hypochondria and neuroticism during the second trimester showed inferior weight gain compared to babies whose mothers had scored in the normal range. The results suggested that emotional stress during pregnancy has a biological influence on the fetus, causing retardation of weight gain after birth. Another study revealed that experimentally induced stress could cause intense uterine contractions in pregnant women. The damage from psychological stress was thought to be a contributor to the higher incidence of stillborn babies among illegitimate, as compared to legitimate, births (James, 1969).

Infants born to mothers who were schizophrenic during pregnancy were compared to infants whose mothers became schizophrenic later and to infants whose mothers had a physical illness (Yarden and Suranyi, 1968). All the children were studied during their first six months while they were being cared for in a special facility for newborns. The children in the first group had the lowest weight gain in the first six months, suggesting that a stress factor operates during the pregnancy of schizophrenic women which later influences the child's development. Interestingly, the girl babies in this study weighed more than the boys, contrary to the usual finding, additional evidence that boys are more vulnerable to adverse conditions.

Numerous studies attest to the effects on unborn infants of various drugs taken by the mother. The widely publicized effects of the sedative thalidomide are a dramatic example. Many pregnant women who took this drug before it was banned gave birth to infants who had a condition called *phocomelia*, in which the hands and feet are attached to the body by short stumps rather than by normal arms and legs. Babies born to narcotics addicts are highly likely to be addicted at birth and to have withdrawal symptoms. They also have a high incidence of prematurity, low birth weight, and mortality (Perlmutter, 1967). Babies born to addict mothers treated with methadone are much less likely to manifest these effects (Blinick, 1968).

A six-year English study found that women users of amphetamines, marijuana, and LSD have a higher-than-average rate of congenitally malformed babies and more stillbirths than nonusers (McCary, 1973). Whether these substances caused such effects in the babies is not clear, however, in that it is possible that other factors in the lives of drug-using women may have contributed to both their drug use and their tendency to have defective infants.

Reports on the effects of maternal smoking on the fetus are equivocal. An early study found that infants whose mothers smoked during their pregnancy weighed less at birth than did infants born to nonsmokers (Montague, 1963). But a later study of eighteen thousand women disclosed that smoking mothers also had had lightweight babies before they started smoking, indicating that the birth weights of these babies might be related to other factors in the smoker, rather than to the smoking itself (Goodall, 1972).

Although there is no direct contact between the mother's nervous system or blood circulatory system and the fetus, many substances can pass from her blood vessels in the walls of the uterus into the umbilical blood vessels which serve the fetus. These include chemical substances as well as food and oxygen. Maternal factors affecting the fetus, aside from gross physical trauma, exercise their effect through this transfer mechanism. Special talents, physical stigmata, or personality traits of the child are not caused by specific maternal exposure to similar or seemingly related events, e.g., artistic talent in a child is not caused by his mother's frequent visits to an art gallery during her pregnancy!

Preparation for Childbearing

In contemporary society many young women grow up with little or no exposure to the verities of childbearing. Smaller families, the decline of the extended family, and the increased mobility of young married couples make it less likely today than in the past that a young woman will be near her mother, older sisters, or other supportive friends and relatives who, though often misinformed, can often give emotional support and offer examples to her as she approaches labor and delivery. It is not atypical for a woman to experience her first pregnancy with very little understanding of the changes in her body and to approach her labor and delivery with practically no idea of what to expect. The usual course of a pregnancy includes monthly visits to an obstetrician in his private office or to a clinic for physical check-ups which monitor the condition of the woman and the fetus. Toward the end of the pregnancy, visits are more frequent, and the patient may be given information about anesthesia, probable length of hospital stay, and other procedural matters. When her labor begins she goes or is taken to the hospital and admitted to a labor room, where her husband may or may not be allowed to stay with her. If she receives general anesthesia, as many women still do, she will have no memory of the experience and will not even see the baby until hours later (Ostrum, 1975). Most hospitals place newborns in a nursery, bringing them to the mother for feeding every three or four hours. Thus there is little opportunity for the mother, and even less for the father, to become acquainted with the baby and to begin to feel comfortable with it before the trip home.

Thus, the impersonality of the hospital, the separation from family and friends, the aura of illness, the strangers attending her, and the often total lack of knowledge about what to expect can frequently be frightening and demoralizing and constitute for many a highly negative introduction to motherhood. That non-preparation for childbearing continues to be the norm was documented in a study which found that of twenty-three hospitals offering obstetric care to a large metropolitan area, only five offered some kind of preparatory course for childbirth (Ostrum, 1975).

In contrast, a growing trend in this and other Western countries provides women with the option of another kind of childbirth experience which includes instructional preparation for both the woman and her husband, his presence at the delivery, minimal or no anesthesia to allow for her full participation in the birth, and immediate contact with the newborn, sometimes continued with the rooming-in of the baby with its mother during the hospital stay. The rationale for this kind of experience includes reduction of pain and anxiety for the mother, elimination of risk to her and to the infant from the use of conventional anesthesia, and the psychological benefits derived from sharing the event with her mate. Advocates of rooming-in also point out that the parents have a chance to become acquainted with the baby before they are confronted with the sole responsibility for it at home.

Two kinds of preparation for childbirth are growing in popularity in this and other countries. Called the Read method and the Lamaze, or psychoprophylactic (PPM) method, they and variants and combinations of the two are variously referred to as "prepared," "participatory," or "natural" methods of giving birth. The term "natural," while older than the others, has fallen into disfavor because of its implications that other methods, particularly those in which anesthesia is used, are unnatural. Neither the Read nor the Lamaze method precludes the use of anesthesia, although the mother's full, conscious participation in the birth is a key element in the training of both methods.

The Read method was introduced by the English physician Grantly Dick-Read through his book *Childbirth Without Fear* (1944). The theoretical basis of the Read method is the elimination of the vicious circle of fear-tension-pain-fear which is the result of ignorance and anxiety about the process of labor. Fear of anticipated pain causes contraction of the uterine muscles, creating a resistance against cervical expansion. The resultant tension state, according to Read, is interpreted by the woman as pain, which increases her fear and tension and augments the pain. The method prevents this cycle from getting under way by focusing on the reduction of both fear and tension. Through learning about the phenomena of pregnancy, labor, and delivery, she loses her "unreal" superstitious fear of the unknown. Beginning about the fourth or fifth month of pregnancy, she is trained in techniques of muscular relaxation, on the theory that if she can completely relax, she will not "fight" against the uterine action, thus permitting the cervical stretching and uterine muscular activity to effect an unimpeded and relatively painless delivery. Deep chest breathing and muscular exercises help the woman to achieve a state of relaxation during labor.

The Lamaze method was first developed in Russia, and was brought to France by the French physician Fernand Lamaze and popularized in the United States by Marjorie Karmel's book *Thank You, Dr. Lamaze* (1959). This method is based on Pavlov's conditioned-reflex work and relies upon re-educating the woman to dissociate pain sensations from labor. Any implication that uterine activity in labor is painful is avoided, and other physiological responses are conditioned to the sensations of labor so that these are not experienced as pain. These include rhythmic breathing or panting and abdominal effleurage (moving the fingers over the abdomen in a light, circular motion). Women are taught the physiology of labor and delivery and are trained to be aware of their body sensations in labor so that they can adjust their breathing and pushing activities accordingly. While both the Read method and the Lamaze method have in common the twin aims of educating the woman for childbirth and reducing or eliminating pain so that she can be conscious during the birth, they differ in that the Lamaze method actively engages the woman in the labor process while the Read method emphasizes relaxation and dissociation from body processes. Both methods and their variations stress the participation of the husband in both the training and the labor and delivery.

How do the participants feel about the effectiveness of such preparation for childbirth? These are some sample quotes from both takers and nontakers of a course (Tanzer, 1973):

Takers

The ride all the way to the hospital was nice because somehow being in the car, breathing, and being with my husband, I was very much in control.

I was pushing all the way into the delivery room, and it was really the most wonderful thing in the world to watch the baby being born. It was just fantastic. And to push with all my might to get him out, and to see him, his little body.

Nontakers

I was lost . . . no medication until then . . . I was screaming purposely . . . hoping one of the doctors would give me medication. It was horrible. I kept thinking I was dying.

I remember being wheeled into the delivery room. The doctor just gave me a shot, and the next thing, he held up the baby and put her on my stomach. I remember yelling, "Take him away!"

Many enthusiastic claims have been made by women who have had a childbirth preparation course. Lamaze training was related to participants' postpartum recall of experiencing feelings of mastery, personal control, and coping power during labor (Oliver, 1972). In another study twenty-two women who took a childbirth course were compared with fourteen who had delivery by conventional methods. Pain reduction was a joint product of taking the course and having a good menstrual history (Tanzer, 1973). In addition, women whose husbands were with them at delivery were more likely to describe it as a "peak" experience, a rapturous gratification of emotional needs. Since neither the Read nor the Lamaze method precludes anesthesia if the woman wants it, and since both result in a more knowledgeable participation in the childbearing process, it is difficult to see how the various components of the training could result in a worse experience than the woman would have had without them. Certainly, the informational aspects of the program and the rehearsals for labor seem to reduce the fear of the unknown and the sense of helplessness and isolation for first-time mothers and to give the father a more intimate role in the bringing forth of the child.

Imitations of Pregnancy

The ambivalence aroused by the phenomena of pregnancy and birth with their multiple meanings are nowhere more apparent than in the psychosomatic disorders and cultural practices whose distinguishing characteristic is an imitation of these great human events. Both females and males can manifest symptoms of pregnancy in the absence of an underlying reality. *Pseudocyesis* or false pregnancy is a psychosomatic condition in which a woman develops all the symptoms of pregnancy, including amenorrhea, abdominal distention, weight gain, and breast changes. It is found in about 0.1 percent of American women who consult an obstetrician (Katchadourian and Lunde, 1975). The *couvade syndrome* is likewise psychogenic, affecting a man during his wife's pregnancy with symptoms resembling those of pregnant women.

Pseudocyesis is an example of the close reciprocal relationship between a woman's emotional life and her body. The hormone-regulating function of the hypothalamus responds to conscious and unconscious feelings to produce many of the profound body changes of pregnancy. The psychodynamic interpretation of pseudocyesis is one which emphasizes the woman's conflict over her wish for pregnancy and her fear of it. Immature dependency and hostility toward her own mother may cause anxiety and a dread of pregnancy and its consequences. On the other hand, a pregnant state permits gratification of succorant and dependency needs. Thus the false pregnancy temporarily resolves the conflict.

Couvade symptoms may occur at any time after the third month of a wife's pregnancy (Enoch, *et al.*, 1967). The physical symptoms, including nausea and abdominal distention, are seen as manifestations of anxiety resulting from the threat of his wife's pregnancy to his own dependency needs, revival of old sibling rivalries, and envy of her new status.

The conscious or deliberate imitation of pregnancy as a superstitious or magic ritual among primitive groups has been observed all over the world (Frazer, 1950). Among the Dyaks of Borneo, if a woman is having a hard labor, a wizard outside the house ties a large stone to his abdomen and then proceeds to imitate the behavior of the woman in labor, moving the stone down his body in the belief that this will facilitate her labor. Several groups accomplish adoption of a child or an adult by an imitation birth ritual. The woman covers herself with a drapery, and the adoptive candidate crawls out from between her legs. The most commonly reported form of couvade, however, is that practiced by the man whose wife is in labor. He takes to his bed or hammock, writhes and moans as if in great pain, and finally "gives birth" in conjunction with his wife. Subsequently, he requires a period of convalescence during which he must be nursed and cared for. Explanations for the couvade include the man's envy of and wish to identify with the woman's creative act, as well as his need to establish a bond with the child through giving symbolic birth.

Sexuality and Pregnancy

Taboos against intercourse with a pregnant woman are very common in undeveloped countries and have historically been observed as part of religious rules among some people. Among the Ashanti of Ghana, the pregnancy taboo begins as soon as the pregnancy is determined. The husbands, tiring of abstinence, often take another wife, and it is not uncommon for women to practice abortion in order to avoid the long taboo (Saucier, 1972).

In our society the continuation of sexual activity by pregnant women is not only common practice but is generally sanctioned by physicians though precautions apply here as in other kinds of physical activity at this time. Although there is no evidence that sexual intercourse and orgasm harm the fetus or cause miscarriage or premature birth, women who have a history of miscarriage may be advised to avoid sexual relations for the first few months. Some obstetricians advise women to abstain during the last few weeks of pregnancy. Reliable studies of actual sexual practice during pregnancy are few, and results are equivocal or contradictory, but some trends emerge which may reflect the experience of a significant number of women.

A study of 101 women revealed an increase in sexual tension and performance during the second trimester which they attributed to the increased pelvic vascularity associated with pregnancy (Masters and Johnson, 1966). But other studies are in general agreement that sexual interest and activity fall off during pregnancy, especially during the last trimester (Solberg *et al.*, 1973). Interviews of 260 women in the immediate postpartum period were conducted for information on frequency of coitus, orgasmic function, sexual behaviors other than coitus, coital positions, and relation of sexual activity to prematurity. For most of the women, coital activity declined, though rate was related to sexual-interest level. Women whose sexual interest level had been high before pregnancy had higher orgasmic rates during pregnancy. Of the 44 women who had used masturbation to achieve orgasm during the two years before pregnancy, more than half did not use it during pregnancy. Hand stimulation by the woman's partner and oral-genital stimulation similarly declined. Side-by-side or rear entry became the preferred positions as pregnancy advanced. Prematurity and condition of the infant at birth were unrelated to sexual behavior of the mother during pregnancy.

Women who reported a change in their sexual behavior during pregnancy gave these reasons: physical discomfort, 46 percent; fear of injury to baby, 27 percent; and loss of interest, 23 percent. Less frequently reported reasons included awkwardness and loss of attractiveness. Of the 260 women, 29 percent were instructed by their physicians to abstain from coitus from two to eight weeks before the estimated time of delivery. Ten percent were advised about positions that might be more comfortable than the male superior position, and 2 percent received suggestions for sexual activities which could be substituted for coitus (hand stimulation for both partners in all cases). These data reveal a notable paucity of discussion between doctor and patient of sexuality during pregnancy.

While the authors conclude that many women experience a generalized loss of libido with advancing pregnancy, they also note that women's sexual interest and behavior during pregnancy is quite variable, emphasizing again the highly individualistic nature of female sexuality and its relative freedom from the hormonal, instinctual, and other nonlearned determinants which mediate the behavior of females of other primate species.

The resumption of coitus after the woman has given birth follows no particular pattern, and its regulation and prescription vary widely from culture to culture. Intercourse with a lactating woman is tabooed among some groups. The Abipon women of Paraguay, for example, nurse their children for as long as three years during which they have no intercourse with their husbands. Where there are no religious or cultural taboos against postpartum intercourse, abstention may be practiced for a few weeks for a variety of reasons relating to the woman's health and comfort (Saucier, 1972). Four out of six women in one study experienced erotic arousal four to five weeks after delivery, but their physiological responses—vasocongestion of the labia, lubrication, and orgasmic contractions—were reduced in degree and intensity. About half of this large sample of 101 women reported a low level of sexual response, their reasons including fatigue, fear, pain, and vaginal discharge. By three months, however, most of the women had returned to their pre-pregnancy level of activity (Masters and Johnson, 1966).

Psychological Aspects of Pregnancy

A number of influences converge to determine and to mobilize the psychological adjustment of the woman during pregnancy. First, the physical changes in body physiology and in body size and shape, which can evoke feelings in part dependent upon her perception of these changes. Second, her pre-existing psychological status, her capacity to handle whatever stresses accompany her pregnancy; third, her real-life situation, marital status and relationship, and the number and ages of her children; and finally, the psychodynamic meaning the pregnancy has for her, with its potential to evoke conflicts around dependency needs, rivalries with mother or siblings, hostility toward the husband, and unconscious attitudes toward the self and female functions. All these variables contribute to the woman's reactions to the pregnancy experience, their relative importance depending upon the individual.

Unfortunately, the research on the psychology of pregnancy is sparse, most of it dealing with unusual or pathological maternal behaviors. The course of a happy, healthy, uncomplicated pregnancy and delivery has only recently attracted research attention (Tanzer, 1973). It has been suggested that benign and uneventful pregnancies were the exception: "Even under the best of circumstances, and whether from professional or social observation, rarely is a pregnancy predominantly a well-timed, gratifying, welcome occurrence, in terms of unconscious attitudes as well as conscious acceptance" (Shainess, 1964, p. 240). Even so, pregnancy and childbirth are normal physiological events, and most are uncomplicated by serious physical or psychological pathology. The experience is not bland, however, and women have a wide range of feelings and reactions which are individual and yet part of a commonly shared experience.

Physical changes during pregnancy which are most closely related to psychological state are changes in gonadal hormone levels and changes in body size and shape. Elevations in estrogen and progesterone in pregnant animals have been shown to be related to decreased levels of norepinephrine (NE), a chemical substance manufactured in the brain. A review of the evidence for an association between decreased NE and depression indicated that many clinical depressions may be related to NE deficiency (Schildkraut, 1965). To test this hypothesis, a biochemical and psychological assessment of twenty-one pregnant women and a control group of nine women, all with no history of psychiatric illness was conducted. Urinary excretion of NE was significantly lower in the pregnant group, and the deficiency was found to be correlated with increased scores for depression in the psychological evaluation. It is hypothesized that the reduction in NE linked to the gonadal hormone changes of pregnancy might be responsible for the increased depression (Treadway *et al.*, 1975). This interpretation is based, however, on the important assumption that depression as measured by test scores of pregnant women is similar to clinically observed depression, and not all of those with reduced NE had test scores reflecting depression. The findings lead to a tentative conclusion that pregnant women have an increased biologic susceptibility to affective (mood) disorders, suggesting that other factors are important determinants of whether or not a given woman actually manifests a depression during pregnancy.

Changes in body size and shape are dramatic in the second and third trimesters, requiring radical alterations of the body image, of the way the woman perceives her physical self. One study found that the pregnant women, compared to the nonpregnant control group, felt less feminine and had increased levels of concern over the body and its functions. (Treadway *et al.*, 1975). Although there are no data bearing on this, we should note parenthetically that the feelings a woman has about her figure changes can be expected to reflect her attitude toward her pregnancy. An emotionally secure woman who wanted to be pregnant may well be proud of the visible evidence that she is expecting a child. On the other hand, a woman whose feelings of worth derive largely from living up to a conventional standard of sexual attractiveness may be anxious about what the pregnancy is doing to her figure. These observations demonstrate the important point that there is no direct causal relationship between the physical changes of pregnancy and the psychology of the pregnant woman. Rather, her psychological status is the result of interaction among the variables we are discussing.

Pregnancy, particularly the first one, is a developmental crisis in a woman's life, in that it ushers in a new stage of life with new tasks and problems which require adaptations and solutions that have yet to be learned. As a crisis, it escalates the total amount of stress experienced by the woman, making additional demands upon her psychological adjustment and coping ability. Consequently, her characteristic psychological status, as it is affected by the additional stress of pregnancy, is one determinant of her adaptation during pregnancy. Women with a history of menstrual symptoms, marital conflict, and anxiety had more physical symptoms during pregnancy, and anxiety during pregnancy was related to the amount of pain relief required during labor (Zuckerman, 1963). In another study a group of pregnant women with hyperemesis (pathological vomiting) were compared with nonvomiting pregnant women. Hyperemesis was more likely to occur in women who had repeated severe life stresses and previous illnesses. They also had a higher rate of prematurity and labor complications (Tylen, 1968).

Women who tend to be anxious and who have a timid or fearful approach to life and to new situations in particular can be expected to show elevations of these reactions to the experience of pregnancy with its perceived and real potential for demanding adaptations and life changes. For example, women who were afraid of pregnancy were more likely to manifest depression when pregnant (Kutner, 1971). But a large-scale survey of attempted suicides found that the incidence of such attempts was not greater for the pregnant group. In only one-sixth of the pregnant women did their pregnancy seem to be the dominant cause of the attempt. For most, the pregnancy was incidental to the attempt, which was related to the same kinds of emotional instabilities and interpersonal problems that characterized the attempts of the nonpregnant women (Whittack and Edwards, 1968).

Reality factors in the woman's life affect her psychological adaptation to pregnancy. Several themes emerged from a group of young married women who were both working to support their husbands and pregnant for the first time. There were concerns over bodily changes and fears about delivery, concerns about the normality of the infant, increase in wanting to be cared for and irritation toward the husband for not meeting this need, and fantasies about the babies and their own ability to function as mothers. Most had not planned on becoming pregnant, and the advent of a child in their lives was clearly disruptive to their present life styles. The same study included a sample of unmarried women who were pregnant for the first time. Their responses brought out the influence of sociocultural factors and attitudes toward unplanned and unwanted pregnancies. These women expressed feelings of depression and dependency, and saw their pregnancy as a disgrace to themselves and their families. Major themes were their desire for a dependent relationship with a man and ambivalence about giving the child up for adoption. Although such pregnancies are easier to terminate now than they were at one time, there is no reason to doubt that the initial feelings they evoke are any less prominent (Loesch and Greenberg, 1962).

In general, first pregnancies present more problems of a psychological nature than later ones do. Women who were pregnant for the first time were compared with women who had given birth before. The former expressed more anxiety about themselves and the baby, while the latter had fewer of these concerns but expressed more generalized feelings of irritability and tension (Erickson, 1965).

Finally, the psychological reactions of a woman to her pregnancy are to some extent dependent upon intrapsychic variables which may be largely unconscious. In addition to the physical and emotional stresses, pregnancy has the potential of evoking old conflicts around dependency needs, relationships with significant others, and feelings about oneself as a woman. Empirical data on the importance of these kinds of influences in pregnancy are practically nonexistent, and most discussions of their potency are hypothetical, based upon clinical observation and speculation. A model of a psychoanalytically oriented approach to the study of the psychology of pregnancy is the following analysis of "tasks" of normal pregnancy and motherhood (Bibring, 1975). Most relevant to pregnancy are the woman's relation to her male partner and to her own mother. The psychodynamic importance of her relation with her husband revolves around the shift caused by the impending child and its meaning. Can she carry the child without feeling abused and exploited as a woman? Can she share her husband's love with a child, or does she wish to be the child herself? Is all her attention now diverted from him to the child itself, as if to say that his function is now completed? Such questions depend on the woman's maturity, her ability to abandon the self-centeredness of childhood, old sibling competitions for the love of parents, and the ability to share her new role.

The woman's relationship with her own mother has moved from the total dependency of infancy to the relative independence of adulthood, sometimes accompanied by chaotic struggles to free herself as well as by regressions to the old safe role of childhood. Pregnancy holds the promise of putting her finally on an equal level with her mother and of achieving a mature relationship with her. Two kinds of relations to their mothers were observed among the pregnant women. One type displayed an increased dependence on their mothers' support and advice, and were overinvolved in their mothers' attention and competitive for it with the other members of the family. As the pregnancy progressed, many of these women began to disengage, to begin to make their own decisions with an accompanying rise in self-esteem. Another type were belligerently independent at first, as if old grievances were evoked bringing out a determination that mother would not interfere with the baby as she had with her daughter. This reaction also ameliorated in time in these normal women, who became more tolerant and accepting of their mothers and expressed increased understanding of them from their own new perspective of impending motherhood. When such submissive or rebellious mother-entanglements are of pathological extent, however, they resist such smooth resolution, carrying over old conflicts into the new mother-child dyad.

We have been discussing the sources of influences which affect the psychological reactions of a woman to her pregnancy. It should be clear that such reactions, both positive and negative, develop from the interactions among these influences and their relative strength as determinants for the individual woman in her unique situation. While it is not uncommon in clinical or educational settings to hear young women express ambivalence or even strong negative feelings about pregnancy, one often finds that these feelings either diminish or are repressed when the woman actually becomes pregnant, particularly if her life situation is compatible with such an event. Childbearing continues to be for most young women a major developmental challenge, with achievement connotations which are often ignored or unrecognized. The motive for doing it well can be quite strong, with positive, maturing consequences for the woman. If she is physically and psychologically healthy, if the pregnancy is a wanted one, if she has a history of relatively satisfying relationships with the important persons in her life, then she is likely to experience this developmental event as rewarding and growth enhancing.

The Postpartum Period

The hours, days, and weeks following childbirth are noteworthy for the personal and emotional adjustments the woman must make, as well as for the physical changes which occur in her body. She is confronted with the reality of the baby, the irrevocable fact that it is here to stay, and that its imperious demands must be met at whatever cost to her own needs and time. Especially with a first baby, her life style changes drastically because of the total dependency of the infant whose needs now come before her own, a state of affairs which can provoke anxiety approaching panic in new mothers. It becomes clear to her that her life will never again be the same, that she is now responsible for the care and well-being of a helpless infant whose very life is in her hands. Under the best of circumstances, with a sharing mate and helping friends and relatives, the postpartum period makes adaptive demands many women find difficult to meet.

Reactions of women in the postpartum period cover a wide spectrum, from transient and mild to lasting and severe. The experience of any given woman is the result of a number of factors with origins in her self, her immediate experience, and the cultural milieu. "Baby blues," with mild depression, tearfulness or crying spells, and irritability are common and usually pass in a few weeks. Feelings commonly reported by postpartum women include inability to concentrate, fantasies of running away, anger toward the baby and her husband, helplessness, inability to cope, and lethargy and fatigue. Serious psychiatric conditions requiring hospitalization and treatment are rare, affecting one or two women per thousand in the postpartum period (Brown and Shereshefsky, 1972).

The high pregnancy levels of estrogen and progesterone drop rapidly after delivery, effecting endocrine changes which can influence mood states. While these have been implicated in postpartum reactions, other factors must be considered in trying to understand individual reactions and the more serious manifestations (Dalton, 1971). A Swedish study of adjustment during and after pregnancy of 165 women found that more than a third had some symptoms of postpartum mental disturbance. Number and severity of symptoms were related to the woman's attitude toward her reproductive function, her relationship with the child's father, and conditions at the time of the birth (Nilsson and Alnigren, 1970).

Further evidence suggests that postpartum adjustment has important determinants other than the physiological. The following "signals" in the background of women with adverse reactions were found: family home broken by death or other separation; previous emotional disorder in self, parents or other immediate family; physical illness or complication of pregnancy; marital differences in religion or age, marked shift on economic social ladder; recent move; older parents; unplanned pregnancy; and acute strains during pregnancy, such as husband away or no outside help in the household (Gordon and Gordon, 1967).

Summarizing, the research findings suggest that a model for explaining and predicting postpartum adjustment must include four major components: the woman's personal vulnerability to stress, immediate environmental conditions, relations with significant others, and biochemical changes.

Breast-feeding

The practice of breast-feeding the infant varies by era and by place. Some primitive groups breast-feed babies for several years, or until a new arrival forces the older child from the breast. In undeveloped societies breast-feeding may be necessary for the child's survival, although artificial feeding has been practiced all during historical times, as attested by finds of clay nursing bottles and other related artifacts. Wealthy Roman women avoided breast-feeding in order to keep the youthful appearance of their breasts, and even today women express anxiety that nursing will cause their breasts to sag. In the United States, the incidence of breast-feeding has fluctuated with availability of alternative methods as well as with fashions and value systems. At the turn of the century, 90 percent of babies were breast-fed for at least a few months. By 1946, when prepared baby foods and canned milk were available in all grocery stores, the figure had dropped to 33 percent, and ten years later, in 1956, only 12 percent of babies leaving the hospital were breast-fed (McCary, 1973). By 1966, the trend turned upward, and 20 percent of mothers were breast-feeding their infants, a phenomenon attributable mostly to middle-class, well-educated women (Mayer, 1972).

The current revival of breast-feeding has a variety of sources, among them the counter-culture movement with its emphasis on simplicity and natural substances, the participatory childbirth movement, loosening of taboos about body parts and functions, and of course, the belief that mother's milk is better for the child. Still, a sizeable percentage of women choose not to breast-feed their infants, and others who want to become discouraged and terminate their attempts after a few days or weeks. Several factors exert pressure against the decision to breast-feed. Most hospitals still separate mother and infant right after birth and bring the baby to her every three or four hours for feeding. The first few days or weeks of the nursing experience may be discouragingly uncomfortable. Swollen, tender breasts and cracked nipples are not uncommon. Hospital medical staff often do not take the time to provide instruction and to reassure the anxious mother who fears the baby is not getting enough milk, or to advise the one whose nipples become sore. Too, some mothers do not wish to be tied down to the baby's feeding needs. Sometimes husbands complain, or relatives decry breast-feeding as too confining or old-fashioned. Considering all these pressures, the wide availability of substitutes for mother's milk, and the less-than-mandatory nature of breast-feeding, perhaps it is surprising that it continues to be popular with many women.

Success with breast-feeding has been closely related to the mothers' attitudes. Those who felt positive about it as new mothers were those who were successfully nursing by the time they left the hospital. Other attitudes differentiated them also. They felt that women have more satisfying lives than men do, and that their labors had been easy. They showed strong interest in their infants, and were more likely to engage in close body contact with them, such as sleeping in the same bed. Furthermore, they were more open in their views of sex and nudity and were more tolerant of sex play and masturbation in their children (Newton, 1968).

Since all these characteristics are consistent with contemporary ideas about the attributes of mature and mentally healthy persons, one might come to the conclusion that not only is breast-feeding better for the baby, but that women who do it successfully are better mothers and persons than those who do not. Such a conclusion is unwarranted. While breast milk helps to confer a temporary immunity from certain infectious diseases, there is no evidence that bottle-fed babies in our society are less healthy or well adjusted in the long run. Mothers with health problems or mothers who work or have large families might find artificial feeding a desirable alternative. A balanced appraisal would support the approach which includes information giving, counseling, availability of options, and sensitivity to the woman's needs and preferences as well as the baby's.

In this chapter we have looked at some reasons why people choose to have children and have reviewed the events, both biological and psychological, which are part of the reproductive sequence. By now it should be plain that in this area of woman's experience, the biology and the psychology of women are so intertwined that it is not productive to try to think of them as discrete sets of events, one belonging to the body, the other to the mind. Pregnancy affects the way a woman thinks and feels, and the way she thinks and feels affects her pregnancy and labor. But neither of these is a sole determinant of the other. A third important source of influence emanates from the society she lives in and its attitudes toward her and toward her reproductive and social roles. We have seen how attitudes toward woman's reproductive role have changed drastically in recent years. These changes are bringing about modifications in her social roles as well as value shifts which are requiring different adaptations of both women and men. These modifications and adaptations as they are reflected in contemporary life styles are the subject of the next chapter.

Life styles: tradition and change

10

[T]he cornerstone of the highest civilization has always been the home, and wifehood and motherhood the happiest estate of woman. To my mind, it is a cruel wrong to a young girl to launch her in life unadvised on these points, and imbued with determination of independence of the other sex. . . .

—Mrs. Burton Harrison, Harper's Bazaar, May 19, 1900

The women of our age in most countries of the same degree of development are outgrowing the artificial restrictions so long placed upon them, and following natural lines of human advance. They are specializing, because they are human. They are organizing, because they are human. They are seeking economic and political independence, because they are human. . . . women will never cease to be females, but they will cease to be weak and ignorant and defenseless. They are becoming wiser, stronger, better able to protect themselves, one another, and their children. . . .

—Charlotte Perkins Gilman, Harper's Weekly, May 25, 1912

The stage and setting for the playing out of women's lives has typically and traditionally been the home. Therein almost all of them have performed with varying degrees of enthusiasm, resignation, indifference, or aversion the perennial primary roles of wife and mother, each generating a host of related specialty or subroles. The variations introduced by the number and complexity of these and by the competence, personalities, and preferences of the women doing them result in a totality of life styles of American women so heterogeneous that no single set of generalizations can describe a majority. But within the roles of wife and mother, the tasks and duties performed by women and the ways they experience them have much in common across age, location, and socioeconomic status. These commonalities still constitute a way of life for the majority of adult women at equivalent stages of the life cycle. While the lives of some American women depart drastically from the traditional model, the lives of many do not, and in between are degrees of conformity and innovation which suggest a spectrum of available and acceptable life styles for women of the seventies.

Excursions of women into the work world outside the home have most often been for economic reasons, adding to their repertoire another role which is usually secondary and often a paid and formalized version of one of the primary roles, such as nurse, teacher, or waitress. The woman who combines a job outside the home with her domestic roles is no longer a curiosity, though the wife and mother with a strong commitment to a demanding career is still in a small minority of unusual women.

But radical social changes are sweeping the old institutions and challenging old beliefs and prejudices, and while the effects are experienced by relatively few so far, demographic and technological developments facilitate the spread of their influence and soften resistance to them. Egalitarian ideology becomes practical as women acquire the means of economic independence and freedom from childbearing. These realities promote redefinition of goals and values and effect fundamental changes in social structure and in the relationships between women and men.

In this chapter we shall examine some aspects of the life styles of contemporary American women in the traditional roles and their variations, and in young, emergent models which may become the norms of tomorrow.

The Traditional Role

A woman enters the traditional female role-dyad of wife and mother through the event of marriage, which occurs in this country at the average age of twenty. The rituals preparatory to and culminating in the wedding are in a sense a *rite de passage* between girlhood and adulthood. Her friends and her mother weep as she is given away by her father to a man whose name becomes hers. She is expected to give up the ways of her childhood and to take up the tasks that are appropriate to an adult woman. The event marks for her a transition into a new status and a new role, that of wife.

Women in American society move into, function in, and abandon roles in a rough chronological order which corresponds to the developmental life cycle. The cycle has changed drastically over the last century as the life span has become longer and the years devoted to childbearing fewer, but its major events are the same. The woman of today spends more years in school, marries younger, has fewer children earlier, and lives longer (as does her spouse) than did her nineteenth-century counterpart (Neugarten, 1972). She has her first child at twenty-one, and her last at twenty-six. She can expect to live forty-six years after her last child starts to school, compared to only thirty in 1890. At that time, too, she was widowed before the marriage of her last child, whereas today she still has sixteen years of married life after that event, greatly increasing the amount of time that she and her husband will be alone with each other.

Co-ordinated with this chronology are the following transitions and stages in the lives of women which define their more important roles at any particular time: from the socializing home and family environment of early childhood to school and work situations; from the multidimensional life of the young adult to a new identity as married woman and housewife; from the life of young wife to that of new mother; from almost total immersion in the care of small children to a stage of increasing competence as housewife, confrontation of children's problems as mother, habituation as wife, and varying degrees of participation in community activities; from full participation in family life, seen as ideal for women, to constriction or loss of roles as children leave home and husband dies; and from being the sole member of a household to one of a variety of life styles until death (Lopata, 1971).

With the exception of that brief interlude before marriage, the stages and transitions characterizing the lives of most women are all described in terms of the roles of wife and mother. The later stages include employment for many women, but its pattern tends to be discontinuous, as women with small children often drop out of the work force and re-enter at a later stage.

The role of housewife

Marriage introduces women to sets of activities and duties which cluster into their customary roles in the home. The expectation that women would move into these roles in the normal course of their lives and would perform the associated tasks gladly and well is traditional in our society and persists to the present time. Coexisting with it for over a century, however, is another view whose proponents see the identification of women with the domestic role as an assignment to a "place" which inevitably precludes equality between the sexes. The extremes of feelings of these views are defined by the two following positions:

First, woman's place is in the home, fashioning it into a clean, comfortable, attractive place where good food is served, order is maintained, and the personal needs of the occupants are met. She does whatever is necessary to manage this, and she does it not for money or personal gain, but because it is her duty to her loved ones. Furthermore, it is an exalted role, the highest that a woman can have. Any woman who does not believe this, who wishes or tries to do something else, is unnatural, immoral, and unwomanly.

Second, the work that is necessary to maintain people comfortably is not special or different from any other tedious and repetitive labor. It can be done equally well by both sexes. The beneficiaries of such work should share in doing it or pay a fair wage to have it done by someone who chooses to do it. The exemption of men from this work and the assignment of it to most women is a major source of oppression and the chief reason preventing women from developing their potential and making their full contribution to society.

While neither of these positions represents a majority view, they reflect climates of opinion which have existed in our society both in the past and in the present, although it is fair to say that the first statement would have found more supporters in the 1800s than today.

Domesticity and skill in the domestic arts were highly prized in young women during the seventeenth and eighteenth centuries; it was lack of ability in this area or expressed interest in some other role that was deplorable. For example, the English journalist William Cobbett wrote in 1829 of how he fell in love with his future wife:

> It was now dead of winter, and, of course, the snow several feet on the ground and the weather piercing cold. . . . In about three mornings after I had first seen her our road lay by the house of her father. It was hardly light, but she was out on the snow, scrubbing out a washing tub. "That's the girl for me," said I . . . (in Klein, 1971, p. 176).

The celebration of the value of housekeeping skills for women was affected by the Industrial Revolution and the resultant technology with its production of labor-saving equipment for the home and its usurpation of many of women's traditional jobs. Factories not only took over the spinning and weaving of cloth, the manufacture of clothes, the processing of food and other products formerly made by women at home, but they also gave women the chance to become economically productive. As housework became easier, and work away from home became available, the role of the stay-at-home woman declined in status. The doors continued to be closed, however, to the kinds of education and work that might interest upper-class women, who became consigned increasingly to lives of barren routine and trivial interests.

Toward the end of the last century, a movement began to appear whose goal was to elevate the status of the housewife role to something approaching equality with the male professions. Women were told, in effect, that housework was real, important work requiring complex skills which were just as vital as those necessary to the practice of law or medicine. The acquisition and practice of these skills in home management was a unique mission of woman, and if approached in these terms, would constitute for her a "career" as deeply satisfying as any that man could aspire to. Books were published on domestic science and domestic engineering, and courses in Home Economics appeared in the curricula of schools and colleges.[1] One book was *The American Woman's Home: Or Principles of Domestic Science,* by the nineteenth-century authors Catherine Beecher and her sister, Harriet Beecher Stowe. While contemporary feminists argued for the legal and economic equality of women, Beecher and Stowe took a different tack. Realizing as well as the feminists did that something was wrong with the lot of the American woman, they sought to improve it by legitimizing her domestic function and by bringing to it some of the dignity that invested male activities:

> It is the aim of this volume to elevate both the honor and the remuneration of all the employments that sustain the many difficult and sacred duties of the family state, and thus to render each department of woman's true profession as much desired and respected as are the most honored professions of men (p. 13).

After describing some of the tasks of "woman's profession," the authors comment on the need for training and standards: "These duties of woman are as sacred and important as any ordained to man; and yet no such advantages for preparation have been accorded to her, nor is there any qualified body to certify the public that a woman is duly prepared to give proper instruction in her profession . . ." (p. 14).

The promotion of the housewife-mother role as the only truly important and rewarding one for women has continued unabated into the 1970s. A study of women's roles in women's magazine fiction from 1940 to 1970 revealed that the only proper role portrayed for women was the role of housewife and mother. The nature of the role involved total dependence on the husband and complete dedication to her family. The role is validated by contrasting it to the "deviant" roles of spinster, divorcee, career woman, or any childless woman. The housewife-mother in these stories might briefly envy such a woman, but when she attempts to emulate her by going to work, taking a trip alone, or even eventually attaining some of her freedom when her children get older, she is brought to a realization

---

[1] Today, women who major in home economics are preparing for a career. I have never heard of anyone taking such a course in preparation for the role of housewife.

of the much greater worth of her position by her family's constant need for her or by her own guilt which she assuages by staying home and/or having another baby (Franzwa, 1975).

A far different evaluation of women's place and the life that went with it had supporters at the same time that the domestic reform movement was attempting to elevate its status and convince women of its high mission. Marxist and socialist ideology included attacks on the family itself as a major oppressor of women. Marxist and feminist writers (see in *The Feminist Papers* [Rossi, 1973]) were vocal critics of women's assigned roles. Friedrich Engels, a nineteenth-century Marxist and bitter critic of the modern family, wrote that it is "founded on the open or concealed domestic slavery of the wife . . ." (p. 486), and the economist John Stuart Mill, reflecting in 1869 on why women had achieved so little, said that the supervising of a household "is extremely onerous to the thoughts; it requires incessant vigilance, an eye which no detail escapes, and presents questions for consideration and solution, foreseen and unforeseen, at every hour of the day, from which the person responsible for them can hardly ever shake herself free" (p. 228). Feminists of the time, while stopping short of attacking marriage itself, were under no illusions about what it meant for women. Sarah Grimke in 1837 commented that women are brought up with the belief that keeping a husband's house and making him comfortable was the end of their being, and called such indoctrination "dangerous and absurd" (p. 312). Two decades later, soon after the birth of her sixth child, Elizabeth Cady Stanton wrote to Susan B. Anthony, "I pace up and down these two chambers of mine like a caged lioness longing to bring to a close nursing and housekeeping cares . . ." (p. 380).

Today, feminists see the confinement of women to traditional roles as major deterrents to the realization of the goals of equality and freedom of choice. They reject the glorification of these roles and the notion that they are the special province of women, who should be responsible for the tasks they include. "[We] women have been brainwashed more than even we can imagine. Probably too many years of seeing television women in ecstasy over their shiny waxed floors or breaking down over dirty shirt collars. Men have no such conditioning. They recognize the essential fact of housework right from the very beginning, which is that it stinks" (Mainardi, 1972, p. 283).

It is difficult to think of any other occupational role which excites such extremes of feeling and comment. Many other jobs in the society rank low in pay and status, and sometimes bitter disputes arise over the conditions associated with the work, but no one gets emotional about the job itself. The matter of who is going to do it and how rarely becomes a political issue. But the role of housewife is not like any other occupational role; its physical and psychological environment, its working conditions, constraints, requirements, and rewards are totally different from those that characterize the occupations both women and men perform outside the home.

In the first place, the society does not provide formalized training or instruction to prepare persons to do the tasks that the role normally requires. Women may become housewives overnight, simply by getting married. There are no particular requirements for the job, and whether one comes to it with many skills or none is irrelevant. It is assumed that one either knows how to run a household or that one will learn "naturally." In one study when the women were asked what training they had received before marriage that was helpful to them in their housewife role, a fifth answered "none." The most frequently mentioned sources of help were their mothers and a school course. A majority of the respondents felt that women were not adequately trained to be housewives, and women with more education were even more likely to see the role as requiring more skill than they had when they entered it (Lopata, 1971).

Second, the specific tasks performed by women in the home are carried out under conditions which require diffusion of attention and effort. Many events may be competing simultaneously for some action on her part. The phone rings, a pot boils over, the baby wakes up, the dog wants to go out, the three-year-old falls down, the second-grader bursts in from school—experiencing all these events at the same time, each demanding her attention, is in the normal course for a housewife. Furthermore, the role requirements are highly repetitive and allow for very little respite or privacy. She is "on call" for whatever needs to be done, twenty-four hours a day.

A third characteristic which differentiates this role from other occupations is that there are no standards or tests of performance, no objective, externally imposed measure of how well the role is performed. And unlike any other job that one can think of, the rewards have no direct relationship to the quality of the performance. A woman who keeps a dirty house and feeds her family hamburgers and soft drinks three times a week does not necessarily lose her job as housewife; on the other hand, her neighbor who maintains a spotless home, cooks gourmet meals, and makes all the children's clothes herself does not necessarily get more material or affectional rewards for her efforts. The job can be done sloppily or perfectionistically without directly affecting the woman's tenure in it. Because of its private, personal quality, it is basically invisible to the larger community.

A fourth feature of the housewife role is its ambiguity. No job description for it exists; whereas other occupational roles include specific rights and responsibilities, the housewife role does not. No wage and hour laws apply to it, nor are its duties prescribed. A woman with grown children and a full-time maid has as much right to the title as has a woman with five children under ten and no outside help. Furthermore, from a list of all possible household tasks a woman may actually perform none, several, or all of them. She may have much help or none, many tools or few. She may do her work at any time of the day or night. She structures the job to her own situation. No union protects her or interferes with her highly individual style of performance. Also, a woman calls herself or is called by others a housewife only if she is not otherwise employed. If she works in a bank or a hospital, her response to the question, "What do you do?" is "I am a banker," or "I am a nurse," not "I am a housewife." This is true even if she performs exactly the same jobs at home that her unemployed sister does. It seems to be tacitly understood that one is designated "housewife" only if one is not something else. All other work-related roles have priority as descriptors of the person.

Perhaps related to this phenomenon is the often-noted low status and devaluation of the role of housewife. The apologetic "just a housewife" suggests that nothing such a person does in that role is of any importance, that it cannot compare in status with a "real job." The housewife's status depends not on what she does but rather on who she is. Elsie Smith has a certain status in the community because she is the wife of Harold Smith, high-school principal. Her status is set by the status of her husband, who has that status because of what he does. One recalls Terman's comment that a good many of the gifted girls in his sample made their most notable achievement in their choice of a husband (see Chapter 6).

Finally, let us note that the role of housewife differs from other occupational roles in that the personal qualities of the woman are not related to her admission to the role category. While the role of, for example, engineer, requires a certain level of intelligence, aptitude, and interest, the role of housewife is unspecialized in this regard. Housewives are not different from women in general. No particular personality, temperament, intellectual level, or set of interests is specified as critical to performance of the role. One does not have to be "suited" to it, either by training or by temperament.

Some special problems for women that can arise from their ubiquitous relegation to the housewife role, and from the role's special characteristics, will be dealt with in the next chapter.

In a study of almost six hundred Chicago-area women, the social roles of wife, housewife, and mother were analyzed (Lopata,

1971). This work offers an empirically based description of these traditional roles of women in contemporary society derived from extensive field investigation of both suburban and urban women, employed and non-employed. Although women are increasing their involvement in economic, political, and educational roles, the women in this study were emphatic in giving the home roles of women the status of greatest importance. In fact, when asked "What are the most important roles of a woman, in order of importance?" most referred only to the roles of mother, wife, and housewife. Only one-fifth even mentioned roles connected with work, or with social, community, or religious organizations. Asked to rank in importance thirteen possible roles of women, the subjects gave the lowest four places to artist (self-expression), career woman, worker, and member of the community. Factors which were important in this rejection of non-familial roles were the respondents' stage in the life cycle, and their educational and economic level. Mothers with young children stressed family roles, as did the poor and less educated. Women who worked were more tolerant of expanded roles for women in general, and women in the higher social classes were more likely to view extrafamilial involvement as important. But basically, the respondents' attitudes were traditional and restrictive, limiting women to home-based roles and devaluing all others.

There was considerable variation when housewives were asked what entrance into marriage had meant for them. Some saw it as primarily a change in the pattern of life: "Marriage has been the biggest change—women have a much more distinct change in their lives than men do" (p. 83). Women who had married quite young thought that marriage had resulted in a change in themselves: "I went into marriage spoiled and opinionated, and I had a great adjustment to make to a mate. I have learned to be more tolerant, patient, and to expect less of myself and others" (p. 83). Interestingly, some women related marital status to personal independence, others to an unaccustomed dependency. These two quite different perceptions are illustrated in their comments:

> Since I have been married, I've had to adjust and make a few changes. You have to learn to share. It's different from when you're home with your brother and sister. You have to learn to give as well as take; to learn to be more independent. I don't depend on my folks as much as I used to (p. 84).

> Life has gone from independence to dependence. Before marriage I did what I wanted. Now, I am dependent on my husband. In the future, I will become more and more dependent as the kids grow up and move away (p. 84).

Likewise, some women felt freer after marriage; others before. The former saw it as an opportunity for independent action; the latter, as a giving up of personal control over oneself and the assumption of a burden of responsibility.

These varied views of the difference marriage makes for women are not at all contradictory; rather, they reflect individual personalities and background, as well as the way the woman feels about her current situation. For example, a young woman whose parents had been oppressive in their concern and protection of her might see marriage as a declaration of independence, as an escape from the status of dependent girlhood to the elevation of equality with her own mother. For another, the move from dependence to independence might be economic. Economic dependence on a husband is not necessarily the same as economic dependence on a father. From dependence on the latter's largesse or lack of it, she might move to a situation where the paycheck is handed to her and she is the arbiter of how it should be spent in the best interests of the new family unit. When marriage is viewed as movement in the other direction, from independence to dependence, again the meaning of the terms for the individual must be considered. A young woman may first experience strong emotional dependence when she moves away from her family and friends to a strange city, and has only her husband to meet her needs for reassurance and personal contact. One who has had her own job and apartment, and freedom to come and go as she pleased, might feel keenly deprived of these after the honeymoon is over.

When the Chicago-area women were asked, "What are the roles, in order of importance, of the man of the family?" there was impressive agreement among suburban, urban, and working women: his main role is provider for the family, followed by father and husband. In fact, the role of man as provider was mentioned more often than the role of woman as mother, indicating a greater consensus among the women in their view of the role of the male.

The women in this study saw the role of the family man today as very different from that of his counterpart three generations ago. The changes, they thought, were focused on a shift in his relation to the entire family. Older, less educated respondents emphasized his loss of power; he is no longer "lord and master." A second group saw the relational change as more than a dethroning of the patriarch, rather involving a redistribution of authority toward a more democratic alignment. The more educated women spoke of changes in the quality of the relationships, using such phrases as "more understanding," and "more interested in the family." Across all vari-

ables of age, housing, and residence, however, the higher the education of the woman, the more positive she was in describing the
changed role of the man in the family.

While the tradition of the male as provider and the female as
domestic manager and worker is less rigid in many families today
than in the past, it is still common to observe that many household
jobs have sex labels. For example, the man of the house may wash
dishes, do the laundry, and run the vacuum cleaner, but he does not
usually do the family ironing or sewing. Furthermore, it is usual to
view the husband's participation in these kinds of activities as "helping" his wife, a linguistic convention which plainly reveals whose job
it really is. In the same study, women were asked specific questions
about the kind of help they received with household tasks. Approximately two out of three husbands helped at least part of the time
with such tasks as family finances, care of children, and shopping.
However, only about one in three ever helped with such housework
as cooking, cleaning, and laundry.

The higher the income, the more likely the husband was to have
sole responsibility for managing the household finances; the wife
usually received an allowance for those expenditures which were her
responsibility. In very low-income homes, where most of the money
went for necessities such as food and rent, the woman usually had
charge of its allocation. While most fathers with young children
helped with their care at least some of the time, we do not know how
many were sharing a parental responsibility and how many were
helping the mother with "her" children.

The role of mother

Occurring usually after a woman has assumed the roles of wife
and housewife, the role of mother is seen by most women as the
most important in the life of the adult female. The responsibility for
the care and socialization of the young and the feeling of importance
deriving from that responsibility are major sources of satisfaction
and self-esteem for many women, at least while the children are
young. But this is only one part of the montage of feelings about
motherhood that can range from despair to ecstasy. The desire to
have children and an interest in rearing them is by no means universal among women. Some are deciding to forego the experience altogether, a decision which would have been considered selfish if not
actually sinful a few decades ago. More common is the decision drastically to limit the number of children borne, with the result that in
1973 the number of babies per thousand women of childbearing age

(fifteen to forty-four) was 69.3, compared to 122.9 in 1957.[2] Although the role of mother dominates much less of the life span of women today, it is still an experience shared by 83 percent of all American women, and its assumption, especially for the first time, is a major life-changing event (Lopata, 1971).

As we saw in Chapter 1, the romanticization of the mother role was a feature of popular American culture during the late nineteenth century, and vestiges of it still survive in Mother's Day celebrations. The early feminists were not ready to attack the mother role, nor to abandon it themselves, but they were well aware of the restrictions it imposed on their own activities. Susan B. Anthony, who was childless, was open in her disapproval of the large families of her feminist friends, as in this excerpt from a letter she wrote to Antoinette Brown in 1858:

> A note from Lucy last night tells me that you have another *daughter*. Well, so be it. I rejoice that you are past the trial hour.
>
> Now, Nettie, *not another baby* is my *peremptory command, two* will solve the problem whether a *woman can* be anything more than a *wife* and *mother* better than a half dozen or *ten even* (Rossi, 1973, p. 383; italics original).

Charlotte Perkins Gilman, writing in 1898, saw clearly the irony in the contrast between the adulation of the mother role and the oppression of women:

> An extra-terrestial sociologist studying human life and hearing for the first time of our so-called "maternal sacrifice" as a means of benefitting the species, might be touched and impressed by the idea. "How beautiful!" he would say. "How exquisitely pathetic and tender! One half of humanity surrendering all other human interests and activities to concentrate its time, strength, and devotion upon the functions of maternity! To bear and rear the majestic race to which they can never fully belong! To live vicariously forever, through their sons, their daughters being only another vicarious link! What a supreme and magnificent martyrdom! (Rossi, 1973, pp. 589–590).

The childbearing histories of most women, however, were less effected by feminist ideology than by medical technology and environmental concern with an emerging belief that it was more acceptable to have few children than many. Even so, as late as 1962, a Gallup survey of the American woman found that childbirth was "the most thrilling event" in the lives of half his sample. One woman explained, "You've done something that's recognized as a good thing to do and you're the center of attention" (Rossi, 1964, p. 152).

[2] U.S. Bureau of the Census, cited in *Parade,* August 18, 1974.

Although today's young women will have fewer children and will spend less of their lives mothering, their role of mother will continue to be the most important focus of their lives when their children are young. The reasons for this are not innately determined by a "maternal instinct," but result from certain conditions of contemporary society. The first of these is that the care of the infant and young child is relegated almost entirely to the mother. While there are many exceptions, the norm is still the nuclear family in which the father is away at work during the day and the mother cares for the young children who are not in school. Thus most of her waking hours are spent with her children, for whom she has the ultimate responsibility. The present mores still favor the mother as primary caretaker, even in the absence of clear evidence that such an arrangement is necessary or even desirable for the well-being of the children (Hoffman, 1974).

Another reason for the salience of the mother role for young women today is the central role of children in the family. With fewer children, and more leisure and affluence, parents can afford to view each one as unique and precious, to consider him or her as an individual who has a "right" to gratification of needs in the best possible environment. Parallel with this development and contributing to it has been the burgeoning of information and guidance contributed by the medical and behavioral sciences, advising mothers on every aspect of child care and impressing upon them the importance of their role in personality development and in the growth of healthy children. Studies by Bowlby (1960), Spitz (1946), Harlow (1967), and others were interpreted by writers for the lay public as proof of the damage that could be caused by inadequate or improper mothering, and this was translated into a popular belief that the child was best cared for by its own mother all the time. The notion that a mother of young children who does anything else on a regular basis other than care for them is guilty of neglect continues to be so influential that every counselor and clinician is familiar with the guilt and self-castigation felt and experienced by the mother who goes back to work or school while her children are still young.

Since the mother has most of the responsibility for care of the children, and since the children are very important, it follows that their physical and emotional well-being are often attributed to her interaction with them. If children have problems, it is almost always the mother who is blamed for them, on account of the enormous influence she is believed to have over them. Such prevailing views about child development have a very sobering effect upon the behavior of young mothers and inevitably upon their extrafamilial aspirations.

When asked about the consequences of becoming a mother, women defined several major areas which could be identified as directly resulting from the event of motherhood (Lopata, 1971). One of these was a redefinition of one's identity, meaning an abandonment of one's own interests into a necessary service of the interests of the dependent one, the infant:

> When you are married and have small children, you have a lot of things you would like to do but can't; you don't have time and facilities. If I could, if I had peace one–two hours a day, I would continue voice, buy a piano, study. Sometimes I feel lost in the shuffle, confused; not the make-a-meal self, but as if I lost identity . . . (p. 192).

Another consequence was described as a more positive change in the self in the direction of greater maturity and ability, and a growth away from selfishness and childishness. These women saw themselves as becoming more responsible, as acquiring traits associated with adulthood as they had to adapt to the needs of others and learn to tolerate frustration.

A third consequence was expressed in terms of a constriction of one's personal world, of being "tied down" by the responsibilities and demands of young children. Future changes anticipated by the women envisioned more freedom to do things they wanted to do, and to have more time, both for themselves and to be with their husbands: "More tied down now, hope to have more freedom later . . . my life is not my own. The demands of the children take time and I have less time for myself. . . . I wish I would get out more" (p. 195). For some of the women, special circumstances entered into their perception of the changes effected by motherhood: having a retarded child, for example, or taking on the rearing of a grandchild at the same time that one or more of her own were young.

Another consequence was the extra labor required for the care of children, leading to changes in other social roles, such as housewife: "When I first married, I was exacting about the house, exact time and spotless; as I had children, I realized that this is not the most important thing; picking on children—vicious circle . . . I learned not to be exacting" (p. 197).

When these women were asked the question, What are the *satisfactions* of the homemaker's role? both the urban and suburban respondents spoke of having children, seeing them grow up, feeling proud of them more than any other satisfactions, including general family relations, husband and happy marriage, and the home itself. Yet when asked about *problems* peculiar to the role, more of them spoke of children than of any other area. The four main categories of problems with sample quotations for each are given in Table 10.1:

Table 10.1 Problems in being a mother.*

1. *Own behavior in the role:*
    "Knowing what to do: the responsibility of proper child-rearing."
    "Trying to understand the needs of children and why they do things."

2. *The child and his behavior:*
    "The children, trying to keep them from being a problem is a problem."
    "Trying to get children to pick up rooms, toys . . ."

3. *Actions of others in the social circle:*
    "Trying to get cooperation from the other family members (over disciplining the youngest child).

4. *Role conflict:*
    "The submergence of one's individual personality to the demands of the family."
    "Being pulled in all directions by all members of the family . . . husband-wife relation is often neglected."

* Adapted from Lopata, 1971.

   While in the long run children are a great source of satisfaction to many parents, their arrival and their presence in the household can impose serious strains on the marriage of their parents. A national survey conducted by the University of Michigan's Institute For Social Research[3] found that young married persons without children were happier than were those with children. Eighty-eight percent of the childless wives and 73 percent of the childless husbands between the ages of eighteen and twenty-nine said that they were "generally happy with life as a whole," compared with 65 percent of the husbands and wives with children under six. Contentment dropped and stress increased when the couples had their first child. As the children grew older, marital happiness increased and continued to increase after children had left home. Studies on marital satisfaction over the life span reveal a U-shaped relationship between satisfaction and time period, with satisfaction scores being lowest when children are young (see Fig. 10.1).

   The blame for this situation should not fall altogether on the fact of parenthood, however. During this period, other conditions contribute to difficulties of adjustment, and the advent of one or more children may exacerbate stress from other causes: economic strains, in-laws, and clashes of cultural backgrounds, personalities,

[3] *St. Petersburg Times* (Florida), December 8, 1974.

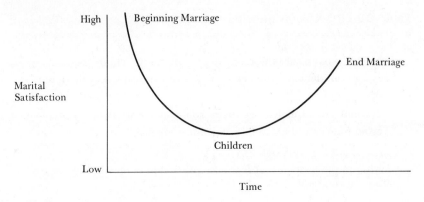

Figure 10.1 Marital satisfaction and the life span. (From Cameron, 1974.)

and expectations as two relatively immature and inexperienced persons learn to live together.

Today, theoretical and empirically based discussions of woman's traditional roles have implications far beyond the academic arena. They stir up or accompany clouds of controversy which prove the importance of the issues involved. At a conference on the older woman in America, for example, a psychology professor stated that sex roles are based on parenthood, which mediates different role directions for males and females: the provision by males of physical security, and by females of emotional security for the young. Questioning and experimenting with familial roles, and a quest for self-fulfillment, must take second place to the emotional development of young children. The post-child period of freedom is time enough for more open discovery of the self, for psychological release, for liberation. In total disagreement a social worker replied that waiting for post-child freedom is not tenable to today's woman; forty or fifty is too late to make changes in the self-image or to begin to develop in new ways. Roles are not an immutable function of biology; rather, women are socialized to be as they are, and few are allowed to develop capabilities beyond those ascribed to them by role stereotypes (Uits, 1974).

And so the argument continues. Almost thirty years ago, the behaviorist B. F. Skinner, in *Walden II,* proposed the complete emancipation of women from family roles in a new kind of community in which the role of mother, while still performed by the woman, would have "no more connection with her daily work than the role of father with his work in the office or factory or field. . . ." As for housework, " [T]he intelligent woman sees through it at once, no matter how hard she wants to believe. She knows very well that someone else could make the beds and get the meals and wash the clothes, and her family wouldn't know the difference. . . ." But in *Walden II,* the place of women has been radically changed: "Some women feel momentarily insecure for that reason. But their new position is more dignified, more enjoyable, and more healthful, and the whole question of security eventually vanishes" (pp. 121–22). We may be in transition to *Walden II,* but we are not yet there.

New Ways To Live

Tradition dies hard, and it is safe to say that a majority of adult women will continue to have as a significant part of their personal history a participation in the roles we have just described. But running through the recent history of human relationships and institutions is the bright thread of revolution, and marriage and motherhood are no exceptions. Marriage and the monogamous nuclear family have been the subject of bitter attack by feminists who see them as major vehicles for the oppression of women. Furthermore, the viability of the traditional marriage relationship as a setting within which individuals can freely grow into their full potential has been seriously questioned, especially by younger, better educated people. Is marriage still a desirable goal? Is marriage ever compatible with freedom and equality? How can marital roles be shared? Not only are these questions being answered, but the answers are empirical, coming out of active experimentation with a variety of life styles reflecting more or less faithfully the ideology of individualism, with its values of personal freedom, self-expression, self-direction, and exploitation of the growth possibilities in a variety of relationships.

Open marriage

The ultimate demise of the patriarchal type of nuclear family symbolized by the phrase "man and wife," in which the man was the "head of the household" and the wife was subservient and economically dependent, was evident by the middle of this century because of "the ESE factor" (O'Neill and O'Neill, 1972). This factor consists of three components: educational, sexual, and economic freedom for women. While none of these freedoms had emerged fully at midcentury, nor yet, for that matter, the precursors were identifiable in the technological modifications of home life and in woman's performance outside the home during and after World War II. Education broadened her interests to the world outside the home, opening the door to the possibilities of work and career; birth-control technology largely liberated her from biological imperatives and gave her a measure of control over her own body processes; and economic freedom, achieved through access to education and jobs, meant that she need no longer settle for old dependency roles. Not only has the ESE factor moved women closer to the goal of equality, but it is "the single most important force affecting change in today's marriage styles" (O'Neill and O'Neill, 1972, p. 195). The realization of these freedoms for women has the potential to make new life styles possible and to fundamentally alter the traditional marriage relationship. Among alternatives to traditional marriage which have already appeared and are being practiced by women and men are the single life; the egalitarian, usually dual-career marriage; and communal and other group forms of living together.

In 1975 the Census Bureau's Population Division reported a 3 percent drop in the number of marriages during the twelve-month period ending in August 1974, the first significant decline in thirty years. The proportion of women remaining single until they are between 20 and 24 years old has increased by one-third since 1960. The number of unmarried women and men living together increased by 800 percent during the 1960s. Statistics on marriage have fluctuated in the past, as a response to war, economic conditions, and changes in life styles, but these recent changes, according to the report, reflect a complex set of circumstances which are new in American life, important among which are changes in the role of women.

"Better dead than unwed" once described the unhappy future in store for a single woman, and not without reason in a time when marriage provided the only path to security that the average women could hope for. The socialization process which left little doubt that marriage was the only acceptable outcome for women was reinforced by the veritable lack of alternative ways of spending one's life productively. When attractive alternatives are available, women are much more likely to delay marriage or to stay single (Bernard, 1971b). Marriage rates are higher among women who are unemployed, and the higher the level of the job and the income, the lower the rate of marriage. As more women develop the values of autonomy and independence, the feasibility of a single life style should improve. Other factors that promote the delay or rejection of marriage are the climate of acceptability which has evolved with the now widespread practice of single persons living together, and the emergence of a singles identity, an awareness by the single person that one is a member of an identifiable group with a legitimate life style (Moran, 1972).

Living the life of a single woman in contemporary society or living with a man in a relationship free of the traditional bonds of marriage does not necessarily convey liberation from sex roles, however. Role assignment on the basis of sex can be a feature of the most sexually liberated social or living arrangement. For example, females in "singles" society found that it catered to men, who still had the option of doing most of the pursuing and choosing from among eligible women (Moran, 1972). College educated couples living together and both working often retain vestiges of the old roles when it comes to housework. Terry and Chick were such a couple. "Like any young housewife, she does most of the cooking, shopping, and laundry. Chick fixes their car. . . ." 'I seldom identify with movements,' says Chick, 'and Women's Lib is no exception. . . . [M]any of the premises are unfounded and incongruous' " (Coffin, 1972, pp. 316–17).

Even though one marriage in three now ends in divorce, marriage is still thought of as conveying status on a woman and providing economic and emotional security. Does marriage have anything other than these advantages to offer women? It is possible to have emotionally and sexually satisfying relationships without marriage. In an increasingly permissive society it is even possible to have children outside marriage either by having one's own or by adoption. As the number of independent and adventurous women increases, and as role models for the single life become more visible, more may opt for a life that is free of the explicit and implicit commitments marriage has always meant.

Open Marriage is a relationship of intimacy based on equal freedom and identity of both partners (O'Neill and O'Neill, 1972). Involving a departure from rigid conformity to the established husband-wife roles, its realization is dependent upon the equality of women and men, and therefore it may be viewed as a logical consequence of the change in the status relations of the sexes caused by the appearance of the ESE factor. Freed of power inequities in the relationship, the couple is able to implement other values which expand on the concept of equality. Living in an open marriage is clearly a "new way to be." A woman may have full equality with a man in their society, yet not have an open marriage, but she cannot have an open marriage without equality. Since equality of women with men is only now possible for the first time in history, open marriage is also only recently possible.

The open marriage model has two purposes: first to provide insights on the *closed*, or traditional, marriage patterns, which presented few options for choice or change; and second, to provide guidelines for developing an intimate marital relationship within which both partners can grow, each supporting the other.

The patterns of traditional marriage include certain expectations, ideals, and beliefs which are impossible fully to realize. These include the ideas that one mate belongs to the other, that one will always "be true," that the ultimate goal of marriage is to have a child, that each plays a different part as a function of biological sex, and that one's spouse can fill all one's needs, economic, physical, intellectual, and emotional. The values in such a relationship of exclusivity, possessiveness, endurance, and security, give it a static quality which inhibits growth and spontaneity, and stifles creativity.

Open marriage, by contrast, includes the expectations that both partners will change; that each will accept responsibility for self and grant it to the other; that one's mate cannot fill all one's needs; that the partners will be different persons, not because one is a husband and one is a wife; that children are not needed as proof of love for each other; that liking and loving will grow out of the mutual respect that the open relationship allows. These expectations reflect the values of individual freedom, flexibility, personal growth, and "undependence" within a dynamic, responsive relationship. Theoretically, the model represents the application of the concept of the self-actualizing environment to marriage (Maslow, 1954). This concept encourages growth to the fullest of human potential. Hence, a couple can go beyond the more traditional relationship, whose form and role requirements can be restrictive to such growth.[4]

The achievement of an open marriage depends upon using guidelines which interact with each other in ways that are mutually augmenting. As a basis for a style of interpersonal relationship between the sexes (although equally applicable to other relationships as well), these guidelines reflect values that are clearly contemporary:

> *equality:* the respect for the equal status of the other, in contrast to the status differences inherent in traditional man-woman relations;
> *role flexibility:* the sharing or exchange of role-associated tasks, both household and economic;
> *open companionship:* each partner having the freedom to relate to others, male or female, outside their own marital unit

[4] Dr. Laura Singer, formerly president of the American Association of Marriage and Family Counselors, was speaking of traditional marriage when she said, "I wouldn't say that marriage and self-actualization are necessarily mutually exclusive, but they are difficult to reconcile" (Lear, 1972).

(this is seen as an auxiliary facilitator of growth, not a replacement for the primary relationship of the marriage);

identity: the development of the individual through the realization of potential and the growth toward autonomy;

privacy: each having personal time and space to be alone when
she or he desires it. This is in contrast to the "togetherness"
mystique fostered by earlier values;

open and honest communication: discussion that is expressive of
one's real feelings, free of defensiveness and the kinds of
minor decptions that are learned in the process of growing
up;

living for now: relating to the mate within the present emotional
and intellectual climate. Reflection on past glories or calami-
ties, or fixation on future materialistic goals will diminish
the personal self which exists only in the present.

trust: an outgrowth of the practice of the other guidelines based
on respect for the integrity of the other.

Note that certain conventional guidelines for the "happy marriage," such as love, sexual intimacy, or personal attraction, are absent from this list. This is because they are results, not causes, of a
truly open, growth-enhancing relationship. They grow out of the exercise of the guidelines, and cannot in themselves ensure or prolong
the kind of relationship defined by the values of the open marriage.

Open marriage is still marriage conceptualized within the
framework of a primary relationship between two persons implicitly
(though not necessarily) male and female, who have a personal commitment to each other which may or may not be legal as well. The
factors of sex of the participants and of legality are irrelevant as far
as the application of the principles is concerned, but the intention of
the developers of the model is to present and to encourage new
kinds of behavior in a marital relationship, to bring marriage out of
an obsolete form into one compatible with contemporary egalitarian
and individualistic values. Thus it would modernize, not abandon or
abolish, the old institution. Its success depends upon the capacity of
the persons involved to free themselves from the stereotypes which
almost everyone growing up in our society so far has learned, and
actually to implement the values which underlie such a marriage.

How can the fundamental goal of equality be realized if there
are children and if the male is the major or only breadwinner? As
long as roles are assigned on the basis of sex, such a situation is
clearly unequal. For example, one woman and her husband moved
from the relative equality of early marriage when both worked and

shared household tasks, to a total separation of roles when children were born and she quit her job to care for them, then finally back to equal status and sharing when she resumed her work on a part-time basis and an agreement was worked out which spread the housework and child-care responsibilities more evenly and allowed for disparities in time, income, and personal needs and wishes (Shulman, 1974).

Proponents of open marriage point out that the separation of roles into "his" work and "her" work makes little sense in today's world. Assigning the total responsibility for the provider and managerial role to the male places a heavy burden of stress on him which not all men are capable of handling and deprives him and the children of each other. The assumption that the wife will have the main domestic responsibility places many women in a role which underutilizes their abilities and restricts their development. They recommend role flexibility, whereby each person can share in both occupational and parent roles, working out an agreement compatible to both. Some couples might find a reversal of roles to their liking, with the man staying at home and the woman working. Or they might exchange chores, she balancing the checkbook, he doing the laundry. The basic idea is that both housework and wage earning must be done, that paid work is not necessarily more valuable than unpaid work, and that couples can work out an equitable agreement which recognizes the talents, wishes, and needs of both.

Clearly the young, less fettered by the past, are more likely to be able to do this—and so are those in increasing numbers who have been the old route and know its traps. It is hard to imagine any significant acceptance of such a model with all its implications by couples who have been married for two or three decades and who have made their adjustments to their marriage and to each other. Not necessarily unhappy, they may feel no need for change at all, and indeed might be quite threatened by such ideas as these. For the male, such change would include giving up a position of power, dominance and authority, and the right to exclusive possession of his wife; for the female, the loss of her dependency status with its guarantee of protection and material security (for as long as the marriage works!). It would require a dissolution of role limitations and the cultivation of undeveloped aspects of personality. Attempts at such change can provoke high levels of anxiety which some persons cannot or will not tolerate. But it may be for many an attractive alternative to a life style with which traditionally there has been very little competition.

Alternatives to marriage

During the past decade many variations from the conventional heterosexual monogamous dyadic relationship have been identified by social scientists and discovered by men and women ready to experiment. None of these is newly invented or unique to twentieth-century experience. Their emergence and their attraction as phenomena suitable for scientific research are peculiar to our times. They are differentiated by such factors as number and sex of partners, residential arrangements, economic characteristics, sexual access, provision for children, and so on.[5] As far as women are concerned, some of them represent new ways to live and some do not. One characteristic which many have in common, however, is the intention of liberation of the participants from sexual possessiveness and exclusivity. Among such alternatives to the conventional dyadic marriage are multilateral, or group marriage, and communal living.

Multilateral marriage is a marriage of at least three individuals, each of whom is "married" to at least two other members of the unit. The individual must perceive her or himself to have a commitment to the others which is essentially analogous to marriage (Constantine and Constantine, 1971). The definition does not specify size of the group, sex, sexual access, or even residence. The essential elements are two or more mates per person, and the perception of a bond of commitment. A study of sixteen such groups revealed that the members were motivated by personal growth opportunities and by interest in having a variety of sexual partners. Psychological examination suggested that the females who chose such an arrangement had higher sexual needs than did their male counterparts, contrary to usual findings in the general population. Some interesting findings emerged with regard to roles and sex differences. Among legally married spouses in such groups, the wives were as likely as the husbands to have initiated involvement. Sex roles were much less differentiated than in the average nuclear family. Men took care of children and did some of the housework, and women were involved in careers and education; an egalitarian ethic guided decision-making and policy-forming activities. Individuals tended to specialize in certain tasks; one woman kept the books, another was the correspondent, while someone else organized the child care. But the residual work that no one wanted to do usually fell to the person who

---

[5] For reviews of recent research, see Constantine and Constantine (1971); DeLora and DeLora (1972); and Smith and Smith (1974).

was least assertive or had the highest need for order—both more likely to be women (Constantine and Constantine, 1974).

Communes and communal living arrangements have become very common since the mid-sixties and have been widely observed and studied. Such experiments in collective living have a long history in American society. More than two hundred were founded in the nineteenth century alone (Muncy, 1973). Families and tribes have always been the most common interest groups, and the recent renewal of interest in communal living may be the desire to return to an extended family or tribal grouping (Ramey, 1974). Those communes which have survived the longest have been groups with a strong unifying drive or theme, often religious, and a strong, usually patriarchal leader. While such communes still exist, the more visible today are the utopian variety, which began to appear in the 1960s, consisting mainly of persons who for one reason or another wish to drop out of the mainstream of the society, either on a temporary or permanent basis. Again, the most successful of these have a structured theme and rely on the leadership of a strong and charismatic leader (Ramey, 1974). Their purpose may be economic, political-revolutionary, religious, sexual liberation, or personal psychological development. A few espouse the principles of women's liberation and attempt the obliteration of roles based on sex.

Contemporary communes exist in such a bewildering variety of forms that no generalizations are possible. Compared to multilateral marriages, however, they tend to be less stable and shorter lived, with a fluctuating membership (Veysey, 1974). They are essentially a living arrangement, typically of fifteen to twenty persons residing together. Sexual access of members to each other may range from completely free to monogamous; a multilateral marriage may be imbedded within its context. Some are familial, applying the incest taboo to sexual relations among members. Several thousand communes exist at present, varying widely with regard to sex-role differentiation. As in other forms of living arrangement, much depends upon whether or not children are involved and the extent to which women are economically productive. In general, the literature does not suggest any radical departure for women from their traditional roles of housework and child care. One account, for example, of a New Mexico commune speaks of the inhabitants as "young bloods and kitchen-weary girls" (Hedgepeth, 1972, p. 321). The most ephemeral groups seem to be those based on complete sexual freedom and drug use, the so-called "hippie" communes. One woman wrote an unnerving account of her experiences living in two of these. In both, the women, married and single, did the cooking and cleaning, and cared for the children, while the men worked for nearby farmers. Among the major problems were male chauvinism and the economic dependence of the women:

> Although communal living appears to be a step in the right direction, the hip commune uses women in a group way the same as the fathers did in a one-to-one way. The communes are too fluid to create any security for a woman. Her stability lost and isolation complete, she cannot be an effective force for change. She must leave or kick the men out. Kicking the men out is hard because they own the land and are the breadwinners. . . . It is hard for the hippie housewife to rebel but it is happening. Almost every women I know has gone home to her parents or moved to her own place. . . . The men look around and wonder where have all the "chicks" gone? (Estellachild, 1972, p. 337).

Recent years have seen a huge proliferation of variants to the basic forms of alternatives to marriage. The most robust of these seem to be the delay or rejection of marriage in favor of living alone, living with another person in a quasimarital relationship but without the legal involvement, and certain forms of group commitments or communal arrangements with common ethos and goals and strong leadership. What they will mean for women remains to be seen. It is plain, however, that the trend is for increasing freedom and flexibility of choice of life style on an individual basis. At the same time, the option of some for innovation in personal relationships should be viewed in the total context of our society. Marriage and conventional expectations for it are still very popular, even if one in three do not work out. But very powerful social, political, economic, and technological forces are producing at the very least a new alignment within the old format, and it seems unlikely that things will ever be the same again. In summary, these forces interact with each other and affect women, men, and marriage:

Technology has freed women from household drudgery and unwanted pregnancies, thus reducing in importance the old roles of housewife and mother.

Liberalization of divorce and abortion laws reflects a lifting of old oppressive sanctions which maintained traditional roles.

Changing views on sexual morality, with increased emphasis on permissiveness and individualism, and decline of the double standard.

The women's liberation movement with its egalitarian and revolutionary goals is supporting educational and economic equality, and optional independence of women from men and children. The movement has also given women some relief from the onus of staying single or of being homosexual.

The effects of these changes will touch almost everyone as old patterns break up, and in the absence of new repression, a truly pluralistic society emerges.

The Future of Motherhood

But what about motherhood, the oldest role of all, in the brave new world? Some see a continuing erosion of the role as technology removes many of its tasks from the home, and a decline in its importance as women have fewer children and more time for other activities, especially jobs and careers. The new scenario for the role of women as mothers is no minor concern, attended to after important matters such as defense and the balance of trade; rather, it is the heart of the matter, a momentous project relevant to the future of the species. Most women will have children, but institutions and fathers will find they must get more involved in their care as women spend less time in the home. A synthesis will evolve in which the principles of "male" strength and "female" nurturance will be found in both sexes, rather than separately specialized in one or the other. Mothering will be a craft for those who enjoy it most, of either sex. Free of the distorting effects of role specialization, "the individual human will be able to develop the psychic wholeness that is urgently needed" if Western society is to face the dangers that lie ahead (Bernard, 1974, p. 365).

This is indeed a grand vision and one whose realization is far in the future. The reduction in numbers of children that women bear, the diffusion of roles, and the availability of alternatives to mother-care must proceed in parallel before the mother role will be significantly affected. Many women will be interested in such alternatives. At the present time, it appears that the first of the three components is proceeding more rapidly than the others. And the second, role diffusion, cannot occur unless surrogate care releases women from some part of the demands of the role.

The research on day care, communal arrangement, and other types of surrogate mothering cannot be reviewed here. But 90 percent of children under six whose mothers worked were in "informal" kinds of care—by friends, neighbors, and other non-kin who were paid for their services. Those in "formal" day care, such as nonprofit centers and commercial facilities, were exposed to a wide variety of quality of care; indeed, quality varied greatly within the various kinds of arrangements, both formal and informal (Emlen and Perry, 1974). And still, the biggest problem of the working mother with young children is, who will take care of them? how much will it cost?

if I leave them, will it help them or hurt them? what happens when they are ill? and on and on. The long conditioning of women to feel that they are solely or primarily responsible for their children, even if someone else has them part of the day, is not likely to be extinguished quickly.

Conservative Adaptations

Between the old stasis of the *Kinde, Küche,* and *Kirche* assignment and the dynamic visions of women's liberation, open marriage, and complete sexual equality are more typical models, with elements of both, which account for the way millions of American women live today. The emergence of women into roles of economic productivity outside the home has forced adaptations of women, men, and the family. These are marked by the residuals of old human problems and the generation of new ones. In some ways they are very traditional, while in others they are different from anything we have had before. But some of the differences are superficial, are more apparent than real, and represent only a slight shift in women's positions in the world of men.

Typically, when women work they are grafting onto their lives a new role in addition to the old ones. Since this would seem to add to the complexity of their lives and make great demands on their time and energy, the reasons why they do so must be rather compelling. Also, for the individual woman, her absence from home and her status as economic contributor both would seem to effect a substantial change in the way housework and child care get done, and in her relationship with her husband. At a deeper level of analysis, one would expect her power to increase to the extent that she attains economic equality with men in general and with her mate in particular. However, the research on motivation for working, how it effects other roles, and the relationship between economic productivity and power suggest that, while we may be on the right road, we still have a long way to go.

Why women work

In 1974, more than half of all adult women were working, and six out of ten of these were married.[6] Since the employment of a married woman outside the home must have some effect upon her domestic roles and upon her marital relationship, it is relevant to

[6] Women's Bureau, U.S. Department of Labor.

consider why so many contemporary women are taking outside jobs. Some reasons are money, aspects of the housewife-mother role, and personality factors (Hoffman, 1974).

Mundane as it may seem, the major reason that a woman works is to meet economic need. If she is the head of a household, or if her husband is unemployed or has a very low income, she may work because she must, simply to provide necessities for the family. Or she may work to reach and to maintain a higher standard of living for her family by supplementing her husband's paycheck with her own. More subtly, a paycheck is tangible evidence of the value of one's skills. It is connected in our society with such attributes as achievement, personal worth, and self-esteem. For many women returning to the labor market after years of domesticity, discovery that someone is willing to *pay* for the work of their hands and brain is a powerful stimulant to growth of their self-image. For the housewife, bringing home a paycheck could be interpreted as a sign of competence and as a tangible contribution to the family (Riesman, 1953).

Certain attributes of the domestic roles of women act as motivators for working away from home. Basic housework is not very creative, and while it can be done at varying levels of competence, it does not require a high level of skill. While it can be embellished by casting it at a level which includes baking one's own bread, designing and making clothing, and decorating the home with needlepoint and other domestic art, the incentive for such activity has been reduced by the ready availability of such items in the market. A woman may feel that she would rather spend her time at a job earning money to pay for such goods and services than to supply them herself. The role of mother, important as it is, has elements which send some women in search of a job. The constant companionship of children, the relentless demands, the isolation, the loss of freedom, the physical labor, the repetitive tasks, the noise level—these can cause feelings of despair and frustration in the most dedicated mother. It is not uncommon to hear working mothers of young children rationalize their need to get away by saying, "I'm a better mother when I have time away from the children. I have more patience with them and enjoy them more when I'm home." Another factor associated with the role is its diminishing importance as children go to school and grow up. The woman may go to work not to get away from the children but because their leaving creates a gap in her life which she feels pressure to fill with something meaningful.

The role of personality factors as motivators toward working is much less clear, inasmuch as the numbers of women who work are so large, and as a group they are so heterogeneous, that one would not expect to find them sharply differentiated by personality from their nonworking sisters. Many women are attracted to work outside the home because of a commitment to a skilled or professional occupation and a need to achieve in it, aside from its economic rewards or its offer of an alternative to staying home all day. A career, for example, is often distinguished from a job by the implication that the woman has a long-term identification with a field of work requiring high-level skills, the performance of which results in feelings of achievement and other personal satisfaction. Several studies have found that working women have a stronger feeling of competence and a less traditional view of sex roles, but it is not clear whether this is a cause or an effect of their working status. Studies of the psychological needs that women cite as reasons for working include status aspirations, the realization of potential, desire to benefit society, high energy level, active orientation toward life, and the need for social contact (Hoffman, 1974). A study of women who were seniors in college found that those who wanted to realize their potential through combining a career with marriage were higher in ego strength than were the more traditionally oriented (Gump, 1972). Again, we do not know whether ego strength mediates the willingness to pursue difficult goals, or whether the decision to do the less usual, to pursue two valued goals, increases ego strength. In any case, ego strength was negatively related to the adoption of the traditional female role.

In addition to money, the housewife-mother role, and personality factors, there is another element: social pressure. In recent years a variety of factors have combined to lift the cultural interdiction against employment for married women whose husbands could support them. One of these is the ideology of feminism, which deplores the economic dependence of women and supports the emergence of the individual woman as a strong, independent, free person who will develop herself to the fullest. Her economic independence from the male through her own achievements will give her choices that her mother never had. The appeal of this line of thinking is strongest to the young and educated, and while it may be considerably attenuated among more conservative groups, one suspects that the college woman who openly states that her only life goal is to be a housewife and mother will be regarded as quaintly archaic or hopelessly reactionary. In fact, a study by the Educational Testing Service of college freshmen women found that the percentage who thought that "women's activities are best confined to the home and family" dropped from 37 in 1970 to 9 in 1973. Asked to make future goal predictions, fewer than one in five of the latter looked forward to being a housewife fifteen years later (Wilson, 1974). Parents of daughters, too, knowing that the rate of marriage failure is high and alimony less certain, are more interested in the education of daughters for future contingencies. The notion that the education of sons is more important is less prevalent today, with almost equal numbers of males and females continuing into higher education.

Whatever the motivation, women are working. The new cultural imperative seems to be that most women will combine marriage with a job or a career. One study found this expectation emerging as a function of age from puberty to young adulthood. A study of junior high, high school, and college women revealed that the youngest group saw marriage as their most important future goal. For the older groups career emerged as an important part of their life pattern, accompanied by increasingly liberal attitudes and desires regarding work for women (Rand and Miller, 1972).

Role adaptations

The traditional family has always exemplified in its structure and function the concept of the division of labor: the man is the provider; the woman manages the household and cares for the children. What happens to this concept in practice when women go to work outside the home? Are role prescriptions modified, or do they vanish altogether, and if so, under what conditions? When mother brings home a paycheck, does father pitch in with the housework? The research in this area yields two major conclusions: first, the employed married woman does less housework than she did when she was not working, and her husband does more; and second, the home and children continue to be viewed by both as primarily her responsibility.

The research on division of labor in homes of working women indicates that in general the results were consistent in showing that working women did less housework while their husbands did more (Bahr, 1974). One study found that the employment of wives results in "substantial decreases in the number of wives who carry sole responsibility of getting the husband's breakfast, doing the evening dishes, and straightening up the livingroom when company is coming. Working wives also tend to do less household repairing and do less grocery shopping by themselves . . ." (Blood, 1963, pp. 287–88).

Some variations were introduced into these basic conclusions by the variables of ages of children and wife's commitment to work. Husbands did more housework when children were small, presumably because there was more to do. Though older children might be expected to take on some of the chores, prevailing child-rearing beliefs promoted to some extent an indulgent attitude toward offspring, at least as they were interpreted by many parents who reported concern that children not be overburdened with household tasks (Roy, 1963). Wives whose work commitment was low, who were working primarily out of economic need, received more help from husbands and children than did wives with high commitment, who would work whether they needed the money or not. Regarding this last finding, there are probably both economic and psychological factors at work. One is more likely to find commitment to work among educated professional women who can afford household help, thus reducing the need for the husband's contribution. And, poignantly, the woman who works to satisfy her personal needs may feel sufficiently guilty that she cannot burden her family with tasks which she would be doing if she had stayed at home.

Though some husbands pitch in with the dishes and laundry, housework and child care continue to be seen as the woman's responsibility. This prediction for sex roles of the future was made more than two decades ago:

> Even if, and it seems possible, it should come about that the average married woman had some kind of job, it seems most unlikely that this relative balance would be upset; that either roles would be reversed, or through qualitative differentiation in these respects, completely erased (Parson and Bales, 1955, p. 15).

Concerning the "myth of the egalitarian family," there is no indication that the overall "relative balance" has been upset (Poloma and Garland, 1971). This study concentrated on a sample of highly educated professional women, a group expected to be among the most liberated of women, and to have a most nearly egalitarian marriage. The data permitted the fifty-three couples to be described in terms of four types of marriages: traditional, neotraditional, egalitarian, and matriarchal. The numbers in each of these types are presented in Table 10.2.

In the traditional families, the wife's career was regarded by

Table 10.2 Distribution of family types*

Family types	Number of families
Traditional	20
Neotraditional	27
Egalitarian	1
Matriarchal	5

* From Poloma and Garland, 1971.

both her and her husband as equivalent to a hobby, with the family's status and income deriving from the husband. The wife's income was not used for family needs. Her principal role was wife-mother-homemaker. Though hired domestic help performed most of the routine chores, she alone was responsible for all other feminine role tasks, such as child care, entertaining, cooking, and so on.

The neotraditional families differed from the traditional in that the wife's income was needed to maintain the standard of living, and her career was given some importance when major family decisions had to be made, such as moving to another city. Though more egalitarian in the division of labor (the husband "helped out"), both considered the wife to be in charge of the home and children. When a woman pediatrician, married to a pathologist, was asked if her husband helped around the house, she said:

> He helps a lot. I don't ask him to clean up the livingroom or to wash the diapers—I have a maid to clean. It's the little things that are most important. If I am tired, he will take the baby . . . and he is not at all demanding. If I am busy, he doesn't mind having a TV dinner for supper (Poloma and Garland, 1971, p. 750).

Let the speaker be male, and substitue "she" for "he". The resulting incongruity will clearly demonstrate whose responsibility the baby and the dinner are.

Only one couple was truly egalitarian in sharing both the provider and child-care–housework roles. The other five families were classified as matriarchal because the wives earned more than their husbands. Even so, the men did not share significantly in the work and responsibility of the household.

The power shift

The totality of human interaction can never be understood without including the pervasive role of power (Jacobson, 1972). Marriage, being the most common and intimate of all human interactions, is a relationship in which roles are invested with greater or lesser power, one determinant of which is economic. While the concept of power is variously defined, or not defined, in the research it generally is held to mean the ability of one person (in the case of a marriage) to influence or control the behavior of the other, or to make more of the important decisions. In marriage, such decisions include, for example, what job the spouse should take, where the family will spend vacation, what kind of car they will buy, whether the children go to public or private school, and what kind of food is eaten.

Considering the distribution of power in the family, two facts emerge as salient. First, in most families, the male is the primary provider of economic resources, and second, most important family decisions involve money. Thus it follows that in most families the male exercises more power than the female does. Although the matter of who supports the family is not the only determinant of power, most of the research supports the conclusion of male dominance, in spite of popular belief to the contrary (Gillespie, 1975).

What happens to this unbalanced situation when the wife is employed? In some cases, she gains power in areas where she had none and loses in areas where she was dominant. In other cases, nothing is different. For example, if her income is critical to the family's well-being or desired standard of living, she gains power in the making of decisions about how money will be spent. On the other hand, if her husband or someone else participates actively in the care of the children, she may lose power in the decisions regarding them. And in the cases of the upper-class professional women where their income was not needed, the fact of their working made very little difference in the power structure of the marriage (Poloma, 1971). This so-called modern family type was not basically different from the traditional model.

An interesting class difference has been observed in the power wielded by working wives. Lower-class wives gain more power when they are employed than middle-class wives do (Bahr, 1974), in spite of the fact that middle-class husbands espouse a more egalitarian philosophy than do their lower-class counterparts (Gillespie, 1975). While the first finding is readily explainable by the assumption that the wife's income is more important to less affluent people, the contrast between deed and word across classes is something of an anomaly. It may be that the lower-class male is ideologically more concerned about presenting a traditionally masculine image but is more willing to concede material power when it is realistic to do so, whereas the educated male adopts the more sophisticated strategy of verbally supporting an egalitarian arrangement while tacitly expecting the traditional perquisites of his sex.

Psyche and society: variations from the norm

11

[T]here is no sharp line between those who act out their conflicts directly and in forms unacceptable to society and all others who struggle with them at some time in their lives, but do not act in this particular way. It is We one studies when one studies any part of the human race, never They.

—Gisela Konopka, *The Adolescent Girl in Conflict*, 1966

In the language of social psychology, norms are ways of behaving which are typical for a group, and which reflect its attitudes about what is right and wrong, good and bad. Normative behavior is behavior which is within the limits defined as normal, that is, limits which include the behaviors displayed by most of the group. Thus it is normative in our society for children to go to school; for parents to care for their own children; for all persons to respect the property rights of others; and for men and women to marry each other and to have only one spouse at a time. Norms are essentially reflections of value judgments which are tacitly agreed upon by the influential members of the society and which establish, among other things, the guidelines for the socialization of children. All human societies have norms which regulate the behavior of their members; violations are more or less severely punished, depending upon the importance of the norm: one who wears inappropriate clothes to a public event may be stared at, while one who wears no clothes at all may be put in jail. Such judgments about behavior vary greatly from one society to another and even between groups in a single society. But they all have one element in common, and that is that they are perceived as necessary for the survival of the group and for the growth to maturity of the individual.

This chapter deals with women whose behavior violates such important norms that they are a threat to the social order and must be segregated and confined; and with women whose behavior causes them to be seen as mentally disturbed and in need of treatment to restore them to normal and to alleviate their psychological discomfort and the concern that others have for them. While women are not uniquely different from men in the crimes that they commit or the mental and emotional disturbances that they develop, the etiology, incidence, and patterns of these, the reactions they evoke, and the ways they are dealt with are sufficiently different to justify special consideration. The observable sex differences that abound in these areas, as in others we have looked at, are outcomes of a complex interaction of individual histories, sociocultural pressures, socialization practices, and biological factors. Although one of these elements may contribute more than the others to a particular case, it is a mistake to look for the single cause as some observers do. It is no more enlightening, for example, to say that a certain woman is suicidal because her father died when she was ten, or because an oppressive society defines her "place," than it is to credit her symptoms to demonic possession. No one, male or female, is exempt from pressures from all these sources and more, and individual variations in morally and socially sanctioned behavior result from the many possible combinations of social and environmental influences impinging upon the unique and vulnerable individual.

Early Life Adaptation of Girls

Culture and biology combine to favor the psychosocial adaptation of girls in our society during at least the first decade of life. Those behavioral and learning problems which are commonly manifested by children and the relative incidence of these in the two sexes are shown in Table 11.1.

The manifestation of behavior which is troublesome either to the child, to her or his parents, or to society, behavior which is regarded as pathological or which brings the child into conflict with laws and mores, is unquestionably less frequent among young girls than boys. The research on sex differences reviewed in Chapter 5 indicates that several factors interact to produce this effect.

1. The additional genetic material on the second X chromosome conveys some protection to females against non-lethal sex-linked disorders which add stress to the life of the affected individual.

2. The lower incidence in girls of congenital neurological abnormalities is reflected in lower rates of mental retardation, learning

Table 11.1   Sex ratio of behavior and learning problems in childhood*

Problem	Age group	Male/female
"Social and emotional immaturity syndrome"—absenteeism, shyness, fatigability, inability to follow directions, slow learning, infantile speech, etc.	First grade	11 to 1
Stuttering	Later school grades	4 to 1
Reading difficulty	"	5 to 1
Speech, hearing, and eye problems	"	4 to 1
Personality disorders	"	2.6 to 1
Behavior problems	"	4.4 to 1
School failure	"	2.6 to 1
Delinquency	"	4.5 to 1
Childhood psychosis	Under 7	2 to 1
Childhood psychosis	Ages 7–12	2.7 to 1

* From data in Anthony, 1970.

disabilities, hyperactivity, poor impulse control, and personality disorganization. Schizophrenic children often shows signs of neurological impairment, such as deficiencies in motor coordination, muscle tone, gait and balance, and the capacity to integrate sensory stimuli. When schizophrenic children are grouped on the basis of whether or not they have these signs, the ratio of boys to girls is higher in the group which has such signs, suggesting that neurological impairment is more often involved in childhood psychosis in boys than in girls (Goldfarb, 1970).

3. The advanced developmental maturity of girls compared to boys facilitates their early learning and socialization, giving them an advantage in developing coping and interpersonal skills. The reinforcement which girls receive for these skills may promote the salience for them of affiliative behavior, reducing the probability that they will alienate significant people by hostile and aggressive behaviors.

4. The "feminine" tone of the early childhood environment, in which girls are cared for and later taught by same-sex models, facilitates the adoption of socially approved roles and reduces the potential for conflict with authority.

5. The cluster of aggressiveness-competitiveness-resistiveness differentiates girls from boys, who have a lower threshold for the evocation of such behaviors. Since a major thrust of socialization practices is control of aggressive and antisocial behavior, girls adapt more easily to the adult expectations of such control. If we assume that the sex difference in aggression among young humans is largely biologically determined,[1] as the research clearly indicates, and that more boys than girls will display a higher rate of such behavior, then it follows that the agents of socialization, parents and other adults, will direct more stringent efforts toward curbing their unacceptable responses, applying nonphysical and physical punishments. In 1972, Eleanor Maccoby reported that fathers were more punishing of aggression in their sons than in their daughters. Thus boys, more frequently subject to methods of aversive control, experience more conflict with authority figures and are more likely to develop attitudes of hostility and resistiveness toward even legitimate authority. Such a snowballing effect can occur when the biological and developmental differences between the sexes in early life are not understood, and when inappropriate or ineffective methods are used by adults in their attempts to modify behavior and bring it into line with whatever their idiosyncratic and prevailing cultural criteria are. To the extent that girls behave differently from boys, they elicit a different kind and level of response from adults, and this also has a cumulative effect, mediating in general a more positive adaptation of young girls to the norms of a demanding society.

These factors taken together should be thought of as an etiological basis for the childhood sex differences in problem behavior. Together, they predict a higher incidence for boys than for girls of such behavior. The persistence of problem behavior into later life is dependent not only on its historical antecedents but also on society's reactions and its attempts to deal with it.

A distinction is made between the kinds of judgments concerning the behavior of young children in our society and those that are imposed on the behavior of older children and adults. Atypical behaviors that give rise to concern in parents of young children are usually classified as behavior disorders, learning disorders, or the more serious childhood psychoses. When young children exhibit an-

[1] As we saw in Chapter 5, this is not as fateful and sinister as it sounds. The role of the biological determinant is very limited indeed compared to the greater potency of experientially determined behavior shaping. Although the participants in socially sanctioned forms of aggression such as sports and war are overwhelmingly male, many individual males and even whole tribes such as the Tasaday of the Philippines are quite unaggressive. The Tasaday, in fact, have no weapons and no word for *war* (MacLeish and Launois, 1972).

tisocial behavior, such as stealing or assault on an infant sibling, they are not labeled delinquents or felons, because they are not considered to be responsible for their behavior. Instead, they are considered to be emotionally disturbed and in need of treatment. Older individuals who violate the property or person of others are more likely to be held responsible for their behavior and to be incarcerated and punished. Disturbances and problems that adolescents and adults have that do not violate a law, such as emotional distress and occupational and marital discomforts, are presumed to be mental illnesses or problems of adjustment amenable to treatment by trained personnel in appropriate facilities. Thus an important dichotomy develops in the classification of behavior problems of older children and adults, some behaviors being classified as delinquent or criminal and others as due to mental or emotional disorders. This developmentally emergent dichotomy does not exist for young children. That it is altogether a social artifact is obvious. But it has important effects for the research findings on later sex differences in atypical behavior: among adults, more males than females go to jail; more females than males go to psychiatrists.

Delinquency and Crime

Nowhere in all the documentation of sex differences does one find more striking examples than in the literature on delinquency and crime. In fact, the differences between males and females in patterns of delinquent behavior, rates of arrest and imprisonment, treatment by the criminal-justice system, and behavior in correctional institutions are so important that attempts to understand delinquency and criminality have had to deal separately with them. Such behavior by men and women cannot be explained by a single model; thus the female offender joins the list of exceptions to theories built upon the observations of the male sex.

Delinquency in girls

Although there exists a very large body of theory and research on delinquency, most of it deals with boys. Studies of delinquency in girls and attempts to explain it have been few. Earlier writers simply ignored it, as if it didn't exist. For example, in 1954, Talcott Parsons explained delinquency in boys as a rebellion against the female-oriented Western family and their difficulty in making an appropriate male identification. The girl had a more favorable opportunity for healthy maturing, since her mother was readily available to model for the functions of wife and mother. While this may be true, it clearly glosses over the occurrence of delinquency in girls. Another study of adolescent behavior blamed delinquency on the long postponement of adult roles (Bloch and Niederhoffer, 1958). Again, it was presented entirely in relation to the boy and his frustration at being barred for so long from the roles of worker and father. Whether or not a parallel situation exists for girls was not considered.

More recently, another theory of the adolescent girl in conflict was presented. It includes four concepts: the unique pubertal biology of girls, the nature of their identifications, the changing cultural position of women, and the "faceless" adult authority with resulting loneliness (Konopka, 1966).

Puberty with its dramatic body changes ushers in the role of sexuality and the possibility of pregnancy. Thus sex has a more pervasive meaning for girls than for boys and acquires intensive romantic connotations as a love offering, a weapon, or an outlet for frustration and rebellion. Parental role models for identification may be absent, inadequate, or so punitive and rejecting that constant conflicts make the development of an emotionally mature sense of self impossible. Changes in the cultural roles of women have led to raised expectations for education and vocational opportunities which may not be available in fact, and increased awareness of double standards in sex roles create resentment and hostility against a society which provides more freedom and access to its goods to boys.

These three conditions apply to all girls but lead to delinquency only under special circumstances. They are potent sources of problems, their resolution dependent on factors in the life of the individual. The girl who seeks love through sexual acting out, who flees from harsh conditions and from physical and emotional trauma, and who sees no way out of her situation comes into conflict with society and its values. She distrusts authority at home, in school, and on the street as inimical, and this distrust grows to include all adults and even peers. The resulting behavior leads to rejection, school failure, and feelings of worthlessness, which in themselves increase frustration and rebelliousness generating further conflict with society (Konopka, 1966).

Juvenile delinquency offers a fertile field for the study of both sex differences in behavior and the double standard of treatment of offenders. On the record, boys are significantly more delinquent than girls, but the reported figures represent only the tip of the iceberg. One study of 522 teenagers in Flint, Michigan, found that 433 of them admitted to almost twenty-five hundred delinquent acts, but only 47 adolescents and eighty of their offenses got into the records (Haney and Gold, 1973). Whether by self-report or official records, however, females are far less likely to engage in most kinds of illegal behavior. An interesting difference appears in girls' self-reports of offenses and court records showing offenses for which they were actually referred to the juvenile authorities. Incorrigibility, running away, and sexual delinquency (fornication) accounted for only 11 percent of the self-reported crime of a national sample of girls (Haney and Gold, 1973) but such offenses, together with truancy and being a "person in need of supervision," accounted for over 50 percent of referrals of girls to juvenile courts (Chesney-Lind, 1974). Only 20 percent of boys were referred for such offenses; primarily, they were charged with larceny, burglary, car theft, or other "adult" crimes.

Thus, the criminal-justice system is more likely to punish girls for offenses which violate sexual mores and parental authority— behaviors which are not criminal when committed by adults. On the other hand, girls are dealt with more leniently when they commit crimes. Police were more likely to refer to court girls charged with their first juvenile offense than girls charged with their first criminal offense (Chesney-Lind, 1974). The paternalistic attitude of society toward girls mediates the view that their sexual and sex-role transgressions call for protective and punitive measures, but traditional attitudes of chivalry result in their actual crimes being dealt with less harshly than boys'. For example, a Pennsylvania study revealed that 45 percent of girls charged with juvenile or sex-role violations were detained before trial, compared to 24 percent of those charged with misdemeanors and 35 percent of those charged with felonies (Chesney-Lind, 1974).

Women and crime

Considering that women constitute more than half the population, they are remarkably underrepresented in crime statistics. Several theories have been advanced to account for this. Cesare Lombroso, a nineteenth-century Italian criminologist, believed that criminals were born with certain physical characteristics which distinguished them from other persons and predisposed them to lives of crime. But he found that his theory did not fit women criminals, who did not differ from moral women with regard to physical anomalies. He attempted to explain this on the basis of women's biology and their social roles. Women showed fewer physical stigmata because they were less deviant from their norms on biological characteristics, and because of a selection factor whereby men choose women who had fewer physical anomalies. They committed fewer crimes because of their sedentary social roles and because of a less active cerebral cortex, which when irritated led to hysteria and sexual problems rather than to crime (Lombroso and Ferrero, 1916). Thus he decided that most female criminals, unlike males, were not born criminals but were led into crime by lovers and husbands. Occasionally, however, a born female criminal would appear who was more diabolical than the male.

Otto Pollack in his classic book *The Criminality of Women*, published in 1950, presented the thesis that the criminality of women is vastly underreported because it is masked in their conventional roles of mother, domestic servant, nurse, shopper, and so on. For example, women have much more opportunity to commit crimes of abuse against children which often go unreported. They can conceal theft in their roles of servant or shopper. In addition, because of women's less active role in society, they are more often instigators of crime committed by men than perpetrators. Thus the real incidence of female crime is not known because of its devious nature, and because of women's protected role.

More recent writers have looked to the socialization of women and to their sex roles for explanations of the degree and kind of their criminal behavior (Payak, 1963; Ward *et al.*, 1969). The feminine model which guides the socialization of women includes the attenuation of aggressive drives and the development of a moral stance which precludes overt acting out against others. Males are often rewarded by peers for resisting authority and engaging in illegal acts, whereas females are not ordinarily encouraged in such behavior. Also, the restricted sphere in which women have traditionally lived in middle-class society has provided them with less opportunity to engage in criminal behavior.

Today female crime has become less of a rarity. The ratio of male to female arrest in 1973 was 6 to 1, compared to 8 to 1 in 1960. The ratio of males to females in correctional institutions in 1973 was approximately 25 to 1,[2] indicating that women who are arrested are less likely to go to jail than men are. Even so, the number of women inmates in federal prisons went up 81 percent in the five years between 1968 and 1973. The rate of female arrests also has increased dramatically in recent years. For example, from 1965 to 1973, female arrests for robbery increased 187 percent; for drunken driving, 211 percent; and for narcotics violations, 1,032 percent.[3]

The increase in female crime has been attributed to a variety of factors, including increased drug use, general letdown of social in-

[2] Federal Bureau of Investigation, *Uniform Crime Reports.*
[3] *Ibid.*

hibitions, and changes in the status of women leading to increased willingness of law-enforcement officials to arrest them.[4] One can hypothesize that as society becomes more open to women their opportunities to commit visible crimes increase, and concomitantly, as society becomes less protective of women and less patriarchal in its attitudes toward them their infractions of the law will be dealt with more stringently.

Women in Prison

The consequences of imprisonment include certain common experiences for both men and women: loss of freedom and autonomy, deprivation of goods and services, separation from family and heterosexual contacts, and removal from home and community to a sometimes alien and often harsh and lonely setting. For women, the disruption of family life and of significant relationships has the effect of undermining or removing their most salient social roles of wife, lover, mother, sister, daughter, and so on, roles to which their identities are tied and within which their affectional and security needs are met. To compensate, women in prison evolve an informal culture which duplicates the interactions of primary social relationships in the outside world and represents a transfer of social roles and statuses into the prison, providing a system whereby women can continue to participate in the familiar rituals of courtship, marriage, and the family (Giallombardo, 1974; 1966; Heffernan, 1972). Such social systems are found both in institutions for delinquent girls and in prisons for adult women with remarkable similarities that suggest their relevance to common needs and problems and reflect the outside social structure. The system is a network of nuclear families and other configurations linked to each other by the overlapping membership of some individuals.

Western, a correctional school for girls, is an example of an institution where an informal social system developed. It is called "chick business," which means all the behavior related to the homosexual alliances and kinship ties formed by the inmates. Individuals are differentiated by the family roles and the sex roles they occupy, and almost all are part of the system of family groups in the institution. A newcomer becomes socialized very rapidly to the inmate culture:

> Some girls are going together as soon as they come on the dorm. For others it takes two days or it could take one week or one month. It

[4] *U.S. News & World Report,* September 23, 1974, p. 45.

depends on what crowd you get into. Some get in the crowd real fast— if they know you on the streets, and if you're friendly and hip (Giallombardo, 1974, p. 224).

Though only a small percentage of the inmates is committed to a homosexual role in the outside world, all but a few adopt a sex role of butch or femme during their stay at Western. The butch is supposed to take the aggressive role in the courtship, and the femme takes the passive role. In all other aspects of the roles, the relationship is patterned after the inmates' cultural expectation of such roles in the outside world. Marriages are formalized by written documents and by a ceremony performed by a "high priest," an older butch who is gay outside as well as inside prison.

Kinship ties occur both in and out of marriage. A couple will start a family soon after their marriage, by asking another inmate, usually a younger one of thirteen or fourteen, to be their child. As the child gets older, she may in turn marry and her mate becomes the son-in-law to the original couple. Thus families grow, and include all the usual components of such groups, such as aunts, cousins, and siblings. These relationships enable the participants to engage in patterns of social behavior similar to those they had in outside life, but particularly they fulfill needs of emotional contact, protection, and security. The family system helps to solve the problems of isolation and alienation which are inherent in the formal organization of the prison:

> It seems more realistic to you. You want to make it as realistic as possible. I guess it gives you self-confidence. Staff don't really know you. It makes you feel more secure. It makes you feel more secure when you know that you can care about someone and someone cares about you (p. 239).

While the inmates describe the adoption of homosexual roles and behavior as temporary expedients to alleviate the distress of incarceration, a transition in their perception of reality occurred. The social structure of the prison quickly became the norm: "In the beginning it seemed like a fantasy—like a fairy tale. But it seems real to me now (p. 231)."

Another social structure developed at Occoquan, the Women's Reformatory of the District of Columbia.[5] The women of Occoquan had a median age of thirty-four, and three out of four were black. Four levels or stages of affective relationships among the women were distinguished: friendship; "play families" that contained all except the conjugal role; pseudohomosexuality or "playing" at having

---

[5] Occoquan is no longer used as a prison for women.

conjugal roles; and overt homosexuality. These were not as clear-cut in reality as they are conceptually, since a "family" may have consisted of persons who were involved at several levels (Heffernan, 1972).

Friends were drawn from a peer group and provided someone to talk to about things, a bond of support, and an opportunity for release of tensions. They were seen as independent of the "family" roles or those of a sexual nature. Only about 50 percent of the women in the study felt that friends were vital; the others expressed the view that friendship was impossible.

Play families reproduced nonconjugal relationships, consisting of play mothers, daughters, and sisters. Not only was the family supportive of its members, but it functioned as an important system of economic exchange of gifts and services. Women working in the kitchen, sewing room, or storehouse were expected to supply goods, information, or other services for which they had the necessary contacts. Some "mothers" limited their support of their "children" to the giving of advice and affection; others assumed almost a complete maternal role, supplying toilet items, treats, and admonitions in a convincing parallel of the conventional mother-child relationship.

"Playing" at conjugal roles was widespread at Occoquan, with estimates by staff and inmates of 37 to 60 percent of the women involved in them to some extent. Sex roles of "husband" and "wife" were adopted, and these tended to follow traditional expectations in the outside world. The housewife-mother-supportive role was regarded as an expression of womanhood even though it seemed to mean that the woman carried a disproportionate share of the burden of the relationship. The "husband's" role required presenting a masculine kind of support, adopting masculine traits and dress and being as much of a "man" as possible. The bond between the two had supportive, affectional, economic, and sometimes sexual elements and was taken very seriously as a close duplicate of such a bond in the outside society. Disruption of the bond by another could provide bitter jealousy and physical reprisals.

Overt homosexuality was punished at Occoquan, although disciplinary episodes were infrequent. It was pointed out that the rate of recorded disciplinary action was no indication either of the actual frequency of such behavior or of the staff's attitude toward it (Heffernan, 1972). The official attitude of the correctional staff was that homosexuality was abnormal and required control by the institution. The concept that it might be a normal adaptation to life with a single-sex population was not accepted, and couples suspected of having a sexual alliance were often separated by transferring them to other dormitory or work assignments.

While dominant-submissive roles in homosexual relationships are common in men's prisons, the inmate social system does not include marriage and a kinship network (Vedder & King, 1967). The roles of violence and the enforced submission of a weaker inmate to a strong one, both characteristic of male inmate culture, do not emerge in the prisons for women. Such sex differences reflect prevalent values in the outside world. As Giallombardo pointed out, since the cultural orientation of males in our society precludes the adoption of a female role, the family systems of the female prison cannot occur. Even in prison, the confirmed homosexual is considered to have sacrificed his manhood, although the "wolf" who is aggressively homosexual as a temporary expedient is consistent with masculine norms, especially since the absence of sentiment in the relationship divests it of the feminine aura that it tends to have in society.

Rehabilitation and release

Differences exist between male and female prisons in regard to rehabilitation programs and release patterns. While prison life can have negative and dehumanizing consequences for both sexes, evidence indicates that women are discriminated against as recipients of certain kinds of services (Howard and Howard, 1974). First, the training opportunities for women in prison tend to be those which contribute to the operation of the facility, rather than preparation for potential employment. While programs for men are also limited and often unrealistic, they usually include a wider range of choices relevant to later employment. Second, work-release programs, in which the inmate works or goes to school during the day and returns to the prison at night, are less widely available to women, although they have been known to be successful in men's institutions. Third, educational opportunities for women in prison are meager, especially for non–English-speaking inmates. Where classes did exist, they were conducted in English, and bilingual teachers were rare (Howard and Howard, 1974). Fourth, therapeutic programs whose aim is to reorient the offender to function in more socially acceptable ways on the outside, while rare everywhere, are more likely to be found in men's facilities. Innovative therapeutic programs are first introduced in men's prisons, and are tried in women's institutions only after their success has been demonstrated with male prisoners.

The practice of allowing conjugal visits is being introduced in some state prisons for men only (Hayner, 1972). So far, the conjugal visit is a male prerogative which women in prison do not enjoy. Also, some states allow men, but not women, to go home on furloughs if they are due to be released soon. Such differential treatment might once have been explained as necessary to avoid pregnancy in incarcerated women, but with today's contraception this is no longer a valid argument. The implication is strong that the sexual needs of women continue to be seen as less urgent, or less important, than are the needs of men in similar circumstances.

Mental and Emotional Disorders

Historically people who behave in strange, unpredictable, "mad" ways have been perceived as threats and have been variously punished, segregated, and "treated." Until fairly recent times, such persons were thought to be responsible for their misery, which they had brought upon themselves by their own wickedness. Thus to the punishment by God was added the punishment by man, and floggings, torture, and murder were common (Zilboorg and Henry, 1941). The notion that such disturbed persons were sick rather than sinful is credited to Philippe Pinel, an eighteenth-century French physician who thought that the revolutionary slogan "Liberty, Equality, and Fraternity" should apply also to the inmates of asylums and persuaded the government to take steps to alleviate their miserable conditions.

Although the change in attitude toward such disorders was certainly an improvement, it became fashionable to label as "sick" all kinds of troublesome behavior from marital infidelity to bed-wetting. This overinclusiveness of the "sickness" concept has caused it to lose credibility among some theorists and students of human behavior, who have advised its abandonment altogether. Thomas Szasz, for instance, has been highly critical of his profession of psychiatry and its treatment of patients, which he has characterized as unethical and oppressive (1961). He has questioned the very existence of mental illness, and compared the examination, diagnosing, and treatment of mental patients to the inquisition, testing, and exorcism rituals practiced on witches by priests of earlier time (Szasz, 1970).

Concepts of mental health or mental illness vary considerably among professionals in our own society, and we have already seen that judgments about what is normal are subject to very different standards in different cultures. Questions such as, "What is normal," and "Who is mentally healthy," ask for definitions of values which cannot be supplied by empirical science. It is said that when Freud was asked what ought a normal person be able to do, he replied, "Arbeiten und lieben" (to work and to love). Most contemporary theories likewise include in their definitions of mental health effective mental and physical functioning and the ability to form satisfying interpersonal relationships. But even these reflect our Western value judgments of the good life. In 1937, Karen Horney pointed out the effect of cultural relativity: "With us a person would be neurotic or psychotic who talked by the hour with his deceased grandfather, whereas such communication with ancestors is a recognized pattern in some Indian tribes" (p. 15).

In our society mental disorders are typically diagnosed in accordance with the classification system devised by the American Psychiatric Association (1968). Examples of mental disorders that we shall discuss will be described in terms of this system and will include several significant categories: the functional psychoses, the psychoneuroses, psychophysiological and psychosomatic disorders, and transient situational disorders. We cannot provide a detailed description of psychiatric diagnoses but will define these selected categories briefly for purposes of the subsequent discussion.

Functional psychosis is a general term for serious mental disorders characterized by some degree of personality disorganization, loss of ability to evaluate reality, and inability to relate effectively to others. The term functional means that there is no known pathology of the central nervous system related to the psychosis. The most common of the functional psychoses is schizophrenia, whose outstanding characteristics are the affected person's disordered thought processes which sometimes make behavior and speech incomprehensible and the inability to express feelings and emotions appropriately.

The psychoneuroses are milder forms of mental disorder than the psychoses. Their chief characteristic is anxiety, either overtly manifested or concealed in other symptoms. Common neurosis symptoms include anxiety, irrational fears, obsessions and compulsions, and depressions without the disorganization of psychotic reactions. Many neurotics experience periods of impaired function owing to their symptoms, but many whose symptoms are milder continue to function adequately without treatment.

Psychophysiological and psychosomatic disorders are characterized by physical symptoms that appear to result from emotional tension or prolonged stress. Events which affect the person psychologically lead to malfunction of body systems and actual tissue damage. Examples are gastrointestinal reactions such as duodenal ulcers, and respiratory reactions such as asthma. While these are not always caused by emotional stress, they are often exacerbated by it.

Transient situational disorders are acute symptom responses to an overwhelming stress situation where there is no underlying pathology. When the stress diminishes, the symptoms do also. This diagnosis is used with people of all ages though unlike the others it is more frequently used for children and adolescents. An example is an acute but transient depression brought about by loss of a loved one or a job.

Earlier we noted the dichotomy that occurs after childhood in the classification and treatment of problem behavior, and how some behaviors come to be seen as criminal and others as symptoms of mental illness. We have already seen that the behavior of women compared to men is infrequently seen as criminal. In the area of mental disorder a differing picture emerges: women are over-represented among the help-seekers, and their diagnoses and treatment are different from those of men.

Rates of mental disorders

It is not a simple matter to assess accurately the incidence of mental and emotional problems in a population, since many persons do not seek treatment, and diagnostic information for those who do may go unrecorded in some cases or may be inaccurate or imprecise in others owing to varying interpretations of patients' syndromes by different practitioners in different treatment settings. Available data, however, show that very large sex differences exist in the proportions of males and females in those diagnostic categories of mental disorder which we have described.

A survey of persons being treated for mental disorders in hospitals and psychiatric clinics in the United States yielded the data presented in Table 11.2. Except for persons admitted to mental hospitals for treatment of transient situational disorders,[6] and psychophysiologic and psychosomatic disorders, females substantially outnumber males. Even for these diagnoses, the ratio of females to males is much higher among persons being treated in general hospitals and outpatient psychiatric clinics.[7]

Among both the psychoses and the psychoneuroses are several disorders whose major feature is depression. Examples of these include psychotic depressive reaction which is distinguished by a depressive mood severe enough to interfere with reality contact and

---

[6] The absolute number of persons admitted to mental hospitals with a primary diagnosis of transient situational disorder is very small, compared to the other diagnoses in this table. Such persons are more likely to be treated on the psychiatric ward of a general hospital or in an outpatient setting.

[7] The sex ratios in this table are derived from figures variously based on rates of admission and discharge. For a full presentation of the data and their sources, see Gove and Tudor (1973).

Table 11.2   Females per 100 males by psychiatric diagnosis and facility*

Diagnosis	Facility†		
	Mental hospital	General hospital	Outpatient psychiatric clinic
Functional psychosis	110	144	121
Psychoneurosis	146	189	173
Transient situational disorder	81	162	163
Psychophysiological and psychosomatic disorder	100	169	135

* Adapted from Gove and Tudor (1973).
† Includes Veterans Administration, state, county, and private hospitals and clinics.

functional adequacy, and depressive neurosis commonly associated with internal conflicts or an identifiable external event, such as loss of a love object. The depressive disorders account for 21.2 percent of all psychiatric diagnoses of women, compared to only 9.8 percent for men. Thus women are more than twice as likely as men to be perceived as suffering from a depressive disorder.[8]

Most persons who receive treatment for mental disorders are treated by physicians in the community without special psychiatric training, and more women than men receive such treatment (Gove and Tudor, 1973). This conclusion was supported by two studies conducted in Monroe County, New York, of psychiatric and emotional disorders among the patients of general practitioners and internists (Locke and Gardner, 1969) and patients seen in general medical clinics (Rosen et al., 1972). The studies were concerned with the prevalence of such disorders as perceived by physicians in non-psychiatric settings. Almost two out of every three patients were women. For most age groups, women were about twice as likely to be perceived as having psychiatric and emotional problems than were men. The percentage of women seen as having such problems peaked in the decade 35–44 years, 25.3 percent and 42.7 percent respectively in the two studies, while the peak for men was the decade 45–54, 15.5 percent and 23.2 percent.

A recent study of psychologists in private practice in the southeastern United States found that the greatest percent of the primary

[8] Statistical Note 92, Survey and Reports Section, National Institute of Mental Health, 1973.

clientele of both male and female clinicians consisted of individual female clients, 37.5 percent and 41.4 percent respectively. Less than 1 percent of the clients of female clinicians, and 12.6 percent of the clients of male clinicians, were individual males (Pendergrass, 1974).

Finally, one other interesting finding relates a sex difference to the incidence of mental disorders among the intellectually gifted. The Terman longitudinal study of gifted children (see Chapter 6) found that as children, the boys had a higher incidence of nervous disorders than the girls. But as adults the rate of psychosis among women was *higher* than the expectancy rate in the general population, while the rate for men was *lower*.

All these data show that women have higher rates of mental disorder in several important categories than men do. When the data are examined by marital status, however, a somewhat different picture emerges. Studies which report marital status of mental patients agree that single, divorced, and widowed women have fewer mental problems than men in the same categories (Crago, 1972; Garai, 1970). Therefore it is the population of married women which accounts for the surplus of women among the mentally ill. The shift from being married to being divorced or widowed has a more negative effect for males than for females, and marriage has a more advantageous effect for males than for females (Gove, 1973). But why would single men have higher rates of mental illness than single women? Staying single does not cause men to have mental problems any more than it does women; rather, for men, the relationship is the other way around: men with serious mental problems are more likely to stay single. For example, male schizophrenics are more likely to stay single than are female schizophrenics (Birley, 1968; Garai, 1970). Taking the initiative in courtship and providing for a home and the support of a family require skills and resources which such a person rarely has. Female schizophrenics, on the other hand, are spread more evenly among the single and married populations of women.

Suicide

Suicide and attempted suicide are behaviors which clearly reflect very serious degrees of personal distress. Though not themselves defined as mental illness, they represent behavioral solutions, or attempted solutions, to intolerable pressures of anxiety, depression, or psychotic distortions of reality often precipitated by or associated with severe environmental stress. Here also the differences between the sexes are remarkable: men commit approximately three times as many suicides as women, while women make about four times as many attempts as men do (Garai, 1970). A simple comparison of suicide rates for males and females does little, however, to enhance understanding of the phenomenon. One could interpret the much greater number of attempts by women as evidence that more women are acutely distressed; but on the other hand, more men are successful. Men are more likely to use violent methods, such as firearms and cutting instruments, while women use less aggressive methods such as pills or gas. Women are much more likely than men to use suicide attempts as appeals to others and as attempts to manipulate relationships (Stengel, 1964). Thus the threat against the self may be a result of powerlessness. Attempted suicide is a weapon that is used when no other seems available. The rate of suicide among women has greatly increased in the United States in recent years though that for men has not (Garai, 1972). Furthermore, women in professional occupations such as medicine and psychology have a suicide rate about three times that of women in general (Schaar, 1974).

Suicide rates are known to vary with marital status, with the lowest rates occurring among married persons, intermediate rates among the widowed and single, and the highest rate among the divorced. While males have a higher rate of suicide than females in all these marital categories, the disparity for males across marital categories is much greater than for females (Gove, 1972). For instance, for the ages twenty-five to sixty-four single females in the United States are 47 percent more likely to commit suicide than married females, while single males are 97 percent more likely to commit suicide than married males. Likewise the disparity for widowed and divorced males compared to married males is much greater than for females in the same categories. For example, the suicide rate for widowed females is about twice that for married females, while the rate for widowed males is over four times that for married males. As with mental disorders, it appears that the change in marital status from married to divorced or widowed has a more devastating effect on men. Likewise, the higher rate of suicides among single men compared to married men can be explained by the observation that men who are at greater risk for suicide because of emotional instability or other personality problems are less likely to get married, thus swelling the numbers of potentially suicidal men among the unmarried.

Social Roles and Mental Disorders

The higher rates for females in such important categories as the functional psychoses, the psychoneuroses, and other problem behavior raise an interesting question: What happened during the course of time to those auspicious beginnings of girlhood, when by all signs she was destined for a smoother developmental course than her brother? Most of the evidence indicates that her advantage begins to be lost during the years of puberty. Several plausible explanations have been presented, all of which have merit. But the search for the single cause is a vain one; a satisfactory theory will need to integrate several interacting factors contributory to this important sex difference.

No one proposes that women are genetically at greater risk for mental disorder than men are. In fact the opposite is more plausible, since the second X chromosome confers protective effects on females who have fewer genetic defects at birth and a lower incidence of central nervous system pathology. Biologically, females have an adaptive advantage which manifests itself in many ways during their life span. But women's biology is different in ways that have been seen as significant for mental health by some (including a White House physician who stated that a woman could never be president because of her "curious mental aberrations" associated with "raging hormonal imbalance").[9] The decline of estrogen premenstrually and during the climacterium seems to be related to mood changes as well as to somatic symptoms in some women, and the high incidence of depression, especially in older women, may reflect a contribution from this source.[10] If the involution of the ovarian function was a major cause of depressive disorders, the incidence should be much higher than it is. Since women's biology is the result of a long process of selection for adaptation, not maladaptation, it is logically improbable that it would have a decisive negative effect on her psychological well being.

Other explanations for the differences in mental health between men and women are based upon observations of sex-differentiated socialization practices, the social roles of adult men and women which are the goals of the socialization process, the ways that the lives of women differ from the lives of men, and the sex-linked expectations of society, all of which are closely related to each other.

The effects of socialization into sex roles become more salient during puberty, when body changes further enhance sex differentiation, and relationships with the other sex and the development of social and interactional skills become critical concerns. Even in adolescence, girls seem to have a greater investment in personal relationships than most boys do. In 1963, Erik Erikson described intimacy as a normal achievement of late adolescence, a capacity to

[9] *Time*, August 10, 1970, p. 13.
[10] For a detailed discussion of the climacterium see Chapters 4 and 12.

commit oneself to affiliations and partnerships, a stage of readiness for "true genitality" with one of the other sex. Many writers have argued that women value intimacy and affiliation more, and thus are more affected by their disruption or loss. Men, on the other hand, invest much of their energy in achievement strivings and the realization of vocational goals, valuing success in these areas as well as success in achieving a truly intimate relationship. Now the capacity and need for intimacy are not in themselves conducive to mental disorders. But girls and women whose identity is primarily maintained through their relationships with others and who have not developed an autonomous self-concept may be especially dependent on their affective environment and thus especially vulnerable to its course. In fact, in one view "failure to achieve intimacy with a man is probably the most serious factor precipitating mental dysfunction in women" (Garai, 1970, p. 134). While the validity of this assertion is yet to be demonstrated, there is little doubt that the achievement of intimacy is an important need for most women.

There is a relationship between adult sex roles and rates of mental disorders, according to one study (Gove and Tudor 1973). Women are more likely than men to have emotional problems because of their roles, for the following reasons: first, most women have a single major role, that of housewife, which includes being a mother. Men have two, head of the household, which includes being a father, and worker. Although a very large percentage of women are employed, most are in low-level jobs whose importance is economic, not central to their self-esteem and identity. Thus if the woman does not find her domestic role gratifying, she typically has no other major source of gratification. Second, since the major activities of the housewife do not require a high level of skill or education, they must be boring and frustrating to many women who are overqualified for the job. Third, the role of housewife is poorly defined and practically invisible. There is no special set of requirements for it, and its very diffuseness permits women to give play to their problems in a way that a structured job, subject to evaluation, would not. Fourth, the married woman who works is usually in a less satisfactory position than the married male. Not only does she earn less in a job with which she is minimally involved, but typically when she comes home she performs most of the household chores, so that her work day is much longer than her husband's. Fifth, the expectations for women are unclear and even contradictory. Their lives seem to be contingent upon what others do, especially family members. Though educated in the same ways as men, they are still not treated as equals and remain essentially in the old institutionalized positions.

Some have noted that the typical emotional state for women is depression, and that the mental health of housewives is "public enemy number one" (Bernard, 1973). In 1942, Jessie Bernard proposed what she called the shock theory of marriage to explain the commonly reported phenomenon of the deterioration of mental health among married women, including the observation that the disparity between such women and their never-married sisters grew greater with age. Some of the conventional ingredients of the shock included the anti-climactic realization after attaining the sought-after status of married woman that she is now just a housewife, a role that involves menial labor and is low in status both to her and to society.

A more recently recognized shock is the fallacy of the sex stereotypes around which she has built her expectations (Bernard, 1971). Just as the child discovers the fallibility of its parents, the wife discovers her husband's weaknesses and dependencies. She finds that he does not really know more than she, that he is not the calm, rational dealer in facts and relevant arguments, that he is not the kind of person the male stereotype pictures him to be. She finds that she is not really the weaker vessel and that often she must be the strong one in the relationship. Thus expectations of the marital relationship, built on stereotypes, and the reality of the roles themselves, result in a dissonance and a disillusionment for women, putting too much stress on those who are vulnerable and who are already at risk for the development of a mental disorder.

The sex-role explanation for higher rates of mental disorder in women is based, then, on the components of the adult role, on the realities of life for the average adult female and their potential for producing stress beyond the coping capacity of many women. The discrepancy between these realities and prior expectations built up by stereotypes is a secondary component of this explanation, a contributor to problems inherent in the role.

Another explanation for the incidence of mental disorders in women is based on the observation that women are freer to express how they feel than men are. In community surveys of mental illness where the data were self-reports of psychiatric symptoms, women reported more symptoms than men did. The investigators questioned whether this sex difference was real, suggesting that it could reflect men's reluctance to admit to unpleasant feelings and sensations, since it is "more culturally appropriate and acceptable for women to be more expressive about their difficulties" (Phillips and Segal, 1969, p. 59).

Clearly, females of all ages in our society are permitted more freedom in the display of emotions of all kinds, although the mode in which the emotion is expressed may differ for the sexes. For example, if a woman is enraged she may cry, become hysterical, or withdraw; a man may shout, curse, or retaliate. The assertion that women are emotional does not really mean that women compared to men are emotional in the sense that emotionalism is a female attribute, like having breasts; rather, it means that women in general are more expressive of feelings. They have permission to show to others that they are experiencing grief, anxiety, excitement, joy, and concern. The male is expected to be more stoic, to look upon emotionally arousing situations almost as if they were problems to be solved. "Take it like a man" means don't cry, *do* something about it; doing something about it, the issuance of an instrumental response, is one way to handle feelings, especially anxiety and fear (Kagan, 1972). An important corollary is that it is more acceptable for women to admit feelings associated with problems, such as depression, inadequacy, guilt, and low self-esteem, whereas men must avoid any show of weakness or inability to cope. Thus there is less dissonance for a woman when she takes the step of seeking help and becoming a patient and a statistic.

The Double Standard for Mental Health

The standards for evaluating mental health are different for males and females in our society. This hypothesis was tested with male and female practicing clinicians. These subjects were given a set of 122 bipolar adjectives, each of which describes a behavior trait or characteristic such as:

> very aggressive . . . . not at all aggressive
> doesn't hide emotions . . . . always hides emotions

The clinicians were divided into three groups. The first group was asked to indicate for each item the pole to which a mature, healthy, socially competent *man* would be closer; the second group was asked to describe in this manner a mature, healthy, socially competent *female,* and the third, a mature, healthy, socially competent *adult,* sex unspecified. The results revealed that the clinicians strongly agreed on the characteristics of healthy men, healthy women, and healthy adults, sex unspecified. But while the concepts of the healthy, mature man and the adult were not different from each other, the clinicians were significantly less likely to attribute to healthy women the same traits that they saw in the healthy adult. Women were seen as more submissive, less independent, less adventurous, more easily influenced, less aggressive, less competitive, more excitable in minor crises, more emotional, more conceited, and less objective—a strange description of a mature, healthy person. This finding suggests that the ideal personality is essentially a masculine model, and that women who conform to the female model are then in the curious position of being "normal" and deviant at the same time (Broverman *et al.*, 1970).

In another study clinicians were given a psychological and educational history of a college student who was always identically described except for sex, John or Joan, and political orientation, left or right politically active. The clinicians ascribed significantly greater maladjustment to the left-involved female than to her male counterpart, and their verdicts for her were more severe than for the right-involved youth of either sex (Abramowitz *et al.*, 1973).

Clinicians are not the only ones who differentially identify and evaluate behaviors and personality characteristics on the basis of sex. College men and women agree on behaviors characteristically seen as masculine and feminine; they value the former higher than the latter; and females tend to see themselves in accordance with the stereotype for their sex, i.e., hold negative values of their worth compared to males (Rosenkrantz *et al.*, 1968).

Occasionally, blatantly immature and unadaptive behavior is viewed as normal for women. For example, one theorist wrote that, in a nonpathological form, the hysterical character (as usually described in the analytic literature: histrionic, pseudosexual, highly dependent upon others for emotional support and concern, competitive with other women for male attention, manipulative, and hyperreactive emotionally to both positive and negative response from others) is developmentally appropriate for women, that it is widespread, comprehensible, and predictable. "The psychodynamics of the hysteric are uncomfortably close to the dynamics of the idealized *normal* feminine personality" (Wolowitz, 1972, p. 313, *italics added*).

As women move into higher-level professional and administrative positions they can find themselves in situations where their responses are labeled deviant simply because they are emitted by females. The anxiety-provoking effects of being the lone woman in a professional, task-oriented peer group have been studied. The six groups studied were highly uniform in their responses to the lone female in their midst:

> Many coping mechanisms carry sex-role labels in our culture. If she acted friendly, she was thought to be flirting....If she apologized for alienating the group she was seen as a submissive woman knowing her place. If she asked for help, she earned a "needy" female label. If she became angry...she was seen as competitive, in a bitchy, unfeminine way (Wolman and Frank, 1975, p. 168).

The double standard of mental health clearly reflects role typing and sexual stereotypes. In summary, it holds, first of all, that the criteria for judging certain kinds of behaviors normal differ for males and females, secondly, that the traits which make up the male criterion are the norm for the healthy adult and are more highly valued in this society, and thirdly, that females who conform to the "feminine" criterion are thus not "healthy" by definition. The woman is put in a precarious double bind: if she is feminine, she embodies a collection of traits which are negatively valued. If she is masculine, she violates the behavioral norms for her sex and becomes subject to all the sanctions imposed upon deviants. Though the double standard is real, part of its identification is attributable to semantics and part to certain concepts that are held both by psychologists and by society. Taken together, these tend to perpetuate inaccurate conclusions with regard to the healthy personality.

The semantic problem lies in the differential designation of behaviors and personality characteristics as masculine or feminine, which implies that males do or ought to exhibit the masculine ones and females the feminine ones. Thus empathy is a feminine characteristic and inventiveness is masculine. The stereotypy here is obvious, since neither of these characteristics, nor dozens of others likewise sexually labeled, is exclusively in the repertoire of one sex and not the other. But the consensus for such designation is very strong, and it gives rise to the serious problem that behaviors are dichotomized along sex lines, thus setting the stage for differential valuing. For example, certain characteristics were agreed upon by college students to be more desirable in American society for males and females respectively (Bem, 1974). Males should be assertive, athletic, individualistic, and self-reliant, while females should be affectionate, compassionate, loyal, and understanding. These are only a few of the traits attributed to each sex. The students' descriptors, with few exceptions, are not strongly negative or pejorative if applied to either sex; that is, it is acceptable for males to be affectionate, compassionate, and loyal, and for females to be assertive, athletic, and self-reliant. But the prevailing values of American society are such that as abstractions the masculine traits are likely to be seen as more valuable because they serve the goals of society. If they are "masculine" in most peoples' minds then we have a double standard.

The other contributor to the double standard which is not part of its reality base is the concept that masculinity and femininity are mutually exclusive, that a person is either masculine or feminine but not both. This highly artificial dichotomy is incorporated into many personality tests so that a person's orientation as measured by her performance on the test is in either a "feminine" or "masculine" direction.

Recently, some personality theorists have introduced the concept of androgyny as a replacement for sex-linked evaluations of personality (Bem, 1974; Spence, 1974). Their view argues that all individuals integrate in varying degrees personality traits that have been called masculine and feminine, and that socially desirable traits instead of characterizing one sex or the other are androgynous in that they characterize the healthy human regardless of sexual identity. Thus both a male and a female might be both assertive *and* yielding, forceful *and* compassionate, ambitious *and* sensitive to the needs of others. Such a person would be flexible, able to adapt to the needs of the situation and to engage in behaviors that were appropriate to it. By contrast, the highly sex-typed person who is motivated to behave consistently with a sex-role standard would have to suppress those aspects of her or his personality which were incongruent with that standard.

Support for such an androgynous model of personality was found when masculinity and femininity as two separate dimensions of personality were studied. College students who ascribed to themselves both instrumental ("masculine") and expressive ("feminine") tendencies were higher in self-esteem (Spence, 1974). College women who scored high on a masculinity scale were no less expressive but were more instrumental than feminine women were (Heilbrun, 1968b). Furthermore, the combination of goal-directedness and interpersonal sensitivity found in the masculine girls defined a more effective personality than that found in the feminine girls.

Perhaps the best androgynous model of personality, incorporating a nonsexist description of the healthy *person,* is based on Abraham Maslow's views of the development of personality (1954). A distinctive feature of Maslow's investigations is its focus on healthy, creative persons, in contrast to the more typical concern of psychologists with the pathologies, weaknesses, and negativisms of humans. Maslow thought that all humans have needs, capacities, and tendencies which are essentially good or neutral rather than evil, and that healthy, normal development consists in actualizing this basic nature, providing the environment in which it can grow from within rather than being shaped from without. When persons become miserable or neurotic, it is because the environment has made them so through ignorance and social pathology.

Maslow studied people who were "self actualized," who had succeeded in developing their basic, healthy inner natures to their fullest expression. He undertook a series of studies whose goal was the discovery of characteristics which distinguish such persons from ordinary ones. His subjects came from all sectors of life; some were historical figures such as Lincoln, Whitman, and Thoreau; while others, such as Albert Einstein, were living. Among those he studied were four women: Eleanor Roosevelt, Jane Addams, Ida Tarbell, and Harriet Tubman.

What are the distinguishing features of the personalities of such actualized persons? They are realistically oriented, accepting themselves, other people, and the natural world for what they are. Their values are democratic, and they can identify readily with all kinds of people. They are at home in the world. They are spontaneous, open, and relatively free of neurotic defenses. Their appreciation of people and things is fresh rather than stereotyped. They have a childlike quality which lets them see and experience and feel as if each time is the first. They are problem-centered rather than self-centered. They are creative and resist conformity to the culture, transcending it rather than merely coping with it. Such self-actualized persons have a few deep relationships with certain important others. Emotionally self-sufficient, they strive for autonomy in their lives. They require privacy and enjoy solitude. With others they are never exploitative, nor do they confuse means with ends. Their humor is philosophical, often at their own expense, rather than hostile.

This is clearly a concept of the healthy personality whose features are independent of sexual identity. Biased toward neither masculinity nor femininity, it suggests that the most valuable traits are human traits, with no sex label, and by implication it advocates the kind of nurturance which freely permits the emergence of individual traits which are not a function of an arbitrary assignment based on sexual category.

An early study suggests how an androgynous model of personality might be manifested in healthy women. He found that women who were high in self-esteem were also tolerant of others, assertive, willing to take initiative, decisive, self-reliant, independent, and ambitious. They permitted themselves a wider range of sexual experience, had no fear of the body or its organs, and eschewed altogether the double standard of sexual behavior (Maslow, 1942). These are characteristics which are valued in our society, and which are seen as descriptive of the healthy person, a far cry from the feminine vision of the clinicians (Broverman *et al.*, 1970). Such characteristics do not preclude those positive ones usually attributed to women, which, whether manifested by women or men, underlie the emergence of empathy and concern for others into human relationships. One remembers again Margaret Mead's proposal that society make possible a broad and flexible range of models which would permit the unfolding of all temperamental variations in the absence of pressures to conform to a model based on sex category.

Women As Patients

The role of the patient is more compatible with the female sex role than with the male sex role. "Patient" behavior includes weakness, dependency, irrationality, childishness, submission to authority, and acceptance of care and attention. The patient, whether the disorder is mental or physical, is not expected to behave like a normal person. Rather, regression to a less effective and competent mode of functioning is expected and permitted. Thus an analysis of the patient role reveals it to be uncomfortably close to the traditional female role. The role of the sick one is less deviant for women than for men. When a woman becomes ill, she goes or is taken to a helper, usually a male, with whom she enters into a relationship that parallels others she has experienced, e.g., father-daughter, husband-wife, all having in common the dyadic male-female constituents who are respectively dominant and submissive, strong and weak, authoritative and yielding.

Not only is her "femininity" reinforced by the role of patient, but her helper, her physician or other therapist, is quite likely to share common social assumptions about her personality and behavior, and to treat her accordingly. For example, when physicians were asked to describe "the typical complaining patient," sex unspecified, 72 percent spontaneously referred to a woman and only 4 percent to a man; 24 percent did not mention the sex of the patient (Cooperstock, 1971).

Women fit so naturally into the role of patient that often their complaints are seen as not "real," as psychogenic in nature and at best uninteresting. One researcher found that women are held in low regard as patients, that less concern is given to their specific conditions and to their health care, compared to males. Included as examples are the observations that women are subjected to a high rate of hysterectomies, often without adequate indications; and that such research questions as the relationship between breast cancer, the second leading cause of death in women, and trauma attract neither medical researchers nor funding. Women were more likely than men to have their depressions and anxieties treated by drugs rather than to be helped to uncover the cause of the symptoms. Stereotyped attitudes and assumptions about "woman's place" pervasively colored the doctor-patient relationship, and women were seen as unreliable personal historians whose emotionality always enhanced their disease—or itself was the disease (Howell, 1974).

Women receive a disproportionate number of drug prescriptions for both mental and physical disorders. In a study of 1.5 million prescriptions written by general practitioners in Australia, 80 percent were for mental disorders, most commonly for depressive neurosis, and the drugs were issued far more frequently for women than for men (Rowe, 1973). In this country, women get 60 percent of the prescriptions for nonpsychoactive drugs and 67 percent of the prescriptions for psychoactive drugs (Fidell, 1973).[11] The heavy involvement of women in drugs tends to be hidden under the guise of legitimacy, since they are procured from physicians.

Perhaps the female-role stereotypes held by physicians influence them to over-prescribe drugs for women. For example, one study found that physicians were willing to prescribe tranquilizers to housewives because they could always take naps and needn't be alert (Brodsky, 1971). Physicians saw daily use of Librium, a strong sedative, as much more legitimate for housewives than for students (Linn, 1971).

Advertising also plays a part in influencing physicians' treatment of women. Increasingly, problems in living are defined as appropriate for drug therapy, with drug advertisements broadening the range of problem situations which allegedly can be helped by drugs. A content analysis of drug advertisements in leading medical journals over a five-year period revealed that men and women were depicted differently in the following ways:

1. Sex stereotypes were confirmed almost without exception in the ads.
2. Psychoactive drugs tended to be associated with female patients.
3. Nonpsychoactive drugs tended to be associated with male patients (despite the fact that women take more of them than men do), this fact implying that men have "real" illnesses, while women have mental problems.
4. The symptoms listed for male and female users of psychoactive drugs were different. Men presented specific, work-related symptoms, while women complained of diffuse anxiety, tension, and depression.
5. Male patients were depicted as older on the average, but in a wider range of ages than female patients.

---

[11] Psychoactive drugs affect mental and emotional states as contrasted to physical or organic conditions.

6. Women's illnesses tended to be shown as irritating to others and as socially embarrassing.
7. Women were shown as recovering from mental illness when they began to reassume sex-stereotypical behaviors and attitudes (Prather and Fidell, 1972).

When a woman becomes a patient, then, for whatever real reasons, she enters a role which is invested with an accretion of assumptions, values and attitudes called forth by her identity as woman. It would be surprising indeed if her treatment did not reflect both the dimensions of the role and that special identity.

Women and Psychotherapy

The term *psychotherapy* is applied to the use of psychological techniques by trained persons—clinical psychologists, psychiatrists, and social workers—to alleviate mental and emotional disorders or problems in daily living. Its usage is very general and is appropriate to a broad spectrum of theoretical orientations. Techniques may include giving emotional support and acceptance, retraining, hypnosis, releasing and interpreting feelings, or simply giving advice and directions. It carries no implication about the seriousness of the problem or the length of treatment. It has been used to describe the treatment of everything from nail-biting to schizophrenia, for periods varying from one session to several years. Almost always psychotherapy implies a personal consultation between a therapist and a client. Implicit in the practice of psychotherapy is the goal of change in the client—change in behavior, attitudes, beliefs, feelings, approach to life, well being, and mental health. While the extent to which psychotherapy of all kinds actually is effective is controversial, it is generally agreed that it is most helpful with younger, better educated clients whose values are similar to those of the therapist. Persons who have a psychoneurosis or a transient situational disorder are usually seen as more suitable for psychotherapy than are persons who are psychotic. The latter are more likely to be treated with drugs or other medically oriented procedures, although drugs are often used in conjunction with psychotherapy for all kinds of mental disorders. Many persons who seek and receive psychotherapy are not mentally disturbed in the clinical sense; they are not suffering from a mental disorder. Such persons are often seeking help in dealing with a problem in their lives, like an unhappy marriage, misbehaving children, or lack of vocational or educational success.

Women have always been the main consumers of psychotherapy from Freud's era onward.[12] On one extreme, psychotherapy and marriage are seen as the two socially approved institutions for American women. In recent years psychotherapy as it affects women has come under critical scrutiny by feminists, especially by feminist therapists. These critics see psychotherapy as reflecting and reinforcing traditional values, beliefs, and attitudes about women and their roles, and thus failing to come to grips with the real problems of women inherent in their traditionally subservient and powerless role. It is the traditional role of women and stereotyped beliefs about women in relation to their role which are responsible for the increasing numbers of women who seek help for mental and emotional problems and for the ways they are dealt with by professional helpers in and out of institutions. To the extent that the values and goals underlying the treatment process reflect those held to be "normal" by the society as a whole, the therapy must reflect the pervasive sexism characteristic of the society (Chesler, 1972).

Although patients and therapists vary widely, analyses show that the larger group of women in therapy are white, educated, middle-class housewives and mothers (Fabrikant, 1974), while the majority of psychologists and psychiatrists are middle-aged, middle-class, married males (Chesler, 1971). Thus both have been socialized within the traditional model of male-female relationships and are likely to share the values and attitudes inherent in that model. For women, the psychotherapeutic relationship is not unlike marriage. Not only is it a male-female interaction, but the therapist has or is perceived by the patient as having power, authority, control, and arcane knowledge which he will use to help her with her problems. Conditioned to expect and to value such attributes in males, she can move into the relationship without violating her sense of the fitness of things. The therapist can be a surrogate father, husband, lover, or priest-confessor for her in a role interaction that is both complementary and respectable. Thus it is not surprising that women, even more than men, are likely to state a preference for a male therapist (Chesler, 1971).

The traditional definition of female sexuality and role behavior, the nature of the psychotherapeutic relationship, and the predominance of male therapists all may contribute to the formulation of goals for female patients which feature adjustment to their place in society. The therapist with traditional assumptions about sex roles, trained in an approach which has as its criterion for restoration to health the patient's ability to function in conformity with society's ex-

---

[12] For a history of women in psychotherapy, see Franks and Burtle (1974).

pectations, may interpret as pathological a woman's expressions of discontent or condemnation of the feminine role.[13] The goal of adjustment to that role places the questioning woman in a very serious predicament. On the one hand she is enjoined to enjoy being a woman, while on the other, evidence all around her convinces her that psychological and physical femininity include a collection of low-valued traits and the relegation to a role and status which not only do not command respect but are mostly irrelevant to contemporary life.

Psychoanalytically oriented psychotherapy which interprets women's behavior through Freudian explanations and concepts has come under the heaviest criticism from feminists. The continuing influence of psychoanalytic theory on contemporary psychotherapy was illustrated by the psychoanalytic treatment of a woman who had become a patient after her former therapist and she had had a love affair. Analysis of this account of the four-and-a-half-year treatment of this woman reveals the patriarchal and authoritarian framework of the treatment model, the assumptions underlying interpretations of the patient's behavior during therapy, and the critieria that defined a successful outcome.

Treatment was based on Freudian theory, with modifications which the therapist thought were necessitated by her periods of regression:

> *having* her sit up; *permitting* her to phone me at any time of the day or night; *prescribing* drugs on one occasion; *insisting* the patient and her husband visit each other . . . *prohibiting* a divorce; *physically restraining* her in the office . . . *demanding* the patient be hospitalized; *insisting* . . . that treatment continue until I agreed to terminate it; and, finally, that the patient adhere to the psychoanalytic method *despite whatever feelings she might develop in the course of the treatment* (Voth, 1972, p. 394, *italics added*).

This insistently controlling and authoritarian approach was thought to be necessary because of the patient's rage and feeling of deprivation which resulted from her father's death when she was very young, and from her former analyst-lover's capitulation to her seductiveness which had ended so disastrously. Her strong penis envy drove her to wish to triumph over men: "She had defeated a man, proved herself superior to men, and had won the forbidden

[13] An exaggeration of this phenomenon is commonly observed in the reactions of the general public to persons who are in the vanguard of social movements. A good example of this tendency is the readiness to label supporters of women's liberation lesbians. A woman who questions or violates normative female behavior is thus seen as deviant, which "explains" her lack of interest in or hostility toward society's definition of her role.

father" (p. 397), but in reality, "she had gotten neither a penis nor her father" (p. 396). At one point the patient attempted to wreck the office and had to be physically subdued. This incident was analyzed as a revelation of her resentment at continuing treatment and having to become more feminine. But when she became aware that termination was near, this plus "the challenge of accepting her feminine gender and feminine responsibilities and commitments" (p. 397) led to several suicidal gestures which were interpreted as a last resistance to acceptance of the fact that she would never get what she wanted, presumably a penis. But finally she said, "I guess it's time for me to shape up and become a woman, wife, and mother" (p. 398). Even so, she continued to talk of committing suicide by drowning. At termination, the treatment was judged to have been fairly successful; "the patient was generally well controlled and friendly. Her child was doing well; she had a reasonably good social life, included in which was membership in a women's club. The marital adjustment was much better; frigidity and bodily symptoms had disappeared; only brief periods of mild depression remained" (Voth, 1972, pp. 399–400).

Recently, the American Psychological Association carried out an investigation of sex bias and sex-role stereotyping in psychotherapeutic practice. Women psychologists were asked to respond to a questionnaire regarding actual incidents and circumstances illustrating sexism in psychotherapy with women. Their responses illustrated five areas of sexist behavior which were of common concern: fostering traditional sex roles, bias in expectations and devaluation of women, sexist use of psychoanalytic concepts, sexual exploitation of female clients, and viewing women as sex objects. The greatest number of complaints was in the first category, with examples of therapists who encouraged women clients to get married, or to perfect themselves as wives, who depreciated the importance of a career, or who used clients' attitudes toward motherhood as evidence of emotional maturity or lack of it. One therapist wrote, "I have had women report to me that they could not continue in therapy (with a previous therapist) because the objective seemed to be for them to learn to adjust better to their role as wives, mothers, daughters (underlings of one kind or another) and they needed to become free persons" (p. 4). Others reported knowledge of male psychologists who encouraged clients to continue to be docile, passive, seductive, and nonassertive, and to stay in professions "open to women" (p. 4). Respondents who had been in therapy themselves reported experiences of being pressured to have vaginal orgasms and of being told that their competitiveness was due to penis envy (Asher, 1975).

Growing awareness of sexist assumptions and biases in the therapeutic situation and their effects on women has begun to result in the introduction of feminist values into psychotherapy with women. Feminist therapists of many different theoretical orientations have changed their ways of interacting with clients to reflect the feminist consciousness of the effect of the historical social oppression of women on their lives. A common goal of therapy illuminated by feminism is to help the client become aware of the social and political context of their psychological problems. Most feminist psychologists, female and male, identify themselves with the broad humanistic movement in psychology, which emphasizes individual growth and awareness of one's feelings and their expression, valuing the quality of individual experience and its importance to the person rather than the dedication of oneself to the pursuit of goals defined by others as valuable. Self-nurturance and attention to one's own needs are encouraged, especially in women who are on the self-defeating course of allowing themselves to be excessively influenced by the needs and expectations of others because they fear the consequences of others' displeasure and the possible loss of love.

Typically, a woman who is involved in feminist therapy begins to see the extent to which external forces have shaped her behavior and are controlling the course of her life. As this insight develops, she experiences anger and frustration along with the realization that her problems are not all her fault, as she may have believed, but are at least partly caused by the fact that she is a woman in a sexist society. The therapist, fully realizing the pressures and demands that diminish women and drive them "crazy," offers the client supportive understanding as she helps her to channel her anger, to identify the obstacles that are preventing her growth, and to seek out alternatives to her present behavior and life style. The client of a feminist therapist does not necessarily become a feminist herself, however, or adopt the value system of her therapist. She may wish to continue in a rather conventional marriage, for example, but under different conditions, such as greater personal freedom and greater involvement in activities outside the home without feeling guilty. Under such circumstances the goal is to help her to grow into the whole person she can be and to have the kind of life which is fulfilling to her, within the context of her personal circumstances and the framework of society. At times, however, the new consciousness that develops so alters a woman's perceptions of herself and her life that nothing short of a drastic change will permit her to take advantage of her revised concept of what her life should be like. In either case, the therapist helps the individual to recognize the choices that are realistically available to her in her situation, and to identify the consequences of each of them. Unwillingness to face the need for change, to experiment with new ways of doing things, is seen as a form of self-betrayal, a refusal to take the risks inherent in the beginnings of growth. The woman must, in a sense, create herself. If her work is boring and unpromising, or a once-important relationship now sterile, she must confront these realities and examine what she can do to change them.

Ideally, the goals of feminist therapy are not different in kind from the goals of all therapy: the alleviation of personal distress and the removal of growth-inhibiting influences and behaviors so that the person can mature emotionally and live effectively, in accordance with her desires and standards. The difference is in the extent to which the feminist therapist places the blame for the client's problem on the structure of social institutions and stereotypes and encourages the client to see how these are affecting her and to challenge their impact on her life. Thus a feminist therapist would place herself in opposition to all the forces which attempt to pressure women toward submission to the status quo. This stance requires that she be aware of these forces and know what they are and what they are doing to women. In this respect, more than any other, she is different from nonfeminist therapists who may never have thought about sex roles as factors in emotional problems, who see sex roles as the natural order of things; if women, and men as well, are not adapted to their roles, then the maladaptation is seen as a problem. The feminist therapist would see the requirements of the role as itself a problem.

There is a need to train all therapists to fill a greater number of roles. They should become experts on the research into sex differences and the psychology of women. Most therapists have little training in these areas and little understanding of the cultural and social antecedents of discrimination. They should be informed about alternative life styles and sex roles. Although trained to be passive with regard to innovative social trends and to avoid imposing their values on their clients, they should be willing to encourage women to seek out paths to self-esteem, even if these threaten to conflict with old family patterns of dominance. Their willingness to help educate the community and to work with groups has more potential for effecting change in attitudes than has the traditional mode of seeing only a handful of patients a week. Finally, more women should be encouraged to enter the mental-health fields at professional levels. Female clients could expect greater sensitivity to their conflicts, and empathy with their feelings; male clients could be confronted with the ways their stereotypes affect them, even within the dyad of the therapeutic relationship (Rice and Rice, 1973).

Consciousness Raising

An alternative kind of help for women began to take shape in the late 1960s as part of the renaissance of feminism. Women began discovering that the sharing with each other of their personal experiences and the examination of their lives in a society which conferred power on men and only indirectly on women was a potent technique for introducing women to the feminist perspective, for generating feelings of mutual supportiveness and sharing, for getting women in touch with each other and for breaking down barriers of suspicion and distrust which had kept them apart.

Consciousness raising (CR) is not therapy in the usual sense. The roles, the relationships, and the setting are all quite different. The CR group typically consists of a small group of women, five to ten in number, who meet weekly in each other's houses to talk. Groups often are very diverse in membership, cutting across lines of age, race, and socioeconomic status. Such diversity enables the group to approach one of its goals, which is to realize the commonalities of experience among women, and the ways that society oppresses all women regardless of the individual differences in their personal situations.

Because of the egalitarian ideology of the women's movement, the groups are leaderless. Each woman is her own authority, knowing better than anyone else her own personal experience. She shares this with the other members of the group, in conformity with certain informal norms: members are not interrupted or criticized; no one dominates or competes for a chance to speak; differences in life styles, backgrounds, and values are tolerated; members are supportive of each other but do not give specific advice.

Some groups use guidelines which offer suggestions for topics, while others deal with issues that arise spontaneously. Some examples for discussion include feelings about other women, experiences with men, feelings about one's self and how one would like to change, sexual experiences, and family arrangements, such as the division of tasks. A major goal is the development of awareness so that one sees oneself and one's experiences in a different light, as shaped by the sexual caste system of society rather than by one's own misdeeds and shortcomings.

The stages of development of CR groups are opening up, sharing, analyzing, and abstracting. At first, members share personal confidences and intimate feelings, which are received by the others without criticism in an atmosphere of warmth and understanding. Barriers to communication disappear as the women learn to trust each other and to know that all feelings will be accepted without evaluation or judgment. In the sharing stage, the focus moves from the individual to the group, as members learn that their problems are not uniquely theirs and are not the result of their own inadequacies but are common problems that have their origin in social conventions and institutions. A spirit of co-operation develops as the members begin to look for ways to effect personal and social change. In the analytic stage, attention is turned to the status of women as a whole, and to analysis of the factors that cause women to be devalued and to remain in an inferior position. Finally, the group begins to abstract from their more personal visions ideas and theories about the structuring of institutions, how they interfere with the growth of human potential, and how they ought to be changed (Allen, 1970).

While these four stages build upon each other, they are not distinctly separated into time periods, but rather mesh together after the initial opening up. Though they move from the concrete experience of the particular person to a consideration of the human condition, they continue to be rooted in the here-and-now feelings of the participants, and their content is validated by those feelings.

The content of the conversation of a small group of women during several sessions of their CR group revealed four main content categories. "Primary statements" synthesized each category. The content categories and their primary statements, with verbatim examples, are as follows:

1. Feelings about other women—women in the group desire support and trust from other women:

> I was really quite glad that you did it—embraced her. Because I've thought since then how difficult it would be for me to reach out and touch someone. And yet there are times when I have wanted desperately to be able to do that and have felt a real sense of restraint. I find it very difficult to touch people physically. . . . I really appreciate the fact that the people in this group have reached out and allowed me to feel free to share some of whom I am and certainly have opened themselves up.

2. Self-perception—women in the group want to strengthen their self-concepts as physically acceptable and worthy individuals, to break out of the passive female role, and to establish themselves as independent mature people:

> No, it's being able to do it, not necessarily to feel that you can do it. I think that to be liberated you don't necessarily have to live alone, you have to be able to live with yourself alone . . . you're accepting responsibility for yourself, for your actions, and not depending upon someone else to motivate you, to make you do certain things, to fulfill you.

3. Feelings about men—women in the group are seeking to restructure their priorities in intimate relationships with men, to seek independence, responsibility and autonomy, instead of security and passivity:

> I guess I reject the idea that a woman has to be a nice guy and suffer in sex and sacrifice and I'm not about to suffer and sacrifice. I'll suffer and sacrifice for somebody I'm into a relationship with and who cares about me and who I care about and who's trying. But I'm not going to suffer and sacrifice for somebody that doesn't, isn't trying, and doesn't care about me and all that.

4. Feelings about motherhood and children—women in the group want to accept motherhood and children as an integral part, but not the sole defining feature, of their identity:

> Having four kids around all the time, it doesn't take very long before you think that you're an ogre when you go through the whole day doing all these hassles and everything . . . you just get so tired of it and the mother is just saying, "Oh, my God, is there nothing else in the world except these little kids . . . it just seems like it's endless and it's so dull a routine (Fish, 1975).

Participation in a CR group is reported to effect remarkable change in self-perceptions, goals, and life styles (Kirsh, 1974). As women learn to see themselves differently, they seek new definitions of self which are independent of the old contingent identities of wife, mother, or daughter, and they begin to move toward independence, autonomy, and self-acceptance. For many, the group has been the first time they have related in a trusting and noncompetitive way to other women; the feeling of a common sisterhood of women becomes strong. Often a new understanding of the mother emerges, evoked by recognition of the constraints under which she too lived. The convention that woman cannot work together or trust each other comes to be seen as a device for keeping women apart, preventing them from gathering strength and thus maintaining them in the old positions of powerlessness and inferiority.

The ideology and goals of consciousness raising derived from a new, informed concern for women, by women, and of women. Clearly it cannot replace therapy for all women who have problems; some women who are in a CR group are also in therapy. Its constituency is mostly middle-class, educated, white women who are psychiatrically normal. It has, however, helped many women to rid themselves of the belief that the problems they have in living are altogether their doing, thus helping to break up old patterns of guilt and self-destructiveness.

In this chapter we have looked at some aspects of the experience and behavior of women who are in conflict with society, with significant others, with themselves, or with all three. We have selected for emphasis those areas which are different for women and men, where the problems and maladjustments of women seem to be related to the roles they are relegated to in the society. The statistics on women in prison and women in therapy reflect these roles to some extent, though it is not possible now to know how many of women's conflicts are role determined and how many result from the pressures in contemporary life which affect everybody, regardless of sex. Research on problems that typically affect women and on the ways women cope with them is only beginning to appear. Research on problems that affect both men and women has usually studied men only. Few studies, for example, deal with women who are alcoholic or who commit crimes of violence. Differences in age, socioeconomic level, and education are obviously important variables in women's problems and conflicts. Much more research is needed across the whole spectrum of problem behavior, so that knowledge can enlighten the efforts of those who try to help.

Middle age and aging

12

In masks outrageous and austere
  The years go by in single file;
But none has merited my fear,
  And none has quite escaped my smile.

—Elinor Wylie, *Collected Poems*, 1932 *

In fairy tales when the princess marries her prince, the story ends. We are told that she lived happily ever after, but the curtain is pulled, concealing forever that last long age of her life. When middle-aged women appear in the stories they are wicked step-mothers or witches, almost never normal, mature women. Ugly to the point of deformity, their personalities are distorted by jealousy and hatred. They have a penchant for cruelty, especially toward young girls, as in "Cinderella" and "Sleeping Beauty." If fairy tales, like myths, are made in the deeper layers of the mind, out of the oldest fears and ruminative concerns of humans, then in them we can see the reflections of feelings of fear and dread toward aging and toward the woman who is no longer young. Though contemporary popular portrayals of older women are relatively bland, especially in children's literature, the signs are many that attitudes toward aging have changed but little. Woman especially has always had good reason to fear the passing of youth. Her most socially valued qualities, her ability to provide sex and attractive companionship, and to have children and nurture them, are expressed in the context of youth, which is endowed with physical beauty and fertility. As she ages, she becomes less physically attractive and desirable, and her reproductive and nurturant functions are no longer relevant. Since traditionally women have not been encouraged to develop those qualities which often improve with age, such as intellec-

* Reprinted by permission, Alfred A. Knopf, Inc.

tual competence and the ability to apply mature wisdom to the solution of problems, it is hardly surprising that depression and feelings of uselessness are identified so frequently in the literature on older women. The problems that women express as they age seem to have in common a motif of loss—loss of children, perhaps husband, loss of youth and physical attractiveness, loss of the regular reminder of femininity in the menopause, loss of purpose in life. The extent to which these changes are problems, however, depends upon cultural definitions and prescriptions for women and their roles, and upon idiosyncratic variables of personality and circumstances. No biological imperative programs women to feel worn out, useless, and depressed during the second half of life.

But women become middle aged and older, as do men, and hardly anyone views the prospect with complete equanimity. What does it mean to a woman to move past youth? What is it like? How does it feel? How do others feel toward her? In this chapter we shall consider some of the physical, psychological, and social aspects of the middle and later ages of women, and, on the basis of current knowledge, identify some of the factors which mediate both their successful and unsuccessful aging in Western society.

Biological Aspects of Aging

The biology of aging is concerned with changes which occur in individuals within a species as a function of the passage of time, and with explanations for characteristic lengths of life.

As persons grow older, they change in appearance because of certain biological changes which occur gradually over the life span. The more important ones of these are increase in connective tissue fibers between the body cells, gradual loss of elastic properties of skin and blood vessels, increase in fat, decrease in muscular strength, and diminution of secretions from the gonads, an effect which is more marked in women and is associated with loss of fertility.

These changes have their onset at different chronological ages and progress at different rates depending upon genetic and environmental variables. In general, such changes as these reduce the individual's adaptability to withstand physical and psychological stress and to recoup strength and recover from illnesses and traumas.

Changes which occur in the central nervous system as people grow older result from quite complex events, including cell death, oxygen deprivation, and chemical changes in the cells themselves. Since these cells do not reproduce themselves, when cells are lost from disease, toxins, traumas, or other causes the diminution in number over time can result in a decrease in the efficiency of the brain's functioning. The most pervasive effect of changes with age is a slowing of central nervous system activity causing, for example, the person's reaction time to become longer. Clearly this change can affect a wide range of behavior, from intelligence-test performance to driving an automobile. Recent longitudinal studies measuring the same persons across time indicate however that those with superior intellectual ability decline hardly at all and may even continue to improve their performance, at least to age 50. Persons of average ability begin to decline slightly after age 30. As one would expect, a more precipitous decline is observed in those with accelerated brain changes owing to disease processes. The important point is that there is no drastic decline in intellectual ability in healthy older persons as a function of age (Kimmel, 1974).

The importance of this fact to the psychology of women is the difference not in ability as compared to men of any age, but in the extent to which ability is used as a resource, is cultivated to broaden interests and to enhance life's satisfactions as the years go by.

Although the life expectancy for humans has increased remarkably in the last century, the upper limits of life span have changed little; that is, the proportion of persons in the population who reach such an advanced age as eighty has not changed much (Birren, 1964). Thus the upper limits of life for the individual seem to be genetically fixed, with the likelihood of living out this potential span dependent upon life conditions and events such as nutrition, medical care, accidents, and so on. As such environmental factors come under improved control, the genetic determinants of longevity emerge more clearly. One of these determinants is sex linked. As life expectancy has increased for both sexes, women have gained more years than men have; at birth, women's life expectancy is six to seven years longer.

Women are the only primates who outlive their reproductive capacity. Females of other species do not have a true menopause (Riopelle and Rogers, 1965). The termination of women's reproductive capability relatively early in life is adaptive for the production of healthy children.

Since the female's ova in immature form are already present in her ovaries at birth, they are as old as she is at any given time. Cells develop defects in their genetic material over time, and ova also are susceptible to processes of aging which would be incompatible with the production of healthy offspring. An example of this is the well-established fact that the risk of bearing a child with Down's syndrome (mongolism) increases remarkably with age (Nortman, 1974). Sperm by contrast are continuously produced in the testes and thus are not subject to the same risk of aging. Thus the termination of ovulation prevents what would otherwise be a rapidly increasing percentage of abnormal offspring.

It is interesting to consider how the phenomenon of a long postreproductive hiatus might have evolved in the human female. What is the selective advantage of termination of fertility in the fifth decade, and why do women live past that time? If men continue to be fertile all their lives, why don't women? When the female is no longer capable of performing her species-serving biological function, why is she programmed to live another thirty years?

One theory of aging proposes that genes which are important as determinants of aging are also important earlier in development; that is, genetic factors which are important in early life processes might also be involved in determining the potential limits of longevity (Birren, 1964). Since these potential limits are to some extent genetically determined, this theory would imply that the genes important in women's longevity have other influences earlier in development. It seems reasonable that one of these is the greater viability of females beginning with conception. The adaptive advantages of the lesser vulnerability of females to disease and trauma are not difficult to trace. The number of children that a woman can have is relatively small, owing to extended pregnancy and lactation periods, whereas the number of offspring that a man can biologically father is almost limitless. A one-to-one ratio of male to female is not necessary, biologically speaking. Furthermore, natural selection would favor the survival of women who could withstand the rigors of reproduction, a characteristic which would be unimportant to male selection. Finally, the nutritional needs and the long dependency of the human infant would also favor selection of durable females but would not affect males. Males would be selected for muscular strength, size, and build, which are uncorrelated with resistance to stress and disease and would not contribute to longevity.

Theoretically, therefore, the female, being more important to the species because of her reproductive role, was selected for traits which mitigated her greater resilience and survival capacity; and the genetic material which served those developmental characteristics could also operate to lengthen life in the postreproductive period. It is possible that female longevity is a developmental counterpart of earlier life-favoring traits which females, more than males, are likely to manifest. Until modern times, women and men alike had short life expectancies because of unfavorable environmental factors. As the toll exacted by plagues, famine, and catastrophes of nature decreased, and as childbearing became safer, the later life counterpart of women's earlier, genetically controlled biological advantage could become manifest. Although the different life styles of women and men probably contribute to some extent to the systematic difference in their life spans, some theorists believe that the greater gain in life span of women in the last few decades compared to men is an emergent characteristic of such genetic determinants (Birren, 1964).

Psychological Reactions

The menopause has been likened to a *rite de passage,* a ritual symbolic of the passage of the person from one role to another (Skultans, 1970). The menopause itself, the cessation of the menses, is a biological event which parallels other events along the course of aging. Although it is the manifest sign of the end of reproductive life, its symbolic meanings invest it with an importance which extends far beyond its biological definition. The cessation of the monthly bleeding after some thirty or thirty-five years comes as a specific physical event at a time when the woman also observes signs of aging in face and body, and experiences drastic role changes as children mature and leave home. Thus the menopause can appear as a sign of change, and the climacterium as a change of life, as it is aptly called by many—change in body, change in role and life style, and often change in the evaluation of the person by both herself and others.

In addition to physical symptoms reported to some degree by about 75 percent of women (Sherman, 1971), a wide variety of other reactions are related, ranging from fear and boredom to relief and renewed vigor. Helene Deutsch, perhaps because of her emphasis on motherhood as the core of femininity, saw the psychological reactions to the menopause as being among the most trying of a woman's life. Others take a positive view of the climacterium. Healthy women, newly freed from the demands of childbearing, can respond to the biological change with an influx of energy which could be directed to new aims, with a new impetus for socialization and learning. The many interests and productions of women after the climacterium, and their improvement in physical and emotional health, were cited as evidence that this period, in a psychological sense, is a developmental phase, a "challenge for the reorganization of the personality" (Benedek, 1959, p. 745).

The problem with most psychiatric and psychoanalytic studies of menopausal women is that they are based on observations of women who either perceive themselves or are perceived by others as having problems and needing treatment. Studies of normal, healthy women are very scarce. On balance, the data are more supportive of the belief that healthy women move effectively through this phase than they are of Deutsch's theory that women mourn the loss of their reproductive capacity and have great difficulty in coming to terms with their changed condition.

A group of 100 white women aged forty-five to fifty-five were studied. A third of the women were still menstruating regularly, a third had not menstruated for at least two years, and the remaining third were in a transitional period. But presence or absence of the menstrual cycle was unimportant in the psychological status of the women; in the larger context of the biological, psychological, and social cues that signify the climacterium, they were more alike than they were different. That is, their life stage with its implications which were common to all of them was more important than the presence or absence of menses. Only 4 percent mentioned the menopause as an important worry, while more than half said that their greatest concern was widowhood. Other fears included cancer, children leaving home, or just aging. Asked about the most positive aspects of the menopause, three fourths named the elimination of the fear of pregnancy and of the bother of menstruation. Some mentioned better relations, including sexual relations, with their husbands. Only 12 of the 100 women were unable to see any positive value. Some reported improvements in mental and physical health with increases in energy and feelings of well being. They attributed these changes to individual variables, not to a general effect of the menopause. Interestingly enough, when asked to compare themselves to "women in menopause," they consistently rated themselves more favorably—they saw the problems in others rather than in themselves. These responses were seen as a defense mechanism which revealed the underlying ambivalence of the women toward the menopause, ambivalence rooted in personal and cultural attitudes toward aging and femininity (Neugarten, 1973).

Though most women take the climacterium in stride and play down the importance of menopause in their lives, about 10 to 15 percent have physical or emotional problems serious enough to cause them to seek medical help (Shafer, 1970).[1] Aside from the readily recognizable physical symptoms which have come to be associated with the menopause, the most frequent and most serious psychological problem of women in this age group is depression. In psychiatric terms depression is characterized by apathy, loss of inter-

---

[1] Seriousness of problems is not the only determinant of seeking help. Attitudes toward symptoms, finances, availability of care, educational level, and personality are also important. For example, one woman might have a very stoic attitude, believing that she must "live with" problems she sees as inevitable; another with the same kind and degree of symptoms might be less willing to endure or be more knowledgeable of kinds of help available.

est and zest, loss of energy and appetite, feelings of worthlessness and guilt, and in serious cases the belief that life is no longer worth living. Feelings of depression and even prolonged depressive episodes are common experiences by no means unique to middle-aged women. But its incidence for this group has been extensively noted for many decades, and a sizeable literature on the phenomenon now exists (e.g., Sherman, 1971).

Depression which lasts longer than a fleeting despondency, or "the blues," is usually interpreted as a response to loss of something of value to the individual; loss of a loved one, loss of self-esteem, loss of purpose and meaning of life. If we look at menopausal depression in the light of this interpretation, we can see at least a partial explanation for it on the basis of role loss. A girl in our society is socialized to be as sexually attractive as possible so that she can find a mate, marry, and become a mother. If she follows this prescription, she faces the inevitable prospect of loss of youthful beauty, loss of children and their need for her, and probably loss of husband. To the extent that she identifies with her roles of mother and wife and evaluates herself by her performance of them to the exclusion of other roles and measures of her value, she is vulnerable to the feeling that her life has lost purpose and meaning when the roles are no longer relevant.

The empty-nest syndrome was revealed in studies involving the cases of 172 affluent married women aged thirty-five to fifty-five who came into treatment for depressions aggravated by social and family changes, including prominently the loss of the mother role when no children were left at home. This problem will become more intense with increased longevity and technological advances that reduce the amount of time required to run a household (Goodman and Goodman, 1972).

But too much free or uncommitted time is only one of the parameters of an epidemic condition. Cultural practices and attitudes, the availability of other roles, the extent of the role loss, and, perhaps most important, the emotional investment or involvement in the maternal role are all implicated in the adaptive outcome for the woman at this time of her life. An extensive study of depression in middle-aged women brought forth evidence on the variable importance of these factors. First, anthropological data on thirty societies and another six cultures were studied for information on menopausal reactions. Second, the hospital records of 533 women between the ages of forty and fifty-nine without previous hospitalization for mental disorder were reviewed. Third, interviews were conducted with psychological testing of 20 of the women to obtain information on maternal role loss (whether a child had recently left home) and type of relationship with children and husband. The results of the study were as follows:

1. Depressions in middle-aged women are due to their lack of important roles and consequent loss of self-esteem, not to the hormonal changes of menopause. In societies where the woman's status was enhanced with increasing age, such depression did not occur. In the two where the woman's status declined, as in ours, the effects were similar to those in Western countries.
2. Those hospitalized women who had a diagnosis of depression were more likely to have suffered a recent maternal role loss than were the nondepressed women.
3. Women who had overprotective or overinvolved relationships with their children were more likely to be depressed in their postparental period than were women who did not have such relationships.
4. Housewives had a higher rate of depression than working women when children left, since not only the maternal role but also the housewife role shrinks as the number of people to be cared for decreases. Working women, on the other hand, were less affected since they had another role in which they were active.
5. When ethnic groups in the sample were compared, Jews had the highest rate of depression, Anglos second, and blacks the lowest. The traditional Jewish mother identifies very closely with her children and is susceptible to feelings of desertion and to self-punitiveness when they leave. The black woman, by contrast, is much less likely to suffer depression in midlife. Traditional patterns frequently include an extension of the mother role by caring for her daughter's or other relative's children while their mother works. Also, since the black woman is more likely to have been employed outside the home while her children were growing up, she might have avoided the intense involvement with her children's lives and the vicarious living through them which characterized the Jewish mothers in the sample (Bart, 1971).

Thus depression is most likely to be found among those middle-aged women who are housewives, who have suffered a maternal role loss, and who had overprotective, overinvolved relationships with their children. Such a supermother has a conventional view of her role, an attitude of dedication, and a readiness for martyrdom. The depression developed because such a woman believed that by subjugating all her own needs to those of her family, especially for her children, she would reap the rewards of such selflessness later. Then when children left to pursue their own interests, she perceived that the pot of gold was not there, that her offering was not recognized; thus, her life seemed meaningless (Becker, 1964). In *Portnoy's Complaint*, contemporary novelist Philip Roth described such a mother as she seemed to her young son:

> It was my mother who could accomplish anything, who herself had to admit that it might even be that she was actually too good. . . . Weeping, suffering, she grated her own horseradish rather than buy the *pishachs* [urine] they sold in a bottle at the delicatessen. . . . The energy of her! The thoroughness! For mistakes she checked my sums; for holes, my socks, for dirt, my nails, my neck, every seam and crease of my body . . . where health and cleanliness are concerned, germs and bodily secretions, she will not spare herself and sacrifice others. . . . Devotion is just in her blood (p. 11).

A broader cultural explanation, applicable not just to super-mothers but to women in general, has become a challenge to psychiatrists and psychologists who treat middle-aged women with depressions. Women become depressed during this period because "they do not have enough *reasons* for satisfying action, and when they lose the one apparent reason upon which they predicated their lives—their femininity—their whole action world caves in. Let us be brutally direct: Menopausal depression is the consequence of confining women to a too narrow range of life choices or opportunities. It is a social and cultural phenomenon, for which the 'designers' of social roles are to blame. We create menopausal depression by not seeing to it that women are armed with more than one justification for their lives" (Becker, 1963, p. 358).

Supporting the above analysis is a reinterpretation of a case of Freud's. A fifty-three-year-old woman became insanely jealous of a young girl working in her husband's factory, believing that he was having an affair with her. Although her accusations were without foundation, she could not put them out of her mind. Freud saw her for two hours and decided that she feared that her attractiveness was waning, particularly her attractiveness to her young son-in-law, with whom she had an unconscious desire to commit adultery. Thus, her delusional accusations toward her husband were a cover for her own forbidden libidinous wishes for the love of the younger man. But there is no evidence in Freud's account of the case that the woman was attracted to her son-in-law. Rather, the crux of the matter probably lay in her feelings toward the young career woman who had violated all the norms but was reaping the rewards of working in a man's world, receiving money, and being treated with respect. The wife, on the other hand, had played by the rules, and her children had now grown up and married, leaving her alone with little to do while her husband continued to work at his factory and to enjoy a useful life. Her whole reason for being in the world had vanished, and her jealousy was a cry against helplessness, against personal and social injustice: "I have been cheated." This jealousy-language, was the only cognitive tool she had to express the undermining of her sense of value as a human being. Yet Freud interpreted it as a cover for unacceptable sexual instincts and put the fault on the woman while maintaining the fiction that the social order was ethical and just (Becker, 1963).

Also analyzed was the guilt often felt and expressed by depressed women. The ordinary, conventional, mild housewife, searching for meaning in a life which no longer has any, takes on the total blame for her failure. Everyone else is good—only she is sinning, worthless, guilty. The key to understanding the paradox of such guilt-language in the absence of an apparent cause is the recognition that by its use the woman is attempting to make sense out of her inexplicable depression. Why should she be depressed? It is obvious that she has everything: a home, husband, children, and the knowledge that she has been patient and faithful in the role for which she was trained. If she now feels useless, it must be because she is evil and deserves nothing for herself. Thus she forefeits all claims of her own, and asks only forgiveness for her sin of existence. The self-punitiveness of guilt, like the obsessional jealousy of Freud's patient, is a special language used by the woman who lacks the words and ideas with which to examine her life. And she lacks them because of the social tyranny which never permitted her to consider that there might be other life plans than the one she carried out. Such interpretation suggests an existential view that human life is motivated by the search for meaning, not for ways to express antisocial urges. In the light of contemporary data, this view better fits the patient's case, without the invocation of unconscious urges which are not susceptible to proof or disproof (Becker, 1963).

If such depressions are artifacts of culture, not a fateful concomitant of aging tissues and ebbing hormones endogenous to the woman, then one would expect differences in reactions among women whose cultural role prescriptions varied. One study addressed the question, Which life style is most rewarding for the middle years, that of a traditional woman whose children are all about her, or that of a modern woman who can choose career, family, or both? The subjects in the study were women from five ethnic groups living in Israel and representing a continuum from traditional to modern: Israeli Muslim Arabs; Persian, Turkish, and North African Jews; and European Jews. These groups were chosen because, though they had a common heritage of tradition, especially traditions shaping the lives of women, they differed in the extent to which they had retained or repudiated the traditions. The traditional woman was subordinate to the male, illiterate, devout, custom bound, and the mother of many children. Progressing through the transitional societies to the modern, the woman had more nearly equal rights, a higher educational level, fewer religious controls, and a smaller, planned family. The groups differed significantly with regard to their perception and evaluation of the changes of middle life, and these differences related to the traditional-modern continuum. The modern women of European background were the most successfully adjusted. Coping actively with the changes of middle age, they welcomed the cessation of fertility and saw their marriages changing for the better. Next were the Arab women, of the most traditional, patriarchal group. Accepting the changes of middle age with equanimity, they saw their status and emotional health improving as they grew older. The most negative reactions of all came from the women in the transitional groups, who had not yet adapted to modernity but could not look forward either to the status of traditional roles for women, especially the role of matriarch. Thus both the traditional and the liberated woman adapted better in a psychological sense to midlife changes than did the woman who was neither. She paid the highest psychic price for her cultural dislocation (Dowty, 1972).

The theory and research on reactions to the climacterium, though they approach the problem from different positions and study widely varying samples have enough commonality of results to permit the development of a summary model presented in Table 12.1, which identifies the elements in society favoring a female pattern of values conducive to negative reactions.

Just as women outlive their reproductive lives, most of them in Western societies also outlive their maternal roles. As women live longer and have fewer children, they can look forward to two or three decades of postparental life. Studies of the reactions of normal women whose children have left home are rare, perhaps because this is a relatively new phase in the family-life cycle. In a study of the quality of postparental life, results were obtained which are markedly different from those described earlier dealing with maternal role loss. A door-to-door survey identified 33 couples between the ages of forty and sixty-five who had had one to four children, none of whom was still living at home. Forty-nine of the spouses were interviewed with questions designed to bring out evaluations of their present life situation, such as "How is your life different now from what it was when the children were at home? and "How did

Table 12.1 Model for negative reactions during climacterium

The society	The woman
Socializes girls to wife-mother role.	Aspires to wife-mother role as ultimate fulfillment.
Youth oriented, values females as sex objects.	Self-esteem based on sexual attractiveness and maintenance of youthful beauty.
Denies or discourages other or additional roles for women.	Leaves job in first pregnancy. No career involvement of her own. Promotes and supports husband's career.
Child-centered, nuclear family.	Dedicated mother. Children are her primary concern.
Values passivity, humility, and self-sacrifice in women.	Subjugates her own needs to family's. Puts self-interest last.
Values masculine, competitive model of achievement.	Identifies vicariously with achievements of husband and child.
Male oriented. Women seen as inferior.	Sees self and other women as inferior. Ready to blame self, feel guilty.
Transitional. Both traditional and modern life styles in evidence.	Matriarchal role not available. Has neither desire nor necessary skills for "liberated" role.
Double standard of aging for men and women.	Fears aging with its loss of status, loneliness, isolation.

you feel when the last of the children left home? Clear evaluation of the postparental stage as better than any preceding stage of the family cycle appeared in 22 of the 49 responses, while negative evaluations occurred only 3 times. Almost twice as many wives as husbands saw their present lives without the children as better than before; on the other hand, wives were responsible for all three of the negative responses as well. Women with positive views saw this period as a time of freedom and time for the self, as in these typical responses:

> There's not as much physical labor. There's not as much cooking and there's not as much mending, and, well, I remarked not long ago that for the first time since I can remember my evenings are free. And we had to be very economical to get the three children through college. We're over the hurdle now; we've completed it. Last fall was the first time in 27 years that I haven't gotten a child ready to go to school. That was very relaxing (Deutscher, 1968, p. 265).

Other responses referred to improved relationships in the marriage and to feelings of accomplishment—of a job well done. The rare unfavorable evaluations centered about the advent of the menopause and aging, definition of oneself as a failure, either in work or child-rearing, and inability to fill a life left empty by the children's departure.

Though much more research is needed, findings such as these suggest that, though women who sit in their empty nests and mourn may attract the most attention, many others, perhaps a majority, have little difficulty in adapting to the reduced responsibilities and new freedoms of postparenthood.

In Chapter 4 when we looked at the physical changes that occur in women during the climacterium, changes which included the menopause and symptoms attributed to the decline of ovarian function, we noted that a well-defined menopausal syndrome predictable for women at this time has not been demonstrated. The research suggests that while women may indeed respond to the body changes of the climacterium and may experience symptoms related to hormonal changes, the psychological reactions that they develop are less definitively tied to biological events than they are to the conditions of their lives. Fears of aging, loss of salient roles, and feelings of uselessness are more important to women's existential experience of themselves at this time than is the menopause itself. Women whose self-esteem is intact, whose lives continue to be interesting and rewarding, and whose work, whatever its nature, helps them to feel that they are making a continuing contribution to the society, are the least likely to have negative reactions to the change of life.

Sexuality and Aging

The sexuality and sexual activity of the older woman are affected by a variety of physical and psychological conditions, as well as by the exigencies of her personal life style and her environment. The menopause and other changes associated with the climacterium in themselves do not produce any discontinuity in sexual desire or behavior. Though interest in sex is commonly assumed to decline with age for both sexes and generally does on a statistical basis, beliefs and expectations regarding this decline are often unrealistic and greatly exaggerated. Attitudes toward sexuality in older people are generally negative in our society, ranging from the view that the aging man and woman become essentially asexual, to the emotional reaction that any erotic interest on their part is offensive, unnatural, and disgusting. Jokes about love-hungry spinsters and dirty old men are plentiful and reveal popular stereotypes in some common themes: salacious interest in the older man who wants to perform sexually but cannot; desire for sexual attention in the older woman who is unable to find a partner because she is no longer attractive.[2] While these images may be painfully true for some, they are by no means universally valid, and perhaps they say at least as much about the prevalent values and anxieties as they do about reality.

Changes in sexual physiology occur with aging in both sexes. Some of these are in common, and are related to the general changes of aging discussed earlier. Strength and energy are reduced, for example, and body responses are generally slowed and attenuated. Basically, however, both men and women continue to respond as before, though frequency and intensity are reduced. Both remain capable of orgasm. Though exceptions to this basic principle exist, they are produced by factors other than normal physiology; that is, the loss of orgasmic capacity is not an inevitable concomitant of aging.

In addition to the thinning of the vaginal walls and reduction in lubrication mentioned earlier, postmenopausal women experience other changes in sexual physiology. The orgasmic platform develops less fully, and orgasmic contractions become fewer and less intense. The uterus diminishes in size, and sometimes uterine contractions in orgasm are reported as quite painful. The labia become thinner, although the minor lips continue to respond with vasocongestion. Clitoral response seems to remain unchanged into old age, though resolution is swift. Most physical difficulties in having sexual intercourse are related to changes in the vaginal walls and mucosa. The thinning out and dryness can make intercourse uncomfortable, even painful. Some women experience irritation of the bladder and urethra after intercourse, resulting in burning sensations during urination. This condition is caused in older women by the partial atrophy of the vaginal walls, with resulting inadequate protection of the bladder. These problems are signs of postmenopausal hormone deficiency and can be substantially corrected or prevented by hormone replacement.

In males, the major concern is potency, the ability to achieve and maintain penile erection. While attaining erection tends to take longer, the older male can often maintain it longer, either from greater experience or from changes in physiological functioning. In any event, this change has the potential of enhancing his perfor-

---

[2] A review of such material cited the observation that there are no "old bachelor" jokes and that the jokes about women are more often negative (77 percent) than are those about men (51 percent) (Puner, 1974).

mance and effectiveness as a sexual partner from the woman's view. Other changes involve chiefly attenuation of responses: fewer orgasmic contractions, less vigorous ejaculation, less marked change in the scrotum and testes, and a shorter resolution stage.

The effects of biological changes, including sex-hormone withdrawal, have only an indirect effect on sexual drive and behavior (Masters and Johnson, 1968). If the change in endocrine level were responsible for fluctuations in sexual activity in menopausal and postmenopausal women, we would see much more uniformity in such behavior. As it is, women vary widely in their responses to endocrine depletion as it affects sexual activity. Menopausal discomforts such as flushing, headaches, and nervous tension may diminish the woman's interest in sex, but this is an indirect result of the endocrine imbalance. Since estrogen level is not directly responsible for the strength of the sex drive, hormone-replacement therapy does not increase libido; rather, the restoration of the woman's sense of well-being may bring with it a renewal of erotic interest as a side effect.

By far the most important factors influencing sexual behavior in older women are the availability of a partner and the opportunity for regular sexual expression. Given these conditions, many women experience in their forty's and fifty's an increased interest in their sexuality for a number of possible reasons. Helene Deutsch thought that the approach of menopause signaled for some women a "closing of the gates," arousing a desire for one more pregnancy as evidence of their femininity. For others, the cessation of the menses brings a freedom from fear of pregnancy so that the woman for the first time can abandon herself to the enjoyment of sex without apprehension. This release from "pregnancy phobia" is probably one of the most plausible explanations for increased sexual interest in postmenopausal women who did not have effective birth-control methods available to them during their reproductive years. Since young women of today have much less reason to fear unwanted pregnancy, their level of sexual activity may not show this later-life increase which has been reported by many observers.

The married woman in this age group may have other fortuitous circumstances which enhance her sexual expression. The problems which beset a young marriage, such as finances, in-laws, and friction in adjusting to the marital relationship, may all be in the past. The draining demands of having and rearing children no longer exhaust and preoccupy her, leaving more time and energy for the renewal of interest in herself and her mate. A revival of sexual interest may be one aspect of a more general awakening to the varied possibility of a mature life.

Thus the healthy, well-adjusted woman who is happily married may experience little or no change in her pattern of sexual activity; in fact, she may find that her sex life has improved with the advent of middle age. But for very large numbers of women the picture is not so bright. The woman who found sex uninteresting and unsatisfying during her reproductive years may use the menopause as an excuse to terminate sexual relations, to rid her life permanently of the embarrassment and frustration which sex has meant to her. Related to this reaction are underlying puritanical beliefs that sex is basically sinful unless it is in the service of reproduction. Thus it would appear particularly unsuitable and repugnant as an interest of the older woman.

Most studies support the idea that women have a more stable sex drive than men have and that it is less susceptible to the effects of aging. Although many men remain potent and sexually active into their eighty's, impotence is a common problem past middle age. Studies of sexual inadequacy revealed that 83 percent of the impotent males were past forty years of age, and 75 percent were past fifty. There are a number of responsible factors for male impotence, chief among them the ego-shattering "fear of failure" which sometimes leads men to seek newer or younger partners in a search for reassurance of their virility. In any case, since women typically marry men who are older than they are, it is inevitable that some who are still as interested in sex as ever will find themselves with a husband who has withdrawn from sexual activity or is directing it elsewhere. Also, husbands in this age group may have physical problems or disabilities associated with advancing age which may make sex impossible for them (Masters and Johnson, 1968).

Because the ratio of men to women declines drastically with age, many older women are without partners. In the fifty-five–to–sixty-four age group, there are about 80 men to every 100 women; in the next decade, the number of men to each 100 women is about 72; and after 75, it drops to 63 (Puner, 1974). Widows outnumber widowers four to one, and only one-third of women over sixty-five in this country are married, compared to two-thirds of the men.

The older woman who is without a partner for whatever reason has a much more difficult time finding one, if she wishes to, than a comparable male does. There is a "double standard of aging." When a woman is in her late teens or early twenties she attracts men of about her age or slightly older, marries, and raises a family. Some years later, if her husband decides to have an affair, he usually does so with a much younger woman. In the event of divorce, his chances of remarriage are excellent, but hers, at age forty or fifty, are not. Men in her age group are either married or seeking younger women. She has become sexually ineligible, whereas a male at the same age may be in no way less attractive than he was at twenty-five. "Boys and young men have little reason to anticipate trouble because of aging. What makes men desirable to women is by no means tied to youth. On the contrary, getting older tends (for several decades) to operate in men's favor, since their value as lovers and husbands is set more by what they do than how they look" (Sontag, 1972, p. 32).

The aging woman, if she is not married, may find it very difficult to develop a sexual relationship. A young man may desire a woman old enough to be his mother, but not his grandmother: "A woman of seventy is no longer regarded by anyone as an erotic object" (de Beauvoir, 1972, p. 39). And yet women of this age are not without sexual desire.

Several studies of sexual behavior in older people (Kaplan, 1974) agree that women after sixty-five, though less concerned with sex than they were at forty, may still seek out and respond to erotic encounters. Erotic dreams are reported, and in sharp contrast to men, women at this age continue to be capable of multiple orgasms. The physical changes of aging are accompanied by comparatively little change in the libidinal aspects of women's sexuality (Kaplan, 1974).

As opportunities shrink, with or without marriage, masturbation often becomes the most important source of sexual release (Masters and Johnson, 1968). The unmarried woman who has masturbated during her teens and twenties usually continues the same activity into her later years. The widowed or divorced woman without heterosexual contacts may revert to the masturbatory practices of her youth to relieve sexual tension. While these authors report that the women they studied deemed the practice less necessary after 60, they observed that the frequency of sexual intercourse or manipulative activity during the postmenopausal years was very variable, and did not seem very important to healthy, active, well-adjusted women.

But whether the reason is lack of a partner, inhibition and shame, or embarrassment over her aging body, the older woman is less likely to have an active sex life than is a man of comparable age. Table 12.2, adapted from data in the Playboy study described in Chapter 7, shows frequency of sexual intercourse for the older married groups in the sample. While the median[3] frequency for the past year was almost the same for males and females in the three age groups, the percentage of persons having no intercourse jumped sharply for females aged 55 and over.

---

[3] The median is the midpoint dividing the top 50 percent from the bottom 50 percent.

Table 12.2   Frequency of sexual intercourse in past year*

	Male			Female		
	35–44	45–54	55 and over	35–44	45–54	55 and over
None	1.0%	4.9%	5.1%	2.4%	5.1%	13.0%
Median (number of times)	102	52	50	99	52	49

* Adapted from *Playboy*, October 1973.

In an earlier study a comparable difference in the older participants was found. Of the fifty-year-old men, 97 percent were still sexually active, compared to 93 percent of the women in that age group. At age sixty, the percentages were 94 for men and 80 for women. The median frequencies per week for men and women reached zero at ages 75 and 65 respectively (Kinsey *et al.,,* 1948, 1953).

Given the present state of knowledge, it is difficult if not impossible to arrive at any definitive conclusions about the relationship between sexuality and aging in women. The statistical studies show that sexual behavior is quantitatively less frequent and terminates earlier for women than for men. Biologically, however, woman's sexuality is less affected by age than man's and has the potential for being part of her experience indefinitely. The important variables are the prevailing cultural attitudes, the way she feels about herself and her body, and the availability of a capable partner.

Widowhood

Widowhood is rapidly becoming almost ubiquitous as a final stage in the marital histories of American women. The facts that many women marry men older than they are, live longer, and are less likely to remarry than are widowed males all help to produce the result that two out of three women over sixty-five in this country are unmarried, and most of these are widows. If a woman under fifty-five is married to a man five years younger than she, there is a 54 percent chance that she will eventually be widowed. If he is five years older, the chance increases to 64 percent. Lastly, there is an 80 percent chance if he is ten years older (Metropolitan Life Insurance Company, 1969).

In 1970, the U.S. Census of Population reported the marital status of white and black American women aged fifty or over. The percentage of those married dropped from 78.8 percent at ages fifty to fifty-four to 10.7 percent at age eighty-five and over. The percentage of those widowed rose from 10.0 percent at age fifty to fifty-four to 76.9 percent at age eighty-five and over. Though the trends for the black and white women are the same for both categories, the percentages for the black women are less for the married and more for the widowed in all age groups, reflecting to some extent the higher death rate for black males.

A detailed analysis of widowhood based upon a sample of 301 Chicago area widows aged fifty and over has been reported. While this is a sociological rather than a psychological study, it illuminates the problems faced by urban widows, describes aspects of their life styles, and identifies the determinants of their re-engagement with social relations after their initial period of widowhood.

The short-term needs of widowed women are summarized as follows:

1. Grief work. The bereaved one should be free to express her sorrow, loneliness, and other feelings activated by the death of a significant person. Family members and friends should allow her to move through the phases from shock to final acceptance and readiness to rebuild her life.

2. Companionship. The widows appreciated someone "just being there." Since widowhood usually occurs after children are grown, the widow has lost the one person around whom her life was regulated. Loneliness becomes a pervasive problem as the woman learns to live alone for the first time in her life. Friends may stay away because of attitudes toward death or because they do not feel comfortable in the presence of grief and bereavement. The widow herself may feel ambivalent, expecting too much from friends on the one hand, or refusing all offers of companionship on the other, out of pride or suspicion that she is being offered charity.

3. Solution of problems. The people around her may want to give her too much advice, or to rush her into decisions, such as selling the house or moving into a retirement community. Only immediate crises should be dealt with, since the chances of making wrong decisions are great, and her view may well change after the period of grieving is past. No one should make her decisions for her, since they may be ill informed or lacking in understanding of her real needs. Furthermore, a take-over attitude on the part of others can have the effect of fostering dependency and undermining her confidence in herself and her ability to solve her own problems—a self-confidence which may be low to begin with and, most of all, in need of bolstering through the experience of successfully making decisions for herself.

4. Re-engagement into social involvement. The extent to which the widow engages or re-engages in social relations and activities reflects her location in the modern social system. Her educational level and her financial and occupational status influence the widow's involvement in her community, her relations with friends and neighbors, and her membership in voluntary groups. Three types of widows are described in terms of the degree of their re-engagement and its relation to the woman's past life situation. The first is adapted by socialization and education to modern society; she is self-initiating, capable of re-examining her life style and goals after her husband's death, and of choosing which aspects of her old roles she will maintain and which she will give up. She is conscious of the need to adjust behavior and relations to her new status, and she initiates changes and retains control of her life, rather than passively reacting to poorly understood external events. The second type of urban widow, living in an ethnic "village" in a traditional life style for which her socialization prepared her, may change very little. Her kin relations, close peer group, and neighborhood system may continue to involve her much as they did before, especially if her world is essentially sex-segregated, as is the case among many groups of lower-class urbanites. The third type of widow is the social isolate who lacks the ability to engage effectively with modern society. Hampered by lack of mobility, finances, or bad health, and socialized into a passive stance with regard to affecting her environment, she cannot develop new social roles as old ones disappear, hence she tends to withdraw into isolation, rarely leaving her home and unwilling or unable to initiate any contact with other persons or groups.

A basic difference between the two extremes of the active, engaged woman and the social isolate was education. A low level of education meant that the woman was likely to have married a man of similar status, and that the family income was always minimal. Marginal to the social system, lacking skills for re-engagement into society, she is dependent for her involvement upon chance and the actions of others. "The best position is that of the widow who was socialized into the modern social system and has enough financial and health resources to participate" (Lopata, 1973a, p. 270).

In another analysis of the data, the popular belief that black women are surrounded by kin and thus by implication would be less likely than white women to suffer from loneliness and isolation was considered. To the contrary, it was found that most of the black women were not part of an enduring kinship structure. Two-thirds of both groups had no children living with them, and about that same proportion reported little or no contact with siblings. Regarding attitudes of the two groups, the white women had more positive memories of their husbands than did their black counterparts, more often responding that he was a good man, that their sex relations were good, and that the marriage was above average. The black women were less likely to agree that decision making was hardest for a widow to learn but were more likely to believe that widows are often sexually propositioned, that other women are jealous of them, and that people take advantage of them. And they were twice as likely to feel sorry for their married friends. Thus the evidence suggests that these black women, most of them migrants from the South and poorly educated, had more negative feelings toward their late husbands and toward marriage in general than did their white sisters. But older widows, both black and white, lead lonely lives (Lopata, 1973b).

The factor of loneliness seems to be more important than any other in influencing older widows to remarry if they have the opportunity. In a study of 100 remarried older couples whose median ages were seventy-one for the women and seventy-six for the men, two-thirds of the women and three-fourths of the men spoke of the need for companionship as a major reason for the marriage (McKain, 1969). An important obstacle to such late-life marriages is the adult children of the couple. About 25 percent of this sample said that they had almost given in to their children's objections or hostility and called off the marriage. But five years afterwards, most of the children who had opposed it had changed their minds and were pleased with the outcome. Perhaps one reason for their reappraisal was that the marriages tended to be happy: three-fourths were rated as "highly successful" while only six were seen as failures.

After Widowhood: An Example

In thinking about and attempting to characterize the later lives of women, as with any developmental period, it is easy to forget that one is generalizing from information gathered on groups of individuals who are alike in some ways and unique in many others. The personal account of the woman presented here does not refute the research; but it does offer a suggestion of the individuality lost in statistical data, and an assertion of the personal spirit whose dimensions transcend the formal rules of scientific inquiry.

Angelina's story, *Angry In Retirement* (Hughes, 1974), tells of the drastic changes in her life after her husband, Armando, died; of her struggle to maintain her dignity and pride; and of her small victories as she battled the enemies of the old: loneliness, helplessness, and dependency. During their fifty years of marriage they had built their own house, with a rose garden and ·fountains like those in Armando's native Italy. Armando worked for a newspaper; Angelina cared for the two children and the house, worked in her church, and did some part-time translating. After their son died and their daughter moved away, they stayed in their home among their friends and lived on their modest retirement income.

Angelina was completely unprepared for Armando's death. Well-meaning friends insisted that her house was too big for her and that she needed a place where she would be taken care of. She felt "tired and weak," pushed into making decisions. Decisions had always been Armando's responsibility; now, it was easier to let others make them. The house was sold, and in a few weeks she moved into a "retirement home," which required that she relinquish all her financial assets in exchange for lifetime residency in a small room with communal bath and twenty dollars per week allowance. The room was cluttered with her personal possessions, and the closet space was inadequate. But why should she worry about clothes, when one of the first questions asked her was where she intended to be buried? Should she tell them she came here to live?

She had to fight to keep drapes, a small rug, and her bookcase, which interfered with "housekeeping." "I can still feel the anger rage inside me. It was hard for me to keep my chin up and maintain my pride. In my own home I was queen, but here I felt like a child" (p. 58). Her helplessness in the face of the power of the staff overwhelmed her. They controlled whether she got an extra piece of toast, a clean towel; they could put her out, indigent, at any time. Worst of all, they controlled how she, and the others, felt about themselves.

She found herself in "crafts" making pincushions and mice out of grey foam rubber. She knitted a cape which was sold for $2.50 at the bazaar. Was this the price of her time and energy? When she questioned what happened to the money made from the production of the residents, she was rebuffed. Old ladies were not supposed to ask questions. But Angelina resisted the deadening conformity which was forced by fear on the other women. She persuaded the administrator to locate a record player to be put in the parlor. "Where there is music, there is life." She recruited other residents to go out with her on her daily walks, even in cold weather. She started poetry reading sessions, and planned for concerts. But there were always the rules regulating their days. She had to ask permission to stay up past ten o'clock to watch the news: "I must go ahead and live!"

A year later, Angelina was feeling less rebellious. Trying so hard to be heard had depleted her energy; she felt choked and unable to express herself. But she still wanted to contribute, to feel a part of her "home." "The music in the parlor is beautiful. We love it. The monotony has lessened. We talk and the music plays softly. Maybe there will be more than pincushions" (p. 59).

Angelina's story is distinguished only by her persistent sense of self and her resistance to relinquishing her freedom. Because the outlines of it are common enough, it reflects rather clearly attempts on the part of Angelina and others to meet her perceived needs immediately following her bereavement. She was unprepared for coping with the problems attendant upon the loss of her husband of over half a century. Instead of allowing her time to work through her grief and to reach a stage of readiness to think about the future, those around her advised and persuaded her to make decisions which she later regretted. She had no time to build confidence in herself by surveying her options and making her own choices. By the time she was ready to "re-engage," she was in an institution for those who have little to do except wait for death. Even there, she tried to maintain her self-esteem and to assert some degree of control over her life and to keep alive hope for the future. Her story demonstrates the interaction of circumstances and personal qualities which determines the course of a life in the later years, after the death of a spouse.

Throughout this book we have discussed the effects on women of certain modal and developmental experiences in their lives. In general we have seen that women's psychological reactions to these events—menarche and menstruation, marriage, pregnancy, childbirth, work roles outside the home, sexuality, and aging—have been inextricably bound up in the social context within which they occur. Widowhood is no exception. In fact, while loss and loneliness are real, their impact on the person and her subsequent adaptation are dependent both upon her own inner resources and strength and resilience of personality, and also, especially for the old and vulnerable, upon her place in the society, her material resources, and the quality of the help and emotional support she receives from others.

Personality and Aging

We have spoken frequently of the social context within which behavior occurs and its importance for the development of patterns of behavior. When the social context changes, and when the passage of time brings physical changes as well as life-style changes, we would expect that some aspects of the person and her characteristic, unique behavior would undergo change also. At the same time, we would expect the healthy person still to be herself, not radically different at sixty from the way she was at forty.

Longitudinal studies of persons across the life span reveal both consistency and change in the characteristic behavior of persons as they grow older. A major study sampled 700 women and men between the ages of forty and ninety who lived in their own homes. Interviews and tests over a seven-year period revealed consistencies across time for individuals, as well as age-related changes.

A central finding was that some aspects of persons were relatively stable across time. These dealt with "adaptive, goal-directed, and purposive qualities of personality," that is, general adaptation, cognitive competence, and characteristic style of interaction with others. Such characteristics as emotional stability and intelligence, and personality traits such as hostility or passivity remain generally consistent across time. This was true in spite of role, status, and other changes related to aging. To this extent, "Behavior in a normal old person is more consistent and more predictable than in a younger one. . . . As individuals age, they become increasingly themselves, and, on the other hand, . . . the personality structure stands more clearly revealed in an old than in a younger person" (Neugarten, 1964, p. 198).

Other studies based on these data found changes in the subjects which were age-related. That is, some general changes characterized the sample as a whole as a function of aging. These include a decline in ego energy, a shift in ego style, and shifts in sex-role perception. The first change was a consistent decline with age of the amount of emotional energy the person had to invest in the outer world. With this decline went a certain withdrawal of responsiveness to outside stimuli, an abandonment of self-assertiveness, and an avoidance of challenge (Rosen and Neugarten, 1964). The second change related to the decrease in ego energy was a shift in ego style from active mastery to passive and inappropriate mastery styles. These three types of ego style were seen as stages on a continuum from the most vigorous and effective type of functioning, through passivity, to stress-laden, maladaptive functioning. These two age-related changes, or directional shifts, characterized both the females and the males in the sample (Gutmann, 1964).

The third age-related change was in the perceptions of the sex-roles of older women and older men. Subjects ranging in age from forty to seventy were shown a picture of four persons, a young man and woman and an older man and woman. Most saw it as a two-generational family. The descriptions of the older man and woman given by the older persons in the sample, those aged fifty-five to seventy, differed significantly from the descriptions of the younger ones, aged forty to fifty-four. The shift was in the direction of a sex-role reversal, with the older respondents perceiving the old man as more submissive, and the old woman as more authoritative, compared to the perceptions of the younger group. For both men and women in the older group, it was almost always the old woman, not the old man, who was seen as aggressive, dominant, and impulsive (Neugarten and Gutmann, 1968). While one cannot infer actual role shift from these data, it was suggested that actual personality changes are implicated, with women becoming more tolerant of their own aggressiveness and impulsivity, and men of their own nurturant and affiliative impulses. As each becomes more detached from the outside world and its influences with a diminished need for mastery over the self and its impulses, the differences between them seem to diminish.

Attitudes Toward Aging

The notion that age and aging mean something different for women than they do for men has been suggested earlier in this chapter. The sexual and social devaluation of women who are beyond the age of youthful beauty, who no longer fit the girl model so adulated in our society, is part of the experience of most women past 35 or so, though that realization is more important to some women than to others, depending upon their other values, sources of self-esteem, and supportive relationships. The true pervasiveness of the horror of being no longer young is difficult to assess. No doubt some part of it is cultivated by the advertising media to promote the multimillion-dollar industries which depend upon women's fear of being seen as old or unattractive to sell products. The ubiquity of the value of appearing young is such that one cannot know to what extent it is an artifact of prevailing pressures, or even how much it will diminish as women become less dependent upon the adulation of others as a sign of their merit. In any case, the phenomenon of an aging appearance affects women more than men in ways that are remarkably different psychologically.

A Sunday supplement (*Parade,* October 6, 1974) contained the following in a question-and-answer column about well-known personalities:

Q. How much older than her husband is actress Faye Dunaway, and why do so many actresses marry younger men?

A. Faye Dunaway is 33. Husband Peter Wolf . . . is 28. Actresses need constant adulation, *particularly when they get on in years,* which is when they are frequently willing to pay for it [italics added].

A liaison between a thirty-three-year-old man and a twenty-eight-year-old woman would attract no age-related comment at all. Nor would such a man be seen as getting on in years. In fact, he would be approaching his prime, which could then last until he reached fifty-five or sixty. This greater freedom of men to age is a result of the unequal distribution of adult roles between the two sexes. The inequality, by which men choose and women are chosen, is reinforced by women, by their attitudes of acceptance and complacency when they are young, and by their embarrassment and anguish when they are older—the latter no less a concurrence in its value than the former (Sontag, 1972).

Is there an alternative? In some societies, people gain in status and prestige as they grow older. In our society, valuing as it does youth and achievement, persons who are no longer young and achieving are no longer accorded status and attention. This especially affects women, who are seen as old before men are, and whose achievements by conventional standards are often not impressive. In this part of their lives as in others, women have been victims, who have taken unto themselves the oppressive values of the majority and thus dread their own entry into the status of older woman. It is as if they say, "Now that I am older, no one finds me lovable, beautiful, or worthy; therefore, I must be unlovable, ugly, and worthless."

Since there is little indication that the values of our society in this regard are going to change very soon or very rapidly or that, specifically, basic attitudes toward aging and toward older women are going to change, then women must find in themselves the alternative to the pain of feeling rejected and worthless. Returning once more to the model of the self-actualized personality, we can hypothesize that the self-actualized woman will be less affected by others' perception and evaluation of her appearance, that her self-esteem will be more independent of such appraisals, that she will more likely be, in Whitman's words, well-possessed of herself. As women develop greater strength, independence, self-sufficiency, and pride in themselves as women, as their identities become less contingent upon their relations to others, as they become freer to let themselves be, then the specter of middle age and aging will be divested of the special meanings that it has for women. It seems, then, that we must help ourselves, each other, and our children to develop our potential as humans and to learn to love ourselves better for how we are and what we do than for the ephemeral qualities of our youth. Then, as Helene Deutsch said, perhaps we can see our aging "not as an inversion but as a harmonious consequence" (1973, p. 216).

On understanding women: contributing sources

13

When we further consider that to understand one woman is not necessarily to understand any other woman; that even if he could study many women of one rank, or of one country, he would not thereby understand women of other ranks or countries; and even if he did they are still only the women of a single period of history; we may safely assert that the knowledge which men can acquire of women, even as they have been and are, without reference to what they might be, is wretchedly imperfect and superficial, and always will be so, until women themselves have told all that they have to tell. . . .

—John Stuart Mill, *The Subjection of Women,* 1869.

Knowledge about women is less imperfect and superficial today than it was when the British philosopher John Stuart Mill exposed prevailing beliefs of his time about the nature of women for what they were: inventions of a patriarchal society whose purpose was to justify and to maintain the social order. Women today are becoming conscious of themselves, of their commonalities, and of the influences, only now perceived and articulated by large numbers of them, which have affected their lives and their destinies. Women have begun to reflect upon themselves and their lives, to formulate their own questions, to study women, and to tell what they know. Perhaps in the past, as Mill suggested, women had a stake in preserving the mystique which lay about their behavior, since their status relative to men was one of subordination. It was wiser not to reveal oneself, one's thoughts and feelings, because such revelation entailed too great a risk to one's already too-vulnerable position. As woman becomes free standing and attains equal status with man, she can afford to let herself be known. Where are we now in the process of understanding women? Some old problems which impeded understanding have been identified, and some still unresolved issues have been raised.

Human behavior emerges from the neonatal repertoire and becomes organized in a social context. It becomes purposeful and responsive and theoretically predictable. Contrary to popular belief, the behavior of women is not more capricious, cryptic, or occult than the behavior of men. It has, however, been less well understood in any scientific sense because theoreticians and researchers shared with men in general certain basic assumptions about women and men which diverted their attention from the critical questions whose answers could have dispelled the mysteries about female behavior; and because no one, until recently, has undertaken seriously to study the phenomena of women and their behavior, to begin to develop a psychology of women.

A commitment to the systematic study of female behavior implies that such study is needed because of past neglect and/or because of the inadequacy of the existing body of theory and knowledge to produce understanding, and that women as a class have in common certain attributes, conditions, and experiences which differentiate them from men and require that they be studied separately if their behavior is to be understood.

Behavioral researchers, most of whom are male, have shown a notable preference for the use of males as subjects. A study of research methods in 226 studies of personality revealed that the ratio of male to female subjects was approximately two to one. Even so, this lopsided attention to the male sex was an improvement over the "serious imbalance in sex composition of samples" (Carlson, 1971, p. 205), which had been found in an earlier review of the literature (Carlson and Carlson, 1960).

Not infrequently, when women have been included in research samples, their performance has turned up inexplicable sex differences which constituted an anomaly to the existing theory.[1] Their behavior did not fit with the model which was supposed to predict the behavior under investigation. Confronted with this embarrassment, what alternatives has the investigator? First, he can regard the anomaly as uninteresting and simply ignore it by studying males only. An example of this is the research on the achievement motive, an area which has drawn considerable attention during the past two decades. At the height of this attention, a major review of personality research contained the following:

[1] Note that in the examples which follow it is female behavior which is the anomaly. Such is the masculine bias which informs inquiry.

> In general, studies of achievement motivation have been confined to samples of males. The few available reports of experiments on women have been ambiguous and inconclusive (London and Rosenhan, 1964, p. 461).

It was not until 1970, that the anomaly of women's achievement behavior began to be understood (Horner, 1970).

A second possibility is to interpret the female anomaly in such a way that it can be fitted into the theory, or even to extrapolate from or to add onto the theory to make it cover the incidental other.

> The female case has often been neglected, and too frequently forced into inappropriate male categories. . . . [P]sychologists have often set up dimensions where the female can only come out as "not male" (weak instead of strong, small instead of large, etc.). And the persistent tendency to read "different" as "deficient" leads to less than rational controversy in this field, especially where it touches on delicate social balances and cherished mythologies (May, 1966, p. 576).

The best (and best-known) examples of personality theories which are basically masculine models are those of Freud and Erikson. In the former, a basic model of psychosexual development based on the male was adapted to fit the female, and the adaptation utilized primarily the fact of her difference from the male. In the latter, the basic model for identity development was the male, the female's being contingent finally upon her selection of him who would be admitted to her inner space. For both of these, the extension of theory to cover the development of women came almost as an afterthought (Chasseguet-Smirgel, 1970). "The great majority of psychoanalytical studies on instinctual drives and the development of the ego have been made with reference to man's development, with merely a secondary adjustment when applying the same results to women" (p. 213). Even the contemporary humanist Abraham Maslow, whose description of the self-actualized person we looked at in Chapter 10, could not free himself from a masculine point of reference. For example, he explained man's old and ever-present need to dominate women by equating his fear of women with his fear of his own unconscious, that is, his own femaleness, softness, tenderness, and so on. "And therefore fighting women or trying to control them or to derogate them has been part of this effort to control these unconscious forces which are within everyone of us" (Maslow, 1971, p. 90). The idea that men live in fear that the old, long-ago-repressed mother identification will reassert itself, that they thus fear woman as a manifestation of that identity and must therefore control *her* is not new. But what does this formulation say about women? What unconscious process is she fighting against? Since she never had to repress her earliest identification with her mother, what process mediates her behavior vis-à-vis the male? Or is she the process itself, in a sophisticated restatement of the old myth of woman as Nature, ancient Eve personifying passion and earthiness (Kasten, 1972)?

The problem with all these ways of trying to explain women is that they have a point of view which imposes an inherent necessity on them to explain women in terms of men, by trying to fit their behavior into a conceptual scheme devised from a male stance to explain male motivations and behavior.

The fact that humans occur in two basic biological types, male and female, has made further comparisons between them irresistible. The very large literature on sex differences attests to the fascination that such inquiry has for scientists as well as for lay persons (e.g., Maccoby and Jacklin, 1974). But the practice of studying woman by looking at the ways in which she is different from man has the clear potential for reinforcing the use of a masculine model as a standard for humans, or even for raising a new standard, now built on female criteria. Neither of these is more acceptable than the other. Further, an emphasis on sex differences implies a categorical distinction, a dichotomy of opposites, which is not justified. Woman is not the opposite of man, each being more like the other than either is like their same sex in any other species. Even at the level of the biological dichotomy which allows us to sort humans into male and female, the evidence is clear that we have a common prototype. As we saw in Chapter 4, the external genitalia and the gonads themselves differentiate from common anatomical structures into female or male forms, and the differences in the hormones accounting for observable differences in morphology are differences in degree, not kind.

Further, a research focus on behavioral differences between the sexes is impoverished as a method for developing information about so heterogeneous a group as women. The intrasex differences in most psychologically relevant variables are so large, and overlap between the sexes is so extensive, that identification by sexual category offers little in the way of prediction of behavior.

Instead of ignoring female behavior, trying to explain it in terms of models developed from studying males, or emphasizing differences between groups of females and males, one can, alternatively, undertake the serious study of women as women, using interdisciplinary conceptual tools and methods that will illuminate the dark spaces in our knowledge about them. Understanding women requires that attention be paid to a number of determinants which interact to influence the behavior of any particular woman or narrowly defined groups of women. These include biology, socialization within a social order, life chances, and personality. As determinants of behavior, they range from the widely shared (biology) to the unique (personality). All these sources of variation are behavioral determinants for men also, but to the extent that they are systematically different for women and men they shape different outcomes for the two sexes.

Biology

In the popular wisdom the psychology of women, their motivations, personality, and behavior, has been closely tied to the events of their bodies. Theorists have attempted to explain women in terms of their bodies, and researchers have looked for the demonstrable effects of women's bodies on their behavior. All of these approaches suggest a basic assumption that for women the relationship between biology and behavior is a uniquely strong and intimate one. While this assumption may be valid, it has yet to be demonstrated as a universal principle by the conventional methods of science.

It is plain that the biological distinctions between the sexes in infancy do not mediate the development of a feminine or masculine gender; rather, with certain rare exceptions (Stoller, 1972) the sense of oneself as female or male grows from innumerable noncontradictory communications from others, which are normally contingent upon the appearance of the external genitalia (Money, 1972). But that sense is less a function of biological sex than it is of parental reaction; thus the crucial factor is psychological, not biological (Stoller, 1974).

Woman's body, however, is productive of a number of uniquely female events, shared by almost all women to a greater or less extent and reflected in their experiential histories and in the patterns of their lives. These events include the menarche and the subsequent rhythm of menstruation, breast development, pregnancy, parturition, lactation, and menopause. All are relevant to woman's role as childbearer and nurturer, and none of them has a counterpart in man's experience of his body. Thus the biological referents of the social roles of mother and father are not even comparable, let alone equal.

Surely all these are important events in the lives of women. But the search for a direct effect of the attendant body changes on the psychology of women has so far been a fruitless one. Rather, the effects are indirect, linked to the consequences of these events and to the meanings they have for the woman and for relevant others.

The menstrual cycle, for example, is a rhythmic reminder to

women of their bodies, and much has been made of its hormonal fluctuations and associated discomforts. But there is no evidence whatsoever that menstruation constitutes a handicap for women in the pursuits of their daily lives or that it noticeably deters them from performing as capably as nonmenstruating people, other factors being equal. As we saw in Chapter 4, research on the premenstrual syndrome has not yet established the existence of a class of behaviors which is correlated with any particular phase of the cycle for groups of women. This is not to say that such behaviors do not exist, but that as a scientific hypothesis the existence of a definable premenstrual syndrome has not been validated. There is an abundance of statements in the literature which simply assume a direct causal relationship between physiological processes and psychological experiences, but neither specify "the nature of the hypothetical mechanism supposed to link physiological and psychological events nor make explicit the underlying beliefs about the conceptually difficult relationship between mind and body" (Parlee, 1973, p. 461). The meaning of menstruation, however, expressed in customs and taboos and in beliefs about its effects has consequences for women far beyond its biological course.

Pregnancy and childbirth are ephemeral events with long-lasting consequences. It is children rather than pregnancy which change women's behavior and their lives. Given the role specialization and other characteristics of the nuclear family and of contemporary society, the woman who has no children, the woman who has one, and the woman who has six lead lives that are profoundly different from each other because of this one factor alone. Changing values, however, with the availability of contraception and abortion, mean that women will have fewer children, and many will have none at all. Thus the psychological correlates of having children will be less important in the overall pattern of women's lives.

In the last chapter we saw that the menopause as a biological event was relatively unimportant to most women. Its psychological effect, again, stemmed from concomitant events of the climacterium, such as role loss as children leave or husband dies, physical changes related to aging which may affect the woman's self-evaluation and the attitude of others toward her, and the general status of older women in our society.

When we speak of the importance of women's biology for the psychology of women we are talking about reproductive biology. Today, the issue is less whether and how her biology affects her behavior than it is how much she is in control of her body and can choose how she will use it. So far, valid and reliable psychological correlates to the biological events of women's bodies have not been demonstrated. Thus there is no scientific basis for the systematic differential treatment of women on the grounds that their behavior is functionally related to the great and small rhythms of their bodies.

The importance of biology for the psychology of women is less in its direct causative effects on behavior than it is in the meanings of biological events, in the psychic representations of those events, and in the feelings that women and men have about them. Since woman's reproductive capability was so impressive and so important, its related physical events were likewise invested with great significance and became intimately associated with everything about her. Her identity, her persona, was inseparable from her body and its uses.

In addition to its identification with reproduction was the sexual potential of woman's body. The attractiveness to man of her body is probably the most potent of the biologically based influences on woman's behavior. In patriarchal societies, where the power was totally vested in males, the woman was dependent on the man for the maintenance of her life, as well as for any pleasure or privilege she might wish to have. Since anything and everything she wanted could only be obtained through him it would have been strange indeed had not the goal of being attractive to him been of singular importance as a determinant of her behavior and as a reinforcer of certain personality traits. Sexual attractiveness began with the body but extended, by cultural definition, to other characteristics which had to be cultivated as long as they were valued by him. In order to have her needs met through him, woman had to learn to behave in ways that were appropriate to her place, to which she was assigned because she was born female.

Sex-Role Socialization

The differential ways that boys and girls are socialized to conform to the appropriate behavioral norms derive primarily from the long history of division of labor along sex lines, which was necessitated by the biological and socioeconomic facts of life. A study of socialization practices in 110 nonliterate societies found that differentiation was not important in infancy, but that in childhood girls were pressured toward nurturance, obedience, and responsibility while boys were taught self-reliance and achievement (Barry, Bacon, and Child, 1957). Such differentiation is functional in societies in which the greater strength of males is put to good use in hunting and foraging activities or in physical defense and conquest; and where the bearing and rearing of children is left to the women. However, in industrialized societies in which physical strength for work or for war is not so important, the rationale for such bifurcation of personality into male and female models seems not only unwarranted but restrictive and growth inhibiting. A general cultural diminution of sex-role differentiation goes along with a greater valuing of the individual and of ideals of personal freedom, such that the boundaries between behaviors designated as "male" and "female" become more permeable and less rigid.

As jobs and other societal roles are less often tagged as male or female, it is inevitable that socialization practices will change too. They will change together, however. There is little point in desexing child-rearing practices unless both boys and girls have the chance to try out their skills along a continuum of ways of being. Nor will the opening of new work roles be meaningful or successful unless the hitherto ineligible persons have the cognitive styles and personalities to function in them.

Many studies have supported the positive value of moving toward androgynous norms for the socialization of children. Men can be permitted closer contact with their feelings and can develop qualities of empathy and greater concern for others, along with an attenuation of *macho* need for dominance and display of high activity level and aggression. Women can help both men and themselves by practicing assertion, independence, and poise, and by abandoning the unnatural postures of childishness, helplessness, and docility.

While many young people are consciously incorporating these changes already, both in themselves and in their handling of their children, other factors, less conscious and less under the control of individuals seem to be working in the same direction. Impressive cross-cultural stability for masculine and feminine ideals was found among six Western countries, Norway, Sweden, Denmark, Finland, England, and the United States (Block, 1973). This result corresponded with the concepts of agency and communion: tendencies of organisms toward individualism, self-protection, self-assertion, and self-expansion on the one hand, and toward mutuality, interdependence, and concern for the joint welfare on the other (Bakan, 1966). But the greatest degree of sex differentiation and agentic description as ideal was in those countries with a strong capitalistic orientation. Denmark and Sweden, both with long-standing commitment to social welfare, placed less emphasis on both sex differences and on agentic characteristics for both sexes. If there is a relationship between capitalism and agency, then a sociopolitical movement toward greater concern with social welfare would in itself have implications for sex norms and socialization practices (Bakan, 1966).

In the long run, changes in models for behavior and in normative limits must be functional for the society if they are to last. This means that androgynous values for human behavior, made real by changes in the socialization of children, must find their counterparts in androgynous social and work roles for adults. When one part of the social system changes, others must change also. New roles must expand to accommodate the time and talents no longer required by old ones, as they diminish in their requirements of personal, individual resources.

Change is often painful, and this one is no exception. The opening up of the world to women was begun by white, middle-class, educated women who had their identities neither with the power elite nor with the most oppressed of their sex. In fact, they fit the concept of "marginal" persons who are essential to social change, and who, in their nonconformity, may represent the best interests and the ultimate values of the group more effectively than the conforming majority (Willie, 1974). It is supportive of this idea to note that it was not the government, the educational system, organized religion, or the psychiatric profession who began the demand for equity and freedom from oppressive stereotypes for women; it was women themselves who took the risks and began to show the way to a more humane life for all persons.

Life Chances

Characteristics such as sex, race, ethnic origin, size, physical handicaps, and so on are socially defined. That is, they are given meaning in terms of social norms. On the bases of these meanings, the individual is provided with differential opportunities, which are called life chances. In the past her sex was always a major determinant of woman's life chances all over the world, the fact that she was born female being the single most important determinant of what she would be doing thirty years hence. Today, the importance of her sex as a predictor is quite variable. The chance that a woman has to escape from traditional role requirements and to exercise some degree of control over her own life depends to a substantial degree on the country, class, and ethnic group into which she was born. Child-rearing practices, important as they are, only reflect these variables and the value systems associated with them.

While the scope of this book has not systematically included comparative studies of culture, class, or ethnicity as they affect the behavior of women, it is relevant to consider one such report, which gives a global perspective and addresses what may be the most important problem of all: the relation between women's equality of opportunity and their fertility in both developed and undeveloped countries all over the world (Dixon, 1975). Based on data gathered for a United Nations report on the status of women, the report contains compelling evidence of a strong relationship between women's status in education, employment, the family, and public life on the one hand, and their reproductive behavior on the other. If one grants that education, employment opportunity, the right to self-determination in one's personal life, and participation in public life all convey power on the person who has them, and that the extent to which one has power or is powerless relative to others is a determinant of behavior, then these factors become important to the psychology of women.

Education

In almost all the countries covered by the report, the goal of equal education had not been achieved even where equality was guaranteed by law. All over the world, females over fifteen were less likely to be literate than males, although the sex differential was less among fifteen- to nineteen-year-olds (see Table 13.1). Except for the African and Asian countries, girls between the ages of five and fourteen were about as likely as boys to be in school but the ratio of females to males in school in the age groups fifteen to nineteen and twenty to twenty-four dropped sharply. Even in the United States, females in the twenty to twenty-four age group were only half as likely to be in school as were their male counterparts (see Table 13.2).

The relationship between women's educational level and their fertility is not a simple one. Each affects the other, and both are af-

Table 13.1 Average ratios of female to male literacy by age and countries, 1960–1970*

Countries	Ages 15 and over	Ages 15–19
African	0.54	0.66
Asian	0.58	0.73
Central and South American	0.94	1.00
Oceanian	0.97	1.01
European	0.88	0.99

* From data in Dixon (1975).

Table 13.2 Average ratios of females to males enrolled in school by age and countries, 1960–1971*

Countries	Ages 5–14	Ages 15–19	Ages 20–24
African	0.79	0.47	0.15
Asian	0.79	0.72	0.44
American** (United States)	1.00 (1.00)	0.89 (0.94)	0.65 (0.51)
Oceanian	1.00	0.89	0.38
European	0.98	0.92	0.57

* From data in Dixon (1975).
** Includes United States, Canada, and Mexico, as well as some Central and South American countries.

fected by numerous other social, cultural, and political pressures. But in general, that aspect of fertility regulation that is most relevant to the issue of equal right to education is delay of the onset of child-bearing, either by delay of marriage or delay of first birth within marriage. For example, the results of a study of 1,600 United States high-school seniors in 1965 who were reinterviewed in 1971 showed that marriage and childbearing severely hindered women from entering and staying in college, and that starting a family had a greater effect on women's education than on men's. Of the married women with children who had started college 75 percent had dropped out, compared to 52 percent of married men with children, 22 percent of single women, and 27 percent of single men (Dixon, 1975). Thus even in a country where conditions favor higher education for women, marriage and motherhood mitigate to a significant degree the probability that women will exercise their rights to equal educational opportunities. In certain African and Asian regions the universal practice of early marriage for all women, plus the lack of a tradition of education for women, combine to assure that almost no women will continue their educations beyond puberty.

But just as delayed childbearing favors attending or staying in school, education has an effect on women's reproductive behavior. In fact, in high fertility countries, it is the educational level of women that is one of the strongest factors affecting their fertility. For example, a national survey of 3,200 married Turkish women under age forty-five found that university graduates averaged 1.4 live-born children, compared with 2.0 for high-school graduates, 2.1 for elementary-school graduates, 2.8 for women with five years of primary school, 3.2 for women with less than five years of primary school, and 4.2 for illiterate women (Temur, 1971). Moreover, the educational level of the wife is more strongly related to a couple's fertility than is the educational level of the husband, suggesting that investment in female education would show a greater effect on limiting fertility than would an equal investment in male education.

Studies show that in the developing countries women with more than high-school education marry later, have fewer children, and know more about birth control than do less educated or illiterate women. But the majority of women of childbearing age in most of the developing countries are illiterate; thus the low birth rate of the educated elite does not substantially affect the overall birth rate for the country. Finally, a highly educated woman may not be inclined to have few or no children unless opportunities to use her skills are available to her. In some countries the most and least educated women had the largest families, leading to a U-shaped relationship between education and family size (Dixon, 1975).

Employment

Although conditions vary greatly from country to country according to their culture and level of economic development, women in general everywhere are less likely to be employed outside the home than men are, though they may do heavy unpaid domestic or agricultural labor (see Table 13.3). Worldwide, one out of two men of all ages is economically active, compared to one out of four women. More than four out of five men in the twenty- to twenty-four age group are economically active, compared to less than two out of five females.

Table 13.3 Percentages of males and females who are economically active, by age and countries, 1962–1972*

	All ages		Ages 20–24	
Countries	Male	Female	Male	Female
African	49.9	26.3	86.9	24.8
Asian	48.6	21.5	86.6	40.4
American**	49.3	17.6	89.1	35.6
Oceania	50.8	15.6	94.1	38.4
Soviet Union	51.5	44.6	(unavailable)	
Europe	57.7	29.4	85.2	58.4

* From data in Dixon (1975).
** Includes United States and Canada, as well as some Central and South American countries.

In examining the relationship between employment and fertility it is difficult to ascertain cause and effect, as it was with education, but some generalizations are possible. If conditions are conducive to female employment but the roles of mother and worker are not compatible (as is the case for many American women), then delayed marriage and effective birth planning would have clear advantages. Marriage alone reduces labor-force participation by women, as in one study in which the percentage of a sample of married childless Chilean women in the work force was 26.3 compared to 68.8 for single women without children.

Small families permit women to work with less likelihood of being overwhelmed by dual responsibilities. Thus the right to determine the number and spacing of births facilitates the free exercise of the right to equal economic opportunity, where that right exists. In rural areas of developing countries, there is little opportunity for paid employment for women, much of it being of the agricultural or cottage-industry type where the number of children may be less important to work activity. In urban areas of the same countries, mothers were more likely to work outside the home, thus requiring child-care assistance. Urban women also had more access to birth-control information and family-planning services. As elsewhere, professional women have fewer children than skilled workers, who in turn have fewer than women in sales, trade, or service occupations (Dixon, 1975).

Marriage and the family

The idea of equal rights for women on entering marriage, during marriage, and at the dissolution of marriage is probably the most sensitive and controversial in the whole area of women's rights. In many countries, women may still lose their civil rights upon marrying, and even in countries with legal equality for women, patterns of male dominance continue to affect actual practice. Legal minimum ages for females at first marriage range from twelve to twenty, with a higher minimum for males in most countries. In general, women in industrialized countries are more likely to marry later or to stay single; but in many regions, such as India and in African tribal societies, girls are married off very young. In general, the younger the average age for marriage of girls is, the greater the gap between age of bride and groom, thus building in a subordinate role for the wife. Already of inferior status owing to sex, her influence is further eroded by marriage to a man of much greater age and experience than she. Also, the practice of early and universal marriage of girls in most developing countries means high levels of fertility.

The relationship between women's equality in marriage and fertility really hinges on the issue of alternative roles for women (Dixon, 1975). Generally, the more resources the woman brings into the marriage, such as education and paid employment, the more nearly equal is her power. Where nondomestic activities are valued and rewarded, her participation in them gives her greater status in the marriage. This in turn creates an interpersonal atmosphere which is more favorable to birth planning, and the resulting smaller family permits a closer relationship between the spouses and less inequality of power and status. In some countries, however, women's status is almost entirely a function of the number of children she has, and infertility or few children can cause her to be ridiculed and scorned. In these areas, too, there are no alternative roles for women—their productivity must be manifested in the one role available to them.

Women's rights at the dissolution of marriage are also related to birth planning and fertility. Where divorce laws are liberal, women with no or few children have the advantage that they do not need to stay in an undesirable marital situation. Birth planning enables women to exercise their rights more effectively if divorce occurs. But in some countries, men have a unilateral right to divorce their wives for such reasons as sterility or failure to bear sons. Having a large number of children may be a form of insurance for a woman who has no voice in whether the marriage survives or not, and no options for herself either, if it does not.

To generalize, it is clear that there is an inverse relationship between the degree of women's equality with men in the marriage relationship and fertility. Before and during marriage, and at its termination, fertility rates are lower where women approach equality. However, other factors affect both of these variables, and the total picture is one of complex interacting relationships.

Participation in public life

Women now have the legal right to vote in most countries, but they appear in only token numbers in the higher levels of government. The masculine character of practically all decision-making bodies attests to the traditional resistance against women in leadership positions, a resistance which has given way very slowly, even in the most sophisticated societies. Here again, the relationship between fertility and public life is a mutual one: women with fewer domestic responsibilities are freer to participate in public life, and those who participate in the wider world outside the home may be motivated to have fewer children (Dixon, 1975). In addition, and perhaps more important, women performing capably in public positions offer a role model which can offer encouragement to other women as well as help to break down stereotypes about women's place and relative competence.

Even a cursory consideration of the relation between women's equality and fertility in various parts of the world heightens awareness of the effects of life chances—of one's birthplace; one's family; one's race, religion, and socioeconomic status; and all the attendant determinants of how one will be reared and by whom, what one will be taught, at what age one will marry and who the spouse will be, events over which many women have no control—on behavior and on the course and pattern of one's life.

In this country social class and ethnic identity affect concepts of masculinity and femininity and the pattern of the relationship between the sexes. These effects are most clearly evident in the lives of black women, particularly of poor black women, and result from their unique history, from their status in the society, and from the availability to them of economic, cultural, and educational opportunities.

A distinctive element in the experience of black women is the relative lack among black people of the strong patriarchal tradition characteristic of the white culture (Yorburg, 1973). The African patriarchal heritage was destroyed when the people were brought to this country as slaves, and since that time black women have been relatively more independent of black men than white women have been of white men. Food and other economic resources were most often distributed by slave owners to women; the black man, having no control of such goods, and being powerless in general, did not assume an authority role over the female. In more recent times her independence was further increased by the fact that she was better able to obtain employment (in low-paying service jobs) and often was the sole economic support of herself and her children. Black women have a history of combining outside employment and motherhood. As doors open to educated black women, one would expect them to have few conflicts about aspiration and achievement.

Activist black women in general have not identified with the goals of the women's liberation movement. The black struggle for identity and equality, they feel, must come first, and its success requires the solidarity of blacks. Compared to the oppression of all blacks, the oppression which white women are complaining about seems trivial to many. Further, the black male needs help in developing the self-esteem he was never permitted to have, and if this means that the black woman will need to "step down" a bit to allow his self-assertion to grow, then that is what she will do. While there is much controversy concerning the relationship between the black woman and black man and the women's liberation movement, one view is the following:

> The role of black woman at this point in history is to give sustenance to the black man. At one time the black woman was the only one that could say something and not get her head chopped off. . . . But the law was strictly against the black man. So he could not do anything. Now that he speaks, we speak together. We cannot separate, and this is what I say to the women's lib movements. . . . The black woman is not undergoing the same kind of oppression that white women have gone through in the homes. The black woman is liberated in her own mind, because she has taken on the responsibility for the family and she works. Black women had to get in the labor force, because black men didn't have jobs. . . .
>
>   The point is, that . . . the struggle of black women and white women is not the same. Because the white woman is oppressed and is only now realizing her oppression. White women, middle class women, have to look at their problem and it is their husbands. He is the oppressor, because he is the system. It's a white male system (Lerner, 1973, pp. 585–86).

Women have in common their hormones and the cycles and events of their bodies. To the extent that systematic *differences* occur in women's behavior across cultures, ethnic groups, and social classes, it is *these* variables that affect life chances and mediate the experiences women have which in turn affect behavior, attitudes, and values.

Personality

The word *personality* is defined and used in a bewildering variety of ways, to mean everything from an evaluation of one's charm and vivacity to a description of a set of characteristics which define one as unique from all others. That personality, unlike constructs in the physical sciences such as electricity, eludes precise definition is generally recognized by psychologists. "[I]t is our conviction that *no substantive definition of personality can be applied with any generality*" (Hall and Lindzey, 1970, p. 9, italics original). But some definitions are more widely used and respected than others, and one of those is that

> personality is the dynamic organization within the individual of those psychophysical systems that determine his characteristic behavior and thought (Allport, 1961, p. 28).

Certain key words in this definition merit attention, especially within the context of thinking about the psychology of women. *Dynamic organization* means that personality is always changing and developing, that it is a process, while at the same time it has a systematic unity which relates its components to each other. This attribute accounts for the stability of a person's behavior across time and situations. *Psychophysical systems* recognizes that personality has both psychic and physical components, its organization drawing from both mind and body and fusing them into a unity. The word *determine* means that personality is an active agent in the patterning of the individual's behavior. Finally, *characteristic* emphasizes the individuality of personality, the uniqueness of its particular organization in the individual.

At this point, an emendation of Allport's definition is in order. Personality alone does not determine behavior. A person, for example, may characteristically be shy and reserved in social situations but under certain conditions may become quite animated and gay. Therefore, to avoid the implication that personality is *the* determinant of behavior, let us change it to read:

> Personality is the dynamic organization within the individual of those psychophysical systems *that intereact with situational variables* to determine an individual's characteristic behavior and thought.

The term *temperament* should be distinguished from personality. *Temperament* refers to dispositions that are largely biologically derived, such as sensitivity and reactivity to stimulation, emotional lability, and so on, dispositions which are manifest quite early in life, before learning has either attenuated or enhanced them. Temperament has been considered to reflect innate, largely hereditary predispositions to behave in certain ways. Thus, along with such attributes as intelligence and physique, it can be thought of as the raw material of personality (Allport, 1961).

To speak of temperament as biologically derived, as a spectrum of genetically determined predispositions to behave in certain ways, should not suggest that personality traits are inherited, and certainly not that the "feminine personality" is passed down from mother to daughter.[2] It is reasonable to assume that the distribution of such predispositions is the same for both sexes. That is, the "raw mate-

---

[2] For a review of studies on the heritability of personality traits, see Lindzey *et al.* (1971). Correlations for personality traits in identical twins, while higher than for fraternal twins, are substantially lower than for other variables, such as intelligence. For example, one study of identical twins reared apart found little resemblance in mode of interpersonal reactions, attitudes, interests, and such personality traits as ambition, aggression, and emotional control.

rial" with which environmental events will interact to shape the person is not systematically different for the two sexes. Although males have a greater predisposition to behave aggressively early in life, they exhibit a wide range of individual differences in the display of aggression, as do females. Clearly, aggressive impulses can be shaped by environmental intervention in the direction either of repression or of release.

Although theorists emphasize different aspects of the various factors which contribute to the development of personality,[3] most would agree that the outcome is determined by the experiential history of the person, the kind and degree and pattern of experiences she has had, impinging upon and affecting the development and maturation of the basic or innate qualities that were there at birth. The behavioral repertoire of the neonate is not large, consisting mostly of motoric and unlearned reflexive behavior like crying and sucking. But individual differences in temperament are observable in very young infants. Thus the uniqueness of the developed personality comes about through the interaction of the person's unique experiential history, which begins at birth, with a unique set of "givens," the result being an infinite array of individuals, no two alike.

The importance of this for the psychology of women is that intrasex variability is very large, a fact that is often forgotten in the enthusiastic search for sex differences. Acting on a spectrum of predispositions which may become manifest at different maturational levels are thousands of complexes of events producing reactions which are themselves events, all shaping the personality of the individual woman.

Although it has been proposed that females are less variable than males on most physical and a few psychological traits (Kagan, 1972), the difference in variability is not great enough to suggest strongly that women are more like each other than men are (Maccoby and Jacklin, 1974). That is, on any given variable such as creativity, one would expect to find as wide a range of differences among females as among males. Therefore, instead of grouping the universe of women under such rubrics as "women are nurturant," and "women are verbal," one line of inquiry could concentrate on studying samples of females to learn what the parameters of female behavior are; that is, to concentrate on the norms and variabilities of female behavior, how personality attributes are distributed in different female populations, and how they mediate different results in different experimental and natural conditions. This approach would essentially correct the bias of psychology toward studying males and

[3] For a review of the major theories of personality, see Hall and Lindzey (1970).

making generalizations and formulating theory based on male samples. As knowledge accumulated about the behavior of women under various conditions, personality theory would be enriched accordingly.

Another approach is to bring attention back to the individual, that is, to attend to individual instead of group differences, or even to return to the now out-of-fashion study of the single person.

Individual differences

The study of intrasex differences in the personality and behavior of women and the interaction of these differences with situational variables deserves more attention than it has had in the past. Comparison of the behavior of male and female groups under certain conditions, and resultant statements that, for example, females are more fearful or more conservative than males, add very little to our understanding of human behavior. Even comparisons of different groups of women, identified on the basis of age or education or some other variable, can lead to misleading or less informative results if individual difference variables are not taken into consideration. For example, consider a study of the effects of social class on women's expectations of success at a given experimental task, involving manual dexterity. A result showing that middle- and lower-class women predict different outcomes for themselves shed little light on the parameters of female behavior in test situations. It is known, however, that anxiety level is related to the threat of failure in some persons (Spielberger et al., 1970). Also, it is reasonable to assume that women within a social class will differ with respect to readiness to develop anxiety in an achievement situation. Thus the individual variable of anxiety level might interact with the group variable of social class to confound results. If, on the other hand, individual differences in the trait of anxiety or predisposition to develop anxiety in test situations were included in the research design, then one could observe the effects across social classes of high, average, and low anxiety in women in test situations. In this hypothetical study, taking into account individual differences in anxiety would essentially refine the results and lead to the generation of more intelligent and interesting hypotheses.

Females differ on such personality and behavioral characteristics as dominance, creativity, conventionality, susceptibility to fear, willingness to take risks, self-esteem, and so on. While this assertion seems obvious, we do not yet know enough about such individual differences and how they interact with other variables to produce behavior.

A related problem concerns the tradition in personality research to consider personality traits to be dimensional, that is, to assume that persons are characterized by some degree of the trait in question. One such trait is "femininity," and most objective personality tests purport to measure the extent to which a person ascribes to herself (or himself) certain descriptions associated with the feminine stereotype. With a few exceptions (Bem, 1974; Spence, 1974), the trait is seen to be unidimensional, and the person's responses to the test place her or him at some point on the dimension anchored by masculine on the one end and feminine on the other. The concept of masculine and feminine characteristics as mutually incompatible implies, just as sex roles do, a bifurcation of personality that is not only unrealistic but also incapable of sampling the possibilities of the individual.

The oft-heard statement "women are dependent" also implies a dependence-independence dimension, with women clustered at one end and men at the other. It should be obvious that dependence can be defined in many ways and that a person can be both dependent and independent, on the basis of her own disposition in the requirements of a given situation. A woman, for example, may be emotionally dependent upon the support and gratification she receives from a special person; at the same time, she may be quite independent in the conduct of her life, in supporting herself, making decisions, and so forth. In personality research on women, individual differences in emotional and instrumental dependence affect responses to situational variables, as do other characteristics of the individual.

The personality of the individual

The definition of personality emphasizes the characteristic behavior of the individual, that by which we know the person and recognize her as different from all others (Allport, 1961). Of all the ways of learning about personality—comparisons of group parameters, experimental manipulations of samples, observance of individual differences as determinants of behavior across various situations—the study of the individual case has been the least favored by researchers. Attempts to understand "the dynamic organization within the individual" have been left to clinicians who believe that they need such understanding in order to help the troubled client. The tradition of study of the individual case, which has come down from European psychiatry and psychoanalysis, has been of little interest to researchers who work within the experimental paradigms of modern psychology. The latter insist that science cannot take account of unique events but must look for statistical regularities, for universal consistencies of behavior which will lead to the discovery of general laws and ultimately to the goals of empirical science, which are prediction and control (Sanford, 1963).

However, it is possible that one could find such regularities and consistencies in the expressive behavior of the individual. One could arrive at generalizations and make predictions for that person by studying the manner or style that uniquely characterizes the individual's performance of an act, such as handwriting, gestures, voice inflections, and so on (Allport, 1961). For example, one's letters and journals could reveal the dominant traits of one's personality. A well-known example of such analysis is *Letters From Jenny*. This book is a study of 301 letters written by a middle-aged woman, Jenny, to a young married couple over a twelve-year period. Because of their importance for the study of individual personality, the letters were analyzed and the most salient traits of Jenny's personality extracted from them. While content analysis could not provide the "golden key" to the riddle of personality, it could bring the person's perceptions of her world into focus and enable the researcher to make better inferences concerning the personality structure underlying her existential experience (Allport, 1965).

More recently, the question, Where is the person in personality research? has been revived (Carlson, 1971). Current methodology for the investigation of personality essentially treats people as "carriers" of the variable under consideration, viewing them as interchangeable for the purpose of research, their idiosyncratic qualities being simply "noise" which, by random assignment to experimental groups, will cancel out. Such treatment, highly impersonal and often employing deception to keep subjects from discerning the real purpose of the study, is incapable of asking or answering questions of any real importance in personality research. A survey of 226 journal articles on personality revealed not a single study concerned with the organization of personality within the individual (Carlson, 1971).

Three suggestions for making personality research more meaningful and more extensive in scope are:

1. The longitudinal study which involves repeated observations of individuals over time. Such studies are capable of revealing the organization and change of personality as it develops over the life span.
2. The use of informal "archival records," such as college application essays, contents of suggestion boxes, and other unobtrusive

measures in natural situations (and presumably such material as those used in *Letters from Jenny*).

3. Willingness to listen to what subjects say about their experiences and what they mean to them. It is reasonable to assume that subjects are willing to tell us more than the simplistic "responses" elicited from them by the currently popular research designs.

This approach holds that the person is there—the whole person—waiting to be discovered by those who are willing to abandon orthodoxy and to invest themselves in the task (Carlson, 1971).

Another paper addressed the impoverished methods of personality research as they apply to the psychology of women. Drawing upon the theoretical formulation of the agency-communion polarity of experience explained below (Bakan, 1966), this paper showed that research methodology as currently practiced is incapable of responding to important questions about human nature. Current scientific operations, such as ordering, quantifying, manipulating, and controlling are called *agentic*—identified with a masculine principle which strives for mastery and ego-enhancement. In contrast, *communal* inquiry involves naturalistic kinds of observation, sensitivity to patterning of phenomena, and personal involvement of the investigator. If psychologists are serious about studying female (and human) personality, according to this viewpoint, they should give up their obsession with agentic methodology and develop communal modes of inquiry which could bring forth new models to further understanding of the person (Carlson, 1972).

We have discussed four sources which influence the behavior of women. At the present time we have no idea what the relative importance of their contribution is to the behavior of any particular woman. Each person, it has been said, is like all other persons, like some other persons, and like no other person (Kluckhohn and Murray, 1949). If we apply this truism to the study of women, we see that its categories describe the contributory sources of behavior that we have been talking about: biology, socialization, life chances, and personality.

From birth woman confronts the world with a body which is more like all other women's than it is like any man's. The socialization pressures of family and school are similar to those experienced by many others in her society. She shares life chances with others of her social class, her race, her neighborhood, and her qualities of health, beauty, and so on. From all this material is organized her ineffable and unique personality, with its substratum of temperamental dispositions.

A general theory of the psychology of women must take all these into account in attempting to formulate explanatory concepts about women. Though women's bodies and their functions are in general more like one another's than unlike, they are not all used in the same way. Women menstruate, gestate, and lactate. But not all women gestate and lactate (Money, 1965). Most women are physically weaker than most men, but some Central African tribes believe the opposite, that men are weaker and not suited for heavy work, which is done by the women (Albert, 1963).

Women are socialized into sex-appropriate behavior, but all societies do not agree on what is sex appropriate. Though Western societies expect men to be sexually aggressive, for example, and women to be passive, resistive, or evasive, some African and American Indian groups believe that women are more highly sexed than men are, and it is the Zuni man who looks forward to his wedding night with fear and apprehension (Albert, 1963). The Iranian male is expected to be sensitive, emotional, and intuitive, while the woman is supposed to be logical and practical (Hall, 1959).

Many behaviors are related to the particular circumstances of one's life. No woman can become a writer or scientist if she is illiterate, a politician if women in her country are secluded in their homes, or Miss America if she is not beautiful. If one girl is born in a migrant labor camp in Mississippi and another in a comfortable suburb in Connecticut, that fact alone and its implications may contribute more than anything else to the later differences between them.

As for personality, each one is different. Yet we have the choice of looking for commonalities (women are dependent) as science has almost always done, or of studying the individual. Considering the sources of diversity, it appears that generalizations about the psychology of women will be valid only for narrowly defined and specified groups. Throughout this book, which has dealt mostly with research in our own society, we have seen how few generalizations about women are possible. This leaves us, then, with the individual. Instead of asking the question, What are women like? shall we direct at least some of our attention to asking, What is *she* like? If we are careful about generalizing, we shall create fewer myths and stereotypes as impediments to the inquiry of the future.

References

ABRAMOWITZ, S. I.; ABRAMOWITZ, C. V.; JACKSON, C.; and GOMES, B. The politics of clinical judgment: What nonliberal examiners infer about women who don't stifle themselves. *Journal of Consulting and Clinical Psychology* 41 (1973): 385–91.

ADAMS, E., and BRISCOE, M. L., eds. *Up against the wall, mother. . . .* Beverly Hills, Calif.: Glencoe, 1971.

ADLER, A. *Understanding human nature.* New York: Greenberg, 1927.

ALBERT, E. M. The roles of women: A question of values. In Farber, S. M., and Wilson, R. H. L., eds., *The potential of woman.* New York: McGraw-Hill, 1963.

ALLEN, P. *Free choice: A perspective on the small group in women's liberation.* Washington, N.J.: Times Change Press, 1970.

ALLPORT, G. W. *Pattern and growth in personality.* New York: Holt, Rinehart and Winston, 1961.

ALLPORT, G. W. *Letters from Jenny.* New York: Harcourt Brace Jovanovich, 1965.

ALLPORT, G. W., and VERNON, P. E. A test for personal values. *Journal of Abnormal and Social Psychology* 26 (1931): 231–48.

ALLPORT, G. W.; VERNON, P. E.; and LINDZEY, G. *Study of values manual.* Boston: Houghton Mifflin, 1960.

AMERICAN PSYCHIATRIC ASSOCIATION. *Diagnostic and statistical manual,* 1968.

ASHER, J. Sex bias found in therapy. *APA Monitor* (April 1975): 1, 5.

AUDEN, W. H., and PEARSON, N. H. *Poets of the English language.* New York: Viking, 1950.

AUERBACK, A. E. Understanding sexual deviations. *Postgraduate Medicine* 43 (1968): 169–73.

BAHR, S. J. Effects on power and division of labor in the family. In Hoffman, L. W., and Nye, F. I., eds., *Working mothers.* San Francisco: Jossey-Bass, 1974.

BAKAN, D. *The duality of human existence.* Chicago: Rand McNally, 1966.

BANDURA, A. Influence of models' reinforcement contingencies on the acquisition of imitative responses. *Journal of Personality and Social Psychology* 1 (1965): 589–95.

BANDURA, A. Social learning theory of identificatory processes. In Goslin,

D. A., ed., *Handbook of socialization theory and research*. Chicago: Rand Mc-Nally, 1969.

BANDURA, A.; GRUSEC, J. E.; and MENLOVE, F. L. Observational learning as a function of symbolization and incentive set. *Child Development* 37 (1966): 499–506.

BANDURA, A.; ROSS, D.; and ROSS, S. A. Transmission of aggression through imitation of aggressive models. *Journal of Abnormal and Social Psychology* 63 (1961): 575–82.

BARDWICK, J. *Psychology of women*. New York: Harper, 1971.

BARDWICK, J. Psychological factors in the acceptance and use of oral contraceptives. In Fawcett, J. T., ed., *Psychological perspectives on population*. New York: Basic Books, 1973.

BARGLOW, P.; GUNTHER, M. S.; JOHNSON, A.; and MELTZER, H. J. Hysterectomy and tubal ligation: a psychiatric comparison. *Obstetrics and Gynecology* 25 (1965): 520–27.

BARRY, H.; BACON, M. K.; and CHILD, I. L. A cross-cultural survey of some sex differences in socialization. *Journal of Abnormal and Social Psychology* 55 (1957): 327–32.

BART, P. Depression in middle-aged women. In Gornick, V., and Moran, B. K., eds., *Woman in sexist society*. New York: Basic Books, 1971.

BARUCH, G. K. Sex-role attitudes of fith-grade girls. In Stacey, J.; Beraud, S.; and Daniels, J., eds., *And Jill came tumbling after: Sexism in American education*. New York: Dell, 1974.

BATES, J. E., and ZAWADZKI, E. S. *Criminal abortion*. Springfield, Ill.: Charles C Thomas, 1964.

BAUMRIND, D. From each according to her ability. *School Review* 80 (1972): 161–97.

BAYLEY, N. Development of mental abilities. In Mussen, P. H., ed., *Carmichael's manual of child psychology*. New York: Wiley, 1970.

BEACH, F. A., ed. *Sex and behavior*. New York: Wiley, 1965.

BEACH, F. A. Hormonal effects on socio-sexual behavior in dogs. In Gibian, H., and Plotz, E. J., eds., *Colloquium der Gesellschaft für Biologische Chemie*. New York: Springer, 1970.

BECKER, E. Social science and psychiatry: The coming challenge. *The Antioch Review* 23 (1963): 353–65.

BECKER, E. *The revolution in psychiatry*. Glencoe, Ill.: The Free Press, 1964.

BEECHER, C., and STOWE, H. B. *The American woman's home: Or, principles of domestic science*. New York: J. B. Ford, 1869.

BELL, R. Q. Relations between behavior manifestations in the human neonate. *Child Development* 31 (1960): 463–77.

BELL, R. Q., and COSTELLO, N. S. Three tests for sex differences in tactile sensitivity in the newborn. *Biologia Neonaturum* 7 (1964): 335–47.

BELLO, F. The magic that made Polaroid. *Fortune* 59 (1959): 124–29.

BEM, S. L. The measurement of psychological androgyny. *Journal of Consulting and Clinical Psychology* 42 (1974): 155–162.

BENEDEK, T. F. Sexual functions in women and their disturbance. In Ariete, S., ed., *American handbook of psychiatry*, vol. 1. New York: Basic Books, 1959.

BERGMAN, J. Are little girls being harmed by Sesame Street? In Stacey, J.; Bereaud, S.: and Daniels, J., eds. *And Jill came tumbling after: Sexism in American education*. New York: Dell, 1974.

BERMANT, G. Behavior therapy approaches to modification of sexual preference: Biological perspective and critique. In Bardwick, J., ed., *Readings on the psychology of women*. New York: Harper & Row, 1972.

BERNARD, J. *Academic women*. University Park, Pa.: Pennsylvania State University Press, 1964.

BERNARD, J. The paradox of the happy marriage. In Gornick, V., and Moran, B. K., eds., *Woman in sexist society*. New York: Basic Books, 1971. (a)

BERNARD, J. *Women and the public interest: An essay on policy and protest*. New York: Aldine-Atherton, 1971. (b)

BERNARD, J. *The future of motherhood*. New York: Dial, 1974.

BERNARD, J. *Sex differences: An overview*. New York: MSS Modular Publications, Inc., Module 26, 1974, 1–18.

BERRY, J. W. Temne and Eskimo perceptual skills. *International Journal of Psychology* 1 (1966): 207–29.

BETTELHEIM, B. The commitment required of a woman entering a scientific profession in present-day American society. In Mattfield, J. A., and Van Akan, C. G., eds., *Women and the scientific professions*. Cambridge, Mass.: M.I.T. Press, 1965.

BIBRING, G. L. Some specific psychological tasks in pregnancy and motherhood. In Hammer, S., ed., *Women: Body and culture*. New York: Harper & Row, 1975.

BIERI, J. Parental identification, acceptance of authority, and within-sex differences in cognitive behavior. *Journal of Abnormal and Social Psychology* 60 (1960): 76–79.

BIRLEY, J. L. T. Early diagnosis of schizophrenia. *British Medical Journal* no. 5625 (1968): 232–34.

BIRREN, J. E. *The psychology of aging*. Englewood Cliffs, N.J.: Prentice-Hall, 1964.

BLINICK, G. Menstrual function and pregnancy in narcotics addicts treated with methadone. *Nature* (London) 219 (1968): 180.

BLOCK, H. A., and NIEDERHOFFER, A. *The gang: A study in adolescent behavior*. New York: Philosophical Library, 1958.

BLOCK, J. H. Conceptions of sex role: Some cross-cultural and longitudinal perspectives. *American Psychologist* 28 (1973): 512–26.

BLOOD, R. O., JR. The husband-wife relationship. In Nye, F. I., and Hoffman, L. W., eds., *The employed mother in America*. Chicago: Rand McNally, 1963.

BOLTER, S. The psychiatrist's role in therapeutic abortions: The unwitting accomplice. *American Journal of Psychiatry* 119 (1962): 312–16.

BOWLBY, J. Grief and mourning in infancy and early childhood. In *The psychoanalytic study of the child*. vol. 15. New York: International Universities Press, 1960.

BOWLBY, J. *Attachment*. New York: Basic Books, 1969.

BRAINE., M. D. S.; HEIMER, C. B.; WORTIS, H.; and FREEDMAN, A. M. Factors associated with impairment of the early development of prematures. *Monographs of the Society for Research in Child Development* 31 (1966): serial No. 106.

BRECHER, E. M. *The sex researchers*. New York: New American Library, 1971.

BROCKETT, L. P. *Woman: Her rights, wrongs, privileges and responsibilities*. Freeport, N.Y.: Books for Libraries Press, 1869.

BRODSKY, C. M. The pharmacotherapy system. *Psychosomatics* 11 (1971): 24–30.

408 References

BROVERMAN, I. K.; BROVERMAN, D. M.; CLARKSON, F. E.; ROSENKRANTZ, P. S.; and VOGEL, S. R. Sex-role stereotypes and clinical judgments of mental health. *Journal of Consulting and Clinical Psychology* 34 (1970): 1–7.

BROVERMAN, I. K.; VOGEL, S. R.; BROVERMAN, D. M.; CLARKSON, F. E.; and ROSENKRANTZ, P. S. Sex-role stereotypes: A current appraisal. *Journal of Social Issues* 28 (1972): 59–78.

BROWN, D. G. Sex-role preference in young children. *Psychological Monographs: General and Applied* 70 (1956): whole no. 421.

BROWN, D. G. Sex-role development in a changing culture. *Psychological Bulletin* 4 (1958): 232–42.

BROWN, D. G., and LYNN, D. B. Human sexual development: An outline of components and concepts. *Journal of Marriage and the Family* 28 (1966): 155–62.

BROWN, L. R. *In the human interest.* New York: Norton, 1974.

BROWN, W. A., and SHERESHEFSKY, P. Seven women: A prospective study of postpartum psychiatric disorders. *Psychiatry,* 35 (1972).

BULLOUGH, V. L. *The subordinate sex: A history of attitudes toward women.* Urbana, Ill.: University of Illinois Press, 1973.

CALDERONE, M. S., ed. *Manual of family planning and contraceptive practice.* Baltimore: Williams & Wilkins, 1970.

CAMERON, M. Family relationships. In *No longer young.* Work Group Reports from the 26th Annual Conference on Aging, Institute of Gerontology, University of Michigan and Wayne State University, 1974.

CAMPBELL, J. *The masks of God: Primitive mythology.* New York: Viking, 1959.

CARLSON, E. R., and CARLSON, R. Male and female subjects in personality research. *Journal of Abnormal and Social Psychology* 61 (1961): 482–83.

CARLSON, R. Where is the person in personality research? *Psychological Bulletin* 3 (1971): 203–19.

CARLSON, R. Understanding women: Implications for personality theory and research. *Journal of Social Issues* 28 (1972): 17–32.

CARTWRIGHT, L. K. Personality differences in male and female medical students. *Psychiatry in Medicine* 3 (1972): 213–18.

CASH, W. J. *The mind of the South.* New York: Random House, 1960.

CASTLE, C. S. *A statistical study of eminent women.* New York: Science Press, 1913.

CHAMOVE, A.; HARLOW, H. F.; and MITCHELL, G. D. Sex differences in the infant-directed behavior of preadolescent rhesus monkeys. *Child Development* 38 (1967): 329–35.

CHASSEGUET-SMIRGEL, J., ed., *Female sexuality.* Ann Arbor, Mich.: University of Michigan Press, 1970.

CHESLER, P. Patient and patriarch: Women in the psychotherapeutic relationship. In Gornick, V., and Moran, B. K., eds., *Women in sexist society.* New York: Basic Books, 1971.

CHESLER, P. *Women and madness.* Garden City, N.Y.: Doubleday, 1972.

CHESNEY-LIND, M. Juvenile delinquency: The sexualization of female crime. *Psychology Today* 8 (1974): 43–46.

CLARKSON, F. E.; VOGEL, S. R.; BROVERMAN, I. K.; BROVERMAN, D. M.; and ROSENKRANTZ, P. S. Family size and sex-role stereotypes. *Science* 167 (1970): 390–92.

CLEMENS, L. G.; SHRYNE, J.; and GORSKI, R. A. Androgen and development of progesterone responsiveness in male and female rats. *Physiology and Behavior,* 1970, 5, 673–78.

COFFIN, P. The young unmarrieds. In DeLora, J. S., and DeLora, J. R., eds., *Intimate life styles.* Pacific Palisades, Calif.: Goodyear, 1972.

COPPERSTOCK, R. Sex differences in the use of mood-modifying drugs: An explanatory model. *Journal of Health and Social Behavior* 12 (1971): 238–44.

CONSTANTINE, L. L., and CONSTANTINE, J. M. Group and multilateral marriage: Definitional notes, glossary, and annotated bibliography. *Family Process* 10 (1971): 157–76.

CONSTANTINE, L. L., and CONSTANTINE, J. M. Sexual aspects of multilateral relations. In Smith, J. R., and Smith, L. G., eds., *Beyond monogamy.* Baltimore: The Johns Hopkins University Press, 1974.

CUTLER, R.; HEIMER, C. B.; WORTIS, H.; and FREEDMAN, A. M. The effects of prenatal and neonatal complications on the development of premature children at two-and-one-half-years of age. *Journal of Genetic Psychology* 107 (1965): 261–76.

DALTON, K. Effect of menstruation on schoolgirls' weekly work. *British Medical Journal* 1 (1960): 326–28.

DALTON, K. Discussion on depression: Emotion or illness. *Practitioner,* 206 (1971): 681–83.

DALY, M. *The church and the second sex.* New York: Harper & Row, 1975.

DAVID, C. A masculine mythology of femininity. In Chasseguet-Smirgel, J., ed., *Female sexuality.* Ann Arbor, Mich.: University Michigan Press, 1970.

DAVID, H. P. Psychological studies in abortion. In Fawcett, J. T., ed., *Psychological perspectives on population.* New York: Basic Books, 1973.

DE BEAUVOIR, S. *The second sex.* New York: Knopf, 1953.

DE BEAUVOIR, S. Joie de vivre. *Harper's Magazine,* January 1972, 33–40.

DEEGAN, D. Y. *The stereotype of the single woman in American novels.* New York: Kings Crown Press, 1951.

DELORA, J. S., and DELORA, J. R. eds., *Intimate life styles: Marriage and its alternatives.* Pacific Palisades, Calif.: Goodyear, 1972.

DE ROUGEMONT, D. *Love in the western world.* New York: Pantheon, 1956.

DEUTSCH, F. A footnote to Freud's "Fragment of an analysis of a case of hysteria." *The Psychoanalytic Quarterly* 25 (1957): 159–67.

DEUTSCH, H. The significance of masochism in the mental life of women. *International Journal of Psychoanalysis* 11 (1930): 48–60.

DEUTSCH, H. *The psychology of women: A psychoanalytic interpretation,* vol. 1. New York: Grune & Stratton, 1944.

DEUTSCH, H. *The psychology of women: A psychoanalytic interpretation,* vol. 2. New York: Grune & Stratton, 1945.

DEUTSCH, H. On female homosexuality (1933). In Ruitenbeek, H., ed., *Psychoanalysis and female sexuality.* New Haven, Conn.: College and University Press, 1966.

DEUTSCH, H. *Confrontations with myself.* New York: Norton, 1973.

DEUTSCHER, I. The quality of postparental life. In Neugarten, B., ed., *Middle age and aging.* Chicago: University of Chicago Press, 1968.

DE VORE, I., ed., *Primate behavior: Field studies of monkeys and apes.* New York: Holt, Rinehart and Winston, 1965.

DICK-READ, G. *Childbirth without fear.* New York: Harper & Brothers, 1944.

DICKINSON, R. L. *Atlas of human sexual anatomy* (1933) 2d ed. Baltimore: Williams & Wilkins, 1949.

DICKINSON, R. L., and BEAM, L. *A thousand marriages.* Baltimore: Williams & Wilkins, 1932.

DICKINSON, R. L., and BEAM, L. *The single woman.* Baltimore: Williams & Wilkins, 1934.

DINER, H. *Mothers and Amazons: The first feminine history of culture.* Garden City, N.Y.: Anchor, 1973.

DIXON, R. B. Women's rights and fertility. *Reports on Population/Family Planning.* The Population Council, 245 Park Avenue, New York, N.Y. January, 1975.

DOHERTY, M. A. Sexual bias in personality theory. *The Counseling Psychologist* 4 (1973): 67–74.

DOUVAN, E. New sources of conflict in females at adolescence. In Bardwick, J. M.; Douvan, E.; Horner, M. S.; and Gutmann, D. *Feminine personality and conflict.* Belmont, Calif.: Brooks/Cole, 1970.

DOWTY, N. To be a woman in Israel. *School Review* 80 (1972): 319–32.

DRELLICH, M. G., and BIEBER, I. The psychologic importance of the uterus and its functions. *Journal of Nervous and Mental Disease* 126 (1958): 322–36.

DUFFY, E. *Activation and behavior.* New York: Wiley, 1962.

ELLIS, H. *Studies in the psychology of sex.* New York: Random House, 1936.

EMLEN, A. C., and PERRY, J. B., JR. Child-care arrangements. In Hoffman, L. W., and Nye, F. I., eds., *The working mother.* San Francisco: Jossey-Bass, 1974.

ENOCH, M. D.; TRETHOWAN, W. H.; and BARKER, J. C. The couvade syndrome. In Enoch, M. P., ed., *Some uncommon psychiatric syndromes.* Bristol: John Wright and Sons, 1967.

ERHARDT, A., GREENBERG, N., and MONEY, J. Female gender identity and absence of fetal hormones: Turner's syndrome. *Johns Hopkins Medical Journal* 125 (1970): 237–48.

ERIKSON, E. H. *Childhood and society.* New York: Norton, 1963.

ERIKSON, E. H. The inner and the outer space: Reflections on womanhood. *Daedalus* 93 (1964): 582–606.

ERIKSON, E. H. *Identity: Youth and crisis.* New York: Norton, 1968.

ERIKSON, E. H. Once more the inner space. In *Life history and the historical moment.* New York: Norton, 1975.

ERICKSON, M. T. Relationship between psychological attitudes during pregnancy and complications of pregnancy, labor, and delivery. Proceedings of the 73rd Annual Convention of the American Psychological Association, 1965, 213–14.

ESTELLACHILD, V. Hippie communes. In DeLora, J. S., and DeLora, J. R., eds., *Intimate life styles: Marriage and its alternatives.* Pacific Palisades, Calif.: Goodyear, 1972.

FABRIKANT, B. The psychotherapist and the female patient: Perceptions, misconceptions and change. In Franks, V., and Burtle, V., eds., *Women in therapy.* New York: Brunner/Mazel, 1974.

FANCHER, R. E. *Psychoanalytic psychology.* New York: Norton, 1973.

FESBACH, N. D. Sex differences in children's modes of aggressive responses toward outsiders. *Merrill Palmer Quarterly* 15 (1969): 249–58.

FESHBACH, S. Aggression. In Mussen, P. F., ed., *Carmichael's manual of child psychology.* New York: Wiley, 1970.

FIDELL, L. S. *Put her down on drugs: Prescribed drug usage in women.* Paper read at the Western Psychological Association Meeting, Anaheim, Calif., April 12, 1973.

FIGES, E. *Patriarchal attitudes.* London: Faber and Faber, 1970.

FINGERER, M. E. Psychological sequelae of abortion: Anxiety and depression. *Journal of Community Psychology* 1 (1973): 221–25.

FISH, S. L. *A phenomenology of women.* Unpublished Doctoral Dissertation, Southern Illinois University, 1975.

FISHER, M. Distribution of women students by major fields. Unpublished paper, Office of Student Affairs, Univerisity of South Florida, 1974.

FISHER, S. *The female orgasm.* New York: Basic Books, 1973.

FORD, C. S., and BEACH, F. A. *Patterns of sexual behavior.* New York: Harper, 1951.

FRANKS, V., and BURTLE, V. *Women in therapy.* New York: Brunner/Mazel, 1974.

FRANZWA, H. H. Female roles in women's magazine fiction. In Unger, R. K., and Denmark, F. L., eds., *Woman: Dependent or independent variable.* New York: Psychological Dimensions, 1975.

FRAZER, J. G. *The golden bough.* New York: Macmillan, 1951.

FREUD, S. *An outline of psychoanalysis* (1939). New York: Norton, 1949.

FREUD, S. Fragment of an analysis of a case of hysteria (1905). *Collected Papers,* trans. Strachey, A., and Strachey, J. New York: Basic Books, 1959.

FREUD, S. *Three essays on the theory of sexuality* (1905). New York: Avon Books, 1965.

FREUD, S. Some psychological consequences of the anatomical distinction between the sexes (1925). In Strouse, J., ed., *Women and analysis.* New York: Grossman, 1974.

FREUD, S. Female sexuality (1931). In Strouse, J., ed., *Women and analysis.* New York: Grossman, 1974.

FREUD, S. Femininity (1933). In Strouse, J., ed., *Women and analysis.* New York: Grossman, 1974.

FREUD, S. and BREUER, J. *Studies in hysteria* (1895). New York: Avon Books, 1966.

FROMM-REICHMAN, F., and GUNST, V. K. On the denial of women's sexual pleasure (1950). In Miller, J. B., ed., *Psychoanalysis and women.* New York: Brunner/Mazel, 1973.

FURTMÜLLER, C. Alfred Adler: A biographical essay. In Ansbacher, H. L., and Ansbacher, R. R., eds., *Superiority and social interest.* Evanston, Ill.: Northwestern University Press, 1964.

GALDSTON, I. Other aspects (psychiatric) of the abortion problem. In Calderone, M., ed., *Abortion in the U.S.* New York: Hoeber-Harper, 1958.

GARAI, J. E. Sex differences in mental health. *Genetic Psychology Monographs* 81 (1970): 123–42.

GARAI, J. E., and SCHEINFELD, A. Sex differences in mental and behavioral traits. *Genetic Psychology Monographs* 77 (1968): 162–299.

GARCIA, C. Clinical aspects of oral hormonal contraception. In Calderone, M., ed., *Manual of family planning and contraceptive practice.* Baltimore: Williams and Wilkins, 1970.

GIALLOMBARDO, R. *Society of women: A study of a women's prison.* New York: Wiley, 1966.

GIALLOMBARDO, R. *The social world of imprisoned girls.* New York: Wiley, 1974.

GILDER, G. *Sexual suicide.* New York: Quadrangle, 1973.

GILLESPIE, D. L. Who has the power? The marital struggle. In Freeman, J., ed., *Women: A feminist perspective.* Palo Alto, Calif.: Mayfield, 1975.

GOLDBERG, S., and LEWIS, M. Play behavior in the year-old infant: Early sex differences. *Child Development* 40 (1969): 21–31.

GOLDFARB, W. Childhood psychosis. In Mussen, P. H., ed., *Carmichael's manual of child psychology.* New York: Wiley, 1970.

GOLUB, S. The effect of premenstrual depression and anxiety on personality and cognitive function. Summary of Unpublished Doctoral Dissertation, Fordham University, 1973.

GOODALL, K. Tie line. *Psychology Today,* March 1972, p. 25.

GOODMAN, M., and GOODMAN, S. Over the hill. In Miller, L., ed., *Fourth International Congress of Social Psychiatry: Abstracts of Papers.* Jerusalem: AHVA Cooperative, 1972.

GORDON, R. E., and GORDON, K. K. Factors in pospartum emotional adjustment. *American Journal of Orthopsychiatry* 37 (1967): 359–60.

GOVE, W. R. Sex, marital status, and suicide. *Journal of Health and Social Behavior* 13 (1972): 204–13.

GOVE, W.R., and TUDOR, J. F. Adult sex roles and mental illness. *American Journal of Sociology* 78 (1973): 812–35.

GRADY, K. I., and YOUNG, W. C. Role of the developing rat testis in differentiation of the neural tissues mediating mating behavior. *Journal of Comparative and Physiological Psychology* 59 (1965): 176–82.

GRAEBNER, D. B. A decade of sexism in readers. *Reading Teacher* 26 (1972), no. 1: 52–58.

GRANT, E. C., and PRYSE-DAVIES, J. Effect of oral contraceptives on depressive mood changes and on endometrial monoamine oxidase and phosphatases. *British Medical Journal* 3 (1968): 777–80.

GREEN, M. R., ed., *Interpersonal psychoanalysis: The selected papers of Clara Thompson.* New York: Basic Books, 1964.

GUMP, J. P. Sex-role attitudes and psychological well-being. *Journal of Social Issues* 28 (1972): 79–92.

GUTMANN, D. L. An exploration of ego configurations in middle and late life. In Neugarten, B. L., *et al.,* eds., *Personality in middle and late life.* New York: Atherton, 1964.

HALL, C. S., and LINDZEY, G. *Theories of personality.* New York: Wiley, 1970.

HALL, E. T., JR. *The silent language.* New York: Doubleday, 1959.

HALLER, J. S., and HALLER, R. M. *The physician and sexuality in Victorian America.* Urbana, Ill.: University of Illinois Press, 1974.

HAMBURG, D. A., and LUNDE, D. T. Sex hormones in the development of sex differences in human behavior. In Maccoby, E. E., ed., *The development of sex differences.* Stanford, Calif.: Stanford University Press, 1966.

HANEY, B., and GOLD, M. The juvenile delinquent nobody knows. *Psychology Today* 7 (1973): 48–55.

HARLOW, H. The heterosexual affectional system in monkeys. *American Psychologist* 17 (1962): 1–9.

HARLOW, H., and HARLOW, M. The young monkeys. In *Readings in psychology today.* Del Mar, Calif.: Communications/Research/Machines, 1967.

HARPER, R. A. *Psychoanalysis and psychotherapy.* Englewood Cliffs, N.J.: Prentice-Hall, 1959.

HATFIELD, J. S.; FERGUSON, L. R.; and ALPERT, R. Mother-child interaction and the socialization process. *Child Development* 38 (1967): 365–414.

HAYNER, N. Attitudes toward conjugal visits for prisoners. *Federal Probation* 36 (1972): 43–49.

HEATHERINGTON, E. M. A developmental study of the effects of sex of the dominant parent on sex-role preference, identification, and imitation in children. *Journal of Personality and Social Psychology* 2 (1965): 188–94.

HEDGEPETH, W. Maybe it'll be different here. In DeLora, D. S., and DeLora, J. R., eds., *Intimate life styles.* Pacific Palisades, Calif.: Goodyear, 1972.

HEFFERNAN, E. *Making it in prison: The square, the cool, and the life.* New York: Wiley, 1972.

HEILBRUN, A. B. Sex role identity in adolescent females: A theoretical paradox. *Adolescence* 3 (1968): 79–88. (a)

HEILBRUN, A. B. Sex-role, instrumental-expressive behavior, and psychopathology in females. *Journal of Abnormal Psychology* 73 (1968): 2, 131–36. (b)

HILL, K. T., and SARASON, S. B. The relation of test anxiety and defensiveness to test and school performance over the elementary school years. *Monographs of the Society for Research in Child Development* 31 (1966): no. 104.

HIMES. N. *The medical history of contraception.* New York: Gamut Press, 1963.

HOFFMAN, L. W. Mother's enjoyment of work and effects on the child. In Nye, F. I., and Hoffman, L. W., eds., *The employed mother in America.* Chicago: Rand McNally, 1963.

HOFFMAN, L. W. Early childhood experiences and women's achievement motives. *Journal of Social Issues* 28 (1972): 129–55.

HOFFMAN, L. W., and HOFFMAN, M. L. The value of children to parents. In Fawcett, J. T., ed., *Psychological perspectives on population.* New York: Basic Books, 1973.

HOFFMAN, L. W., and NYE, F. I. *Working mothers.* San Francisco: Jossey-Bass, 1974.

HOGELAND, R. W., ed., *Women and womanhood in America.* Lexington, Mass. Heath, 1973.

HONZIK, M. P. Prediction of individual abilities at age 18 from early family environment. *Proceedings of the 75th Annual Convention of the American Psychological Association,* 1967, 151–52.

HORNER, M. S. Femininity and successful achievement: A basic inconsistency. In Bardwick, J. M.; Douvan, E.; Horner, M. S.; and Gutmann, D., eds., *Feminine personality and conflict.* Belmont, Calif.: Brooks/Cole, 1970.

HORNER, M. S. Toward an understanding of achievement-related conflicts in women. In Stacey, J.; Gereaud, S.; and Daniels, J., eds. *And Jill came tumbling after: Sexism in American education.* New York: Dell, 1974.

HORNEY. K. *The neurotic personality of our time.* New York: Norton, 1937.

HORNEY, K. *Neurosis and human growth.* New York: Norton, 1950.

HORNEY, K. *Feminine psychology,* New York: Norton, 1973.

HORNEY, K. The problem of feminine masochism (1935). In Horney, K., *Feminine psychology.* New York: Norton, 1973.

HORNEY, K. The overvaluation of love (1934). In Horney, K., *Feminine psychology.* New York: Norton, 1973.

HORNEY, K. The flight from womanhood (1926). In Horney, K., *Feminine psychology.* New York: Norton, 1973.

HOWARD, E. M., and HOWARD, J. L. Women in institutions: Treatment in prisons and mental hospitals. In Franks, V., and Burtle, V., eds., *Women in therapy.* New York: Brunner/Mazel, 1974.

HOWARD, S. *The silver cord.* New York: Charles Scribner's Sons, 1927.

HOWELL, M. C. What medical schools teach about women. *New England Journal of Medicine 291 (1974): 304–7.*

HUGHES, E. Angry in retirement. *Human Behavior* 3 (1974): 9, 56–59.

HUNT, M. *Sexual behavior in the seventies.* Chicago: Playboy Press, 1974.

HUNT, M. Sexual behavior in the 1970's. *Playboy* 20, no. 10 (October 1973): 84–88, 197–207.

HUNT, M. Sexual behavior in the 1970's. *Playboy* 20, no. 11 (November 1973): 74–75.

HUNT, M. Sexual behavior in the 1970's. *Playboy* 20, no. 12 (December 1973): 90–91, 256.

HUNT, M. Sexual behavior in the 1970's. *Playboy* 21, no. 1 (January 1974): 60–61, 686–87.

HUNT, M. Sexual behavior in the 1970's. *Playboy* 21, no. 2 (February 1974): 54–55, 176–77.

IGLITZIN, L. B. A child's eye view of sex roles. Paper presented at American Political Science Association Annual Meeting, Washington, D.C., 1972.

INGIULLA, W.; ADEZATI, L.; FORLEO, R.; and INGRASSIA, F. Menopause and male climacteric: Some physiological and clinical aspects. *Giornale de Gerontologia* 35 (1966): 5–60.

JACKLIN, C. N., MACCOBY, E. E., and DICK, A. E. Barrier behavior and toy preference: Sex differences (and their absence) in the year-old child. *Child Development* 44 (1973): 196–200.

JACOBSON, W. D. *Power and interpersonal relations.* Belmont, Calif.: Wadsworth, 1972.

JAKOBOVITS, I. Jewish views on abortion. In Walbert, D. F., and Butler, J. D., eds., *Abortion, society, and the law.* Cleveland: Press of Case Western Reserve, 1973.

JAMES, W. H. The effect of maternal psychological stress on the foetus. *British Journal of Psychiatry* 115 (1969): 811–25.

JANEWAY, E. *Man's world, woman's place.* New York: Dell, 1971.

JANEWAY, E. On "Female sexuality". In Strouse, J., ed., *Women and analysis.* New York: Grossman, 1974.

JANOWSKY, D. S., and DAVIS, J. M. Progesterone-estrogen effects on uptake and release of norepinephrine by synaptosomes. *Life Sciences* 9 (1970), 525–31.

JERSILD, A. T., and HOLMES, F. B. Children's fears. *Child Development Monographs* 20 (1935).

JONES, E. *The life and work of Sigmund Freud,* vol. 1. New York: Basic Books, 1953.

JONES, E. *The life and work of Sigmund Freud,* vol. 2. New York: Basic Books, 1955.

JONES, E. *The life and work of Sigmund Freud,* vol. 3. New York: Basic Books, 1957.

JOSLYN, W. D. Androgen-induced social dominance in infant female rhesus monkeys. *Journal of Child Psychology and Psychiatry* 14 (1973): 137–45.

JOST, A. A new look at the mechanism controlling sex differentiation in mammals. *Johns Hopkins Medical Journal* 130 (1972): 38–53.

JOURARD, S. M. *Disclosing man to himself.* Princeton, N.J.: Van Nostrand, 1968.

KAGAN, J. Acquisition and significance of sex typing and sex role identity. In Hoffman, M., and Hoffman, L., eds., *Review of Child Development Research,* vol. 1. New York: Russell Sage, 1964.

KAGAN, J. *Change and continuity in infancy.* New York: Wiley, 1971.

KAGAN, J. The emergence of sex differences. *School Review* 80 (1972): 217–27.

KAGAN, J., and KOGAN, N. Individuality and cognitive performance. In Mussen, P. H., ed., *Carmichael's manual of child psychology.* New York: Wiley, 1970.

KAGAN, J., and MOSS, H. A. *Birth to maturity: A study in psychological development.* New York: Wiley, 1962.

KAPLAN, H. S. *The new sex therapy.* New York: Brunner/Mazel, 1974.

KARMEL, M. *Thank you, Dr. Lamaze.* Philadelphia: Lippincott, 1959.

KASTEN, K. Toward a psychology of being: A masculine mystique. *Journal of Humanistic Psychology* 12 (1972): 23–43.

KATCHADOURIAN, H. and LUNDE, D. *Fundamentals of human sexuality.* 2d ed. New York: Holt Rinehart & Winston, 1975.

KAUFMAN, S. A. *The ageless woman.* New York: Dell, 1967.

KELMAN, H. Karen Horney on feminine psychology. *American Journal of Psychoanalysis* 27 (1967): 163–83.

KIMMEL, D. C. *Adulthood and aging.* New York: Wiley, 1974.

KIMURA, D. Functional asymmetry of the brain in dichotic listening. *Cortex* 3 (1967): 163–78.

KINSEY, A. C.; POMEROY, W. B.; and MARTIN, C. E. *Sexual behavior in the human male.* Philadelphia: W. B. Saunders, 1948.

KINSEY, A. C.; POMEROY. W. B.; MARTIN, C. E.; and GEBHARD, P. H. *Sexual behavior in the human female.* Philadelphia: W. B. Saunders, 1953.

KIRK, H. D. Differential sex preference in family formation. *Canadian Review of Sociology and Anthropology* 1 (1964): 31–48.

KIRSH, B. Consciousness-raising groups as therapy for women. In Franks, V., and Burtle, V., eds., *Women in therapy.* New York: Brunner/Mazel, 1974.

KLEIN, V. *The feminine character,* 2d ed. Urbana: University of Illinois Press, 1971.

KLUCKHOHN, C., and MURRAY, H. A. *Personality in nature, society, and culture,* 1st ed. New York: Knopf, 1949.

KNOX, C., and KIMURA, D. Cerebral processing of nonverbal sounds in boys and girls. *Neuropsychologia* 8 (1970): 227–37.

KOHLBERG, L. A. A cognitive-development analysis of children's sex-role concepts and attitudes. In Maccoby, E. E., ed., *The development of sex differences.* Stanford, Calif.: Stanford University Press, 1966.

KONOPKA, G. *The adolescent girl in conflict.* Englewood Cliffs, N.J.: Prentice-Hall, 1966.

KOONTZ, E. Statement before the D.C. Commission on the Status of Women. November 4, 1971.

KREUZ, L. E., and ROSE, R. M. Assessment of aggressive behavior and plasma testosterone in a young criminal population. *Psychosomatic Medicine* 34 (1972): 321–32.

KUHN, T. S. *The structure of scientific revolutions.* Chicago: The University of Chicago Press, 1970.

KUMMER, H. Two variations in the social organizations of baboons. In Jay, P. C., ed., *Primates—studies in adaptation and variability.* New York: Holt, Rinehart and Winston, 1968.

KUTNER, S. J. A survey of fear of pregnancy and depression. *Journal of Psychology* 79 (1971): 263–72.

LAMBERT, W. E.; YACKLEY, A.; and HEIN, R. N. Child training values of English Canadian and French Canadian parents. *Canadian Journal of Behavioral Science* 3 (1971): 217–36.

LAMPL-DE GROOT, J. The evolution of the Oedipus complex in women (1928). In Ruitenbeek, H., ed., *Psychoanalysis and female sexuality.* New Haven, Conn.: College and University Press, 1966.

LEAR, M. W. Save the spouses rather than the marriage. *The New York Times Magazine,* August 13, 1972.

LENNANE, K. J., and LENNANE, R. J. Alleged psychogenic disorders in women—A possible manifestation of sexual prejudice. *The New England Journal of Medicine* 288 (1973): 288–92.

LERNER, G. *Black women in white America: A documentary history.* New York: Vintage Books, 1973.

416 References

LERNER, I. M. *Heredity, evolution, and society.* San Francisco: W. H. Freeman, 1968.

LEVINE, A. G. Marital and occupational plans of women in professional schools: law, medicine, nursing, teaching. Unpublished Ph.D. Dissertation, Yale University, 1968. Cited in Hoffman, L. W., and Hoffman, M. L., The value of children to parents. In Fawcett, J. T. ed., *Psychological perspectives on population.* New York: Basic Books, 1973.

LEWIS, M. Parents and children: Sex-role development. *School Review* 80 (1972): 229–40.

LEWIS, O. Manly-hearted women among the north Piegan. *American Anthropologist* 43 (1941): 173–87.

LINDZEY, G.; LOEHLIN, J.; MANOSEVITZ, M.; and THIESSEN, D. Behavioral genetics. In Mussen, P. H., and Zweig, M. R. R., eds., *Annual review of psychology.* Palo Alto, Calif.: Annual Reviews, Inc., 1971.

LINN, L. Physician characteristics and attitudes toward legitimate use of psychotherapeutic drugs. *Journal of Health and Social Behavior* 12 (1971): 132–40.

LIPMAN-BLUMEN, J. How ideology shapes women's lives. *Scientific American* 226 (1972): 34–42.

LIPPSETT, L., and LEVY, N. Electrotactual threshold in the neonate. *Child Development* 30 (1959): 547–54.

LOCKE, B. Z., and GARDNER, E. A. Psychiatric disorders among the patients of general practitioners and internists. *Public Health Report* 84 (1969): 2, 167–173.

LOESCH, J. G., and GREENBERG, N. H. Some specific areas of conflict observed during pregnancy: A comparative study of married and unmarried pregnant women. *American Journal of Orthopsychiatry* 32 (1962): 624–36.

LOMBROSO, C., and FERRERO, W. *The female offender.* New York: Appleton-Century-Crafts, 1916.

LONDON, P., and ROSENHAN, D. Personality dynamics. In Farnsworth, P. R.; McNemar, O.; and McNemar, Q., eds., *Annual Review of Psychology.* Palo Alto, Calif.: Annual Reviews, Inc., 1964.

LOOFT, W. R. Sex differences in the expression of vocational aspirations by elementary school children. *Developmental Psychology* 5 (1971): 366.

LOPATA, H. Z. *Occupation: Housewife.* New York: Oxford University Press, 1971.

LOPATA, H. Z. *Widowhood in an American city.* Cambridge, Mass.: Schenkman, 1973. (a)

LOPATA, H. Z. Social relations of black and white widowed women in a northern metropolis. *American Journal of Sociology* 78 (1973): 1003–10. (b)

LUNDE, D. T. Sex hormones, mood, and behavior. Paper presented at the 6th Annual Symposium, Society of Medical Psychoanalysis, New York, 1973.

LYNN, D. B. A note on sex differences in the development of masculine and feminine identification. *Psychological Review* 66 (1959): 126–35.

LYNN, D. B. The process of learning parental and sex-role identification. In Schaeffer, D. L., ed., *Sex differences in personality: Readings.* Belmont, Calif.: Brooks/Cole, 1971.

MACCOBY, E. E. Sex differences in intellectual functioning. In Maccoby, E. E., ed., *The development of sex differences.* Stanford, Calif.: Stanford University Press, 1966.

MACCOBY, E. E., and JACKLIN, C. *The psychology of sex differences.* Stanford, Calif.: Stanford University Press, 1974.

MACLEISH, K., and LAUNOIS, J. Stone age cavemen of Mindanao. *National Geographic* 142 (1972): 219–48.

MAINARDI, P. The politics of housework. In DeLora, J. S., and Delora, J. R., eds., *Intimate life style: Marriage and its alternatives.* Pacific Palisades, Calif: Goodyear, 1972.

MARSHALL, D. S., and SUGGS, R. C., eds. *Human sexual behavior.* New York: Basic Books, 1971.

MASLOW, A. Self-esteem (dominance feeling) and sexuality in women. *Journal of Social Psychology* 16 (1942): 259–94.

MASLOW, A. *Motivation and personality.* New York: Harper & Row, 1954.

MASLOW, A. *The further reaches of human nature.* New York: Viking, 1971.

MASTERS, W., and JOHNSON, V. *Human sexual response.* Boston: Little, Brown, 1966.

MASTERS, W., and JOHNSON, V. Human sexual response: The aging female and the aging male. In Neugarten, B., ed., *Middle age and aging.* Chicago: University of Chicago Press, 1968.

MASTERS, W., and JOHNSON, V. *Human sexual inadequacy.* Boston: Little, Brown, 1970.

MAY, R. Sex differences in fantasy patterns. *Journal of Projective Techniques* 30 (1966): 576–86.

MAYER, J. Better-educated mothers lead trend toward breast feeding. *Houston Post,* August 20, 1972.

MCCARY, J. L. *Human sexuality.* New York: Van Nostrand, 1973.

MCCLEARN, G. E. Genetic influences on behavior and development. In Mussen, P. H., ed., *Carmichael's manual of child psychology.* New York: John Wiley and Sons, 1970.

MCCLINTOCK, M. K. Menstrual synchrony and suppression. *Nature* 229 (1971): 244–45.

MCINTYRE, A. Sex differences in children's aggression. *Proceedings of the 80th Annual Convention of the American Psychological Association* 7 (1972): 93–94.

MCKAIN, W. C., *Retirement marriage.* Storrs, Conn.: Storrs Agriculture Experiment Station, University of Connecticut, 1969.

MEAD, M. *Coming of age in Samoa.* New York: William Morrow, 1932.

MEAD, M. *Sex and temperament in three primitive societies.* New York: William Morrow, 1935.

MEAD, M. *Blackberry winter.* New York: William Morrow, 1972.

MEAD, M. On Freud's view of female psychology. In Strouse, J., ed., *Women and analysis.* New York: Grossman, 1974.

MEAD, M., and HEYMAN, K. *Family.* New York: Macmillan, 1965.

MEANS, C. C. A historian's view. In Hall, R. E., ed., *Abortion in a changing world.* New York: Columbia University Press, 1970.

MEDNICK, M. T. S., and WEISSMAN, H. J. The psychology of women—selected topics. In Rosenzweig, M. R., and Porter, L. W., eds., Annual Review of Psychology. Palo Alto, Calif.: Annual Reviews, Inc., 1975.

MEDNICK, M. T. S.; TANGRI, S. J.; and HOFFMAN, L. W. *Women and achievement: Social and motivational analyses.* Washington, D.C.: Hemisphere, 1975.

METROPOLITAN LIFE INSURANCE COMPANY. Chances of dependency. Statistical Bulletin, 50 (January 1969): 10–11.

MILL, J. S. On the subjection of women (1869). In Rossi, A., ed., *The feminist papers.* New York: Columbia University Press, 1973.

MILLER, J. B. *Psychoanalysis and women.* New York: Brunner/Mazel, 1973.

MILLETT, K. *Sexual politics.* New York: Avon, 1971.

MINTON, C.; KAGAN, J.; and LEVINE, J. A. Maternal control and obedience in the two-year-old. *Child Development* 42 (1971): 1873–94.

MINTURN, L., and HITCHCOCK, J. T. The Rajputs of Khalapur, India. In Whiting, B. B., ed., *Six cultures*. New York: Wiley, 1963.

MISCHEL, W. Sex typing and socialization. In Mussen, P. H., ed., *Carmichael's manual of child psychology*. New York: Wiley, 1970.

MITCHELL, J. Women: The longest revolution. *New Left Review*, Nov./Dec. 1966, 11–37.

MITCHELL, J. On Freud and the distinction between the sexes. In Strouse, J., ed., *Women and analysis*. New York: Grossman, 1974. (a)

MITCHELL, J. *Psychoanalysis and feminism*. New York: Pantheon, 1974. (b)

MONEY, J. Psychosexual differentiation. In Money, J., ed., *Sex research: New developments*. New York: Holt, Rinehart and Winston, 1965.

MONEY, J. Determinants of human sexual identity and behavior. In Sager, C. J., and Kaplan, H. S., eds., *Progress in group and family therapy*. New York: Brunner/Mazel, 1972. (a)

MONEY, J. Identification and complementation in the differentiation of gender identity. *Danish Medical Bulletin* 19 (1972): 265–68. (b)

MONEY, J., and EHRHARDT, A. *Man and woman, boy and girl*. Baltimore: The Johns Hopkins University Press, 1972.

MONROE, R. *Schools of psychoanalytic thought*. New York: Dryden, 1955.

MOORE, M. Aggression themes in a binocular rivalry situation. *Journal of Personality and Social Psychology* 3 (1966): 685–88.

MOOS, R. H. Typology of menstrual cycle symptoms. *American Journal of Obstetrics and Gynecology* 103 (1969): 390–402.

MORAN, R. The singles in the seventies. In DeLora, J. S., and DeLora, J. R., eds., *Intimate life styles: Marriage and its alternatives*. Pacific Palisades, Calif.: Goodyear, 1972.

MORTON, J. H., ADDISON, H., ADDISON, R. G., HUNT, L., and SULLIVAN, J. J. A clinical study of premenstrual tension. *American Journal of Obstetrics and Gynecology* 65 (1953): 1182–91.

MOSS, H. A. Sex, age, and state as determinants of mother-infant interaction. *Merrill Palmer Quarterly* 13 (1967): 19–36.

MOSS, Z. (pseud.). It hurts to be alive and obsolete: The aging woman. In Morgan, R., ed., *Sisterhood is powerful: An anthology of writings from the women's liberation movement*. New York: Vintage Press, 1970.

MONTAGUE, A. Smoking, pregnancy, and sex. *Sexology*, November 1963, 220–22.

MUELLER, E. Attitudes toward the economics of family size and their relation to fertility. Unpublished manuscript, University of Michigan. Cited in Hoffman, L. W., and Hoffman, M. L. The value of children to parents. In Fawcett, J. T., ed., *Psychological perspectives on population*. New York: Basic Books, 1973.

MUNCY, R. L. *Sex and marriage in utopian communities: 19th century America*. Bloomington, Ind.: Indiana University Press, 1973.

MURAI, N., and SATO, T. Psychological study on pregnancy-relationship of maternal emotional characteristics to body weight gain of newborn infants. *Journal of the Japanese Psychosomatic Society* 11 (1971): 25–29.

MUSSEN, P. H., and RUTHERFORD, E. Parent-child relations and parental personality in relation to young children's sex-role preferences. *Child Development* 34 (1963): 589–607.

NAHUM, L. H. Amniocentesis in prediction of chromosomal and behavioral abnormalities. *Connecticut Medicine* 34 (1970): 10, 12.

NEUGARTEN, B. L. Summary and implications. In Neugarten, B. L., et al., eds., *Personality in middle and late life*. New York: Atherton, 1964.

NEUGARTEN, B. L. Education and the life cycle. *School Review* 80 (1972): 209–16.

NEUGARTEN, B. L. A new look at menopause. In Tavris, C., ed., *The female experience.* Del Mar, Calif.: Communications/Research/Machines, 1973.

NEUGARTEN, B. L., *et al.*, eds., *Personality in middle and late life.* New York: Atherton, 1964.

NEUGARTEN, B. L., and GUTMANN, D. L. Age-sex roles and personality in middle age: A thematic apperception study. In Neugarten, B. L., *et al.*, eds., *Personality in middle and late life.* New York: Atherton, 1964.

NEWSON, J., and NEWSON, E. *Four years old in an urban community.* Harmondworth, England: Pelican Books, 1968.

NEWTON, M. Breast-feeding. *Psychology Today* 2 (1968): 34, 68–70.

NEWTON, N., and NEWTON, M. Childbirth in crosscultural perspective. In Howells, J. G., ed., *Modern perspectives in psycho-obstetrics.* New York: Brunner/Mazel, 1972.

NILSSON, A., and ALNIGREN, P. Para-natal emotional adjustment—A prospective investigation of 165 women. Pt. II. *Acta Psychiatrica Scandinavica* 220 (1970): 65–151.

NORTMAN, D. *Parental age as a factor in pregnancy outcome and child development.* Reports on Population/Family Planning. The Population Council, 245 Park Avenue, New York, N.Y., August, 1974.

O'BRIEN, J. S.; OKADA, S.; FILLERUP, D. L.; VEATH, M. L.; ADORNATO, B.; BRENNER, P. H.; and LEROY, J. G. Tay-Sachs disease: Prenatal diagnosis. *Science* 172 (1971): 61–67.

OETZEL, R. M. Classified summary of research in sex differences. In Maccoby, E. E., ed., *The development of sex differences.* Stanford, Calif.: Stanford University Press, 1966.

OLIVER, W. A. Childbirth expectancies and experiences as a function of locus of control and Lamaze training. (Doctoral dissertation, Ohio State University, 1972). University Microfilms No. 72-27074. *Dissertation Abstracts International,* Ann Arbor, Michigan.

O'NEILL, G., and O'NEILL, N. *Open marriage.* New York: Avon, 1972.

OSTRUM, A. Childbirth in America. In Hammer, S., ed., *Women: Body and culture.* New York: Harper & Row, 1975.

OVERSTREET, E. W. Female sterilization. In Calderone, M., ed., *Manual of family planning and contraceptive practice.* Baltimore: Williams & Wilkins, 1970.

PARKE, R.; O'LEARY, S.; and WEST, S. Mother-father-newborn interaction: Effects of maternal medication, labor, and sex of infant. *Proceedings of the 80th Annual Convention of the American Psychological Association,* 1972.

PARLEE, M. B. The premenstrual syndrome. *Psychological Bulletin* 80 (1973): 454–65.

PARSONS, T. *Essays in sociological theory, pure and applied,* 2d ed. Glencoe, Ill.: The Free Press, 1954.

PARSONS, T., and BALES, R. E. *Family socialization and interaction process.* Glencoe, Ill.: The Free Press, 1955.

PAULEY, F. R. Sex differences and legal school entrance age. *Journal of Educational Research* 45 (1951): 1–9.

PAYAK, B. Understanding the female offender. *Federal Probation* 27 (1963): 7–12.

PENDERGRASS, V. E. Women as clinicians in private practice. *American Psychologist* 29 (1974): 533–35.

PERLMUTTER, J. F. Drug addiction in pregnant women. *American Journal of Obstetrics and Gynecology* 99 (1967): 569–72.

PHILLIPS, D., and SEGAL, B. Sexual status and psychiatric symptoms. *American Sociological Review* 34 (1969): 58–72.

POHLMAN, E. H. Influencing people to *want* fewer children. Paper presented at the American Psychological Association Convention, Miami, Florida, September 1970.

POLLACK, O. *The criminality of women.* Philadelphia: University of Pennsylvania Press, 1950.

POLOMA, M. M. The married professional woman: An empirical examination of three myths. (Doctoral Dissertation, Case Western Reserve University, 1971). University Microfilms No. 71-19042. *Dissertation Abstracts International,* Ann Arbor, Michigan.

POLOMA, M. M., and GARLAND, T. N. The myth of the egalitarian family: Familial roles and the professionally employed wife. In Theodore, A., ed., *The professional woman.* Cambridge, Mass.: Schenkman, 1971.

Population council annual report. New York: The Population Council, 1973.

Population council annual report. New York: The Population Council, 1974.

PORTEUS, S., and BABCOCK, M. E. *Temperament and race.* Boston: Gorham Press, 1926.

PRATHER, J., and FIDELL, L. Put her down and drug her up. Paper presented at American Sociological Association Meeting, New Orleans, Louisiana, August, 1972.

PRINGLE, M. L. K.; BUTLER, N. R.; and DAVIE, R. *Eleven thousand seven-year olds.* London: Longmans, 1966.

PUNER, M. Will you still love me? *Human Behavior* 3 (1974): 6, 42–48.

RAINWATER, L. *Family design: Marital sexuality, family size, and contraception.* Chicago: Aldine, 1965.

RAMEY, J.W. Communes, group marriage and the upper-middle class. In Smith, J. R., and Smith, L. G., eds., *Beyond Monogamy.* Baltimore: The Johns Hopkins University Press, 1974.

RAND, L. M., and MILLER, A. L. A developmental cross-sectioning of women's careers and marriage attitudes and life plans. *Journal of Vocational Behavior* 2 (1972): 317–31.

RICE, J. K., and RICE, D. G. Implications of the women's liberation movement for psychotherapy. *American Journal of Psychiatry* 30 (1973): 191–96.

RIESMAN, D., GLAZER, N., and DENNY, R. *The lonely crowd.* Garden City, N.Y.: Doubleday, 1953.

RIOPELLE, A. J., and ROGERS, C. M. Age change in chimpanzees. In Shrier, A. M.: Harlow, H. F.; and Stollnitz, F., eds., *Behavior of non-human primates.* New York: Academic Press, 1965.

RIVENBARK, W. H., III. Self disclosure among adolescents. *Psychological Reports* 28 (1971): 35–42.

RODGERS, D. A., and ZIEGLER, F. J. Psychological reactions to surgical contraception. In Fawcett, J. T., ed. *Psychological perspectives on population.* New York: Basic Books, 1973.

ROGERS, K. *The troublesome helpmate: A history of misogyny in literature.* Seattle: University of Washington Press, 1966.

ROSE, R. M.; GORDON, T. P.; and BERNSTEIN, I. S. Plasma testosterone levels in the male rhesus: Influences of sexual and social stimuli. *Science* 178 (1972): 643–45.

ROSEN, B. S.; LOCKE, B. Z.; GOLDBERG, I. D.; and BABIGIAN, H. Identification of emotional disturbance in patients seen in general medical clinics. *Hospital and Community Psychiatry* 23 (1972): no. 12, 364–70.

ROSEN, D. H. *Lesbianism: A study of female homosexuality.* Springfield, Ill.: Charles C Thomas, 1974.

ROSEN, J. L., and NEUGARTEN, B. L. Ego functions in the middle and late years: A thematic apperception study. In Neuarten, B. L., *et al.*, eds., *Personality in middle and late life.* New York: Atherton, 1964.

ROSENBERG, K. M.; DENENBERG, V. H.; ZARROW, M. X.; and BONNIE, L. F. Effects of neonatal castration and testosterone on the rat's pup-killing behavior and activity. *Physiology and Behavior* 7 (1971): 363–68.

ROSENBLATT, J. S. The development of maternal responsiveness in the rat. *American Journal of Orthopsychiatry* 30 (1969): 36–56.

ROSENKRANTZ, P.; VOGEL, S.; BEE, H.; BROVERMAN, I.; and BROVERMAN, D. M. Sex-role stereotypes and self-concepts in college students. *Journal of Consulting and Clinical Psychology* 3 (1968): 287–95.

ROSSI, A. Equality between the sexes: An immodest proposal. *Daedalus* 93 (1964): 607–52.

ROSSI, A. *The feminist papers: From Adams to de Beauvoir.* New York: Columbia University Press, 1973.

ROTH, P. *Portnoy's complaint.* New York: Random House, 1967.

ROTHBART, M. K. Birth order and mother-child interaction in an achievement situation. *Journal of Personality and Social Psychology* 17 (1971): 113–20.

ROTHBART, M. K., and MACCOBY, E. E. Parents' differential reactions to sons and daughters. *Journal of Personality and Social Psychology* 4 (1966): 237–43.

ROWE, I. L. Prescriptions of psychotropic drugs by general practitioners. *Medical Journal of Australia* 1 (1973): 642–44.

ROY, P. Adolescent roles: Rural-urban differentials. In Nye, F. I., and Hoffman, L. W., eds., *The employed mother in America.* Chicago: Rand McNally, 1963.

RUBIN, J. Z.; PROVENZANO, F. J.; and LURIA, Z. The eye of the beholder: Parents' views on sex of newborns. *American Journal of Orthopsychiatry* 44 (1974): 512–19.

SANFORD, N. Personality: Its place in psychology. In Koch, S., ed., *Psychology: A study of a science.* New York: McGraw-Hill, 1963.

SARVIS, B., and RODMAN, H. *The abortion controversy.* New York: Columbia University Press, 1973.

SAUCIER, J. F. Correlates of the long postpartum taboo: A cross-cultural study. *Current Anthropology* 13 (1972): 238–49.

SCHAAR, K. Suicide rate high among women psychologists. *APA Monitor* 5 (1974): 1, 10.

SCHILDKRAUT, J. J. The catecholamine hypothesis of affective disorders: A review of supporting evidence, *American Journal of Psychiatry* 122 (1965): 509–22.

SCHULZ, D. A. *The changing family: Its function and future.* Englewood Cliffs, N.J.: Prentice-Hall, 1972.

SCULLY, D., and BART, P. A funny thing happened on the way to the orifice: Women in gynecology textbooks. *American Journal of Sociology* 78 (1973): 1045–50.

SEARS, P. S., and FELDMAN, D. H. Teacher interactions with boys and with girls. In Stacey, J.; Bereaud, S.; and Daniels, J., eds., *And Jill came tumbling after: Sexism in American education.* New York: Dell, 1974.

SEARS, R. R.; RAU, L.; and ALPERT, R. *Identification and child-rearing.* Stanford, Calif.: Stanford University Press, 1965.

SHAFER, N. Helping women through the change of life. *Sexology* 36 (1970): 54–56.

SHAINESS, N. Feminine identity and mothering. In Masserman, J. H., ed., *Science and Psychoanalysis,* vol. 7. New York: Grune and Stratton, 1964.

SHANAN, J.; BRZEZINSKI, H.; SHILMAN, F.; and SHARON, M. Active coping behavior, anxiety, and cortical steroid excretion in the prediction of transient amenorrhea. *Behavioral Science* 10 (1965): 461–65.

SHEPHERD, W., and PETERSON, J. Are there sex differences in infancy? *JSAS Catalog of Selected Documents in Psychology* 3 (1973): 121.

SHERFEY, M. J. *The nature and evolution of female sexuality.* New York: Random House, 1972.

SHERMAN, J. *On the psychology of women.* Springfield, Ill.,: Charles C Thomas, 1971.

SHIELDS, S. A. The variability hypothesis and sex differences in intelligence. Unpublished manuscript, 1974. (Available from Department of Psychology, Pennsylvania State University, State College, Pennsylvania.)

SHIELDS, S. A. Functionalism, Darwinism, and the psychology of women. *American Psychologist* 30 (1975): 739–754.

SHOPE, D. F. *Interpersonal sexuality.* Philadelphia: W. B. Saunders, 1975.

SHULMAN, A. A marriage agreement. In Perrucci, C. C., and Targ, D. B., eds., *Marriage and the family.* New York: David McKay, 1974.

SIDEL, R. *Women and child care in China.* Baltimore: Penguin, 1973.

SINGER, I., and SINGER, J. Types of female orgasm. *Journal of Sex Research* 8 (1972): 255–67.

SINGER, J. E.; WESTPHAL, M.; and NISWANDER, K. R. Sex differences in the incidence of neonatal abnormalities and abnormal performance in early childhood. *Child Development* 39 (1968): 103–122.

SJOVALL, E. Coitus interruptus. In Calderone, M., ed., *Manual of family planning and contraceptive practice.* Baltimore: Williams & Wilkins, 1970.

SKULTANS, V. The symbolic significance of menstruation and the menopause. *Man* 5 (1970): 639–51.

SMITH, E. M. A follow-up study of women who request abortion. *American Journal of Orthopsychiatry* 43 (1973): 575–85.

SMITH, J. R., and SMITH, L. G., eds. *Beyond monogamy.* Baltimore: The Johns Hopkins University Press, 1974.

SOLBERG, D. A.; BUTLER, J.; and WAGNER, N. N. Sexual behavior in pregnancy. *New England Journal of Medicine* 288 (1973): 1098–1103.

SONTAG, S. The double standard of aging. *Saturday Review* 55 (1972): 39, 29–38.

SORENSON, R. C. *Adolescent sexuality in contemporary America,* (The Sorenson Report). New York: World Publishing, 1973.

SPENCE, J. T.; HELMREICH, R.; and STAPP, J. The personal attributes questionnaire: A measure of sex-role stereotypes and masculinity-femininity. *JSAS Catalog of Selected Documents in Psychology* 4 (1974): 43.

SPIELBERGER, C. D.; LUSHENE, R. E.; and MCADOO, W. G. Theory and measurement of anxiety states. In Cattell, R. B., ed., *Handbook of Modern Personality Theory.* Chicago: Aldine, 1970.

SPITZ, R., and WOLF, K. M. Anaclitic depression: An inquiry into the genesis of psychiatric conditions in early childhood. In *The psychoanalytic study of the child,* vol. 2. New York: International Universities Press, 1946.

SPRANGER, E. *Types of men,* trans. Pigors, P. J. W. Halle: Niemeyer, 1928.

STACEY, J.; BEREAUD, S.; and DANIELS, J. *And Jill came tumbling after: Sexism in American education.* New York: Dell, 1974.

STAFFORD-CLARK, D. *What Freud really said.* New York: Schocken, 1965.

STEIN, A. H., and BAILEY, M. M. The socialization of achievement orientation in females. *Psychological Bulletin* 80 (1973): 345–66.

STENGEL, E. *Suicide and attempted suicide.* Baltimore: Penguin, 1964.

STEVENSON, H. W.; HALE, G. A.; HILL, K. T.; and MOELY, B. E. Determinants of children's preference for adults. *Child Development* 38 (1967): 1–14.

STOLLER, R. J. The "bedrock" of masculinity and femininity: Bisexuality. *Archives of General Psychiatry* 26 (1972): 207–12.

STOLLER, R. J. Facts and fancies: An examination of Freud's concept of bisexuality. In Strouse, J., ed., *Women and analysis.* New York: Grossman, 1974.

STROUSE, J., ed. *Women and analysis.* New York: Grossman, 1974.

SUTHERLAND, H., and STEWART, I. A critical analysis of the pre-menstrual syndrome, *Lancet* 1 (1965): 1180–93.

SWANSON, H. H. Effects of castration at birth in hamsters of both sexes on luteinization of ovarian implants, oestrous cycles and sexual behavior. *Journal of Reproduction and Fertility* 21 (1970): 183–86.

SZASZ, T. S. *The myth of mental illness.* New York: Hoeber-Harper, 1961.

SZASZ, T. S. *The manufacture of madness.* New York: Harper & Row, 1970.

TANNER, J. M. Physical growth. In Mussen, P. H., ed., *Carmichael's manual of child psychology.* New York: Wiley, 1970.

TANZER, D. Natural childbirth: Pain or peak experience. In Tavris, C., ed., *The female experience.* Del Mar, Calif.: Communications/Research/Machines, 1973.

TAUSSIG, F. J. *Abortion, spontaneous and induced.* St. Louis: C. V. Mosby Co., 1936.

TAYLOR, C. W., and BARRON, F. A look ahead. In Taylor, C. W., and Barron, F., eds., *Scientific creativity: Its recognition and development.* New York: Wiley, 1963.

TEMUR, S. Socio-economic determinants of differential fertility in Turkey, The Second European Population Conference, Strasbourg, 1971.

TERMAN, L. M., and ODEN, M. H. *Genetic studies of genius,* vol. 4. Stanford, Calif.: Stanford University Press, 1947.

TERMAN, L. M., and ODEN, M. H. *Genetic studies of genius,* vol. 5. Stanford, Calif: Stanford University Press, 1959.

THOMPSON, C. Cultural pressures in the psychology of women (1942). In Green, M. R., ed., *Interpersonal psychoanalysis: The selected papers of Clara Thompson.* New York: Basic Books, 1964.

THOMPSON, C. Some effects of the derogatory attitude toward female sexuality (1950). In Green, M. R., ed., *Interpersonal psychoanalysis: The selected papers of Clara Thompson.* New York: Basic Books, 1964.

THOMPSON, C. Sullivan and psychoanalysis (1952). In Green, M. R., ed., *Interpersonal psychoanalysis: The selected papers of Clara Thompson.* New York: Basic Books, 1964.

THOMPSON, C. Working women (1953). In Green, M. R., ed., *Interpersonal psychoanalysis: The selected papers of Clara Thompson.* New York: Basic Books, 1964.

THOMPSON, C. Problems of womanhood: In Green, M. R., ed., *Interpersonal psychoanalysis: The selected papers of Clara Thompson.* New York: Basic Books, 1964.

TREADWAY, C. R.; KANE, J. F., JR.; JARRAHI-ZADEH, A.; and LIPTON, M. A. A psychoendocrine study of pregnancy and the puerperium. In Unger, R. K., and Denmark, F. L., eds., *Woman: Dependent or independent variable?* New York: Psychological Dimensions, 1975.

TROLL, L. E.; NEUGARTEN, B. L.; and KRAINES, R. J. Similarities in values and other personality characteristics in college students and their parents. *Merill-Palmer Quarterly* 15 (1969): 323–36.

TYLDEN, E. Hyperemesis and physiological vomiting. *Journal of Psychosomatic Research* 12 (1968): 85–93.

UDDENBERG, N., ALMGREN, P. E., and NILSSON, A. Preference for sex of the child among pregnant women. *Journal of Biosocial Science* 3 (1971): 267–80.

UITS, C. Self image and roles. In *No longer young.* Work Group Reports from the 26th Annual Conference on Aging, Institute of Gerontology, University of Michigan and Wayne State University, 1974.

VAN DE CASTLE, R. L., and KINDER, P. Dream content during pregnancy. *Psychophysiology* 4 (1968), 375.

VANDENBERG, S. G. Primary mental abilities or general intelligence? Evidence from twin studies. In Thoday, J. M., and Parkes, A. S. *Genetic and environmental influences on behavior.* New York: Plenum Press, 1968.

VAN DE VELDE, T. *Ideal marriage, its physiology and technique.* Browne, S., trans. (1926). New York: Random House, 1930.

VEDDER, C. B., and KING, P. G. *Problems of homosexuality in prisons.* Springfield, Ill.: Charles C Thomas, 1967.

VESSEY, M. P. Oral contraceptives and stroke. *New England Journal of Medicine* 288 (1973): 906–7.

VEYSEY, L. Communal sex and communal survival. *Psychology Today* 8 (1974): 73–78.

VOGEL, I. *When I grow up.* New York: Western Publishing, 1968.

VOTH, H. M. Love affair between doctor and patient. *American Journal of Psychotherapy* 26 (1972): 394–400.

WALBERG, H. J. Physics, femininity, and creativity. *Developmental Psychology,* 1 (1969): 47–54.

WALDROP, M. F., and HALVERSON, C. F., JR. Intensive and extensive peer behavior: Longitudinal and cross-sectional analyses. Unpublished manuscript, Child Research Branch, National Institute of Mental Health, Washington, D.C., 1973.

WALTERS, R. G. *Primers for prudery.* Englewood Cliffs, N.J.: Prentice-Hall, 1974.

WARD, D. A.; JACKSON, M.; and WARD, R. E. Crimes of violence by women. In Mulvihill, D., ed., *Crimes of violence.* Washington, D.C.: United States Government Printing Office, 1969.

WARD, W. D. Variance of sex-role preference among boys and girls. *Psychological Reports* 23 (1968): 467–70.

WARD, W. D. Process of sex-role development. *Developmental Psychology* 1 (1969): 163–68.

WATSON, J. B. *Psychology from the standpoint of a behaviorist,* 2d ed. Philadelphia: Lippincott, 1924.

WATSON, J. S. Operant conditioning of visual fixation in infants under visual and auditory reinforcement. *Developmental Psychology* 1 (1969): 408–16.

WEITZMAN, L. J.; EIFLER, D.; HOKADA, E.; and ROSS, C. Sex role socialization in picture books for preschool children. *American Journal of Sociology* 77 (1972): 1125–50.

WELTER, B. The cult of true womanhood, 1820–1860. In Hogeland, R. W., ed., *Women and womanhood in America.* Lexington, Mass.: Heath, 1973.

WERNER, E. E. Sex differences in correlations between children's IQs and measures of parental ability and environmental ratings. *Developmental Psychology* 1 (1969): 280–85.

WEST, J. A child's day. In Schneiderman, B. K., ed., *By and about women.* New York: Harcourt Brace Jovanovich, 1973.

WESTOFF, L. A., and WESTOFF, C. F. *From now to zero: Fertility, contraception, and abortion in America.* Boston, Mass.: Little, Brown, 1971.

WHITING, A. W. M., and CHILD, I. L. *Child training and personality.* New Haven, Conn.: Yale University Press, 1953.

WHITING, B. B., and POPE, C. P. A cross-cultural analysis of sex differences in the behavior of children aged three through eleven. *Journal of Social Psychology* 91 (1973): 171–88.

WHITTACK, F. A., and EDWARDS, J. E. Pregnancy and attempted suicide. *Comprehensive Psychiatry* 9 (1968): 1–21.

WHITMAN, W. *Leaves of Grass.* New York: Modern Library (Random House), 1944.

WILLIAMS, J. H. Sexual role identification and level of functioning in girls. *Journal of Personality* 41 (1973): 1, 1–8.

WILLIE, C. Marginality and social change. *Behavior Today,* February 25, 1974.

WILSON, K. M. Today's women students: New outlooks, options. *Findings,* Educational Testing Service, Princeton, N.J. 1 (1974), no. 4.

WINGETH, C., and KAPP, F. T. The relationship of the manifest content of dreams to duration of childbirth in primiparae. *Psychosomatic Medicine* 34 (1972): 313–20.

WINICK, C. The biege epoch: Depolarization of sex roles in America. *Medical Aspects of Human Sexuality* 3 (1969): 73–74, 78, 80.

WOLBERG, L. R. *The technique of psychotherapy,* 2d ed., vols. 1 and 2. New York: Grune & Stratton, 1967.

WOLFF, C. *Love between women.* London: Duckworth, 1971.

WOLMAN, B. B. Clinical psychology and the philosophy of science. In Wolman, B. B., ed. *Handbook of clinical psychology.* New York: McGraw-Hill, 1965.

WOLMAN, C., and FRANK, H. The solo woman in a professional peer group. *American Journal of Orthopsychiatry* 45 (1975): 164–171.

WOLOWITZ, H. M. Hysterical character and feminine identity. In Bardwick, J. M., ed., *Readings on the psychology of women.* New York: Harper & Row, 1972.

Women on words and images. *Dick and Jane as victims: Sex stereotyping in children's readers.* Princeton, N.J.: Princeton University Press, 1972.

WOOD, C., and SUITTERS, B. *The fight for acceptance.* Aylesbury, England: Medical and Technical Publishing Company, 1972.

World Medicine 8 (1973): 55.

WYLIE, P. *Generation of vipers.* New York: Holt, Rinehart and Winston, 1942.

YARDEN, P. E., and SURANYI, I. The early development of institutionalized children of schizophrenic mothers. *Diseases of the Nervous System* 20 (1968): 380–84.

YORBURG, B. *Sexual identity: Sex roles and social change.* New York: Wiley, 1974.

YORKE, P. C., and THOMSON, D. Anne (1665–1714). *Encyclopaedia Britannica.* Chicago: William Benton, 1958.

YOUNG, W. C.; GOY, R. W.; and PHOENIX, C. H. Hormones and sexual behavior. In Money, J., ed., *Sex research: New developments.* New York: Holt, Rinehart and Winston, 1965.

ZILBOORG, G. Masculine and feminine: Some biological and cultural aspects. In Miller, J. B., ed., *Psychoanalysis and women.* New York: Brunner/Mazel, 1973.

ZILBOORG, G., and HENRY, G. W. *A history of medical psychology.* New York: Norton, 1941.

ZUKERMAN, M.; NURNBERGER, J.; GARDINER, S.; VANDIVEER, J.; BARRET, B.; and DEN BREEIJEN, A. Psychological correlates of somatic complaints in pregnancy and difficulty in childbirth. *Journal of Consulting Psychology* 27 (1963): 324–29.

ZUNICH, M. Children's reactions to failure. *Journal of Genetic Psychology* 104 (1964): 19–24.

Index